Missionary for Freedom

Missionary for Freedom

◆

THE LIFE AND TIMES OF WALTER JUDD

by

LEE EDWARDS

PARAGON HOUSE
New York, New York

First Edition,

Published in the United States by

Paragon House
90 Fifth Avenue
New York, NY 10011

Copyright © 1990 by Lee Edwards

Library of Congress Cataloging-in-Publication Data

Edwards, Lee.
The triumph of freedom: the life and times of Walter Judd/by
Lee Edwards. — 1st ed.
p.   cm
Includes bibliographical references.
ISBN 1-55778-031-5
1. Judd, Walter Henry, 1898- . 2. Legislators—United States—
Biography. 3. United States. Congress. House—Biography.
4. Missionaries—China—Biography. 5. Missionaries—United States—
Biography. I. Title.
E840.8.J83E38   1990
328.73'092—dc20

[B]   89-72184
                                                         CIP

Manufactured in the United States of America

The paper used in this publication meets the minimum requirements of American National Standard for Information Sciences—Permanence of Paper for Printed Library Materials, ANSI Z39.48-1984.

DEDICATION

To Anne and her grace, good humor and wisdom.

Contents

Acknowledgments　　　　　　　　　*ix*
Foreword　　　　　　　　　　　　*xi*

1: A Country Boy　　　　　　　　　　1
2: Call to Arms　　　　　　　　　　13
3: The Middle Kingdom　　　　　　　21
4: Marriage and the Mayo Clinic　　　42
5: China for Good　　　　　　　　　48
6: Sounding the Alarm　　　　　　　65
7: Reluctant Candidate　　　　　　　75
8: Wartime Washington　　　　　　　85
9: Struggle for Power　　　　　　　109
10: Waging the Cold War　　　　　　131
11: Politics at Home and Abroad　　　156
12: I Like Ike　　　　　　　　　　185
13: The "China Lobby"　　　　　　　204
14: Containment and Liberation　　　216
15: Nearly Vice President　　　　　　245
16: A Last Hurrah　　　　　　　　　263
17: Still a Missionary　　　　　　　282
18: In "Retirement"　　　　　　　　310

Postscript　　　　　325
Notes　　　　　　　327
Bibliography　　　　349
Index　　　　　　　357

Acknowledgments

I AM INDEBTED TO Walter and Miriam Judd, whose cooperation at all times has been without fail. I am particularly grateful to Miriam Judd for sharing stories and memories of her husband of close to sixty years. I also thank the Judd daughters, Mary Lou Carpenter, Eleanor Quinn, and Carolyn Judd for their personal insights into their father.

The amount of available material and information about Walter Judd and his career is daunting, and I would have been unable to cope without the assistance of a number of splendid librarians and archivists. First in the pantheon are Elena Danielson and Pruda Lood at the Hoover Institution on War, Revolution and Peace. Next, in not necessarily descending order, I thank the Minnesota Historical Society, St. Paul; the archivists of the Minneapolis Collection at the Minneapolis Public Library; Maura Porter of the John Fitzgerald Kennedy Library, Boston; Benedict K. Zobrist, director of the Harry S. Truman Library, Independence, Missouri; Martin M. Teasley, assistant director of the Dwight D. Eisenhower Library, Abilene, Kansas; and Susan Catto of the Oral History Project at Columbia University's Butler Library. I am also grateful to the staffs of the George C. Marshall Research Library, Lexington, Virginia; the Library of Congress; the Mullen Library at The Catholic University of America; the library of *The World and I,* and the Rochester Historical Society.

ACKNOWLEDGMENTS

Hundreds of people have talked to me about Walter Judd. I cannot name them all, but I would be remiss if I did not single out B.A. Garside, Marvin Liebman, Michael Thompson, John Fulton Lewis, Dorothy Bageant, Robert Morris, Boyd Crawford, Edward Derwinski, Carl Curtis, and Anthony Kubek. Among many old friends and colleagues in Minnesota, I would like to acknowledge the special help of Robert Bjorklund, Douglas Head, Sally Pillsbury, and Virginia Meyers for her recollections about the Republican Workshop. In the Republic of China, I am most grateful for the assistance of Chin Hsiao-yi, director of the National Palace Museum, and Konsin Shah, former ambassador to the United States.

Among those who read the manuscript-in-progress, I thank first and foremost George Nash for his thoughtful comments and recommendations. I am also indebted to Paul Gottfried for his suggestions and to John Felczak for his research assistance.

I would not have been able to write this book without the generous financial support of the Historical Research Foundation, the Earhart Foundation, the Marguerite Eyer Wilbur Foundation and the Heritage Foundation.

I wish to thank the editors at Paragon House Publishers for their help, particularly copy editor Peter Borten for his editing skill, and publisher John Maniatis for his initial encouragement.

Finally, the research and writing of this biography has truly been a family endeavor. My daughter Elizabeth, whose own books I look forward to reading one day soon, conducted major research at the Hoover Institution and carefully read the manuscript. My wife Anne pored over files and folders in Minneapolis, conducted important interviews, and made many sensible suggestions about the manuscript, all of which have made this a far better biography.

*

A linguistic note: because it is what Walter Judd learned in language school in Nanking in 1925 and used throughout his life, I have employed the Wade-Giles system rather than the new *pinyin* system for the transliteration of Chinese words. Therefore, Mao Tse-tung is Mao Tse-tung, not Mao Zedong; Peking is Peking, not Beijing.

Foreword

SOME THIRTY YEARS AGO, I heard a congressman from Minnesota give a speech at the Republican National Convention in Chicago that I shall never forget. I still remember his vibrant voice, crackling with energy, the historic sweep of his remarks, ranging from Lincoln and Lenin to Eisenhower and Mao, the way he had of suddenly raising both arms as though beseeching the heavens, how he hurled a series of pointed questions about the role of Democrats in war and peace at the audience, bringing everyone in the huge arena to his feet cheering. It was magnificent partisan oratory that stampeded the convention and nearly obtained the vice presidential nomination for that congressman. How different the history of the nation and the world would be if, in 1960, Richard Nixon had picked the indefatigable Walter H. Judd rather than the indolent Henry Cabot Lodge as his running mate; many political analysts believe that Judd would have gained Nixon the electoral votes he needed to defeat John F. Kennedy for the presidency. Nixon later admitted as much to Judd.

In the succeeding years, I came to know Walter Judd and admire him, as many did, for his integrity, his honesty, and his insights into the human condition, particularly his personally gained knowledge of communists and communism. For nine years, I worked with him as secretary of the Committee of One Million (Against the Admission of

Communist China to the United Nations) and its successor organization, the Committee for a Free China, of which he was chairman. I learned of his encyclopedic knowledge of foreign affairs, not just of China, for which he was best known, but of Europe, the Middle East, and other Asian nations. I discovered that he was not so much a twentieth-century conservative as an eighteenth-century liberal, a disciple of Thomas Jefferson, who believed in limited government, individual liberty, and the duty of government to help those who could not help themselves. Although a medical missionary in China for ten years, he never flaunted his faith, preferring, as he had been taught by his New England mother, to let his deeds speak for his commitment to God and the Gospel. He was an American original with roots that went back 350 years to the freedom-seeking Pilgrims.

It seemed as though he had known every American leader of his time: presidents from Franklin Roosevelt to Ronald Reagan, secretaries of state from Dean Acheson to Henry Kissinger, politicians from Arthur Vandenberg to Barry Goldwater, generals from George Marshall to William Westmoreland; he knew foreign leaders, too, like Chiang Kai-shek, Jawaharlal Nehru, and the Dalai Lama. I learned about his service in Congress, where he was a "political missionary," and authored or cosponsored historic proposals regarding the United Nations, the World Health Organization, the Voice of America, technical assistance to underdeveloped nations, and the removal of all racial discrimination clauses from U.S. immigration laws, the first civil rights law in eighty years.

I knew that since leaving Congress he had been far from idle (that was as foreign to his nature as boasting), serving as a "missionary-at-large;" moderating a daily radio program that was broadcast from coast to coast; writing for *Reader's Digest;* working with professional, religious, and political organizations; speaking, always speaking, to young people on campuses about their obligation to protect and pass on America's freedoms as preceding generations had done. I joined with others in urging him to write his autobiography. He had a duty, we argued, not only to tell his spellbinding stories about living as a prisoner under the Japanese, facing death at the hands of Chinese bandits, and his life-long battle against facial cancer, but to record his reflections as to how and why the United States emerged from its isolationist cocoon to become the leader of the free world in the post-World War II period. What advice could he, who knew Asia so well, offer to the leaders and people of the United States as they entered what many called the "Pacific

Century"? How could Congress, brought so low by personal scandals and institutional arrogance, regain public esteem? Liberals and conservatives alike were saying, in the wake of *glasnost* and *perestroika,* that the Cold War was over. Had a political millennium arrived; could we now trust the communists? We gave him a thousand reasons for writing his autobiography, and the answer was always the same: he had too much to do. Besides, he wasn't a writer, he agonized over every word that he wrote and rewrote. He might start, he said, but he would never finish his autobiography.

The years went by, and Walter Judd never seemed to show his age, certainly not on that sunny October day in 1981, when he received the Presidential Medal of Freedom from President Reagan, who lauded him for his skills as a healer, his eloquence as a communicator, and his lifelong opposition to tyranny and support of freedom at home and abroad. I often saw Dr. Judd and would argue the importance of writing his autobiography, but to no avail. Finally, one autumn day in 1985, I said, with some exasperation, that he was not getting any younger (he was then an amazingly youthful eighty-seven) and if he didn't want to write his life story, I did. I had recently gone back to college to earn my doctorate in world politics. While working on my dissertation, about the impact of the U.S. Congress on the origins of the Cold War, I read about the major role that Congressman Judd had played in winning congressional approval of the Truman Doctrine, the Marshall Plan, and NATO, initiatives that have given form and substance to the U.S. policy of containment from 1947 to the present. I determined that his story had to be told. To my delight, Dr. Judd did not reject my offer, but promised to consider it. After reflection, he agreed to work with me on an authorized biography, not, he emphasized, to perpetuate his name and his memory, but to bring about a better understanding of the leaders and historic events with which he had been associated "for this and future generations."

This has not been an easy book to write. First, there is a Matterhorn of material, a researcher's dream and nightmare, 313 boxes of correspondence, notes, speeches, clippings, pamphlets, audio tapes, and films, at the Hoover Library of Stanford University, where the Judd papers on national and international affairs are located; another 50-odd boxes at the Minnesota Historical Society, which houses the Judd papers on local affairs; and several filing cabinets overflowing with papers, letters, and other material in his home. Apparently, Walter Judd never threw anything away in his life: I have found lecture notes dating back to the early 1920s when he was traveling about the country on behalf of the Student Volunteer Movement. Second, there was the challenge of writing about a man who has done so much for so long in so many different fields. Not having the time to write a multivolume, Douglas Southall Freeman-like biography, I have left out many details of his private life: his musical performances for three summers on the Chautauqua circuit as a student, homely letters to his family when he was a new member of Congress, acts of kindness and generosity to neighbors and friends. Rather, I have concentrated on the public life of a quintessentially public man whose story is the story of twentieth century America. Third, there is the question of objectivity. While not all biographers fall in love with their subject, many come to admire and even wind up sounding like the man or woman whose life they are describing. In the process, sympathetic biographers can become sycophantic. The problem of objectivity is compounded when one has worked closely with one's subject, as I have. The final judgment rests with the reader, but I have striven to write a balanced political biography of a remarkable American who accomplished many extraordinary things during a very long life.

For example, he understood, far better than most, the nature of the communist adversary with which we have been locked in protracted conflict for decades. He faced danger and death in China at the hands of the Japanese and the Chinese. He made a difference in Congress because he was willing to work harder and longer than almost anyone else, and was always prepared for the debate of the day. He was invariably eloquent, often brilliant, seemingly tireless, a perfectionist who was never completely satisfied with his own work or that of others. He had extraordinary foresight, predicting the war with Japan and the loss of China and Vietnam to the communists. He was not a saint: he often lost his temper, he sometimes took a drink, and he liked a salty medical story. His greatest personal flaw was that he placed the demands of his missionary work, whether in China, Congress or elsewhere, before everything else, including his family, whose members, particularly his children, sometimes suffered from his absence. Like most leaders, he was possessed of a monumental ego that sustained him during those times when the rest of the world did not accept his apocalyptic predictions and revolutionary solutions. He made mistakes, sometimes important ones, as when he failed to press his own case for the vice presidential nomination because he had been trained as a physician not to promote himself. Still, I believe that he inspired and informed more

Americans longer—from the early 1920s through the late 1980s—with his speeches, radio broadcasts, television appearances, and magazine articles than any other public figure. Walter Judd was a missionary, a modern St. Paul, and his mission was based on the words of Thomas Jefferson, carved in giant letters on the corona of his great white marble monument in Washington:

"I have sworn upon the altar of God eternal hostility against every form of tyranny over the mind of man."

CHAPTER ONE

$\blacklozenge$

A Country Boy

THERE IS SOMETHING about the wide prairies and long winters of the upper Middle West that produces national leaders of strong convictions and passionate speech, men like William Jennings Bryan, William Borah, Hubert Humphrey, and Walter Judd. Their vision is as unbounded as the horizon; their oratory is as inexorable as the winds that sweep across the plains. Whether they come from big cities or small towns, they are of a kind—ebullient, eloquent, opinionated. If you mix this midwestern populism with New England discipline and reserve, you produce a powerful, purposeful personality who is certain to affect profoundly the lives of those around him and even the course of history.

Rising City, Nebraska, has always been a small town; the 1900 census put its population at 499. It is a farming town, located fifty miles northwest of Lincoln, the state capital, in fertile, flat prairie land that stretches to the horizon. At the turn of the century, the principal crops were wheat, corn, and oats. It was small but important enough to be a stop on the Union Pacific Railroad with two passenger trains and one freight train each day. Rising City had what many up-and-coming midwestern towns had: two hotels, two doctors, a lawyer, a weekly newspaper, two banks, several retail stores, two barber shops, a lumber yard run by Horace H. Judd (Walter Judd's father), and four Protestant churches: Methodist, Lutheran, the Disciples of Christ, and Congrega-

1

tional. The latter had been an active church, but during most of his boyhood the Sunday school classes, especially the ones taught by Mary Elizabeth Judd (Walter Judd's mother), were the only formal church activity that remained.

In a literal sense, the story of Walter Judd begins in Rising City, his birthplace, but to capture the full measure of the man, we must go back several hundred years, before the Civil War, before the Revolutionary War, to the origins of America, the time of the Pilgrims, the *Mayflower,* and the Massachusetts Bay Colony. About 1633, Thomas Judd left Tunbridge Wells, England, for Massachusetts Bay and what is now Boston. He moved from Cambridge, Massachusetts, to Hartford, Connecticut, and about 1644 joined with two others in founding the town of Farmington, seven miles west of Hartford. Deacon Judd was a substantial farmer and an influential man in the community who was, among other things, a deputy to the Connecticut General Court. He was a prominent member of the Congregational Church in Cambridge and Hartford, until "a church was gathered at Farmington on October 13, 1652," where he served as deacon until his death. His was a solemn responsibility, for the Pilgrims believed that members of the congregation should share in the management of the church's affairs and that each church was self-governing and independent of any outside authority. Thomas Judd had six sons, the third of whom was John Judd, from whom Walter Judd is descended. Deacon Judd's name is on a monument on the capitol grounds in Hartford, erected for the men who founded Connecticut; in fact, his is the first name listed.[1] Deacon Judd set a high standard for future Judds to follow: he was a man of abiding faith who founded a church, a deeply patriotic man who loved his new country, a citizen politician who served his fellow citizens.

Eager to settle new lands, one of Deacon Judd's grandsons, Phineas, moved west into New York and then to the present site of Indianapolis, Indiana. He had three sons and died of typhoid at the age of thirty; his widow Elizabeth reared the boys, one of whom was Warren, Walter Judd's grandfather. Warren Judd and his wife Elizabeth moved in the 1850s to a farm in Worth County, northern Missouri. Following a family tradition (three Judds served in the Continental Army that defeated the British in the Revolutionary War), Warren Judd fought bravely for the North in the Civil War, becoming a captain in the Missouri National Guard. He had three children by Elizabeth, who died, and then married Martha Ann Hendrey, the granddaughter of an Irish immigrant. Their son, Horace Hunter Judd (Walter Judd's father), was born on February 18, 1862, in West Point, Missouri, while Warren was in the Union Army.

Warren Judd had been a good soldier during the Civil War, and he was again pressed into service in the postwar period. Jesse James and other members of his gang were robbing banks and trains and terrorizing the people of Missouri. The state government was weak and unwilling to go after James, so the people set up a vigilante group, making Warren Judd its "captain." The James gang retaliated by marking Captain Judd for death and forcing him for safety to leave Missouri with his family. The Judds first settled on a farm near Sidney, Iowa, and then moved to Nebraska, where in 1880, Warren Judd bought a quarter section of land for a few dollars an acre near the small town of Surprise. "It was called Surprise," explained Walter Judd, "because the land was so flat you could see almost forty miles in every direction, but all of a sudden there is a little dip, a narrow valley, with a small stream and every traveler called it a 'surprise.' "[2]

Right across from the Judd property, the Greenslit family had also bought a piece of land. Like the Judds, the Greenslits had roots deep in America, tracing their ancestors back to Thomas Greenslade, a sailor and fisherman who emigrated from Devonshire, England, to Casco, Maine, south of the present Portland, in the 1640s. Greenslade married a Maine girl named Ann (there is no record of her last name) and had five children. When Thomas Greenslade died in 1674, Ann married Jacob Pudeator, a successful Salem, Massachusetts blacksmith who owned two houses. They lived happily until 1681, when Pudeator died; he expressed great affection for his wife in his will, making her his sole executrix and giving ten pound legacies to her five children by her first husband. But the person who wrote the will misspelled the children's last name as "Greenslit" rather than "Greenslade," so that they were forced to change their name to receive their bequest.

In the "dark days" of 1692, when Salem was filled with rumors of evil women who sold themselves to the Devil and were plotting the destruction of church and state, Mistress Ann Pudeator, who had returned to her former profession of nursing, was charged with being a witch. Although professing her innocence, she was arrested, tried, and hanged along with seven other women on September 22, 1692. Her final petition to the court, in which she firmly denied the testimony of several witnesses, has been acclaimed for its clarity and charity. She concluded: "I am altogether ignorant of and know nothing in the least measure about . . . the crime of witchcraft for which I am condemned to die, as

3

will be known to men and angels at the great day of judgment. Begging and imploring your prayers at the throne of grace in my behalf . . . your poor and humble petitioner shall forever pray as she is bound in duty for your happiness in this life and eternal felicity in the world to come."[3] More than 260 years later, following appeals by Congressman Walter Judd among others, the Massachusetts state legislature passed a bill clearing Ann Pudeator and the other Salem women of all taint of witchcraft, enabling every Greenslit, as one family member put it, to "look the whole world in the face and never again . . . be called the 'son of a witch.' "[4]

Like the Judds, the Greenslits looked west, and in 1878, James Henry and Marcia Maria Fuller Greenslit settled in Surprise, Nebraska. They had several children but no one to teach them, so James Greenslit sent for his sixteen-year-old sister, Mary Elizabeth, who lived in Scotland, Connecticut, and wanted to be a teacher. It took the slender girl (who had never been farther west than Waterbury) three days and two nights on the railroad to get to Seward, Nebraska, twenty miles from Surprise. In the latter part of the nineteenth century, trains did not run at night; they stopped at railroad hotels where the passengers stayed overnight until the trains started up again in the morning. "It is remarkable when you think about it," commented Walter Judd. "A sixteen-year-old girl all alone. But Mother was resourceful. Nothing ever got her down."[5]

Mary Elizabeth Greenslit taught for several years in Surprise and then returned to Connecticut to earn a degree at New Britain Teacher's Training School (now the College of New Britain); upon graduation, she returned to Nebraska. When Walter Judd once asked his mother why she went back, she smiled, a little embarrassed, and replied, "Well, I had your father on the string."[6] While waiting to tie the string, she taught a dozen children in a one-room country school; parents liked her quiet authority and unflappable ways, which were put to a severe test in the winter of 1887–88. One afternoon, snow began falling so heavily that the children and the young teacher could not leave school: they were caught in the worst blizzard in Nebraska history. They stayed in the schoolhouse all night, without food, with the snow piling up around the door and the windows, blocking exit and entry. Mary Greenslit remained New England calm, telling stories to the children, making them as comfortable as possible, turning what could have been a terrifying experience into an adventure. It was not until the following afternoon that parents were able to dig through the banks of snow and rescue the children and their still unruffled teacher.

Horace and Mary Judd were married on November 22, 1888, in Surprise. Opposites had attracted. He was tall, dark, outgoing, with a ready smile. She was short, fair and reserved, rarely wasting a word. He had little formal education: "I got about as far as the fourth grade," he once told his son, and only went from Christmas time to March because of the farm chores. Although Horace Judd had little "book learning," he had an enormous amount of common sense. Mary Judd was unusually well educated for a young woman of the time, having earned the equivalent of a college degree.

Horace started out as a farmer and then bought a little grocery store in Surprise, which he ran successfully for several years; but he always kept his eye open for something better. Mary's older brother, Walter, owned a small retail lumber yard in Surprise that began to attract more and more business after the Northwestern Railroad came through. Soon trains were bringing in hard pine from the south and soft pine and fir from the west. Seven miles away, in Rising City, another lumber yard was up for sale, and Horace Judd decided it was going to be his. He had saved the impressive sum of four thousand dollars, and he borrowed two thousand more from his father, three thousand from Grandpa Greenslit, and another three thousand from an Iowan brother-in-law to buy the yard. He moved his family to their new Rising City home in 1892.

Horace and Mary settled into a contented cycle of running a small business and raising children. In their first nine years of marriage, they had six children, Myrtle, Clarence, Carroll, Russell, Gertrude, and Walter Henry, who was born on September 25, 1898, to the calm delight of his parents and the mild interest of his brothers and sisters, except for Gertrude, who deeply loved her baby brother from the first day. There was to be one more child, Maurice (Jim), five years later. They lived in a comfortable two-story wooden frame house only a block and a half from the lumber yard. The house was heated in the winter by a cast-iron coal stove in the living room, and lit by kerosene lamps. Mrs. Judd cooked on a coal stove and pumped water from a nearby well. There was no indoor plumbing; everyone used the outhouse in the backyard. The Judds were a close-knit family whose life revolved around the home, the church, and the lumber yard.

After school let out, the Judd kids always came home before they went out to play. "Mother would have baked some cookies," remembered Walter Judd, "and we would have one or two and check in with her before going off to play baseball or go fishing or go out with air rifles

5

to shoot at a sparrow or something. There was never a day, no matter what happened, but when we came home she was there. That was the way New Englanders were brought up and so were we."[7]

His mother made sure that he and the other children said their prayers, read the Bible, and attended church. She taught Sunday school, and for twelve years, until they both went away to college, Walter and Gertrude went every Sunday morning. His father was a nominal Baptist (Grandpa Judd had been a serious "footwashing" Baptist) but a man of obvious faith who knelt beside his bed and prayed every night. But he never joined the church. Many years later, when Walter was home visiting, he asked his mother why his father had never joined a church, although he always attended. She explained that there used to be revival meetings where people came forward to confess their sins, "be saved" and shout "Glory Hallelujah!" But when Horace Judd had come forward—once in his late teens and once after he was married—there was no exultation, no rhapsody, no descending of the Holy Spirit.

Horace Judd decided that if for some reason God did not give him such an experience, then he was not "saved," and he was not going to be a hypocrite and join a church. But he kept praying. "He never unloaded that on us," remarked Walter Judd. "They were strong people, my father and mother, who did their duty. They talked about issues, about the country, the problems of the day, like the eighteenth amendment— Mother was a great worker for that and a member of the Women's Christian Temperance Union—but never about their personal problems." Their practice of keeping private things private deeply impressed young Walter, who as he grew older adopted a similar reserve.

Horace Judd was a strong Republican and enthusiastic supporter of U.S. Senator George Norris, a Republican populist, who called for the direct election of senators as well as presidential primaries, and was the author of the twentieth amendment, abolishing lame-duck Congresses. Norris favored tight restrictions on private power and fathered the Tennessee Valley Authority. His dictum was: The people "ought to be independent of all parties." Walter Judd was influenced by Norris's populism and faith in the native wisdom of the people, but later questioned the wisdom of the direct election by the people of senators, arguing that it made them too sensitive to the daily wishes and wants of their constituents, just like representatives.

People came to rely on Horace Judd's integrity, common sense, and willingness to offer a helping hand to anyone. Even preachers came to him with their problems. One cold winter night when his wife fell sick, Reverend Seidel, the Methodist preacher, called on Horace Judd, who along with a friend, worked a railroad pump car eleven miles to David City, the county seat, to get Dr. Beede and bring him back before daylight to treat the ailing woman. "Why did they come and get my dad?" wondered young Walter. "Why didn't they go to their own deacon?" They would be at the dinner table, he recalled, "and somebody would come to talk with my father about a problem he had with his business or his family. The men always came to my father. And the women all came to my mother." The lesson was imprinted on young Walter: you were expected to help people, and with as little fuss and fanfare as possible.

Walter Judd also learned at an early age how fragile life could be. He was only two when his brother Russell, aged five, was thrown from a horse and hit his head on a rock. Seemingly he recovered from what Dr. Judd decided years later must have been a skull fracture; of course, there was no X-ray machine in Rising City. Six weeks later, the boy, who slept in a small bed alongside his father and mother, woke up, complaining of a terrible pain in his head. Horace Judd went for the doctor, but by the time they returned, Russell was gone, the victim of a massive hemorrhage. The grieving father walked for hours with a neighbor alone through the Nebraska prairie.

"My earliest memory," said Dr. Judd, "is of Russell's funeral, which was held in our home. Before the neighbors arrived, we all went in to say goodbye. I remember seeing this little white casket, and they say that I hid my head in my father's shoulder. He reached up and turned my head around. I looked down, saw my brother and said, 'Russie.' "[8] The family also said goodbye to Carroll and Clarence, who died of typhoid when they were in their teens. The obligation to serve others was joined in the mind of young Walter with the belief that a doctor could heal even the very sick.

The four surviving children grew closer but delighted in disagreeing with each other. "We were the darndest arguers," remembered Judd. "When Miriam came [to Rising City] after we were married, and all four of us were there to meet the new girl, Miriam said afterwards, 'I thought you were all mad at each other.' We were strong-minded," Judd conceded. "The only time I ever saw my mother cry was on a Saturday during winter, when we were all home with nothing to do, except argue back and forth, and she cried, 'Why do you children have to quarrel so?' "[9] A large part of the answer lay in her New England way of speaking her mind plainly, which all of the children, especially Walter, imitated.

The children were also influenced by their father's uncompromising integrity. Walter worked at his father's lumber yard in the afternoons and on Saturdays for a dollar a day. Once a load of soft pine came in on the railroad from Oregon, but it had not been properly dried out and was already curling at the ends. Horace Judd immediately said: "We'll have to cut this up and sell it for kindling wood." "Oh, no," the hired hand protested, "let's lay out the planks with rocks on top and bottom, straighten them out, and sell it. Nobody'll be able to tell." Shaking his head firmly, Horace Judd responded that the wood was bound to warp, and he wouldn't sell one piece of it. He took the considerable loss without another word.[10] Horace helped support four families with the lumber yard—his own, those of Grandparents Judd and Greenslit and the family of the Iowa friend who had also lent him money, sharing the profits with them year after year while they received many times their initial investment. He paid himself a modest monthly salary of one hundred dollars at first, and raised it to two hundred a month after Grandpa Judd sold his share back, the only investor to do so. Horace Judd never complained about the profit-sharing; he had made a deal and stuck to it.

Walter shared in the family chores, including the daily grocery shopping. He would ask his mother what she needed and then get the money from his father, fifty or seventy-five cents, once in a while a whole dollar. "I never bought any oranges because we couldn't afford them. But we had apples and peaches and prunes and plums of our own and in our little garden, we grew radishes, lettuce, onions and potatoes. We had potatoes twice a day, every day—that was the mainstay." Lunch was at ten after twelve and dinner at six o'clock exactly, reflecting Mrs. Judd's sense of order.

Walter began attending grade school in 1904 when Theodore Roosevelt was president. He was always a top student, usually receiving A's in every subject but one—deportment. "I learned quickly because I heard my brothers and sisters talking about things. I could recite the names of all the presidents when I was seven." Mathematics was his best subject; he liked its logic and provability. Rail-thin, he had inexhaustible energy which he poured into everything he did. The only thing quicker than his mind was his tongue, which accounted for his C's in deportment; he was even sassy in Sunday school. One Sunday morning, in a talk about

8

propriety, his mother remarked, "Never do in private what you wouldn't do in public," at which Walter piped up: "How about taking a bath?" In medical school, years later, when the professor was talking about malaria and its symptoms, Walter asked: "Do the mosquitoes have chills, too?"

By the time he was seventeen and a senior in high school, Walter was an often brilliant student, a fierce debater at school and at home, a (usually) dutiful son, and a practicing Christian. But there was something missing. He was at the same time obedient and rebellious. He was bursting with energy, but often channeled it in the wrong direction. He got into so many pranks and scrapes at school that he was automatically blamed for every one, whether he was involved or not. His older sister Gertrude, to whom he was closest of all his brothers and sisters, had gone off to Doane College and then to the University of Nebraska, and he supposed that he would follow. But he was unsure as to his field of study; in fact, he was unsure about his entire life. What did he want to do with it? What should he do with it?

As a young boy, he had read and been impressed by a biography of David Livingstone, the great medical missionary and explorer in Africa. He admired Livingstone for not reckoning success by the number of his conversions but by true pioneering, opening up new ground and leaving natives to carry on from there. Livingstone had set his heart on going to China, and had been deeply disappointed when the London Missionary Society sent him to Africa. Walter daydreamed of distant exotic lands: Japan, India, China. Decades later, he still remembered the maps on the wall in his Sunday school that showed St. Paul's travels all over the Mediterranean world. "The first journey was in red, the second was in yellow, the third in blue, and the last one, to Rome, was some other color; I think it was purple. I suppose that had an impact on me—a little boy in a country town dreaming of places that he might someday go to, where the need was great."[11]

His father thought he would make a pretty good farmer, and of course there was the lumber yard in which he had been working since he was a boy. But his mother had always encouraged him to look beyond the horizons of their town, of Nebraska, and even of America. It was in this unsettled, questioning state of mind that Walter Judd traveled to Lincoln to attend the first YMCA State Conference of Older Boys. There, on the Sunday afternoon after Thanksgiving Day, 1915, he heard Arthur J. (Dad) Elliott speak, and his life was changed forever. "I signed a piece of paper that day saying that whatever I had, whether it was an ounce or a ton, I was going to give as best I could in service to other people who had far less advantages than I. I suppose it was what in the olden days would have been called a conversion."[12]

The talk that converted Walter Judd was called "The Quitter." It was the story of the rich young man who came to Jesus and asked what he had to do to share in everlasting life. Jesus perceived his preoccupation with possessions and said to him, "Sell all you have and give to the poor. . . . Then come and follow me." The man debated with himself, but he was unwilling to move "things" from the center of his life. He turned away, said Dad Elliott, and walked out of history, never to be heard of again—a quitter. Elliott asked the four hundred high school students sitting before him if they were going to be quitters, or if they would answer Jesus's call to use their talents, however large or small, to help the less fortunate.

"Some forty boys came forward," Elliott remembered. "The last to come was a boy who seemed to me to be the most unpromising boy in the group. I recall distinctly the thought that came to my mind when I took him by the hand—'If you ever amount to anything, God has a big task on His hands.' "[13] God was equal to the task. Within two weeks, Elliott received a letter from the teacher of that "unpromising" boy, Walter Judd, describing "the most remarkable change" in a student's behavior that she had witnessed in a lifetime of teaching. There were no more pranks, his deportment improved dramatically, and he became a leader, organizing a "Hi-Y" Club. The mischievous, undisciplined youth disappeared, replaced by a serious young man who committed himself to seeking first the Kingdom of God.

His parents rejoiced in his transformation, but then his father, whom he admired so much, tested him in an unexpected way. The whole family knew that he had decided to become a medical missionary. To accomplish that objective, he had thought he would attend the University of Nebraska in Lincoln as Myrtle and Gertrude had before him. However, although his father had paid the tuition and other expenses of the girls, he now soberly stated that he would not do the same for his son. Walter tried, unsuccessfully, to contain his anger: it wasn't fair!

"Son," his father explained, "I've watched you pretty carefully, and I think you could make a good doctor. Your mother and I are pleased you have that in mind. We feel you'll make something of yourself if you discipline yourself. But you could become a playboy. I hope you'll make good in school, but we're not going to help you with money. You've got to work to get through and if you do, you'll stay straight." Walter thought long and hard about his father's decision. Gradually, and after much prayer, he realized that his father was treating him differently than his sisters because he *was* different. "He risked incurring resentment, rebellion from his own son, in order to do the right thing for me. I became grateful for it; in the long run, I admired him for the way he handled me."

So in the fall of 1916, not knowing how he would earn the money to stay in school, but resolved that he would prevail, seventeen-year-old Walter Judd took the train to Lincoln and walked five blocks to a university building where the YMCA was located. Walter explained to the YMCA representative that he needed a job, badly. The man replied that a half hour before, the university cafeteria manager had called and said he was looking for someone to wipe dishes down in the basement. The job paid twenty cents an hour. Was he interested? "I got off the train at 10:30," remembered Judd, "and I was wiping dishes at 12:15." Walter plunged just as quickly into his classes and soon established himself as one of the university's best students. In fact, in between washing dishes and playing coronet in the university band and participating in YMCA activities, Walter Judd compiled the highest grade point average of any undergraduate in the history of the university up to that time. Again, mathematics and the sciences were his best subjects.

His life revolved around the demands of the cafeteria. He rose at six in the morning, did his devotions, and was at the cafeteria by a quarter to seven. Classes began at eight. "I didn't have a date the whole first year until the last week of school," he remembered, "because I had to be at the cafeteria. And I liked girls. I always did."[14] He washed dishes in the basement until someone who worked upstairs clearing tables left; Walter took his place, still at twenty cents an hour. The person behind the hot table was promoted, and Walter was selected to pass out the meat, vegetables, and hot rolls. "The next year, they made me the cashier. That same year, the war started and the manager volunteered for the army. They needed somebody to keep track of the surplus and so on, and I was promoted to manager, for thirty cents an hour." All those years of shopping for the family paid off.

There was another reason why he did not have many dates: he was self-conscious about his very noticeable adolescent acne. One day he visited a skin specialist who had recently bought an X-ray machine. "We've got a new way of clearing up acne like that," the doctor said, "X-ray exposure." Well-intentioned and unaware of the danger, he began to give the eighteen-year-old massive doses. After several visits, the young student's face began to swell and became hot, dark red, and tight. "That's a good healthy reaction," said the specialist, who continued the weekly treatments. At last, he stopped them when Walter's face began to toughen and dry. The skin doctor had cured the acne, but had killed many normal cells, hair follicles, and glands, leaving hundreds of white scars or red blotches where small blood vessels had shrunk. Belatedly, the doctor realized that radiation was far more powerful than he supposed. "He felt just terrible," Dr. Judd recalled. "He was a wonderful man. It's just that doctors knew so little about X-rays then; it was new. That's how they learned, of course."

Walter looked in the mirror and saw a prune face: "I wanted to crawl into the ground." He had a faint hope that the condition was temporary, or might be corrected. But at that time there was no such thing as plastic surgery, and the scarring became more pronounced as he progressed at the university. "Finally," he recalled, "I took myself in hand and said: 'You'll have this face for the rest of your life. You've got to live with it or go into hiding. And you aren't going to go into hiding.' "[15] He began dating and engaging in as many public activities as possible, overcoming a crisis that would have shattered a less determined and disciplined young man. He was to confront an even more serious consequence of the doctor's misuse of X-rays years later.

In his sophomore year, Walter Judd had an opportunity to practice what his parents had taught him about service to others. Once the United States entered World War I, the YMCA was put in charge of entertaining the armed forces. It set up an entertainment center at every camp where a soldier could write a letter home or play billiards or enjoy an evening musical show produced by the YMCA. The YMCA tried to raise money for its entertainment centers at the University of Nebraska, but failed to obtain much help from senior students. However, one sophomore responded in his typically enthusiastic way. "I began organizing the students," Judd remembered, and in a couple of weeks "we had a parade and a big meeting at the city auditorium—I got them to donate its use for free—and we raised $17,000, the highest amount of any university in the United States. Well, this put me right up in the front row. But I didn't do it to be in the front row. I did it for the cause. I believed in it. I have always been a cause-oriented guy."[16]

CHAPTER TWO

◆

Call to Arms

THE YOUNG IDEALIST was increasingly drawn to the cause of the day, World War I, the war to end all wars. "[President] Wilson was convinced we had to go in," remembered Judd, "and I was convinced he was right." In April 1917, he went down to the recruiting station located in Lincoln's City Hall and declared that he felt he should join up. The recruiting officer looked carefully at the thin, earnest student with the glasses standing before him.

"Well, I don't know," he said, "we're not going to be short of men. I'm not sure you ought to join now. It's more important, I think, for the long run, for the country, for you to go ahead with your medical training. If we get in a jam, where there's a desperate need, then come back."

Reluctantly, Walter returned to his studies at the university. All that school year, he carefully read the papers about the course of the war. The recruiter had been right about one thing: there was no shortage of American soldiers. President Wilson called for a Selective Service Act, which required the registration of all men between the ages of twenty-one and thirty, excluding nineteen-year-olds like Walter Judd.

In the summer of 1918, he came into direct contact with hundreds of American draftees when the Red Triangle of the YMCA put him in charge of providing entertainment for three military groups based in

Lincoln. He was required to present a different program every day for each of the three groups, a total of twenty-one programs a week. It would have been a formidable challenge for a Florenz Ziegfeld, let alone a pre-med student from Rising City. But as usual, Walter got the job done, presenting singers, musicians—including his sister Gertrude who sang and played the guitar—slide shows, and lectures. It was rewarding, but in September, after watching dozens of soldiers leave for overseas, he could restrain himself no longer and joined the army. He was still in training as an enlisted man in Lincoln when an army officer came through camp, recruiting for the nation's artillery officer's training school in Louisville, Kentucky. "I was No. 2 in command of the University ROTC and thought that with my experience," he recalled, "I'd be qualified for officer over most of the men brought in by the draft. So about twenty to twenty-five of us at the University of Nebraska signed up."[1] Shortly after they arrived in Kentucky and began their training, the November 11 armistice was declared and the great war was over. But Walter and most of the other members of his training class decided to complete their three months of training scheduled to end in January 1919. "I wanted to get my commission as a second lieutenant, and I got it." He never liked to leave things undone.

He arrived back at the University of Nebraska one week after the second semester classes had started in February, but confident they would accept him because "I had a pretty good record." Although he had missed a complete semester, he made up the academic ground by working extra hard that spring and by going to school that summer. He entered the University of Nebraska Medical College in Omaha that fall of 1919 and received his B.A. in 1920, graduating Phi Beta Kappa. Still making his own way, he immediately began looking for a job. He and his roommate, Max Gentry, fell into something a little different: they became undertakers. Anyone in the state who died without identification was shipped to the university and placed in the medical school mortuary. "Max and I would embalm them and if no one identified them, they would be used for dissection in freshman anatomy class." Max put a sign on their door: "State Undertaker."[2]

In his sophomore year at medical school, Walter again worked in a cafeteria, this time at the hospital, but in his third year he moved up the job ladder, becoming the telephone operator for the hospital five evenings a week. To make ends meet, he also worked on the weekends.

That was not all. Besides handling the heavy academic demands of medical school (he again finished at the top in his classes), Walter Judd became a teacher. There was a small Presbyterian College, the University of Omaha, that sent about fifteen pre-med students to his medical school every year. One day the dean called Walter in to explain that a teacher at the University of Omaha had fallen ill and had arranged for someone to teach all of his courses with one exception—comparative anatomy of vertebrates. The dean asked Walter if he would like to take the anatomy class and assured him that the task of filling in and lecturing every weekday afternoon from four to five o'clock would be temporary, until the regular teacher recovered.

"I think you're good enough," the dean said, "that by working on Saturday and so forth, you can make up what you'll miss in class. There's a girl who can handle the anatomy lab on Saturday if you set it up. And they'll pay you fifty dollars a month." Whatever hesitation Walter might have had about the added workload disappeared when he learned the salary: fifty dollars a month was a fortune. As it turned out, the teacher's illness was fatal, and Walter lectured twice a week on comparative anatomy all through the next four years in medical school and his year of internship at the university hospital. "I was proud of the fact," he said, "that every single year one or two of the leading freshmen in medical school came, not from the University of Nebraska training in Lincoln, but from my little class at the University of Omaha."

To supplement his income and because it was fun, Walter also went on the road in the summer, playing coronet in the band and singing bass with Ralph Dunbar's White Hussars on the Chautauqua circuit. In July 1921, he visited Washington, D.C. for the first time, walking up and down the 898 steps of the Washington Monument and visiting the White House. There was a long line waiting at the entrance to see President Warren Harding, too long for Walter and his young friends. There was then no fence around the White House and no guard at the main entrance on Pennsylvania Avenue so he and another White Hussar walked in. A guard, seeing no badges on the young men, politely but firmly escorted them out. Recalling the incident many years later, a friend asked: "How many times, Walter, have you [since] been 'kicked out of the White House'?"[3]

Things were going marvelously for Walter Judd. He was certain to graduate with honors, he was helping others to become doctors through his teaching, and he was putting himself through school, justifying the confidence of his parents that he could do so without their financial help. Who could ask for anything more? He received a surprising answer on a date in his sophomore year. He took a nurse friend to a

15

movie and on the way home, she said: "Walter, I've always admired you a lot. You were active in the YMCA and Christian Endeavor and other religious activities at the university in Lincoln. But you're not doing that here, in medical school. You're just studying and working hard. You're not as good a Christian as you used to be."

Walter was stunned by the girl's words. "What do you mean?" he asked, haltingly.

"I can understand it," she responded, trying to soften the impact. "You're just thinking, 'I can't do all these outside things here. Instead, I need just to study to become the best doctor I'm capable of becoming.'"

The girl's words sank into the heart of the young medical student. Sitting at his desk later that night, he turned them over and over in his mind. Yes, it was true that he was concentrating on his medical studies. He was determined to be the best physician he could be. But that was because of his commitment to be the best missionary he could be. "I picked up my Bible," he recalled, "and it opened near the end of the first chapter of Mark, where he describes Jesus's first day as a 'medical missionary,' as I suddenly thought of it. Jesus came into the synagogue and 'they brought him the many to be healed.' The Bible says that 'all the city was gathered at the door and he healed many that were sick of diverse diseases and cast out many demons.' The next verse says, 'And in the morning, rising up a great while before day, he went out and departed into a solitary place and there prayed.' I realized that if Jesus, the Son of God, had to go out alone and spend time on spiritual development, who was I to imagine that I could be a good missionary without doing the same thing? I wrote down on a piece of paper: 'I've got to make huge provision for the cultivation of my soul.'"[4]

Walter made immediate changes in his work schedule so that for the next three years, he led the monthly spiritual meetings of the young people's group that met Sunday evenings at his church. He made another spiritual commitment while at medical school: he became more active in the Student Volunteer Movement for Foreign Missions, a private-sector forerunner of the Peace Corps. Founded in the 1880s by five Princeton students, the movement had by the 1920s inspired more than ten thousand young American men and women to become foreign mission workers under the sponsorship of their own denomination's mission boards. In December 1923, the Student Volunteer Movement held its ninth quadrennial convention in Indianapolis; the student vice chairman and keynote speaker of the convention was Dr. Walter H. Judd, newly graduated from the University of Nebraska Medical College in Omaha and an intern at the hospital there. This was not just another convention, but a coming together of over seven thousand young Christian leaders from forty-one states as well as Canada, China, Japan, South America, and Africa. That Walter Judd was picked to deliver the keynote address was testimony to his speaking ability and his commitment to the missionary life. He was equal to the task, challenging the students to "blaze new trails and endeavor to make the world see Jesus's way out of the world troubles of today."

As he usually did, the soon-to-be medical missionary began by asking questions: "What is wrong with the world? How did it get in such a mess? What is the way out?" His answers resonated with the theme of "The Quitter": "The world must have a spiritual regeneration," he declared, "or it is going to smash, at least that part of it which we call civilized. The greatest need of the world, I say, is the spiritual awakening on the part of the average American student. Instead of living comfortably, happy with social gaieties, he should really be concerned about the affairs of the world. . . . students should have vision, then conviction enough to be willing to lay down their lives for this conviction. . . ." The huge audience of young men and women sat enthralled as the young orator described a "conviction" that meant giving up selfish ambition and the opportunity to become rich, famous, and popular; and choosing instead poverty, obscurity, and even death. Here was no armchair Christian but one willing to sacrifice all, as David Livingstone had given all in his missionary work in Africa. With his words pouring forth almost faster than they could be understood, he looked out at the hushed crowd and concluded: "The way out may be radical. It may be revolutionary. If it is Christ's way, let it be radical and revolutionary. His way was radical and revolutionary when He walked among men on earth. Let us blaze new trails. There is great need for missionaries, but unless we are better here, now, in our own homes, there's no use going to the mission fields. Let us cast our net into the deep."[5]

As the applause swelled and filled the Cadle Tabernacle, Walter Judd thanked God for being able to bring his message to so many young Christians. And the Student Volunteer Movement thanked God for the gift of an eloquent, dedicated young man who agreed to become a traveling secretary for the movement in the 1924–25 school year before he left for China. Walter traveled back and forth across the country, visiting some one hundred college campuses, speaking in chapels, talking about the missions, urging the young men and women in the audiences to cast out their nets. In the early spring of 1925, he came to

Mount Holyoke College in western Massachusetts and was met at the train station by Miriam Barber, a Holyoke junior who had also decided to become a missionary.

"There was an annual conference of colleges in the Connecticut Valley," recalled Miriam Judd, "for students who might be interested in serving abroad. Walter was a principal speaker. I was asked to meet the speaker at the trolley and take him to his guest room in the dormitory where he would stay for the weekend. I was also to see that he got to chapel on time the next morning to deliver his speech. (I've been seeing that he gets to meetings on time ever since.)

"He was dynamic and spoke with conviction. His sense of conviction is the thing that has always affected audiences any place. He seemed to know where he was going, or where he should be going. I sat there with my eyes wide open and thought, 'Boy, what a guy.' Someone said at the end of the meeting, after he finished talking about missionary work and what he hoped to do in China, that any girl in the audience would have gone with him immediately. I didn't 'fall' in that sense, although he was very stimulating, because I had the India 'bug.' "[6]

What Walter Judd talked about at Holyoke and all the other colleges and universities he visited was why American students should leave what he called "non-Christian America" for the Orient. He confessed that when he first determined to become a medical missionary at the age of seventeen, he thought that the purpose of missionaries was to bring to "supposedly unfortunate peoples" all the benefits and advantages of Western civilization, including Western medicine, education, industry, and religion. But World War I brought disillusionment. "I became," he admitted, "painfully conscious of the great chasms of iniquity here at home, the paganism of our industrial system, our un-Christian measurement of success, our perverted standards of patriotism and inhumane social order." He was forced to re-examine his missionary purpose from top to bottom, and at first concluded that becoming a foreign missionary was useless until there was first a "cleanup in America." He did not want to throw his life away by going abroad. But the more he reflected, the more he realized that the way to reform America was not only to be found in America. No country, not even the great United States, was an island unto itself.

In an interdependent world, the modern missionary had a special mission. In teaching the Gospel to foreigners, he should eliminate Western additions and interpretations and present the New Testament unadorned. "That is," said Judd, "he goes [to Asia] not to take our special brand of *theology,* but our *religion.*" After all, he said, trying to shock his fellow westerners, Christianity "was an Oriental religion in the first place." The modern missionary, he argued, should respect the ideas and customs of the foreign land in which he labors: "he does not say or believe that all our ideas and customs are right and all theirs are wrong." In an age filled with warnings about the "yellow peril" and condescending remarks about "savage heathen," this was radical and even revolutionary talk; but Walter Judd had studied the history of China and other Eastern civilizations and knew that many of their habits and customs were "far better suited to them than any we could bring from our lands." The goal of the missionary, he insisted, was to center his message "around the person and principles of Jesus, leaving [the Asians] to work out their own concrete expressions of what they find in Him, and to build their own theology and religious system and civilization under the inspiration of His life and the guidance of His teachings, as *they* understand them. Please God, what they build will be *better* than what the West has built."[7] The young missionary's call for partnership, not paternalism, invariably inspired the young men and women whom he addressed, but created serious problems when he took up missionary work in China. For many old-time missionaries, paternalism was a way of life and of salvation.

He was going to China, he explained, because that was where the needs were the greatest and the workers were the fewest: there was only one Western doctor for every twenty thousand people in China, compared with one doctor for every thousand people in America. He was leaving his family, friends, and home to go halfway around the world because "my study of the [world's] needs and of myself convinced me that the place where I can work to the best advantage of the whole cause is in China. Not because I love America less but because I love her more, I go to the Orient."[8]

Walter and Miriam saw each other casually a few times after that, in connection with their work for the Student Volunteer Movement, but their thoughts were more focused on the Far East than each other. After college she went to teach in India where she had been born, the daughter of the YMCA secretary in the then capital of Calcutta. They did not meet again for six years, during which time they only exchanged letters once. In the summer of 1925, Walter Judd booked passage for China, and the country boy from Rising City, who had studied the colored maps of St. Paul's journeys in his mother's Sunday school classes, had been inspired by Livingstone's heroic expeditions in Africa, and had accepted Dad Elliott's challenge to give unstintingly of his talents, found himself in an ancient land that was undergoing the most revolutionary changes in all of its four-thousand-year history.

CHAPTER THREE

◆

The Middle Kingdom

IN OCTOBER 1911, Sun Yat-sen and other Chinese revolutionaries proclaimed a Republic of China and within six months abolished a 2100-year-old monarchy. Sun quickly discovered the old political truth that revolution is easy but governing is hard. The first to try ruling the unruly four hundred millions of China was Yuan Shih-kai, who, as John K. Fairbank wrote, "knew how to make the old system work but . . . had no vision of a new system."[1] Yuan assassinated opponents, dismissed military governors in the southern provinces, dissolved the Nationalist Party or Kuomintang (KMT) created by Sun, acceded partially to humiliating Japanese demands for territory and authority, and finally announced he would become emperor. Armed opposition quickly formed to his imperial designs, and in March 1916 Yuan suddenly retired, amid demonstrations against him in Peking. In the ensuing political vacuum, political factions vied for power, warlords strengthened their arms and armies, Sun looked for help in the West and the East, and the "world's largest nation appeared to be on the verge of disintegration."[2]

Foreign influence inevitably grew amid the chaos. Shanghai, China's most populous city, was run by a municipal council dominated by the British. Most of China's big cities were treaty ports and protected by British, American, and other foreign gunboats. Westerners were not the

21

only ones to take advantage of China. Japan argued that a weak China had exposed all of the Far East to greedy barbarians. Because China had failed to exert leadership, the Japanese declared, it must now accept the role of follower and give part of its vast territory to the new leader, Japan. The central issue, Tokyo insisted, was not Chinese sovereignty but Japanese losses. After all, more than one million Japanese had died in the Russo-Japanese War; the German naval base at Tsingtao had been secured in 1915 with the lives of two thousand soldiers and sailors. These sacrifices had been caused by China's weakness, asserted the Japanese, and they must be compensated for.[3] A more enlightened foreign influence in China was a network of several hundred Protestant missionary schools and hospitals located throughout the provinces; however, the missionaries shared many of the same privileges as the foreign businessmen and military. They too were protected by treaty provisions which made foreigners and their property and servants subject only to the laws of their own countries and immune to Chinese law except through their own foreign consulates.

Chinese patriotism finally erupted on May 4, 1919, when some three thousand Peking students demonstrated against a secret deal between Japan and the corrupt Anfu government in Peking. The student manifesto declared: "China's territory may be conquered, but it cannot be given away. The Chinese people may be massacred, but they will not surrender. Our country is about to be annihilated. Rise up, brethren."[4] The Peking riot touched off nationwide demonstrations, boycotts, strikes and other manifestations of anti-Japanese sentiment. This patriotic fervor helped the Nationalists gain political power in the following years, but the strong anti-Japanese feelings created serious problems for a nation which, despite its formidable size and enormous population, remained weak and divided.

Sun seized the opportunity presented by the May Fourth movement to begin a tour of Canton and other provincial capitals in South China, the political base of the Kuomintang. He reminded military governors and the people that his party had won a majority in the last free elections before Yuan had carried out his coup in 1913. He promised to restore order and eliminate chaos. The Chinese communists also attempted to capitalize on the May Fourth movement, but their radical politics, small numbers, and sparse military support prevented them from winning a broad following. Their cause was also weakened when the Kuomintang accepted Marxists as members, obviating the need for Chinese communist leadership. All these advantages, plus a divided and legally questionable government in Peking, by 1925 enabled the Kuomintang to control "territories more valuable, in terms of population and resources, than any the communists could claim until 1940."[5]

In forging his Nationalist coalition, Sun accepted aid from the new Bolshevik government in Moscow, in part because he was rebuffed by the U.S. State Department, which adopted a policy of "strict impartiality as between the local leaders of political factions in China."[6] The Nationalist leader welcomed a contingent of Soviet military advisers and weapons aid, and agreed to a "united front" with the Chinese Communist party. There seemed to be little risk in accepting communists: they had after all only 1000 party members compared with the Kuomintang's 150,000; their military failures in the Yangtze Valley contrasted sharply with Kuomintang successes in Canton. Sun sent his top aide, Chiang Kai-shek, to Moscow in October 1923 to work out the details of the Soviet military aid program that was linked to the united front with the Chinese communists. Upon his return, an alarmed Chiang reported to Sun and other members of the KMT standing committee that the Soviet Communist party was not to be trusted and that the Chinese communists he met in Moscow always spoke slanderously of Sun. He said: "The Russian Communist Party, in its dealings with China, has only one aim, namely to make the Chinese Communist Party its chosen instrument. . . . It is the policy of the Russian Communist Party to turn the lands inhabited by the Manchus, Mongols, Moslems and Tibetans into parts of the Soviet domain; it may harbour sinister designs even on China proper."[7]

Chiang Kai-shek's anticommunism remained a driving force of his political philosophy as long as he lived. It made him in later years a major target of those in the West who saw communism as the wave of the future in China. These apologists did not like to be reminded that in the early 1920s, Chiang perceived dangers in communism that they would not admit even after the Stalinist purges of the 1930s and the Nazi-Soviet Pact of 1939. But Chiang's blunt warning about Russian intentions did not carry much weight in the early 1920s as the Kuomintang sought to consolidate its power.[8]

Central to this consolidation was the Northern Expedition to defeat the warlords of the north and unite all China under one government and one party, an initiative approved at the KMT party congress in 1924. While trying to raise money for the expedition and at the same time to negotiate with a northern warlord, Sun fell ill and died of cancer in Peking in March 1925. He was soon canonized as the Father of the

Nation by both Nationalists and communists. The struggle for succession immediately began, but Chiang Kai-shek was not among the leading candidates. Chiang was young by Chinese standards (in his late thirties), a soldier not a politician, and not a prominent party man, although of course a member of the party. However, as Fairbank wrote, "the times called forth the man." A military politician was needed to conquer the warlords and create a central government. Chiang had the "qualities of patriotic determination to unify China plus qualities of personal leadership, decisiveness, foresight, and chicanery that were needed in the late 1920s and early 1930s if warlordism was to be liquidated."[9]

It was at this precarious time in its history that Walter Judd set foot for the first time in the Middle Kingdom. He was eager to go immediately into the field, but was required to spend one year at the Chinese Language School of the University of Nanking. With sixty other young missionaries, male and female, he learned the language, speaking only Chinese for five hours a day, and studied Chinese history and culture. Impatient as always, he finally realized the wisdom of the program: "Instead of being plunged headlong into the concrete responsibilities of a station, and forced to work out our own salvation almost as if we were the first missionaries in China, we [were] given a year for gradual induction into them." Such careful instruction had not been given to most earlier Christian missionaries, who took up their duties lacking any real knowledge of those they were supposed to succor but filled with zeal to convert the "heathen."[10]

The Nanking school pointed out that for more than 2500 years, the Chinese had articulated and practiced Christian ideas such as monotheism, the brotherhood of man, the Golden Rule, the failure of force, the omnipotence of love in human relationships, and the supremacy of the spiritual over the material. Slowly, the young Protestant missionaries began to understand the Chinese people, not only academicians and intellectuals, but workers and farmers as well, and to note their remarkable patience and irresistible good cheer. "Take a drizzly, cold morning," wrote Judd, "the fifth in succession, perhaps, without a letup. One glance at our faces reveals that it has put a pretty hard strain on many Christian dispositions. We are feeling pretty 'low.' And here [a Chinese] comes pulling his ricksha through the mud and slush, barefoot, drenched, shivering with the cold but smiling, joking, and 'on top of the world.' "[11]

The young Americans learned the history of the Protestant missionary movement in China, a story of remarkable growth founded on extraordinary fervor. In 1800, not a single Protestant Christian lived in China—no Anglicans, no Methodists, no Presbyterians, no Congregationalists. The only Christians in China were some 250,000 Catholics, scattered across the country, and a few Orthodox; but by 1889, Protestants numbered nearly 40,000. K.S. Latourette and other scholars have credited the success of the Protestant missions to their indefatigability and increased freedom of movement.[12] There were periodic xenophobic reactions to the growing influence of the missionaries, culminating in the Boxer Rebellion of 1900, when placards read: "Catholics and Protestants have vilified our gods and sages ... conspired with the foreigners, destroyed Buddhist images, seized our people's graveyards. This has angered Heaven." There were calls to "wipe out the foreigners," and before the death and destruction were stopped by an international army, 250 foreigners, mostly missionaries, and 32,000 Chinese Christians had been killed.[13] However, the deaths and heroism of the Boxer Rebellion aroused the determination of Christians in the United States and Europe to continue and even expand their efforts in China. Education became a central concern. The number of primary schools was sharply increased, reaching a high point in 1920 with over 6,000 schools and almost 175,000 pupils, four times as many children as in 1905. Just before the start of the Sino-Japanese War in 1937, the number of secondary school students was over 74,000. At the higher education level, Protestant institutions led the field with thirteen universities.

Medical care and training also received heavy emphasis. Before the Japanese plundered and the communists confiscated, Protestants had some 300 hospitals in China with nearly 500 male doctors and 150 female doctors working in them. In addition, they set up six medical colleges with a total of more than 500 students. The printed word, always a key element in evangelization, was not neglected in China, despite the translation difficulties. In 1924, some nine million copies or parts of the Bible were distributed; in 1937, distribution was more modest, with about 68,000 Bibles and an equal number of New Testaments. The total number of Protestant Christians in China during the mid-1930s was just under half a million, serviced by 5,700 foreign missionaries and about 16,000 Chinese evangelical workers.[14]

Confronted with the vastness and complexity of China, young American missionaries usually reacted in one of three ways. Some refused to admit the Christ-likeness they found among the non-Christian Chinese, as though such an admission would somehow detract from the supremacy of Christ. Some went to the other extreme, saying, "Well, I guess the Chinese don't need Christ since they are about as well off in most respects—even better in some—than we are who came to bring Him." The third and smallest group, which included Walter Judd, decided to study the best and the worst in China, "not as compared to what exists at home or to what we thought existed here, but only as compared to Christ." They would abide by the conclusions of their study, "no matter how different they may be from what we expected or perhaps wanted." For Judd and other open-minded missionaries like him, the message of Christ was not contrary to the teachings of the Chinese sages but beyond them. Sounding one of his essential missionary themes, he later wrote in the *Student Volunteer Movement Bulletin:* "Unless we are willing to meet the Chinese on this basis of building on their best and allowing them to develop their own church organizations and forms of worship as they are led to God, we might almost as well pack up and go home."[15] His analysis was in the spirit of David Livingstone, who encouraged the natives of Africa to run their own churches, but the advocacy of such independence in China did not sit well with many missionaries, particularly of an older generation, who still regarded the Chinese as heathen who needed Western help to enter the kingdom of Heaven. Because he always insisted on speaking his mind once it was made up, Judd found himself increasingly unpopular among some more conservative missionaries.

There were plenty of things for the missionary students to do outside of the classroom. They taught Sunday school classes for the children of foreign missionaries and businessmen, worked with the Christian Endeavor Society, served as scoutmasters for the Boy Scouts, and coached the youngsters in basketball and football. They socialized with the young diplomats of the many foreign missions in Nanking and competed against them in sports. They taught English to Chinese students in classes organized by the YMCA, Nanking University, or Southeastern University, the large coeducational institution sponsored by the Nationalist government. Judd participated with the four other doctors in his class in two medical clinics held at least twice a week. It was a demanding year, but he emerged from it with his enthusiasm and commitment intact and with the title of class president. He was posted to the Shaowu Mission in the town of Shaowu, Fukien Province, so far into the interior that it could only be reached by a ten-day boat trip up the Min River. He arrived in early October 1926 and spent the next five years in Shaowu, caring for the sick and the dying, working under a saintly but anachronistic older missionary, facing death at the hands of bandits, debating ideology with communists, going for months without seeing another white face, and falling deeply in love with China, until, his life threatened by persistent malaria, he reluctantly came home to the United States.

Fukien was one of the most rural and mountainous of all the provinces in China. It was said that there was not a level place ten miles square in the entire province except in the delta near the mouth of the Min River where the capital city of Foochow was located and near Amoy, the other major port. Outside Foochow, travel was by narrow dirt roads, sometimes paved with cobblestones, through the valleys and over the mountain passes. The province was also divided by language: of China's four hundred dialects, two hundred of them were reportedly spoken by the people of Fukien. Beyond every ridge was another valley in which could be found villages with populations ranging from a dozen families up to five thousand people in a central market town. Each valley raised enough food for itself and had little or no contact with the next valley, ten or twenty miles away. Shaowu was more sophisticated: "From our area," Judd recalled, "they shipped rice or tea by small boats down the river to the coast, and then, propelled by poles or pulled by tow ropes, brought back cloth, salt, kerosene and a few manufactured products."[16]

In Shaowu, he joined Dr. Edward Bliss, who had been a medical missionary in China for decades. "He was one of the finest, most benevolent, loving men that ever lived," remarked Judd, "but from my point of view, he was a failure as a missionary because he did things *for* people, always *for* people. He had been there almost forty years, and not a single [Chinese] boy or girl had gone away from there to study medicine. I didn't try to argue with him because he was too saintly a man. But I did with the [Mission] Board. You never can send enough American missionaries to deal with the health problems out there. [The solution is] helping Chinese to become doctors and nurses."[17]

One day, he watched a patient who had been given some medicine by Dr. Bliss walk out into the street and pour it on the ground. He asked the man why he had done that. "It can't be any good," replied the Chinese. "He gave it to me for nothing." Judd suggested to his older colleague that they charge their Chinese patients something for the medicine "for their self-respect." Dr. Bliss was uncertain. "If the medicine is worth a dollar," he asked, "you don't give it to them for ten cents or five cents, do you?" "Sure," said the younger missionary, "let them pay that or two cents or whatever they can afford. Don't make them feel inferior by our 'philanthropy.' "

He believed, as a missionary and later as a member of Congress, that there were three basic questions to be considered when providing assistance to peoples and nations. First, how much did they need? The answer, in almost all cases, was a great deal. Second, how much could they effectively use? The answer was, not as much as they needed. The third and most important question was, how much could they receive without feeling inferior as human beings. Often, the answer was not very much. He learned from the Chinese that it was better to teach a man how to fish than to give him a fish. He despaired of the arrogant American approach. "We're always the great benevolent benefactors," he commented. "They're always the humble backward inferior recipients. That doesn't build human beings."[18]

Because of such firm convictions, Judd's missionary career was almost a crusade aimed as much at missionaries as non-Christians. He saw his mission as not just "to treat patients every day—that was a means and was good in itself—but to build a kingdom on earth as Christians." He tried to think of tomorrow as well as today. "My father used to say, 'wisdom consists of foresight.' And for whatever reason, I seem to have always had foresight. I could see what was coming." What he saw fast approaching for American missionaries in China was their condemnation as imperialists like so many other foreigners in the country. The crisis came faster than even he expected. In the wake of the Shameen incident in Canton in 1925 (when foreign troops fired on and killed hundreds of innocent Chinese civilians), the newly organized All-China Students' Federation passed a resolution branding the missionaries and their academic establishments as "tools of imperialism" and calling on Chinese students to boycott them.[19]

A year later, shortly after his arrival in Shaowu, Chiang Kai-shek's troops moved through the city on their Northern Expedition to unify China. Some of the men were communist or communist-influenced and preached revolution, calling for the removal of all foreign influences, including missionaries. The American Board of Commissioners for Foreign Missions, to which Walter Judd and Edward Bliss both reported, as well as the U.S. Consulate in Foochow advised and then urged all missionaries, especially those with families, to leave the interior. They feared there might be a bloody repetition of the Boxer Rebellion.

Because Dr. Bliss's family was in the United States and Judd was not married, the two of them remained in a bandit-ridden, war-torn territory, in which the wise man stayed close to the walls of his city. In a letter to his parents written on Christmas night, 1926, Walter Judd described how the "head men" of Shaowu tried to close down the Christian schools and to set up their own schools. "Terrific pressure has been put on these [Christian] students and their parents but no one ever saw finer loyalty anywhere on earth. These youngsters are made of true gold." He told of a big anti-Christian parade featuring banners that read "Down with Christianity" (literally, "strike down the church"). But several Christian girls hastily made banners that read, "On with the church" and joined the parade. "The workers who marched," wrote Judd, "were just obeying instructions; they were shouting, 'Kill the foreigners, kill the Christians, kill the foreigners' slaves,' and grinning at me at the same time." Still, he admitted, the present situation was close to anarchy, with uniformed bandits wandering about the missionary houses at all hours of the day and often taking what they wanted.[20]

In the early spring of 1927, Nationalist soldiers, inspired by communist propaganda against the British government and resentful of the longtime British presence in China, came to Shaowu looking for British citizens and thought they had found one—in Walter Judd. He was bound and taken to the river bank to be shot. "I protested the best I could that I was not a Britisher. They didn't believe me. I tried to get my passport, but they wouldn't let me loose. I was talking full speed. It is amazing how well you can talk Chinese when you have to!"

A crowd gathered to watch the execution, among them a farmer whom Judd did not recognize but had treated for a boil some months earlier. The farmer heard the foreigner protest that he was not an Englishman but an American, from "Meikuo" [America]. The man did not know what or where "Meikuo" was, but he realized it could save the foreigner's life. "He got down on his knees," remembered Judd, "and hit his forehead on the rocks until the blood ran out. He grabbed [the soldiers] by their knees. One man grabbed him by the back of his coat while another stabbed his bayonet through the coat next to his skin. They hit him with the butts of their guns. He did not stop. He just *knew* I was from America!" The farmer delayed things enough so that more senior officials at last came and after listening to the medical missionary's explanations, apologized and let him go; they hadn't intended to kill any Americans. "You can do a lot for people," said Judd, "who will risk their life to save yours."[21]

Shortly after, a strongly worded proclamation was issued by General

Chiang Kai-shek ordering the protection of all foreign and Chinese lives and property. But Chiang's order was so casually obeyed that in March, April, and again in May, Nationalist units occupied mission property and caused damage in the thousands of dollars. Despite his vulnerable position, Judd did not hesitate to criticize the Nationalist government and its leaders when necessary. Writing in June 1927 for the *Shanghai Times,* for which he was a regular monthly correspondent, he concluded that in the six months since the Nationalist army had arrived in Fukien, conditions for the common people were worse and not better. "It is no kindness to China or to the world," he wrote, "to whitewash facts no matter how disappointing and painful they are. The situation is all the more pathetic because of the many splendid, high-minded Chinese in the movement, true patriots they are, whose ideals and efforts are being reduced to worse than nought by the army of utterly selfish seekers after power and position and soft jobs with big salaries."

Nor did he spare his fellow missionaries when he felt that they had lost sight of their mission in China. Unable to contain himself any longer, he wrote a nineteen-page, single-spaced letter (he was never a man of few words) to the Reverend William E. Strong, head of the American Board for Missions in Boston. In this extraordinary epistle, Pauline in its insistence on Christ and not a legalistic Christianity as the keystone of faith, the young missionary poured out his passionate beliefs about the true role of a foreign missionary and pointed out that he had predicted, accurately, the decline and near fall of the Protestant missionary system in China. He stressed his disappointment, not in the Chinese for their threats against foreigners, but in missionaries for their "always-has-been, always-must-be, maintain-the-status-quo smug complacency." He expressed amazement that so many missionaries should be surprised by the depth of the antiforeign sentiment. "To me," he wrote, "the most pathetic thing of all is that when we wake up, instead of standing like men and taking our medicine, shouldering our share of the blame (which in my judgment is about 95 percent of the total) we start whimpering like spoiled babies, shaking our heads together in great sorrow, wondering why we should have to suffer all this when we are so entirely undeserving, lamenting that the Chinese are so ungrateful and no longer carry us around on little pedestals, etc., etc., etc."

He also criticized those who, in an emotional overreaction, now counseled that missionaries should turn everything over to the Chinese and immediately leave. It made far more sense to him to stay on the job "to work under them as they have worked under [us] these many years, helping . . . to get them through the difficulties which I fear are likely to prove too much for many a group unassisted." Their Chinese flock, he declared, had the right to expect more from their foreign leaders than a pious prayer, a somber hymn, or the recitation of the Creed: "Apparently," the young American wrote with disdain, "the proper thing to do is rather to drop everything and flee for our own lives at the first threat of danger." If that was the case, he added, in the logical way that was to gain supporters and frustrate opponents in Congress, then the Congregationalists should "quit making heroes out of the Pilgrims" and "destroy the biographies of David Livingstone" and similar missionaries who had risked privation and even death and "still stuck at their posts."

For himself, he would leave Shaowu if and only if the Chinese Nationalist government asked him to leave ("I am ready to be ordered out but not to be scared out"); the U.S. government adopted a policy of withdrawing all its citizens from China ("I was not called to China by my government nor will I be called out by it, unless its reasons become more cogent than anything yet put forth"); the mission or the American Board asked him to withdraw (in such a case, he said he would consider offering his services to the Nationalist army "if that could be done without my giving specific or implicit approval to those features of their program to which I object"); the Chinese Christians asked him to go because they were being persecuted for their relationships with foreigners; and it became apparent that he could serve "the Cause for which I came to China better by leaving than I can by staying." His belief that that moment had not come was reinforced by the leading Chinese pastor in Shaowu, who told him, "We, of course, have felt that more and more of the responsibility should be turned over to us, but what can we do with all this mass which is suddenly dumped on us and for the handling of which we have been given no training?"

He concluded by saying that one of his main reasons for coming to China was to seek in its young church "the heart of what it means to be a Christian" and then returning home "to show us in the West the way." He had found what he hoped he would find, "a vigorous faith and real religious experience." He did not anticipate the slightest danger in staying on, but if there were risks to be run, it was worth taking them: "I should far rather have my career end here and now, by whatever method, than I cause one of these, my brethren, even the least, to stumble. I certainly do not want anyone to feel sorry for me. Come what may, this is enough for me. 'The Lord is my shepherd. I shall not want.' "[22]

The letter was a declaration of independence by the young missionary, a defiant assertion that he would not be bound by traditional approaches to spreading the gospel in China; he would continue to do all that he could to penetrate the prevailing self-satisfaction and stagnation among his fellow missionaries. It is a measure of Walter Judd's persuasive rhetoric and his effective service in Shaowu, and Dr. Strong's appreciation of both, that there was no reprimand from Boston and no more suggestions that he leave the interior.

He did not want for opportunities to practice medicine or his faith during the four more years that he remained in Shaowu. In the winter of 1929, Dr. Bliss, then in his sixties, fell very ill, and it was decided to take him down the Min River to Foochow where he would receive better care. There was danger on the river from bandits looking for foreigners who would bring a handsome ransom, but there was certain death for the aged missionary if he stayed in Shaowu. The first two days of travel passed without incident, but on the third day, the two Americans were stopped by roughly dressed men carrying weapons. "If they take me up on the hills," thought Judd, "I'm young and perhaps can talk them out of it. But if they take this sick man, he will die in one night of midwinter exposure." Miraculously, he recognized among the bandits a former hospital patient in Shaowu who had become a friend. Knowing that no Chinese liked to be thought of as a bandit, he decided to apply some Oriental psychology.

"My," he said, "I am glad I ran into you. I was nervous about things. This old doctor with me is very ill. I had to bring him down the river. I heard there were bandits down here. I was afraid we might run into some."

"That's right," the man replied. "There *are* bandits down here. You ought not to be here."

"I know it," said Judd, "but we had to come. Can't you do something to help us through the bandits?"

He knew that the man was a bandit. The bandit knew that the American knew that he was a bandit. But neither admitted it. The Chinese had the opportunity not only to save face but to save the two foreigners and thereby to place them deeply in his debt. A fierce discussion among the bandits ensued. The missionaries overheard talk about carrying them off and demanding a ransom of $50,000; the Chinese believed that all foreigners were rich and that was the going ransom rate—$25,000 a barbarian. They argued back and forth for two hours, and at last Judd's onetime patient, a bandit but withal one with honor, prevailed. He placed four of his men on the missionary boats and told them to proceed "slowly," enabling him to send runners ahead to tell the main body of bandits farther down the river not to shoot or capture the foreigners. "We didn't see any of the bandits as we went along. But of course they were there in the grass looking at us."[23]

He accompanied Dr. Bliss all the way home to the United States and visited his parents in Rising City before going on to Boston where the American Board warmly welcomed him and scheduled talks at several Congregational churches to raise money for the missions. Then it was back to China and Shaowu where he was now the only Western doctor. He talked Chinese, ate Chinese (taking his evening meals in a Chinese home), thought Chinese, and dreamed Chinese. He floated in a sea of yellow. One morning, he woke up and went into the washroom to shave. He looked into the mirror and was jolted to see—a white face! During these many months of immersion and isolation, he became as Chinese as it is possible for a foreigner to become. He asked himself as every visitor has asked himself: Why is China the way it is? What makes China so different from the West? Why is there so much chaos and anarchy? Why can't the Chinese people get together? He organized his reflections about China, its people, its history, its philosophy, into a talk called "A Philosophy of Life That Works," which he delivered to young Christians upon his return to the United States.

China, he pointed out, had built and maintained for over four thousand years a civilization on the assumption of an unchanging world, unlike the West, which was based on the assumption of a changing world. China was surrounded and protected by natural barriers, the Himalayas, the Tibetan plateau, the Gobi Desert, the Siberian plains, and the Pacific Ocean. China did not need to change because she lived as if on a separate planet. But with the coming of the steam engine and the steamboat, the West abolished the barrier of the Pacific, and Chinese civilization was doomed. Her civilization was the best the world had ever seen, he argued, "for a stationary world," but it was utterly inadequate for a "rapidly changing world."

Secondly, her civilization was built around the natural unit of the family, while that of the West was built around the political unit, the state or nation. In the old China, as long as a man maintained the peace and paid his taxes, there was no interference by the government. "His family, his clan, his little neighborhood, ran themselves quite satisfactorily for four thousand years with a minimum of organization." Furthermore, China had no one centralizing religion, as did Japan, but emphasized ancestor worship or reverence. Everything in China, said Judd, was disunified, decentralized, decontrolled.[24]

The third major contrast between China and the West revolved around the question, "What is the chief virtue?" The West stressed abstract principles like honor, integrity, truth. In China the chief virtue was loyalty to one's family—what the Chinese call "filial piety"—and to one's friends. The sudden changes of allegiance by Chinese political or military figures which were often seen as "treachery" by Westerners were considered acts of loyalty to family or friends by the Chinese.

The fourth contrast concerned the question, "How does one achieve happiness?" In the West, the determination to overcome or conquer one's environment "gives us a great drive," Judd asserted. But inevitably one ran up against something that could not be changed or overcome, "and we have not learned how to yield." Chinese civilization was based on Confucius's Doctrine of the [Golden] Mean—moderation in all things. "When you came to something too difficult, the thing to do was ... to adjust yourself to it.... To master your inner soul was more important than to master the things of your external environment." He readily admitted that such a system had its disadvantages, encouraging people to give up too easily in the face of obstacles and not to take failures too seriously.[25]

But many Chinese were determined to change their nation and their people, to bring them into the twentieth century. One group advocated a capitalistic system of private property and competition. Another group urged communism, the nationalization of natural resources, industries, transportation. Conflicting solutions burst forth as if an intellectual dam had been broken. Which one was right for China? Who would decide what was best for China? Someone once complained to Judd, "What is the matter with China? Why doesn't she ever get a great man, an Abraham Lincoln, a George Washington, or even a Mussolini?" With all due respect to a great American, the medical missionary responded, "Abraham Lincoln's task was a little afternoon tea party as compared with the task of Chiang Kai-shek, the erstwhile president of China. Let no man think China has no great men. Chiang Kai-shek is a giant—[he] would stand out among any Western leaders I have ever seen as a giant—and there are others. ... no other political leader in the history of the human race has ever tackled anything even remotely approaching in magnitude and difficulty and complexity this task— essentially the same task on a vastly magnified scale that Moses had out in the wilderness for forty years—making a *nation* out of a people."[26]

Judd delivered this tribute to Chiang Kai-shek without ever meeting him, after the Shaowu mission had been wantonly damaged by Nationalist forces, and after almost losing his life twice at the hands of bandits because the Nationalist government was unable to maintain order in Fukien Province. Nevertheless, he perceived in the Nationalist leader many of the same strengths and weaknesses that had been present in Sun Yat-sen.

In June 1929, on returning to China after taking Dr. Bliss home to the United States, Judd stopped in Nanking to attend the formal dedication of a gigantic marble tomb to Sun, the father of modern China. "I was welded," he recalled, "as never before with the heart of the Chinese people." He traveled to Foochow with C.J. Lin, the president of Fukien Christian University, who admitted that he had been discouraged that spring when they had graduated only twenty young men, but who now declared that the ceremony in honor of Sun had rejuvenated him. "He was only one man," said Dr. Lin, "but for forty years he never swerved a hair's breadth from one great ideal and devotion. And he, one man, changed the whole face of China. . . . He was a man of absolute integrity." Judd used the same words about Chiang—calling him a man of integrity, devotion, idealism, and flaws—in the course of the years. He agreed with Dr. Lin that there was no hope for China except in such men, and "no way of building men of character adequate for the task save as they are introduced to and follow Jesus Christ. I believed that before. I am dead sure of it now."[27] He was also certain of Chiang's central importance in building a new China because of his keen understanding of modern man's most cunning enemy—communism.

Judd had many communists as his patients in Shaowu and was always impressed by their discipline and their dedication. The communists first came through his city in 1926, when they were part of Chiang Kai-shek's united front against the warlords. "They were the first military outfit I ever saw," he said, "that never had a case of venereal disease." When the communists tried to take over the Nationalist government in 1927 and were purged by Chiang, some of them wound up in the interior of Fukien Province. Sometimes, his communist patients tried to brainwash the young American doctor. They would say to him: "You capitalists"—given Judd's minuscule salary of $500 a year that always amused him—"think that Karl Marx thought up a theory, that communism is a doctrine, a philosophy. No, it's more than that. Karl Marx discovered a *law*." Poring over the history books in the library of the British Museum, Marx noticed a consistent pattern in history: there was

35

always war when some people owned property and other people sold their labor for wages. The communists argued with Judd that when one man tries to get more for himself and his family while another tries to get a better home, they clash. This was why people had wars. "Don't you want peace?" they asked the American. "If so, you must change your system. You capitalists have a system which makes war inevitable."

One communist in particular, articulate, reasonable, persistent, repeated all these arguments to Judd, who finally replied: "Well, sir, I know you believe this, I'm sure you do. And I have to admit, it sounds reasonable. But I can't accept it." "Why?" asked the communist. "Because," the missionary said, "I think it's against human nature." The communist's eyes blazed as he retorted: "Human nature, human nature, you capitalists always talk about human nature. *There is no such thing as human nature!*" With those words, the communists earned the undying opposition of Walter Judd to communism. He knew in his heart, his soul, and his mind that human nature did exist and that it came from God. The Chinese communist continued to speak: "Human nature's what you make it; it isn't anything genetic. As capitalism produces acquisitiveness, greed, clashes, and war, communism will produce concern for the masses, a good society, and everyone will be well-taken-care-of." Judd often wondered whether that communist lived to taste the bitter fruit of Mao Tse-tung's communism, under which tens of millions of Chinese died.[28]

In mid-1930, he learned how the communists tried to convert a town or area to communism. Chu Teh and Mao Tse-tung, with about five thousand men, returned to Fukien Province after a foray into south Kiangsi. They captured Tingchow and advanced toward Shaowu to the north. Writing in the *Shanghai Times,* Judd described the communist pattern. First, burn the [town hall], destroying if possible all records, property titles and so forth. Second, wipe out bandits and shoot without argument all members of the Kuomintang, in retaliation for its "repudiation of Russia, splitting with the Communists and massacres of Reds in Canton and elsewhere." Third, burn or make unfit for occupation all foreign property, residences, schools, hospitals, usually holding foreigners for ransom, since they are worth more alive than dead. Fourth, slaughter all "capitalists," distributing their belongings and all rice among the "common people." Not even lawless bandits, he reflected, visited such death and damage on the people.[29]

Aside from debating communists, writing newspaper articles, and worrying about the future of foreign missionaries in China, Judd helped run the North Gate Hospital in Shaowu, conducted an outpatient clinic, and made house calls. In 1927, for example, he treated more than eight thousand patients at the clinic, including eye, ear, nose, throat, obstetrics, gynecology, and urology; he treated over a hundred patients at the hospital, conducting 7 major and 346 minor operations, and he made approximately 600 house calls. As he commented in his personal report for 1927, 10,000 treatments in one year were "about 6000 too many for one doctor," who was in fact physician, laboratory technician, druggist, and even nurse in the majority of cases. He was grateful for his early training on a Nebraska farm where if any piece of equipment went wrong, it could be fixed with a piece of baling wire "if one had to." He learned in Shaowu that one could make a dressing stay in place on any part of the human anatomy with a piece of string, in the absence of bandage and adhesive. He summed up the year: "One can discover unrealized resources all about him in an emergency, but I shall be glad when this particularly lengthy emergency [caused by six different occupations by military forces] is over, and I hope never to have to practice medieval medicine again with only a twentieth-century training."[30]

At the same time, Judd counseled against building a modern hospital and maintaining foreign staff in Shaowu because of the uncertain political conditions in China and the decline of foreign missions donations in the United States, caused by the economic ripples spreading from the Great Depression. He made it clear that whatever was decided by the Missions Board, he would not return to Shaowu for a second term. A large part of the reason was physical: by 1930, his malaria had become so persistent that he seriously questioned whether he could remain in a climate where the disease was epidemic.

In October 1930, he became ill with his 44th and worst attack of malignant malaria, with the nearest doctor a twelve days' journey away. He had been taking quinine daily for years, but "this time the quinine was like water—and weak water at that." Amid the mounting fever and delirium, he wondered if he would die. "You are so miserable and lonely and far away, if you could just die and have the pain over with, what a relief. Yet something in your training won't let you give up." Before losing consciousness, he was able to instruct a Chinese nurse, a graduate of the Methodist Hospital in Peking, to obtain enough "good quinine" for eight or nine days from her uncle, who ran a medicine shop. "She went out to get the quinine. That is the last I remember for four days. But she got it—and she kept her head." Gradually he gained strength, and by December 1, he was able to get around a little: "It was like driving a car uphill with brakes on. You *can* get there, but there isn't much pickup in the old motor."[31]

A few days after his recovery, his life was again placed in jeopardy. For most of that year, Shaowu was under the control of Lu Hsin Ming, a bandit chief and "the most cruel, vicious man I ever saw." At the head of eight hundred bandits, Lu seized the city after Nationalist troops were withdrawn by Chiang and sent north to help put down a major revolt. Lu kept order, collected "taxes" to support himself and his men, and generally left the American mission and hospital alone. Fortunately for Judd and the other foreigners, the bandit chief contracted a bad case of conjunctivitis and took some Chinese medicine which made it worse. He came to the American doctor who was able to clear up the eye inflammation and place the petty warlord under some obligation to him. Meanwhile the fighting in the north ended, and the Nationalist troops began returning south in October, meaning that Lu's days in Shaowu were drawing to a close. Foreigners and the well-off among the Chinese grew apprehensive; Lu was certain to take them into the hills and hold them for ransom. Normally Judd could have survived, but after the last and almost fatal attack of malaria, "I knew what would happen to me in two days of exposure in the middle of the winter." Christmas passed and the day before New Year's arrived. A secretary in the bandit headquarters whom he had befriended told the American medical missionary that the Nationalist troops were only twenty miles away, and Lu intended to loot the city and leave with his prisoners, including Walter Judd, that very night. There was nothing he could do—he was in too weakened a condition to try to escape—but wait.

That evening, Lu himself came into the dispensary of the hospital and without preliminaries informed Judd that he need have no fear. "You have been fair with us and have taken care of us in the hospital here, and I know you are not getting any money out of it. . . . You have been sick yourself. If you had to live the way we will have to live, up on the hills in the middle of the winter, you wouldn't live long. I know it. Hence I am not going to take you." Then he said the most astonishing thing of all: "How much do we owe the hospital?" Lu paid $170 for services rendered, and left the city after midnight when the shops were closed and his men could not loot them. He did not take a single man or woman with him for ransom.

"I could think of only one thing as Lu sat there," recalled Judd, "Francis Thompson's 'Hound of Heaven.' It had been after him, and he could not do what he had planned." The American thought to himself, "If God can change the heart of such a man, he can change anybody."[32]

On January 21, 1931, Walter Judd reluctantly submitted his formal resignation from the Shaowu mission to the North Fukien Synod of the Church of Christ in China, giving three reasons: the work of the Christian church in the district would advance more rapidly and substantially if the foreign staff withdrew "for a few years"; a higher grade of medical work could be developed if the Chinese had complete responsibility and "set themselves to the task" without depending upon a foreign physician; and four years of frequent malarial attacks had made his health so uncertain that it would be "most unwise" to build up a medical practice around him. The first two reasons flowed from arguments he had been making for at least four years. As he had written in a letter to Shaowu missionaries several weeks earlier, there could be no significant change for the better at Shaowu and other missions "until a measure of mutual confidence and cooperation" was established between the church and missionaries on one hand and the Chinese on the other; but such confidence and cooperation were not possible because of the widespread distrust, especially among young Chinese, of the present foreign missionaries. "I can help the cause of Christ in Shaowu" the most, he said, "by getting out of the way of it. . . . I have faith in Christ and the Shaowu people to believe that a living Church can be built here by the Chinese Christians and our successors, men and women probably no better or freer from error than ourselves but with *clean slates*— something which we can never again have here."[33]

Writing his letter of resignation had been difficult and painful, but Walter Judd had been trained to look at a patient, determine what was right or wrong with him or her, prescribe treatment, and if permitted, carry out the treatment. It was clear to him after six years in China that most foreign missionaries in China had become paternalistic, condescending, and insensitive to the hopes and dreams of their Chinese brothers and sisters and would better serve Christ and his church if they went home. That was what he planned to do. But he had lost so much weight from malaria (some thirty pounds, as well as most of his hair) that he decided to spend the summer in Japan, studying and building up his strength: "I did not want to come home looking like a skeleton."

Judd joined a group of about thirty Chinese and Western students at the Imperial University in Tokyo for a six-week course in Japanese and Oriental culture, history, and economics. His professors included the former Japanese ambassador to the League of Nations, and Baron

Kijuro Shidehara, the current foreign minister, who talked about the importance of Japan and China getting along together, of Japan's expanding leadership role in all of Asia, and how Japan had reversed the current of human history by winning the Russo-Japanese War. The students were told that the war was "the first time that white men went out against a colored people—and were turned back."[34] Based on his years in China where foreigners had so often lorded it over the Chinese, Judd could understand this fierce Japanese nationalism. But, he asked himself, if the Japanese government translated its rhetoric into action, what would be the result for China and the United States? It seemed that Tokyo was talking about controlling everything from Korea down to Singapore, gaining access to rice, iron, rubber, and oil, assuring Japan what she had always wanted but had never so far attained—economic self-sufficiency. How far were the Japanese prepared to go to achieve their goals? He received his answer in September 1931 when Japan manufactured an incident outside Mukden, the largest city in South Manchuria, and proceeded to occupy all of Manchuria, which made up one-fifth of China and accounted for nearly half the country's railroads and four-fifths of its iron production. Many Chinese demanded that Chiang Kai-shek respond to this national humiliation, but Chiang refused, knowing that in a conflict with the far superior Japanese military, the Kuomintang army would lose and that would mean the end of the Nationalist government.[35]

Back in the United States, Judd was deeply disturbed by the Japanese seizure of Manchuria and what it portended for China and the world. With uncanny foresight, he wrote the following to a friend on Thanksgiving Day, 1931:

"If the Japanese military party gets away with this straight steal in Manchuria—as it appears they almost certainly will—. . . then disarmament is out of the question and we idealists would do well to face that fact squarely. . . . A victory for the Japanese military party means the world, although it doesn't yet realize it, has chosen the road of *force* instead of peace. We aren't willing to take the risks of peace. Covenants will have been demonstrated to be of value only when there is no problem for them to solve. The Japanese military party will be as drunk with its *proven* power as was the German after their rattling of the mailed fist got quick results in the Tripoli dispute. The powers save a penny and within twenty years will lose the lives of thousands of their sons and billions of dollars in having to bring the Japanese military machine to its knees."[36]

Rarely have more prophetic words been written. Ten years later, the Japanese bombed Pearl Harbor and began a bitter and bloody war that took 41,322 American lives and 170,596 casualties in the Pacific, and 321,999 dead and 800,000 wounded, captured, or missing in all theaters.[37] Walter Judd took no satisfaction in his prediction, but was compelled to make it because he had made a careful diagnosis and could make no other prognosis. Under the present circumstances, he wrote, he could not favor disarmament—it would be like "whistling to keep my courage up." What was needed were agreements that would cost something if they were not honored. "I am for a world of peace—hence I do not see how I can speak for disarmament at the present juncture because it accomplishes little or nothing." He was to make the same essential argument for peace through strength in the U.S. Congress throughout the 1940s and 1950s.

He ended his letter on a personally jubilant note with references to doors "previously padlocked" that were now ajar and to things once "out of the question" that were now in a different category. His final words were: "Someone—who all unknowingly almost broke the lock six years ago—[has now] walked in. Ah, boy, ain't it a grand and glorious feeling." The medical missionary with a passion for truth, commitment, and service had fallen in love.

CHAPTER FOUR

Marriage and the Mayo Clinic

UPON HIS RETURN to America in the summer of 1931, Walter Judd renewed contact with the Student Volunteer Movement. In August, he traveled to Hightstown, New Jersey, to attend the planning meeting for the quadrennial national convention to be held in Buffalo at the end of the year. During a break, he walked down to the tennis courts and recognized a slim, attractive girl who was swinging her racket with considerable skill. "Oh," he remarked to a friend, "there's that girl who used to be Miriam Barber. What's her name now?" "It's still Miriam Barber," came the reply. Judd smiled and settled down to wait until the young women were through playing. It had been six years since the two young missionaries had seen each other. He had heard that she had married an Englishman serving in Africa, but obviously that wasn't so. Well, they certainly had a lot of catching up to do. By the end of the Hightstown meeting, the couple realized they had more in common than their missionary experiences, but, as Miriam Judd recalled, "It took us the month of September to really get around to fundamentals." Things then moved quickly for the co-workers and by the Buffalo convention at which Walter spoke, they were engaged to be married. It all seemed quite natural; indeed, it would be hard to find two people who were more compatible.

Miriam Louise Barber was the daughter of Benjamin Russell Barber and Miriam Loretta Barber, both active Methodists and aspiring missionaries in their youth. Benjamin attended Northwestern University where he became president of its Young Men's Christian Association (YMCA) and met Miriam Clarke, who came from Point Edward, Canada, and was president of the university's Young Women's Christian Association (YWCA). They were married in 1899 after graduation and, under the sponsorship of the YMCA, went to Calcutta, the capital of British India, where Barber helped coordinate the city's thirteen "Y" branches in India. He raised money, oversaw personnel, and attended to the needs of the students, Anglo-Indians, sailors, and others who came to the YMCA. Miriam was born on August 28, 1904, in Simla, the summer seat of the British government, which was located in the shadow of the Himalayas. She had two brothers, John Clarke and Charles Edmund, also born in India, and a famous Irish grandfather on her mother's side who had fought in the Indian Mutiny fifty years earlier. Andrew Clarke was only seventeen when his family gave him permission to enlist for service in India. He was decorated by the British government for his feats on the battlefield. He later received a medal from the Turkish government and the French Médaille Militaire for heroism in the Crimean War. Miriam's father also proved himself a hero. A fanatic student tried to stab Sir Andrew Fraser, the governor-general of Bengal Province, at a YMCA meeting, but Benjamin Barber saved the official's life by throwing the attacker to the ground, and was himself slightly wounded. Edward VII sent a gold medal which was presented to Barber at the annual honors ceremony in Calcutta.

One of Miriam Judd's most vivid memories was the coronation of King George and Queen Mary as emperor and empress of India in 1911. "The ceremonial parade was in the Maidan, the central park of Calcutta, with all the Indian princes and princesses in their magnificent livery and jewels riding on elephants in a parade such as would dwarf the parades on Inauguration Day here. I was taught to curtsy and given a new dress, and I went through the line and curtsied to Queen Mary." She stayed up all night, looking at the buildings of Calcutta which were ablaze with necklaces of colored glass cups, their lighted wicks floating in oil. Soon after, when the Barbers went home on leave, their seven-year-old daughter was so ill with malaria that doctors advised that she not return to India. The Barbers had no intention of endangering their daughter's health and unhesitatingly gave up the work in India. Benjamin Barber became administrative assistant for the next forty-three years to the famed Dr. John R. Mott, head of the international YMCA, in New York City; the family resided in Montclair, New Jersey. "[Their decision not to return] is one of the reasons," explained Miriam Judd, "why I felt I ought to go back to India and continue their mission there. Which I did after I finished college in 1926."[1]

Miriam taught English at the American school at Kodai Kanal in southern India in the Nilgiri Hills, 8,000 feet above sea level. She loved her time in India, accepting its many contradictions. There were leisurely visits to Calcutta and Lahore during the long vacations and unpleasant encounters with resentful nationalistic Indians who thought all white people were British. One particularly dark memory was a trip to the great coal and iron Tata works north of Calcutta. Their party's descent into the mines was delayed by half an hour, she later learned, to give the many child workers time to hide from the foreigners, who might be distressed at such abuse.[2] When she returned from India two years later, Miriam received a different challenge. She was engaged to be married to an incandescent speaker who was able to ignite five thousand students at the Buffalo convention. One observer wrote of his remarks: "We . . . began to realize with him that all peoples are essentially alike, that we all stand or fall together, that the only solution of the problem lies in persons, and that it is the way of love that works."[3]

The once and future missionary told the assembled young people, echoing the words spoken fifteen years earlier by Dad Elliott, that they had but one life to live and should not throw it away. He recounted that although he had faced sickness, danger, and even death, he had started each day with a simple prayer that began, "O Master, let me walk with Thee in lowly paths of service free" and ended, "In peace that only Thou canst give, with thee, O Master, let me live." The way of love works, he told the vast assemblage, but often "it is the way of the cross. . . ." However there was no need to fear, because "a living Christ" walked with them. He reminded them of Jesus's promise: "Lo, I am with you always, even unto the end of the world." He ended with simple words, "It is true. Do not be afraid." The thousands of young men and women were briefly still, and then began clapping and did not stop for a very long time.[4]

At the end of the conference, Walter and Miriam went to the New York City offices of the Student Volunteer Movement to help write a final report, and to discuss their future plans. Walter had received a three-year fellowship at the renowned Mayo Clinic in Rochester, Minnesota, starting April 1. They decided to get married before Walter began studying surgery at Mayo, and on March 13, 1932, they were married in Miriam's parents' home in Montclair. They agreed that Miriam should complete her master's degree in teaching at Columbia University by attending summer sessions; for six weeks in the summers of 1932 and 1933, Miriam commuted from Montclair to Columbia's campus in Manhattan while Walter learned the art of surgery at Mayo. It was a very modern arrangement for the early 1930s, reflecting the deep respect the young couple felt for each other.

When Judd first applied to the Mayo Clinic, the admissions board hesitated; he had completed school in 1923; this was eight years later. They normally granted such fellowships only to young doctors right after medical school and internship. "I could see," recalled Judd, "[they were] afraid I wouldn't be willing to do the basic tasks," like testing urine samples. His scholastic record was good enough, even for Mayo; he had taken the examinations for a medical license in Nebraska and had scored in the nineties—the next highest score was seventy-eight. As always, he went to the heart of the problem—in this case, Dr. Louis Wilson, the director of admissions "Sir," he said, "would you have taken me if I had applied right out of medical school and internship?" Wilson said, "Yes." "Well," replied Judd, "I am more useful to you *now*, because now I know what I don't know." While in Shaowu, he would have given anything to know how to perform this or that surgery. Often he had had no choice: his patient would have died "if I didn't operate. . . . So I did the best I could and sometimes was able to pull them through." When he returned to China (he was determined that he would), he wanted to be able to operate with the skill and confidence that only the specialized training at Mayo would give him. He was glad to do all the routines (including the urine samples) in order to get the chance to learn the rest. They took him in on a trial basis, and "that helped change the policy of the Mayo Clinic. Now about 10 percent of each class are people who have been in practice but who want to learn the latest techniques. They come from all over the world, not just the United States, but Sweden, England, Japan and so forth. All these years, I've broken the ice on any number of things without intending to. I just figure out what I believe it is best to do, and in the long run other people agree."[5]

He learned more than surgical procedures at Mayo. The clinic did not have fixed charges for its services but billed according to the patient's ability to pay. "Dr. Will" Mayo had a rule that no patient should be allowed to leave unhappy with his bill. Judd remembered treating one man from Oklahoma who "looked one notch above a tramp." Uncertain how poor his patient really was, he called the business office and suggested they might want to check his credit. "Don't worry," came the reply, "we already know." The "tramp" had recently discovered oil and was now a millionaire, but he had been poor and was still very careful with his money. He had dressed like someone off the streets because he feared that the clinic would overcharge him. Judd resolved that when he returned to China he would ask every patient, no matter how poor, to pay something—if only a few coppers—for his self-respect and equal status as a human being.

While learning the finer points of surgery and fees at the Mayo Clinic, he kept up with events in China. Chiang Kai-shek and the Nationalist government seemed to have defeated warlordism and established a national administration in Nanking, creating "a new atmosphere of hope."[6] But there were also enormous problems. Government spending was dominated by the military budget and debt service, the former caused by the Japanese conquest of Manchuria and the cost of continuing Nationalist resistance to attempted subjugation by the communists. Illiteracy was endemic. In Shanghai, the most cosmopolitan city in all China, only 213 of every 10,000 residents had attended high school. There were only 103 colleges and universities in the entire country, half of them private and usually established by Christian missionaries. The country's shipping industry remained largely in the hands of foreign interests, and banking was dominated by British institutions. Three-fourths of all the farmers in China were tenant farmers.[7] Nanking had to promote modern agriculture, transportation, communications, and equal opportunity for all regardless of sex or age, in the most tradition-bound society in the world and perhaps the history of mankind. However, it could not do all this and fight the Japanese. As John K. Fairbank wrote: "In an era of peace and order the Nanking Government might have ridden the crest of modernization, but its fate was determined almost from the first by the menace of Japanese militarism."[8]

Fairbank made this judgment in the 1980s with the advantage of historical hindsight. Judd made a similar point in April 1934 while at the Mayo Clinic in Rochester, Minnesota, predicting that in the absence of effective protest by Western powers, "the Japanese military machine" will "be walking into North China in the next few months or years. . . ." Three years later, in July 1937, the Japanese seized upon a minor fracas at the Marco Polo Bridge outside Peking to invade North China and begin the eight-year-long Sino-Japanese War. As he did so often, Judd used a medical analogy to criticize the West's inaction in

1934: "To consent by silence to the actions of the Japanese government during the last two and a half years [since the seizure of Manchuria in 1931], just in order to save *our* pieces of work here and there, is just as short-sighted and suicidal in the long run ... as it is to ignore the presence of a cancer just because to attack it would injure some overlying healthy and innocent skin." He specifically cited missionary groups for their inaction while conceding that his criticism might result in his not being asked to return to medical missionary work in North China. "Yet speak I must, when the very stones cry out."[9]

In May 1934, Judd received a cable in Rochester, Minnesota, from the American Board of Missions informing him that Dr. Percy T. Watson, head of the Fenchow hospital of the North China Mission, had had a serious heart attack and would have to return home to the United States. Would he be interested in taking Dr. Watson's place and running a 160-bed hospital, the largest the Congregationalists had in China? It would mean giving up the last six months or so of his three-year fellowship at the Mayo Clinic. He and Miriam would have to say goodbye to the many friends they had made in Rochester, leave their families, leave America, and travel with their new daughter, Mary Lou, halfway around the world to reside in a country still living in the nineteenth century and close to war. He did not hesitate, the clinic consented, and he swiftly sent back his acceptance. He was eager to return to China and put into practice what he had learned at the Mayo Clinic and what he had learned about missionary work in Shaowu. He was determined to develop Chinese doctors and nurses to administer as well as heal, to be conscious that he was a foreigner in a foreign land, to emphasize to his fellow missionaries that Americans do not always know what is best for the Chinese, and to remember that Christ had been an Oriental, not an Occidental. Despite his excitement, he was disturbed when Dr. Watson came to Minnesota in August and told him that what the hospital in Fenchow (almost bankrupt) needed most was a new kitchen, an artesian well, and a new nurses' home. "Things," Judd said to himself, while listening politely, "why do so many missionaries always talk about things?"[10]

CHAPTER FIVE

China for Good

RIDING THE TRAIN for twenty-four hours from the historic northern capital of Peking to the city of Fenchow in Shansi Province, Walter Judd was very aware of the heavy responsibilities that awaited him. He would administer the largest Congregational hospital in China, meet a payroll that included foreign and Chinese doctors and nurses, run a nursing school, handle an average of 110 inpatients and 75 outpatients a day, supervise the maintenance of the hospital's physical plant, and attempt to raise money in American churches in the middle of the Great Depression. He arrived, in fact, in the midst of a financial crisis for the hospital. For many months, the hospital had been failing to make ends meet. Foreign (that is, U.S.) gifts had plummeted from $33,000 (Chinese) in 1932 to $6000 in 1934. With more than half of its budget coming from such gifts, the hospital faced either a drastic reduction of its services or the closing of its doors. As Judd realized, it was the end of an era during which the mission hospitals and mission work in general depended on abundant financial support from abroad. He determined to build up operating income until equal to expenses; otherwise, medical works in China would never become self-supporting. "Only then," he asserted in the mission newsletter, "can the hospital have a foundation that is secure—secure because it has sunk its roots as deeply into the hearts of Chinese here as it has had them all these years in the hearts of its friends in America."

The new superintendent shifted the emphasis of the hospital from things to people even though that meant, he conceded, that for a while running water was limited, its electric plant sometimes "sputtered" and stopped, and plants and shrubbery were neglected. Two Chinese doctors left but others took their place; a Chinese nurse was hired when it was decided that obtaining another American nurse was very improbable; the training of some forty nursing students was continued. The average daily number of inpatients was reduced to less than eighty by getting the cured back to their homes quicker and restricting the hospital stay of the incurables. As a result, in the first nine months of 1935, the Fenchow hospital treated more individual patients than in the same months of the preceding year; however, the average length of stay remained high—twenty-four days—because of the relatively large number of tuberculosis patients. Through it all, Judd insisted that every patient pay something. As a result, he reduced the percentage of overseas financial support from two-thirds to one-third of the total budget, a remarkable achievement. In the face of skepticism and resistance, he instituted many of the reforms he had been talking and writing about for nearly ten years, particularly his maxim that the key to helping people lies in working *with* and not *for* them.[1]

Miriam Judd was hardly less busy than her apparently tireless husband. There was much to do in the large American compound, which included the hospital, a kindergarten and primary school, a boarding high school for boys and girls, and a Bible school for the Chinese being trained to be itinerant preachers in the countryside. Fenchow, located in the Fen River valley which raised crops for much of the province, was an ancient city, perhaps a thousand years old, whose five-mile-long perimeter wall was 60 feet high and wide enough at the top for two automobiles to pass each other. "We used to take the kids up in the late afternoon," Miriam recalled, "and walk around the wall with them on a donkey and watch the sun set." She taught English in the high school as well as to the Chinese nurses who kept the patients' charts in English. She also gave piano lessons and taught the organ to the male nurses who wanted to play in church. Until they were ready, she pumped the old foot organ on Sunday mornings. She knew the music, but because the words were in Chinese, "I would sometimes get stuck because I didn't know whether it was time for 'Amen' or another verse."

Although she spent much of her time with the dozen Americans who lived at the mission, Miriam also made Chinese friends. Once, she invited the wife of a Chinese doctor to come and visit with her small children, who were about the same age as the Judd girls. The children played together while Miriam talked with the doctor's wife in her halting Chinese. She enjoyed the visit and the girls seemed to like each other so she again invited the Chinese woman who responded, to Miriam's surprise, that she could not come to the Judds' house any more. "You have so many things for your girls," she explained, "dolls and carriages and games and things to ride on. I don't want my girls to grow up discontented." Each of her daughters, she said, had one special thing: one girl had a doll's perambulator, in which she put sticks and stones for dolls; the other had a little wooden tricycle she could sit on and pedal. The Chinese mother's comments profoundly affected the young American mother. "I had been talking about my poor children and how they didn't have what they would have in America. I realized how happy those Chinese girls were without all the things we had. It set me on a different path of thinking. I learned you could do all sorts of things, like decorating your Christmas tree with cotton and popcorn and red paper chains, and get greater satisfaction than if you ran down to the dime store and bought them."[2]

After little more than one year, Walter Judd was beginning to see his reforms in medicine and missionary work bear fruit when once again the communists entered his life. At the end of the Long March in the summer of 1935, the Chinese communists, under Mao, had finally settled in Yenan, in northern Shensi, about 120 miles from Fenchow. Now, in February 1936, with most of China's forces celebrating "New Year" holidays, the communist armies suddenly attacked across the Yellow River, crossing into Shansi, only eighty miles to the west. Their obvious goal was to surprise and seize Taiyuan, the capital of Shansi, which had the second largest arsenal in China. Fenchow, which lay between the communists and Taiyuan, was the headquarters of a division of pro-Nationalist Shansi troops and normally well defended, but the commanding general had placed most of his men on the other side of the Yellow River. Judd had few illusions about what would happen to Fenchow if the communists seized it. They had captured Shaowu three weeks after he left in 1931 and held it for two years, destroying the social and economic structure of the area.

On February 20 and 21, the communists crossed the ice-filled Yellow River in ferry boats, and the border defenses collapsed. They moved rapidly into counties just west and southwest of Fenchow, whose anxious citizens wondered: would the Shansi troops or the communists arrive first? Walter's anxieties were heightened by the fact that Miriam was due to have their second child any day. He decided to induce labor, and Carolyn Ruth Judd was born without incident on the early morning of February 26. On February 28, rumors swept the city that the communists were only six miles from undefended Fenchow. Two Chinese doctors and the Chinese business manager of the hospital fled with their families; the remaining Chinese doctor was urged by his family to follow suit. Judd had no intention of leaving, but faced a personal dilemma. The missionary residences were in a different compound than the hospital. Martial law was so strict that anyone on the street after dark was shot on sight, no one knowing how many communist sympathizers were inside the city and ready to open the gates for them. "If there were to be disorder," recalled Judd, "[I] naturally wanted to be with [my] family in one compound; but at the same time [I] wanted to be in the hospital compound where [my] job was, trying to protect as much as possible the lives of some three hundred people—patients, staff and families, nurses—and the hospital plant and property." He couldn't move the hospital, but he could move his family. He decided to take Miriam and the two girls to a sister mission in Taiku, fifty miles to the east.

They left after dark and arrived in Taiku four hours later, delayed by detours, a frozen radiator, and a carsick amah. Walter put Miriam and three-day-old Carolyn in the hospital, left Mary Lou with missionary friends, and returned to Fenchow early the next morning just as the gates were being closed against the communists. Had he been an hour later, he would have been locked out and left to the mercy of the contending armies. Tension increased as the city awaited the arrival of either friendly or hostile forces. In the end, the winter cold and heavy snows in the mountains saved Fenchow, slowing the communists so that a battalion of government troops arrived six hours before them and two days after Judd moved his family to Taiku. After careful reconnaissance, the communists, who had no artillery or airplanes, decided not to attack the walled city, but they did not leave the area. After three weeks of fighting southwest of Fenchow, much of it within earshot, the communist army changed its tactics and split into smaller fighting units, launching a series of lightning raids. On March 19, about two thousand communists suddenly drove northward, passing ten miles east of Fenchow. They succeeded in advancing to within thirty miles of Taiyuan and only twenty-five miles from Taiku. Once again, Walter decided to move his family and telegraphed from Fenchow, advising Miriam to take the children to Peking. Within the hour the wires were cut, and Fenchow was without communication to the outside world for a week. Miriam and the children took a seemingly endless thirty-three-hour trip on a train packed with refugees, that was complicated by the illness of the children and Miriam's concern about Walter in isolated Fenchow.

In truth, the doctor was doing fine and so were his patients. At the end of April, the communists returned to their Shensi base as suddenly as they had come. "The amazing resilience of the Chinese people once more demonstrated itself," wrote Judd to friends. People in need of care again poured into the clinic and the hospital, taking up life as if there had been no communist incursion. Part of the reason was that the communists had altered their search-and-destroy tactics from the Fukien days. There was no persecution of the church or of Christians as such. "Their rallying cries were all [now] directed against the Japanese and the few remaining warlords." However, Judd made a distinction between shifting tactics and permanent strategy; he never forgot the blazing eyes of the communist in Shaowu who tried to convert him.

As for the Japanese, their increasing arrogance and use of oppression in North China made it clear to Judd they would soon create an incident that would "give them a pretext for striking," while Europe was "absorbed in its own difficulties." His foresight was once again confirmed with the alleged shooting of a Japanese soldier at the Marco Polo Bridge outside Peking in 1937; it was seized upon by the Japanese as a pretext to begin a war they thought would not last more than a year. Judd could have warned the Japanese not to underestimate the Chinese will. In a letter dated June 18, 1936, he said that he sensed "a rapidly rising tide of [Chinese] determination . . . to refuse to give in much longer to Japanese aggression." The younger generation was insisting that China could not retreat much farther "without losing its soul." But what chance had China, still struggling to emerge from the nineteenth century, against the modern war machine of Japan? "Most of us believe . . . the Japanese military and naval forces simply cannot be defeated now." It was hard to suggest what China should do. "One can only sympathize deeply with her as she is forced into perhaps the most crucial hour in her whole magnificent history. . . . [Miriam and I] would not be elsewhere. We only hope we may be found worthy of our task and opportunities."[3]

Even Chiang Kai-shek, who had always insisted that the communists must be defeated and the nation united before engaging the Japanese, was not immune to the growing calls for armed resistance; he had, in fact, drawn up plans for a war he now deemed unavoidable. Chiang's plan of strategic withdrawal was based on two premises: one, China was far weaker than Japan, the aggressor, and could not confront her directly; and two, a combination of ever-growing casualties and extended lines of supply would eventually weaken the Japanese enemy and force him to withdraw. But the Nationalist leader was unable to forget Mao and the other communists in Yenan. When the warlord Chang Hsueh-liang did not appear to be waging a sufficiently aggressive campaign against the communists, Chiang decided to come north and personally evaluate the situation. Chang urged action against the Japanese and quarreled openly with Chiang, finally causing the Nationalist leader to set up a base in Sian in early December 1936 to personally direct anticommunist operations. In retaliation, Chang had Chiang kidnapped and presented Nanking with an ultimatum: revive the united front with the communists to fight the Japanese, or else Chiang would be turned over to the communists.

Historians disagree as to what transpired next in Sian. In *Red Star Over China*, Edgar Snow depicts an apprehensive Chiang, who turned "pale" when Chou En-lai turned up to deliver the communist demands. The Generalissimo and Madame Chiang, in their narrative, *Sian: A Coup d'Etat*, describe a calm Chiang Kai-shek, who read the Bible and was ready to die rather than sign a humiliating agreement with his longtime enemies. In the end, both communists and Nationalists compromised to end the crisis and allow Chiang to be released, but the Nationalists conceded more. Mao, who wanted to execute Chiang, agreed to join a united front with the Nationalists and theoretically put the Red Army under his old enemy. Chiang did not accept the eight points presented by his captors, but agreed to stop trying to "exterminate" the communists and invited them to send a delegation to the National People's Congress scheduled for November 1937. Most critical of all, plans were laid for a united front against the Japanese. In later years, Chiang bitterly regretted his decision, believing that the communists were so weak in 1936 that one more campaign would have eliminated them.

Following the Sian incident, the communists gained national and international prestige and committed China to a war against Japan which they were confident would mean, as one analyst has written, "the defeat and humiliation of the Nationalist armies, the loss of vast areas, and the destruction of Chiang's administration."[4] Mao knew that a war against Japan was a war the communists could not lose. O. Edmund Clubb wrote that the communists, in entering the new coalition, "had

... not abandoned [their] aim of introducing socialism and, ultimately, communism into China."⁵ Fairbank put it more bluntly: "Far from combining with the KMT ... the separate armed forces of the [Chinese Communist Party] would develop their own bases and popular support while riding the wave of national resistance to the invader."⁶

Just how cynically the communists exploited the war was revealed by Congressman Judd on the floor of the House of Representatives ten years later when he released a secret directive issued by Mao Tse-tung in October 1937, which read: "The Sino-Japanese war affords our party an excellent opportunity for expansion. Our policy should be 70 percent expansion, 20 percent dealing with the Kuomintang, and 10 percent resisting Japan."⁷ The Mao directive set forth the policy which was followed by the communists throughout the Sino-Japanese War. Even Theodore H. White and Annalee Jacoby, in their sympathetic book about the communists, *Thunder Out of China,* state flatly: "The Communists fought when they had an opportunity to surprise a very small group of the enemy.... But during the significant campaigns it was the weary soldiers of the Central Government who took the shock, gnawed at the enemy, and died. During the campaigns of 1937–38 or the eastern China campaign of 1944 more than 70 percent of Japanese effort was concentrated against the troops of Chiang Kai-shek."⁸

In August 1937, the Japanese army began to move west from Peking toward Shansi Province and the city of Fenchow, prompting the U.S. State Department to advise all American women and children to leave. The Judds agreed: not only did they have Mary Lou and Carolyn to consider, but Miriam was pregnant again. "We always said," remembered Miriam Judd, "that whenever we were having a baby, China got into trouble." In early September, they began a harrowing three-day journey by automobile, ferry, train, and truck to Hankow, more than 500 miles to the south, from which Miriam and the girls hoped to catch a plane to Hong Kong and then board a ship home to the United States. Crossing the river, before reaching Taiyuan, they divided into two groups, Walter taking one child and Miriam the other, so that "in case one or the other didn't survive," recalled Miriam, "we would have a partial family left." They arrived in Taiyuan, but the Japanese had already bombed the railroad station and tracks; the closest the trains could approach the city was three miles out in the country. They went to the home of missionary friends to rest. They had no sooner begun settling down for the night when an urgent message came: "A train has arrived—come right away!" They piled their children and luggage into rickshaws and traveled three miles in the darkness to the train which turned out to be the last one out before the Japanese cut the railroad.[9]

The train was filled with hundreds of wounded Chinese soldiers and took two very long days to reach Hankow. It was forced to stop overnight in a little village that was gaily decorated for the mid-autumn harvest festival, one of the most popular Chinese holidays. The moon was full and bright, and scores of Chinese were standing about in the open, "certain in their naive way," Miriam recounted, "that the Japanese would not attack. Up to that time [the Japanese] had not used airplanes from Peking at night." But out of the sky roared a squadron of planes, and, guided by the harvest moon, they dropped scores of bombs, killing hundreds of civilians. None of the Judds, who had stayed inside, was hurt.

Arriving at last in Hankow, Walter, Miriam, and the girls waited anxiously to get seats on the one German plane that flew only three times a week to Hong Kong. In a scene out of *Casablanca*, Judd went every day to the airport to find out if there was any space on the next plane. He was one of hundreds of worried foreigners who besieged the airline for seats for their wives and children. While waiting, the Judds stayed in a large missionary house that served, in the emergency, as a transient hotel for those trying to leave China. Carolyn, their youngest daughter, came down with diarrhea, and spent most of the time upstairs in their room. One day, Walter called from the airport to ask how much Carolyn weighed. Miriam had no idea because since she was sick, the child had had nothing to eat but boiled milk. Why did he want to know? Because, came the reply, plane tickets were sold based on weight, not age—they could buy a half-price ticket if she was below a certain weight. Miriam took Carolyn downstairs and weighed her on a big luggage scale in the hallway while Walter waited on the phone. A few nights later, at a dinner given by Bishop Root, the head of the Episcopalian church in central China, a British lady remarked to Miriam: "You know, the most awful thing is going on in our hotel. There's an American couple there and they are starving their child to get it down below weight and take it half-price on the airplane." "Yes, I know," replied Miriam, "that's us!"

The Japanese added to the chaos by bombing Hankow, taking care to drop their missiles not on the Chinese airfield or the Hanyang Arsenal or other military targets, but in the middle of the tenement districts where there were between two and three thousand people per square mile. They bombed at four in the afternoon when there were no able-bodied men at home and targeted dwellings so flimsy they burst into flames when hit. There was minimum risk to the Japanese airplanes because the Chinese had not thought to put their antiaircraft guns in the middle of slums. One day an air raid caused nine hundred deaths in twenty minutes, with many more wounded and injured. An emergency call for doctors was broadcast, and Judd stayed at the hospital for forty-eight hours, once operating for sixteen straight hours. Of the twenty-nine people from whom he removed jagged scraps of steel, only two were men. "The intent was obvious," said Judd, "to terrify the population"[10] and force the Chinese to give in.

Despite the death and destruction all around them, some missionaries still hoped that things would calm down, but Judd insisted, "This is for good." Older Americans attempted to dismiss their younger colleague as an alarmist and a pessimist, saying, "We've been through this kind of thing before. This is just another uprising." But Judd, having studied the Japanese, knew better; they had openly declared they would not be satisfied until they controlled not only China but all of East Asia— Korea to Singapore. They called their objective, "The Greater East Asia Co-Prosperity Sphere."

At last, after ten days filled with rumor, worry, and mounting tension, Walter obtained three precious airplane tickets for Hong Kong. "I dressed these two little tykes, two and four," remembered Miriam, "in all the clothes they could wear—we weren't allowed any luggage— coats and dresses and sweaters, and when we got to Hong Kong the temperature was about 120 degrees." The young, pregnant mother took off in a plane full of strangers, not knowing whether she would ever see her husband again. But she was the daughter of missionaries, the wife of a missionary, and had been a missionary herself. She tried to keep her priorities straight. "I couldn't do much for Walter or Fenchow or the people we left behind. I could do something about our children. If Walter came back in a month or six months or a year or ten years, I wanted to be able to say to him, 'Here are your kids and they're decent and they're growing up all right.' "[11]

The parting was wrenching for Walter. "One of the two toughest moments of my life was when they took off in that plane, Miriam and two and a half kids. . . . I wondered whether they would get there and would I ever see them again." However, he felt then, as he did throughout his life, that he had no real choice: as much as he loved his family, his mission came first. "I had work to do. My responsibility was [in

Fenchow]. I was superintendent of a hospital; we had worked like Sam Hill to get it from being heavily supported by American money to the reverse. The mission had been established by three graduates of Carleton College in Minnesota. My responsibility was there." He knew that Miriam understood; he hoped that the children would one day understand. He put them out of his mind as best as he could and returned to Fenchow by roundabout train, mule, cart and foot, the main railroad having been blocked. He learned several weeks later through a ham radio operator that Miriam and the girls had arrived safely in America and were in Montclair, N.J. with her parents. He thanked God that he had sent them home as he treated an increasing number of Chinese soldiers wounded by the advancing Japanese army and discovered through them the barbarities visited by the invaders on an unarmed people.

He remembered one incident in particular. In a little village near Fenchow, the townsmen fled with their wives and children when word came that the Japanese were approaching. However, the head of the village refused to go, saying, "The stories are not true." As soon as the Japanese swept through the gates, their commanding officer demanded of him: "Where are the women?" "There are no women left in town," the Chinese replied. "What about you? Haven't you got any women?" "Only my wife," he replied. "Bring her out," the Japanese ordered. The wife was dragged out, terrified, from an inner room, and was raped eight times, while her husband was forced to look on. Then one of the soldiers shot him.

This was not an isolated incident. He treated little girls of nine and grandmothers of seventy, all rape victims of Japanese soldiers. At first he was appalled by such senseless brutality, but at last he realized that to the militarists it was not senseless. The Japanese were not wild sexual fiends but soldiers under coldly calculating warriors who knew that the most vulnerable spot in Chinese society was the love of family. If they could weaken Chinese resolve by rape and pillage and thereby bring the war to a quicker end, and thus save lives, the Japanese militarists, not the Japanese people, would commit "atrocities" without hesitation and without end. What made the rape of China by the Japanese all the more unbearable to the Judds was the realization that America was making it possible by trading scrap iron, oil and other "war" materials to Japan. Someone, he decided, had to tell the American people what was happening in China and mobilize them against the United States providing Japan's militarists with the wherewithall to fight this kind of war.

There was a lull in the fighting during the early winter months, and then the Japanese began advancing again, arriving at the ancient stone walls of Fenchow in mid-February of 1938. They bombed and shelled the city with six-inch cannon for several hours. There were direct hits on the roof of the American hospital, despite the huge bright red crosses painted on the windows; one bomb landed in the room where Miriam would have been if she had stayed and delivered her baby in Fenchow. Once the American flag became wrapped around the pole atop the hospital, and Judd climbed onto the roof and up the pole and unfurled it while the Japanese cannons roared; he was not hit. The end was inevitable. At last, on February 17, after four hours of shelling had produced a great gap in the city wall, the Japanese troops came through and took Fenchow. Thus began five months of captivity for the American doctor, who discovered immediately how much respect the conquerors had for the Geneva Convention.

During the fighting, a wounded Chinese soldier rolled down the sloping inner side of the city wall into the American compound. After the battle was over and Japanese guards had been set up, Judd went out with an American flag, a Red Cross flag and a hospital stretcher to bring the wounded soldier into the hospital for treatment. "I was driven back," he remembered. "I thought that this first guard was a little shaky because of the so recent battle, and that I would wait until they changed the guard. Again I was driven back. . . . [Next] Chinese civilians tried to get permission to get to all the wounded men and give them food and water and bedding; but guards were set up and no one could go near them until they had died which, mercifully, was within forty-eight hours in the middle of winter." Here was a new kind of war far different from the old "gentlemen's wars in the west"; for the Japanese militarists, every Chinese was a military target.

Because the Japanese did not take prisoners, Judd worked with the Chinese to smuggle nearly thirty wounded soldiers out of his hospital through a hole in the wall and to safety in the nearby hills. But he still had three soldiers left, so crippled, blind or legless that they would never fight again and therefore represented no threat to the Japanese. He waited for the right opportunity to plead their case. One day the Japanese commanding officer who was known for his love of flowers, came for tea. Judd showed his visitor the garden where he became entranced by an unusual white flower. "He bent down to smell it in rapture. This, I thought, was the right moment. But at mention of the three men his face hardened, and he told me to take up the matter with another officer." Judd brought the crippled Chinese to the Japanese who said they would take care of them. The next morning he went to the Japanese headquarters to ensure that the three men had been safely released. At first he could not get a satisfactory answer but at last a guard said, "We sent them away in a special train." A "special train," he realized, could mean only one thing—execution; he never forgave himself for the three men's deaths.[12]

But he saved far more lives than he lost. Once he was visited by a terror-stricken Chinese man who revealed that the Japanese wanted to send his daughters of nine and eleven to Japan to be "taught the right things." This was another part of the Japanese plan to destroy China: to keep from the mind of every growing child any knowledge of Chiang Kai-shek, the Chinese revolution, and the rich traditions of China. Judd devised a plan to keep the girls in Fenchow. "Tell the sergeant that I took them. And when he drags you up here—as he surely will—you must demand that I give them up." Later, when the Japanese sergeant came blustering along with the Chinese, the father began crying, "Give me my daughters. I want my children. Give them to me!" The Chinese man's loud protests and Judd's firm refusal to return the girls persuaded the Japanese soldier to leave the children with the Americans, the soldier believing that he was advancing the Japanese campaign to separate and divide the Chinese whenever possible. He did not consider the possibility that an American missionary would risk his displeasure and much more to preserve one small Chinese family. Thereafter the father frequently visited his daughters in the American compound.

Even in his privileged position, Judd found himself the target of the psychological warfare that the Japanese continually waged. The day after the city's capture, he was taken to Japanese headquarters and asked to sign a document stating that it was not the fault of the Japanese that American property in the city had been damaged; it was the fault of the Chinese for resisting. When he refused to sign, Judd was taken under guard to a room where several Chinese were strung up by their thumbs with their toes barely touching the floor and was asked to reconsider his refusal. He was left among the pain-wracked Chinese for six hours. "I wondered what I would do," he remembered. "I didn't see how I could withstand such torture." He had talked about being willing to give his life, if necessary, for Christ. Had his hour come? At last, a Japanese officer entered the room, looked at the American doctor for a moment, and then said slowly, "You can leave." They never threatened him again; he had passed, he supposed, an important test.[13]

As the days and weeks went by, he noticed that the Japanese garrisoned the little towns around Fenchow during the day but always returned to the city at night for fear they might be killed by Chinese guerrillas, many of them members of the Eighth Route Army, the former Red Army, now ostensibly part of Chiang's Nationalist forces. He had the opportunity to meet with leaders of the Eighth Route Army whose discipline and skill he had to admire. At one meeting, the subject of conscription came up because the Japanese had demanded that each village send five men to join a native militia they were organizing, plus two women for the sexual pleasure of the Japanese army. After considerable discussion, the Chinese solved the problem by sending five opium addicts from each village to help form the militia. To select the women, they raised a purse and asked for volunteers; the purse went to the families to help compensate them for their shame. "There is no question about it," Judd later said, "the Eighth Route Army does have spirit in fighting and a great facility for getting close to the people." What many Americans did not understand was that their end goals were always directed at their objective of creating a communist China, not just the defeat of Japan.

Another Japanese tactic used to undermine China was the reintroduction of opium. No opium had been grown in Shansi for nearly thirty years when, ten days after the Japanese had arrived, Judd saw soldiers passing out free seed and compelling Chinese farmers to plant it along the railroad. "Within five months," he said, "one field out of every five or six was white with the poppy." The opium traffic was operated by Korean racketeers from the north who, at the direction of the Japanese army, soon produced thousands of Chinese addicts. Having introduced opium, they turned to its more deadly derivative, heroin. For two months, they offered heroin free to any villager who wanted to try it. At the end of that period, they began to charge for the heroin, confident they could collect from the many who had become addicts. "It [was] a systematic debauching, enslavement, and demoralization of a people," Judd said.[14]

As he watched with growing horror the attempted annihilation of the Chinese army with the use of U.S. war materials (the Japanese had entered Fenchow in Ford and Chevrolet trucks), the forced use of narcotics, the calculated rape and humiliation of women, and the deliberate elimination of Chinese learning and culture, he felt real despair for the first time in his life. Everything around him seemed to mock his work as doctor and missionary. He had done all that anyone could do as the prisoner of an oppressor who gloried in death and destruction; he believed he could be more useful in America to the overall cause. In a letter to Rowland Cross of the American Board in Boston, shortly before the Japanese captured Fenchow, he expressed his increasing feeling that he ought to return home to tell the American government and people how Japan was using American trade to help her defeat China and to urge an immediate end to such a wrong policy. He recalled that he had come to China, "believing that I, with my particular abilities and inabilities, could thereby render greater service not only to China but to America as well. In this present crisis in China and the world, my hope for the Christian Gospel in China lies in *America*. Not because I love China less ... but because I love [it] more I [want to] go to America. ..." The decision to leave was painful and not taken lightly or quickly: "the determining factor has been the inner tornness and disquiet all these months when every fiber of my being has strained to be at the task in America. ..."[15] But how was he to get home? To his further dismay, an ominous-looking growth had developed just below the border of his lower lip, the result, he suspected, of the X-ray treatment for acne he had received as a college student. He had no equipment either to assess or remove his new growth, and no way to get expert attention.

Judd's communications with the Japanese those long months were through a Korean who spoke Japanese and English. One day, the Korean came to him and said that the commanding general of the Yamahoka division headquartered in Fenchow wanted to see him at the hospital, but privately and at night. He was puzzled by the request but naturally agreed. The following night, the general walked into Judd's office, accompanied only by the Korean, and revealed that he had contracted a venereal disease from a Chinese woman and would like to be examined and treated. Obviously he didn't want to go to his military doctor who would report it, causing him disgrace and probable punishment. The Japanese army had an inflexible rule that if anyone, officer or enlisted man, contracted a venereal disease in China, he could not return to Japan for "rest and recreation" for two years. Would the American doctor help him?

Despite his strong feelings about what the Japanese army was doing to the Chinese people, Judd did not hesitate to treat the general for his

61

affliction; he was a human being in need. And as a practical matter, it would not have been wise to refuse someone who could make life uncomfortable or worse, not only for him, but for the 1,500 Chinese Christians who were crowded into the American mission compound. The only treatment available (this was before antibiotics by mouth) was to irrigate the urethra, the canal through which urine is discharged. He told the general that he would have to abstain from alcohol and sexual relations and come every night for at least two weeks, perhaps more. It was not "very exalting for a great Japanese general, under the son of Heaven, the emperor of Japan, to come in after dark to a foreign hospital, take down his pants and have an American irrigate his genitalia."[16] In the course of the treatment, which fortunately was successful and without complications, he and the general talked about a good many things. Once, the Japanese officer asked: "Why is your government always writing letters, sending telegrams, to my government, protesting what we are doing over here in China? We're trying to save China from the communists." Unmoved by the transparency of the argument, Judd replied, "Well, it's aggression and in violation of treaties, so we have to be opposed to what you're doing." The general shook his head and said: "My father is a purchasing agent of my government. He's in the United States right now, purchasing the things that enable us to do what your government writes letters saying we shouldn't be doing." The general and other Japanese had concluded that the U.S. letters and cables of protest were the usual hypocrisy of a government trying to salve its critics. They thought the central issue was the money that the United States was making by selling oil, scrap iron, silk, and other materials to Japan.[17] Judd could not blame them for reaching that conclusion. He saw that the Japanese would continue to misread the true feelings of the United States people and government until U.S. policy was changed. But he couldn't help change what he believed to be a wrong policy of his own government as long as he remained a prisoner in far-off Fenchow; he had to get home. In answer to his request the general gave him permission to leave Fenchow and return to the United States, thereby displaying Japanese magnanimity and removing someone who knew a damaging secret about him. He even allowed Judd to make a special trip to Peking to obtain medical and other supplies for the hospital and the mission. While in Peking, he had experts remove from his lower lip what turned out to be a squamous cell cancer; it was the first but far from the last malignancy that would appear as a result of the X-ray treatment he had received in college. Back in Fenchow, he arranged for the future administration of the hospital by the Chinese doctor whom he had trained to replace him and the head nurse, Emma Noreen, an American, also from Minnesota and the Mayo Clinic.

Finally, on July 4, 1938, truly a day of independence for him, Walter Judd left Fenchow on a military train carrying wounded and dead soldiers, the latter in a uniquely Japanese form. "The Japanese believed," he explained, "that you can become a god by fighting and dying for the emperor, who is himself descended from heaven. And it is important that their ashes be consecrated at the sacred Yasukuni Shrine in Tokyo." He found himself the only live passenger in a railway car stacked high with the boxed ashes of dead Japanese, guarded by silent soldiers who stood motionless for two hours at a stretch, all the way to Peking. It was not a quick trip. At two different places in Shansi, where the railroad went over a bridge above a gorge, the Chinese guerrillas had destroyed the bridge. Each time, the train stopped; soldiers removed the boxes of ashes and carefully carried them down into the gorge and up the other side to the undamaged end of the bridge where another train was waiting. There the soldiers reverently loaded on the remains of their fallen comrades. He pondered the paradox between the profound respect of the Japanese for their own dead and their savage war against the Chinese people.

Arriving in Peking, he sent word to Montclair that he was coming home, and began to consider what he should do upon his return. He had expected to start a medical practice, to provide for his wife and young family, and to live something like a normal life after so many arduous years abroad. But how could he ignore what was happening there in China? It was no wonder that Japan thought the United States approved of its actions. We were shipping it virtually all the essentials for carrying on the war; without our scrap iron, our petroleum products, and other materials, the Japanese could not have continued their assault. And that was not all. The Japanese violated treaties with the United States, they humiliated and even killed U.S. citizens, they destroyed or confiscated mission property. Yet we continued to sell them the goods that made such outrages possible.

Although he had no way of knowing it, the Japanese general had set free a determined crusader who made 1400 speeches in forty-six states over the next two years urging the American people not to give Japan the means with which to conquer China and get control of Asia. Never before or since has any private citizen delivered so many addresses, often six a day, on a single foreign policy issue as Walter Judd did from September 1938 until December 1940. It was a schedule that would have exhausted the most ambitious of presidential candidates, but he was not running for public office. He wanted Americans to stop giving Japanese militarists the wherewithal to slaughter the Chinese and to discourage their lust for expansion that would one day, if unchecked, surely entangle the United States.

CHAPTER SIX

◆

Sounding the Alarm

NEARLY ONE YEAR HAD PASSED since he had last seen his family when he arrived in the United States in August. He went immediately to Montclair, where Miriam and the children were staying with her father and mother. He was especially eager to see six-month-old Eleanor, who although she had never seen her father quickly approved of him. He spent a few days resting but soon began talking about his plans, not to practice medicine and provide for his family, but to tell the public about America's stake in the Far East and to urge his country to stop arming Japan. As always, Miriam was supportive, but there were many questions. How would he support himself and his family? Where would they live? To whom was he going to speak? Did he really think that he, an unknown medical missionary who had spent ten years in China, could change U.S. policy? Why was he turning away from the profession for which he had trained so long and so hard at the University of Nebraska and the Mayo Clinic? Weren't such things as foreign policy better left to the president, Congress, and the Department of State? Couldn't he practice medicine and make some speeches in his spare time? Was what he wanted to do so important that he was justified in putting it first, and his profession, his wife and three small children, perhaps his entire future, second? Walter and Miriam wrote down on a legal-sized piece of yellow paper the reasons why he should and should not go ahead with

65

the "crusade" and spent days discussing them. It became clear to them that they should try.

The Barbers said that Walter, Miriam, and the girls could live in their home so they would at least have a roof over their heads. As for money, a gift of a thousand dollars that Walter's grandfather Greenslit had given him when he was fourteen had more than doubled because of interest. They could live on that for least a year; beyond that, well, the Lord would provide. Walter wasn't too concerned about finding audiences; he would start out talking to church groups and go from there. He didn't know whether he could change U.S. policy about Japan, but he had to try. He could not remain silent about the bits and pieces of American steel which he had removed from innocent Chinese women and children. He was not "giving up" medicine; he was simply putting it aside for a while because the greatest need now was to stop providing Japan's military the tools of war. As for leaving foreign policy to the experts, well, that was what the American people had done so far, and the results were unacceptable. Yes, he could practice medicine and speak in his spare time, in the evenings and on the weekends, but that would be a half-hearted effort and what was happening in China and would undoubtedly happen to America demanded more than a half-hearted crusade. Finally, he had always tried to live by Jesus's words from the Gospel, "Seek ye first the kingdom of God, and his righteousness, and all these things shall be added unto you." He knew that God would provide for his family if he served Him. He was certain that in the year 1938 he would serve Him best by pointing out to his fellow Americans that without U.S. scrap iron, petroleum products, and other materials the Japanese could not continue their assault on China and that "a strong and independent China will be a stabilizing force in the Far East. With the Chinese people free and secure, we need never be concerned about the imperialistic program of military Japan."[1]

He began putting together what he thought of as the Speech, and gave it for the first time in September when a friend asked him to address his Kiwanis Club in Brooklyn. It is an invariable Kiwanis rule that luncheon speakers limit their remarks to thirty minutes, maximum, so that the men can return to their offices promptly by 2 P.M. His speech, "America's Stake in the Far East," ran almost eighteen single-spaced pages, and even Judd, who could speak at a breathtaking rate of 250 words per minute, could not deliver it in less than an hour. Nevertheless, the thin, bespectacled former medical missionary held the Brooklyn businessmen spellbound as he described the new kind of war that Japan was waging against China, in which every Chinese regardless of age, sex, or profession was a "military objective." He called it "totalitarian war" (one of the first times that the phrase was ever used) and he asserted that America was supplying the Japanese with the bulk of the materials for their total war. By now, he had the rapt attention of the Kiwanians. He reassured his audience that he was not calling for the United States to "save" China by sending over its army and navy. "China never suggested or expected us to come to her military assistance; but on the other hand she did not expect that [we] . . . would turn out to be in her darkest hour her enemy's major ally. She didn't expect that *we* would furnish the bulk of the indispensable military supplies which alone enable Japan's military machine to destroy China in violation of the very treaty we sponsored and persuaded China to accept." He talked of being bombed by "American airplanes" because most Japanese planes were made in America. He said that one-third of the scrap iron used in Japanese bombs was American, and described how he had removed bomb fragments from "the bodies and brains of Chinese men and women and children. You could not have stood in my shoes and said it is none of America's responsibility.

"What should we do?" he asked. "Stop our decisive assistance to Japan in the Far East. . . . We don't need to knock Japan out. All we need to do is to stop holding her up and her military adventure collapses for lack of supplies." As *customers,* he said, we should stop financing the war by boycotting Japanese goods. American women should stop buying cultured pearls, tuna fish, crab meat, Christmas-tree ornaments, cheap rayon and, most of all, silk. "Sixty percent of Japan's sales to us are silk, and 74 percent of that goes into silk stockings. Here . . . women have a choice between their silk stockings now or their sons later." As *citizens,* he said, we should let our elected representatives know what "we think our country's action should be in the Pacific. . . . Ask them to pass legislation to stop the sale of war materials to Japan as long as they are being used to destroy the sovereignty and independence of a country, China, whose sovereignty and independence the United States is obligated by solemn treaty [the Nine Power Pact] to respect."

He addressed the natural fears that such actions might lead the United States into war with Japan, arguing that since she had been unable to defeat China *with* our assistance, she could not defeat China and the United States *without* our assistance. "It is just because Japan cannot go to war with us *now* that I urge that we take this action, not as a way to war, but as the way away from war." He stressed that no action by

Japan "*at this time*" would require or justify "our going to war with her." He counseled that "all we need to do is shut off money and materials, sit tight, hold steady, and wait." Isolationism, he insisted, was no longer possible because American inventions like the steamboat and the airplane "had jammed us into one neighborhood with the rest of the world." The Sino-Japanese war, he said, was one issue in international relations where "non-military methods can succeed in solving a dispute. There is no hope for peace and order," he declared, "except as somewhere, sometime, one of these military cliques is checked by non-violent means. There will never be a better opportunity" than in China. "It is the fate of all humanity that is at stake, its hope for decent and peaceful orderliness and security down through the decades ahead."[2]

His speech was based on the two basic ingredients of every successful American foreign policy—idealism and realism. He appealed to the idealist with his description of the terrible plight of the Chinese, the injustice and arrogance of the Japanese, the obligation of Americans to help an old friend and ally, China. He spoke to the realist by listing the specific actions that the ordinary consumer and citizen could take, and by insisting that no military action by the U.S. government against Japan was needed. The reaction of Kiwanians was immediate and enthusiastic: they sent letters to other Kiwanis Clubs across the country and within a few weeks, he was delivering his speech at luncheon meetings and dinner meetings across the country. His speaking schedule expanded dramatically when Harry B. Price, executive secretary of the American Committee for Non-Participation in Japanese Aggression, a national citizens' organization headed by former Secretary of State Henry L. Stimson, got in touch with him and suggested that he speak under their auspices. He agreed and was soon addressing chambers of commerce, trade unions, peace societies, universities and colleges, churches and any other group willing to listen to "the most effective speaker on China now lecturing in America," according to Brewer Eddy, secretary of the American Board for Foreign Missions.[3] During a two-week period in December 1938, for example, he spoke in St. Louis, Chicago, South Bend, Indianapolis, Evansville, Louisville, Cincinnati, Columbus, Pittsburgh, and Wilmington. He received his expenses and an average gift of ten dollars per speaking engagement, which enabled him to stretch his grandfather's gift to cover the family's expenses for two years.

In forums across the country, Judd took on pacifists who feared any U.S. action would lead to war, isolationists who misquoted George

Washington about avoiding *permanent* overseas commitments, businessmen who echoed Calvin Coolidge that the business of America was business, and racists who remarked that what yellow people did to each other was of no concern to America. He pointed out that in 1937, the United States furnished 54 percent and in 1938, 56 percent of Japan's war materials, with a total value of over $300 million. He emphasized that he and other members of the American Committee for Non-Participation in Japanese Aggression were not advocating war or a hands-off stance but a middle course, nonparticipation, that would leave China free to achieve her own independence "which she doubtless can and will do against an unaided Japan." This middle course, he insisted, did not represent any effort to "injure or crush Japan" but "would relieve them of the mounting burden and oppression of war." Once China's sovereignty was restored and assured, the way would be open to help solve the serious economic problems of both China and Japan. But first, he insisted, America's "support to Japanese aggression must end."[4]

In April 1939, he was invited to Washington to testify before the Senate Foreign Relations Committee and the House Foreign Affairs Committee, of which he would later be a leading member. He appeared first before the House committee, presenting himself as an "eyewitness" to a new kind of war in China and arguing that the United States had a responsibility to help end the aggression there, not by military but by economic means. He focused on the key role of the American truck in the Japanese offensive against the Chinese:

"The single, most decisive factor in the interior provinces where I have lived, for instance, and all of the other areas away from the seacoast and rivers where the Japanese Navy operates, is the American truck. My province [of Shansi] lies behind a mountain range on the east, and on the north, the most easily defensible of all of the provinces that the Japanese have succeeded in conquering. The Chinese soldiers were on foot, pushing wheelbarrows, leading donkeys or camels. The Japanese were on tens of thousands of the latest model American wheels. They could get to those 10 or 12 crucial passes first. I saw the six or eight million people living behind the mountains in the area where I worked lose their homes and freedom and things that are dearer than life itself; and it could never have happened without . . . the American automobile."[5]

The subject of the House hearing was "American Neutrality Policy," and Judd took the offensive, insisting that America could not remain neutral in the Far East because China had abided by the Nine Power Pact while Japan had violated the treaty. He was not suggesting that the United States "police the world," but that it should police itself by not giving Japan the tools of war. "What incentive is there for a nation or men to keep contracts if they can break them with impunity and have exactly the same treatment that the other nations get who have gone to the trouble of keeping their contracts?"[6]

Five days later, he appeared before the Senate Committee on Foreign Relations, which was holding hearings on "Neutrality, Peace Legislation and Our Foreign Policy," and made much the same arguments he had to the House committee, adding a caveat about Japan's global designs: "Anyone familiar with Japan's military and also her people's psychology knows that a strong arrogant Japan victorious in China and in the East Indies will continue on its dream and program of world conquest. No nation or man afflicted with this disease, which, for want of a better name I sometimes call 'Alexander's itch,' has ever stopped until it was checked. Neither will nor can Japan. *If she is not checked by nonmilitary measures now, she will have to be checked by military measures later.*" [Emphasis added.]

He so impressed committee members that Sen. Lewis B. Schwellenbach (D-Wash.) declared: "It was the unanimous opinion of those present . . . that the testimony of Dr. Judd had been so outstanding, and had so clearly and exhaustively outlined the situation in the Far East, that there was no need to call any other witnesses upon the Chinese-Japanese problem."[7]

His testimony before the two congressional committees represented the principled internationalism that would dominate U.S. foreign policy after World War II, but it was greeted with great skepticism and even hostility in mid-1939 when members of Congress and other Americans still hoped that the United States could continue to pursue a policy of isolationism. Samuel Eliot Morrison wrote that the average American felt sorry for "John Chinaman" and detested the "Japs" but felt that if 450 million Chinese could not defend themselves against 73 million Japanese "there was nothing he should or could do about it."[8] President Roosevelt did not agree. Particularly after the Japanese took Shanghai and began treating Americans and other Westerners with increasing contempt, the president began considering economic sanctions against Japan as a warning to her leaders. On July 26, 1939, only three months after Judd's congressional testimony, Roosevelt denounced the commerce treaty with Japan, receiving almost unanimous public approval, even from isolationists. But no action was taken to cut off the flow of war supplies that enabled Japan to penetrate deeper and deeper into China.

The Chinese, led by a stubborn Chiang Kai-shek, kept fighting, although their losses were terrible: over two million soldiers were killed or died of wounds in the first three years of the war. More than forty million Chinese were forced to leave their homes, with five to ten million of them dying from disease and starvation.[9] Japan also paid a high price: in early 1940, Tokyo estimated its losses in all engagements as eight hundred thousand killed, wounded, and missing.[10] By the end of 1941, just before Pearl Harbor, the number of Japanese dead was put at 1.15 million.[11] Tokyo extended peace offers to Chiang in 1938 and again in 1939, but he firmly rejected them, confident that eventually his strategy of "trading space for time" would wear the Japanese out and ultimately succeed. In the meantime, he was forced to wage an increasingly defensive war from his mountain-ringed capital of Chungking in Szechwan. He kept the Japanese at bay, but left the Chinese communists relatively free to consolidate their position in the north while carrying out dramatic but militarily unimportant guerrilla operations against the Japanese. To many Chinese and an increasing number of foreigners, it looked as though the communists were fighting while the Nationalists were hiding in the hills. But the Japanese knew who their real enemy was, as reflected in this evaluation by Japanese military writer Masanori Ito: "Although inferiority in weapons and lack of training had caused the Chinese forces to suffer heavy losses, this did not prevent the Chinese [Nationalist] army from maintaining a first-line strength of 7 million, harassing the Japanese army to exhaustion."[12]

Political developments outside China began to affect the Sino-Japanese war. The fall of France and the Netherlands in 1940 created a vacuum in French Indochina and the Dutch East Indies which the Japanese immediately moved to fill. Nazi pressure on Great Britain via sea and air left Malaya, Singapore, and Burma open to attacks which the Japanese quickly launched. Lines of supply for China were cut one by one until only the Burma Road remained. If it were captured, only the Soviet route across Central Asia would be left open, although there was some talk about flying in supplies over the Himalayas, a suggestion dismissed as impossible until U.S. planes and pilots successfully and regularly flew "over the hump" during World War II. The Japanese move into Southeast Asia produced fewer offensive operations in China throughout 1941, but Tokyo did not reduce men and weapons in "the main arena of activity," China.[13] Estimates vary, but Japanese forces in China numbered at least 1.25 million until the very end of the war.

In later years, Judd often referred to the "failure" of his two-year crusade to persuade Americans to stop arming Japan, but in September 1940, President Roosevelt issued an executive order (Congress never having acted) against Japan, prohibiting the trading of airplane fuel and engines, truck tires, machine oil, various metals, and assorted other war materials. His efforts and those of other members of the American Committee for Non-Participation in Japanese Aggression had had their impact. Miriam Judd could also take some of the credit for Roosevelt's action; she not only kept track of Walter's speaking schedule and cared for their three girls but became the leader of a national women's movement against wearing silk stockings, which accounted for most of the Japanese silk exported in the prewar period. It was estimated that each pair of silk stockings gave the Japanese enough currency to buy four rounds of ammunition. Walter always mentioned in his speech that his wife had found someone in New York who would provide lisle cotton stockings to anyone who joined the boycott of silk stockings. Hundreds of women began writing to Miriam for the address of the New York manufacturer. "More than fifty years later," she remarked, "I still meet women who say, 'I wore lisle hose with you, Miriam, because we were going to do our private boycott of silk.' "[14]

For the rest of 1939 and most of 1940, Judd continued his coast-to-coast speaking schedule, hoping to mobilize enough public support to convince Congress that it could and should take economic steps against Japan. He wrote his first article for *Reader's Digest,* under the title, "Let's Stop Arming Japan!" He pointed out that, according to a Gallup Poll, "82 percent of the American people favored the shutting off of war supplies to Japan," but had failed to convey their opinion to Congress and the administration. The time to make their wishes known was now, before the election of 1940, to let elected officials know "they have the people's full support in throwing the weight of America's moral and material power on the side of law and justice and freedom."[15]

He was also the main subject of a remarkable five-part newspaper series, "The Rape of China," published in the *New York World Telegram* in February 1940. Publisher Roy Howard had heard Judd speak at a private dinner in New York City. He was so moved that the next morning he ordered one of his top reporters to interview the former medical missionary and tell the one million readers of the *World Telegram* about the plight of China. Featuring photos of Chinese refugees,

Japanese soldiers operating cannons made with American metal, and the bomb-damaged roof of the Congregational hospital in Fenchow, the series began: "The Japanese are not waging war in the accepted sense of the term—army against army and soldier against soldier. They are attempting to exterminate an entire people, a culture, a way of life." At the end Judd passionately declared: "The time has come for America to take some action in the name of humanity. I have seen the people of a great nation butchered, tortured, humiliated. I have seen their homes destroyed, their families scattered, their culture desecrated. And I know who is responsible for this—my country! America must stop sending war materials to Japan—if America is to remain the land of democracy, freedom and common sense."[16]

But America still hesitated. After Hitler launched his attack on Poland in September 1939, the American people seemed to be justified in their noninvolvement by an ensuing period of inaction which prompted Senator Borah to speak of the "phony war" in Europe and Churchill of "the winter of illusion." However, in the spring of 1940, Nazi Germany invaded Scandinavia and then Belgium, the Netherlands, and finally France. In Samuel Eliot Morison's words: "In one month Hitler's mechanized armies had done what the Kaiser's forces had been unable to accomplish in four years."[17] By now the great majority of Americans wanted the defeat of Germany and the other Axis powers, but they still resisted direct participation in the war. In the Far East, President Roosevelt's partial embargo produced a sharp cutback in Japanese bombing attacks on Chungking. After nearly four years of strategic retreat and isolation and mounting economic, social, and political problems, Chiang Kai-shek and the Nationalist government saw hope and even rescue in the escalating crisis in Europe. If they could hold on a little longer, they told themselves, something would happen which would require the United States to become a direct participant in the war. Their hopes seemed justified, for step by step the United States abandoned its posture of neutrality in the Sino-Japanese War. In late 1940, the Export-Import Bank extended a credit of $100 million to China. The following March, President Roosevelt approved Lend Lease aid to China. On July 25, 1941, the president issued another executive order freezing all Japanese assets in the United States, in effect creating an economic blockade of Japan. A majority of the Japanese military became convinced that war against the United States was necessary. Nevertheless, talks proceeded between Secretary of State Cordell Hull and Admiral Kichisaburo Nomura during most of 1941. The key point was whether

Japan would withdraw from Indochina, which Nomura said she would do if Chiang Kai-shek surrendered and American trade resumed. But Chiang had no intention of surrendering just when it seemed that he would gain the United States as an ally and turn defeat into victory, while the United States insisted that it would not resume trade until after Japan had withdrawn from French Indochina.

Meanwhile, Judd had reluctantly decided, in the fall of 1940, to give up his crusade to change U.S. policy toward Japan. Roosevelt's partial embargo was certainly welcome, but the former missionary felt that it misled people into thinking that it solved the problem. Simply put, the embargo did not go far enough: the war in China continued, the Japanese had extended their influence throughout Indochina, all the conditions for confrontation between Japan and the United States persisted. "I knew," Judd recalled, "that unless some miracle took place there was going to have to be a war." He had done all that anyone could ask: he had made hundreds of speeches, participated in radio debates, given newspaper interviews, written magazine articles, made appearances before congressional committees. His grandfather's gift was almost gone; he was past forty and had yet to practice medicine in the United States. For the first time in his life, he put his family ahead of the cause, moved to Minneapolis, where they had made many friends while he was at the Mayo Clinic, and took over the practice of Dr. Youbert Johnson, who had been called up for the draft and wanted his practice held for him until his return.

CHAPTER SEVEN

◆

Reluctant Candidate

LOCATED ON THE BANKS of the upper Mississippi, Minneapolis is a prosperous, progressive city, a trade and industrial center of the Middle West, with flour milling and dairy products its two main industries. It is Minnesota's largest city, and its congressman wields significant political power in the state and in Washington, D.C. Between World War I and World War II, the Fifth Congressional District, which included about three-fifths of the city, was usually represented by a Republican although it went Farmer-Labor several times during the Roosevelt years. Oscar Youngdahl, a Republican with a well-known Scandinavian name in Minnesota politics (one younger half-brother was later elected governor and another was a very prominent clergyman), won the seat in 1938 and was re-elected by a comfortable margin in 1940. Youngdahl was a typical Minnesota Republican of the time, an isolationist who voted "no" in 1941 on the extension of selective service. He looked like a safe bet for re-election in 1942: Republicans usually won the general election, and who could successfully challenge him in the Republican primary?

Judd did not stop speaking once he started practicing medicine in Minneapolis in January 1941, and as Japanese-American tensions increased through the summer and fall of 1941, he became the most popular public speaker in the city. At the same time, his practice grew

75

until it was more than any one man, except perhaps Walter Judd, could handle. Throughout 1941, he spoke in the evenings, in between delivering babies, and at breakfasts before office hours, and on Sundays before church groups. His message was usually the same: there would almost certainly be war in the Far East because the United States had spent years arming and building up Japan. Although we now recognized that Japan had become a threat to us, he said, and had taken some steps to contain her expansionism, it was essentially too late. As he told his audiences: "If you're going to arm a country, if you're going to give a man a revolver, don't slap him in the face. If you're going to slap him in the face, don't give him a revolver."[1] His pessimism about the future was reinforced by the Japanese's brutal treatment of the remaining missionaries in China: he learned that fifteen Chinese missionaries, including a doctor, who were based not far from Fenchow had been taken out by Japanese soldiers and executed.[2]

On Sunday morning, December 7, 1941, he spoke at the Mayflower Congregational Church, and afterwards as he drove to the hospital to see a critically sick patient, he turned on the radio and learned that the Japanese had attacked Pearl Harbor. "I had tried so darn hard to prevent it, but it had happened." He had promised to appear the following Sunday in the pulpit of his own church, Plymouth Congregational, in downtown Minneapolis. The church was filled with people and anticipation as he said, surprising many with his message: "I have more hope for my country today, dark as the outlook is, than I have had since the latter days of the First World War, for at last we have been stabbed awake and we are on the march. We have seen our task, and I have faith in our will and ability to fulfill it."[3] Miriam Judd remembered that people went around saying: "We didn't listen to that crazy Judd because he was too far out. We didn't think it would ever be possible for a little bunch of volcano islands over there in the Pacific to attack the great United States. He was right and we were wrong."

There was fitful talk among liberal Republicans as well as Democrats and Farmer-Laborites about a challenge to Youngdahl, but opposition was not well defined and had not yet coalesced around anyone. Members of the Republican, Democratic and Farmer-Labor parties were split on the isolationist issue, even after Pearl Harbor; while all three parties officially supported the war, some members grumbled that the United States could and should have stayed on the sidelines. The Democratic party was weak and without impact and later formed a coalition with the Farmer-Labor party. People kept asking, "How did this happen to us?" Judd explained all over Minneapolis that it was the result of America's providing the sinews of war to Japan and that we should never again build up our enemies at the expense of friends like China. More and more people began remarking that the city and the state needed representatives in government like Walter Judd, who had first-hand experience of Asia.

"This was a perfectly ridiculous idea to Walter and me at the start," remarked Miriam Judd. "Although we were tremendously interested in international affairs and making a better world, we had never been interested in the nitty-gritty of politics and elections. We had not lived in Minneapolis long enough to vote. We didn't own any property in Minneapolis. . . . He was a physician, not a politician."[4]

Walter also had other things on his mind, like Miriam's fourth pregnancy. They were concerned about her abnormal increase in size until an X-ray revealed that she was going to have twins. The girls were informed and immediately began debating what their names should be; Miriam took inventory and decided that she had enough "baby things . . . even for twins." However, in late January, with three months still to go before delivery, Miriam became so uncomfortable that she went into the hospital. Bed rest and intravaneous feeding seemed to be working, and there was talk about her going home, when suddenly the membranes burst. Since the early months, Miriam had had too much water in the uterus, accounting for her excessive size, even with twins, and her extreme discomfort. She was taken to the delivery room, and two very tiny girls were born within an hour. Several specialists did their best, Walter staying with them, but both infants lived only nine hours. The next day, Walter took Mary Lou, Carolyn, and Eleanor, into the mortuary chapel where they looked at the "tiny rosebuds, so natural and so perfect and so beautiful and pink." As he told Miriam later, he explained to the girls that the twins were tiny flowers that hadn't had time to unfold in this world but would go on and develop and grow in another one.[5]

Shortly thereafter, a group of citizens who believed that a fight should be made against the isolationism of the state's congressional delegation held a luncheon at the Minneapolis Athletic Club. Present were members of the Committee to Aid the Allies and similar organizations, Republicans, Democrats, and independents. None of them was a politician or active in politics. Walter Judd attended, not knowing exactly what would be discussed but sharing their concern about the foreign policy direction of Congress. As the politically inexperienced but frustrated group talked, a consensus began to emerge that a slate of candidates should be run in the forthcoming Republican primaries against all of the isolationist incumbents. Finally, Gideon Seymour, a seasoned newspaper editor who had been silently listening, decided that it was time to inject a large measure of realism. The talk about a "slate," he said, was nonsense. No one there had any influence in any party or could raise the necessary money to finance one primary campaign, let alone campaigns in half a dozen districts. Besides, he said, the slate idea was hopeless because while people might back one or perhaps two candidates, they would never support the wholesale overthrow of the entire Minnesota delegation.

"If you really want to do something," he said, "start by trying to find a candidate in *one* district—your own, right here in Minneapolis—and get behind him and make a fight to nominate him." As a matter of fact, he said, he had a candidate: the man sitting across the table, Walter Judd. "Thousands of people have heard him and would come to hear him again," he said. "He is talking authoritatively about things the people are most interested in. A lot of women would work for him. The tide is moving toward the views he stands for. He would get a big independent vote."[6]

A surprised Judd responded firmly that he was not interested in running: he was a physician, not a politician, he didn't know anything about politics and campaigning, he had no money, and he had been a Democrat all his life until he had voted for Wendell Willkie and against FDR's third term in 1940. The meeting broke up inconclusively, but a rumor soon began floating around the city that Walter Judd was going to run for Congress. People came up after his talks and said they hoped it was true. He insisted he had no intention of running, but the rumor would not die and soon those who were urging him to declare his candidacy included an energetic young lawyer, a young advertising man, and other rising leaders of Minneapolis.

"I didn't want to do it," the reluctant candidate later explained. "To get into public life was the last thing I'd ever thought of doing. I had been nineteen years in medicine, my whole bent and training were in science. I'd been forced step by step into this public speaking through situations in which I had found myself unintentionally. Finally a couple of young men ... came to see me one afternoon ... [and] said, 'We'll put on the campaign, we'll raise the money, we'll arrange the meetings, we'll do the advertising, and all the rest, you just go and debate the issues as you're doing anyway.' Still I was reluctant."

Why was he so reluctant? He seemed to have all the necessary attributes for a congressman. He was a gifted public speaker capable of igniting audiences large and small. He had as thorough a knowledge of important foreign policy issues as most officials of the State Department and far more than most members of Congress, including Oscar Youngdahl. He knew from American history that the Founding Fathers had emphasized the importance of private citizens serving in government, particularly in Congress. After all that he had confronted in China, including his own death on more than one occasion, he did not find the prospect of challenging an incumbent congressman very daunting. He even believed that he might make a pretty good congressman; perhaps that was why he hesitated. He was determined to return to China, but that day might be postponed a long while if he ran and won a seat in Congress. There was another personal reason: he had been trained as a doctor not to boast of and certainly not to advertise his ability as a physician or surgeon. A candidate for Congress was expected to ask people for their vote and their money, to promise them things, to attack his opponent, to do all the things that politicians naturally do. He couldn't be that kind of a candidate; he wouldn't be that kind of congressman. Could such a nonpolitical candidate win an election?

Undeterred by his reluctance, his unofficial campaign team approached Harlan Nygaard, a young Minneapolis businessman who had been active in Republican politics on behalf of Governor Harold E. Stassen, about becoming chairman of a Judd for Congress Committee, if one were formed. Nygaard agreed to serve temporarily. Judd kept temporizing while four other groups and Carleton College's influential president urged him to be a candidate, but also kept making speeches about the solemn responsibilities of Americans in the current crisis. At last, a young General Mills executive, after hearing him address a dinner meeting, called on him the next day and told Judd bluntly: "You have no right to go around our community, stirring us up, making clear to us what *our* civic duty is, and yet you refuse to do *your* civic duty. We want to send you to Congress as our spokesman." As Judd said afterwards, "I was not willing to shut up, so I had to put up," and run for the Republican nomination. He did one last thing before committing himself: he called his father whose advice and counsel he respected above all others. Horace Judd told his son that there had been members of the Judd family in every war since the American Revolution because they thought the country was worth preserving and worth fighting for. He didn't think there was anything but grief in it for Walter, but if a

79

responsible group of people wanted him to run for public office and would help him make the effort, he didn't see how his son could do anything but say, 'Yes.' "[7]

Just before the Fourth of July, Walter Judd formally announced that he would be a candidate for the Republican nomination to the Fifth Congressional District. Explaining that these were not "ordinary times" and that every man and woman should work where he or she would be most useful in the war effort, he declared that he would leave his profession of medicine for public life if the voters believed that their interests and those of the nation would be best served with him as their representative in Congress. The guarded, conditional language was far from the usual rhetoric of an eager candidate, but was quite acceptable to the citizens of Minneapolis who ardently believed in civic responsibility and service.[8]

The Judd Committee rented a vacant storeroom in downtown Minneapolis for a few dollars and opened a headquarters for volunteers which was quickly staffed mostly by enthusiastic young women. Judd formulated, with help from Seymour, Nygaard and others, a platform that was reprinted in full in the *Minneapolis Sunday Tribune,* which praised it as a "challenging statement" about the issues of the day. A series of evening "open houses" was held, at which the candidate would answer questions and stay on to socialize over coffee and doughnuts. The first meetings attracted only a few people, mostly friends mixed with the usual curious citizens and freeloaders. But the numbers quickly increased to become overflow audiences. More and more VIPs began to drop into campaign headquarters; business leaders invited him to lunch to talk to their friends. "People who heard him were persuaded," recalled a campaign assistant. "Campaign contributions began to come in from men of means who usually said, 'He hasn't a chance—but he makes sense and we want to help.' "[9]

The Republican organization remained cool to the newcomer and largely committed to Youngdahl, but Nygaard worked hard to find experienced precinct and ward workers who after meeting and talking with Judd agreed to help him. Most of the inner circle believed their man would not win, but they were young and it was their first real campaign and everything—the long hours, the incessant telephoning, the cajoling of volunteers, writing press releases, missed meals, little sleep—was fun. They smiled and shrugged when some Republican veterans began to say, "Judd is going to be nominated." The Stassen forces were friendly but did not intervene openly, sharing the conventional wisdom that in the end Youngdahl would prevail. Judd refused to give up his medical practice so that frequently he would finish a campaign speech, rush to a hospital to deliver a baby, and hurry on to the next engagement where the waiting crowd would be given reports on the progress in the delivery room. Sometimes there were medical complications, and Miriam would have to take his place at the podium, once prompting the newspaper headline, "Mrs. Judd Delivers Speech, Dr. Judd Delivers Baby." Every morning, he went to the hospital to operate and then spent hours in his office seeing patients before the day's campaigning started. Often, he worked from midnight after the last speech to early morning, writing out his talks in longhand. Radio was the mass medium of the time and at first presented a problem. Because of his inexperience and his habit of using a hundred words when fifty would do, he often spoke too long and was cut off before finishing. With editing help from Gideon Seymour, he learned to tailor his remarks to the available time. He was probably the most rapid-fire public speaker in America, and because of campaign exhaustion sometimes misspoke. With his quick mind, he usually but not always recovered; once he blurted, "This [campaign] is like a snow-ball rolling downhill—it's catching fire!"

Although Judd steadfastly refused to make any mention of his opponent's heavy drinking, sticking to the issues, the Youngdahl campaign organization did not hesitate to circulate charges that Judd had been sent to live in Minneapolis by "big New York interests," that his real name was "Jude," that he was not a "true Republican" but a front for the Democrats and the Farmer-Labor party; and that he was supported by "official Chinese money" because he would let Chinese labor into the country to work for twenty-five cents an hour and undercut the American working man. Commented Miriam in a letter to her parents: "The general feeling now is that the [Youngdahl] opposition has been very stupid in spreading dirt, for it is starting to boomerang and they are beginning to lose even among their own supporters."[10]

In his final radio talk on Labor Day, Judd asked the voters to choose leaders of "vision and judgment and integrity" and promised, if nominated and elected in November, to do three things: to help win the war "quickly and conclusively" by fighting all "half-measures and half-mobilization"; to help win "a lasting peace" by working to make America part of a decent world order (a "United Nations") and not to allow her to separate herself from the world as in the past; and to promote the interests of the district and its people within the context of the "national good" that is the deepest concern of every citizen.[11]

On the morning of September 8, 1942, primary day in Minneapolis, he told his inner group, "Well, it has been a good fight, and a worthwhile one. We won't win, but I hope we don't get beaten too badly, because all of you have worked so hard. I don't really want to get nominated, I don't have any desire to go to Congress, but I do believe in the ideas I have advocated. It would be ideal if I could lose by, say, five hundred votes. Then I could go back to China as a medical missionary and feel that I had done something for my country." There was, of course, no possibility of his returning to China while the war was on. As for serving his country, both U.S. Army intelligence and the medical corps were trying to persuade him to take a commission and put his knowledge of China and the Chinese to use in the war effort. If he had not been elected to Congress, he would have entered the military in some special capacity.

But he did not have to ponder any such decision: he defeated Oscar Youngdahl in the Republican primary by a margin of three to two. It was a remarkable victory for someone who had only lived in the city for twenty months and who had never voted in the district until he went to the polls to vote for himself. Old-line politicians had dismissed him scornfully as "a missionary," a rank newcomer who dared to take on an established Republican with a good Scandinavian name and following, a man who had come up through the political ranks the hard and proper way. It would have been an impossible victory in ordinary times, but the times were far from ordinary and so was the "missionary" who had once again taken on and bested the establishment. He campaigned and won the Republican nomination as an internationalist and a progressive in the "good government" tradition of most Minnesota public officials. Even so, as one Minneapolis newspaperman observed, his victory would not have occurred "at any other time than in that first balloting after Pearl Harbor, in a grim hour of American history—or in any other congressional district but the cohesive, highly literate Fifth of Minnesota. Certainly it couldn't have been done by anybody but Walter Judd."[12]

In November he outpolled his two opponents, Farmer-Laborite Joseph Gilbert and Democrat Thomas P. Ryan, by a nearly two to one margin. An unusual but effective campaign framework was established that was strictly adhered to for twenty years: Judd would campaign as hard as he knew how on the issues, but would never personally attack his opponent; he would never ask for anyone's vote but would explain where he stood on an issue and why he voted for this or that bill and would welcome a person's support if he agreed with him; he would not raise one dime in campaign funds or put one cent of his own money into any campaign. For their part, the Judd campaign organization kept the political machinery running, raised the money, scheduled the candidate, sometimes spread rumors about the opposition, and derived the great satisfaction of keeping in office the best representative that Minneapolis and Minnesota had had in many years, maybe the best ever. Such an unorthodox arrangement would not have worked amid the machine politics of New York City, Chicago, or Boston, but it prevailed in Minneapolis, proud, public-spirited, and liberal Republican, for two decades. Women were a key group in Judd's first campaign, entering politics as they entered other professions during the war to take the place of their men who were fighting overseas. Emerging from their participation was the Republican Workshop, which spread over the Midwest and the Southwest. Workshop leaders explained the benefits of politics to other women who had never before been interested in the electoral aspects of government. In the years to come, the Republican Workshop provided thousands of workers in congressional districts throughout middle America.[13]

Judd's victory attracted the close attention, among others, of a young political science professor with electoral ambitions. One day, he was visited in his office by Hubert H. Humphrey, who candidly admitted that he was seeking political, not medical advice. He had been urged by colleagues at the University of Minnesota to "run for office," but he had no money, no organization, and wasn't even sure what office he should seek. He revealed that he had voted for Willkie in 1940 "because I opposed a third term for Roosevelt" and had also supported Republican Harold Stassen three times for governor. He was impressed by the new Republican coming out of nowhere and winning a congressional seat. What advice could the congressman-elect give him? As many would be in the coming decades, Judd was impressed by Humphrey's personal warmth and ebullience and said that the only election coming up soon was for mayor of Minneapolis, a nonpartisan office. Humphrey was immediately enthusiastic, and Judd said he would be glad to set up a meeting with some of his campaign leaders. At a luncheon at the Minneapolis Athletic Club, Ronald Welch, Nygaard and three others were so taken with Humphrey that each man put up fifteen dollars to cover the young professor's fifty-dollar filing fee for the mayoralty, with twenty-five dollars left over for his campaign chest. Although owing his start in politics to Walter Judd, Democrat Humphrey never followed his philosophical lead, becoming a champion of liberalism when he was elected to the U.S. Senate in 1948.[14]

In January 1943, Walter and Miriam Judd and their three girls moved to Washington, D.C., where he intended to be the representative of *all* the people of his district and not the agent of any group or bloc, no matter how vocal, well organized or powerful. He liked to quote Edmund Burke that "your representative owes you his judgment as well as his industry. He betrays your best interest if he sacrifices his judgment to your opinion."[15] It would be his political code as long as he was in Congress.

CHAPTER EIGHT

Wartime Washington

WRITING IN *The New Republic,* Malcolm Cowley declared that "Washington in wartime is a combination of Moscow (for overcrowding), Paris (for its trees), Wichita (for its way of thinking), Nome (in the gold-rush days) and Hell (for its livability)."[1] In many ways, Washington, D.C. looked like a city in peacetime, with traffic jams, food in the stores (despite ration cards for everything from sugar to gasoline), parties, and movies; but high-ranking officials in the executive branch and in Congress often worked around the clock as they helped manage a multifront war in Africa, western Europe, Russia, and the South Pacific that had gone badly in 1942. Miriam Judd described the air-raid shelters marked with large signs, the singing of the national anthem at the close of church services, the antiaircraft guns set up in "little parks all through the city," the railroad and bus stations "just teeming with people of all kinds." Shocked by the high rents (at least $250 a month for anything like their Minneapolis home), they decided to buy a large old house with fruit trees and "a good yard" near the National Cathedral in northwest Washington, six miles from Capitol Hill, but near a trolley line "that will take Walter direct to [his office]."[2]

Although the Japanese attack on Pearl Harbor brought the United States into the war, and one might have expected widespread demands to move quickly against the nation that stabbed America in the back, most Americans in and out of government accepted Roosevelt's strategic tilt toward Europe. In those days the president proposed and disposed foreign policy. In addition, few Americans knew much about the Far East or Japan. One of the exceptions was a freshman Congressman from Minnesota named Walter Judd, who broke tradition by not waiting the usual six months but delivered his maiden speech on February 25 as more than a hundred congressmen listened, a large audience for any member, especially a first-termer. His rather immodest theme was "How Can We Win in the Pacific?" It centered on the national psychology of America's enemy there, the Japanese military. He offered three basic insights into the Japanese character.

First, the Japanese are a people of small stature, and like many people of small stature or with physical disabilities, he said, have a strong "inferiority complex." They reacted by trying to conquer the world, not so much to show the world as to "reassure themselves that they were not inferior men." He noted how the Japanese officer rode the tallest horse possible or carried an oversize sword that clanked on the ground "to bolster up his own ego."

Second, Judd saw the Japanese as an unimaginative, uncreative people. He readily conceded that they were efficient, disciplined, and as resolute as any people in the world, but they "never yet produced a single major basic invention." In contrast, the Chinese devised printing, the compass for sea navigation, and gunpowder, three inventions that molded modern European civilization. The lack of Japanese creativity was the result of centuries of regimentation, of the "complete control of all life and thinking by the government."

Third, because even nature had conspired against Japan in the form of typhoons, earthquakes, and volcanic eruptions, the Japanese, according to Judd, had developed a "true persecution psychosis." They had brooded over their troubles, real and imaginary, until they had become "the most moody, self-pitying and morbidly introspective people in the world." They had achieved everything the hard way, by sheer determination and unrelenting struggle, and therefore believed they could conquer America which had become so soft and pleasure-loving it could no longer "take it."

Given these characteristics, Judd suggested that the United States ought to take the offensive, thereby throwing Japan's military machine off stride. "Centuries of regimentation have left Japan's men, especially her officers, [unable to react] once a plan goes awry." To hold on in the Pacific until Hitler was defeated in Europe, "we must understand our allies far better than we have thus far." It was critical, he agreed, to keep Russia in the war: "If Russia went down, it would be a disaster for us in Europe and equally a disaster for us in the Far East." It was no less important to keep China in the war because she tied up more than one million Japanese troops on the mainland and because China neutralized "an enormous amount of Japanese manpower and the shipping and the factories in Japan necessary to supply those men."[3]

Judd's analysis elicited generally favorable comment from other members, except for some fellow Republicans in the Minnesota delegation who, still resenting his upset victory over their former colleague Youngdahl, blocked his assignment to the House Foreign Affairs Committee, where his background and experience would have been best used. However, a very important Washingtonian, Eleanor Roosevelt, liked his initial speech so much she invited the Judds to Sunday dinner at the White House. Walter and Miriam supposed they would be attending some large function for new members of the 78th Congress, but when they arrived they discovered they were one of four couples for a several course meal (oysters on the half shell, roast beef and Yorkshire pudding, ice cream and cake but no wine) and presided over by Mrs. Roosevelt, who read the *Congressional Record* every day and wanted to hear the rest of Congressman Judd's speech, particularly his thoughts about China. The president did not join them, but afterwards the Judds went upstairs and talked briefly with him.

What struck the new Congressman most forcefully was that Roosevelt was "much more crippled than I had realized," and could not walk even with crutches "except by sheer dogged determination." The president was certainly to be praised for having overcome so serious a handicap, Judd readily conceded, but in triumphing over a personal affliction, Roosevelt had acquired "undue confidence" that he could overcome any political or strategic obstacle.[4] As was his custom, Judd wrote a warm note of thanks to the First Lady which, although he did not plan it, helped him get an appointment soon thereafter with the president. Refusing to play politics as usual, he wanted to see Roosevelt about making more medical facilities available for the Minnesota-Iowa national guard soldiers being brought back wounded from North Africa. Roosevelt began by remarking: "You wrote an awfully nice note to my missus, and she appreciates it. Now what about this hospital you're needing in your area? How about a few hundred more beds at that VA hospital in North Dakota?" The President seemed to Judd to be more interested in getting kudos for a Democrat running in North Dakota against an incumbent Republican senator than the best disposition of hospital beds. Always thereafter, Judd sought to find the real reason for an action or position taken by Roosevelt.

Unusual things continued to happen to the freshman congressman: that summer he spent two weeks on the road with a future president, Harry S. Truman. Concerned that the United States might retreat into isolationism following the war as it had after World War I, four senators, Republicans Joseph H. Ball of Minnesota and Harold H. Burton of Ohio and Democrats Lister Hill of Alabama and Carl A. Hatch of New Mexico, introduced a resolution declaring it to be the sense of the Senate that the United States should cooperate with other nations after World War II to bring into being "a world organization" through which peace-loving nations could pool their strength against lawless or aggressive actions by any nation. It was decided that bipartisan teams would fan out across the country explaining the case to the people and mobilizing their support; if the Republican was a senator, the congressman would be a Democrat, and vice versa. It was a mark of his swift acceptance as a foreign policy leader that Judd (who had been working on a similar resolution in the House) was paired with Senator Carl Hatch, one of the authors of the resolution. Hatch and Judd started their tour in Iowa on a hot July morning, but that first day, Senator Hatch became ill and had to leave. A Democratic senator not on one of the regular teams took his place. Harry Truman was not as well known as Hatch, and he wasn't much of a public speaker; but he supported the resolution and was available.

Judd and Hatch had worked out a division of labor which Truman readily accepted; the congressman discussed why a world organization was needed, followed by the senator who dealt with how the Senate would help form such an organization. As Judd recalled:

> I'd try to get them steamed up as to why we couldn't go back to the isolationist pattern of the past. Then it was Mr. Truman's turn. He [would] get up and say: "For me to make a speech following this stem-winder, Judd, always makes me feel like the man who went to the funeral of his wife and the undertaker told him he'd have to ride to the cemetery in the same car with his mother-in-law. The man protested, but the undertaker insisted there was no other place for him to ride." And then Mr. Truman would always scratch his head and go on: " 'Well,' the old fellow said, 'I *can* do it, but it sure is going to spoil the whole day for me.' "

For two weeks, Judd and Truman traveled through the Midwest, addressing an estimated ten thousand civic leaders people at 27 meetings in 19 different cities. "Hundreds of business people were turned away because of lack of facilities to accommodate them," reported the tour's director.[5] At night, the two men shared a bedroom and talked politics; every evening, Truman would telephone his wife Bess to tell her what had happened that day. Their trip went smoothly until they were scheduled to appear in Kansas City, right next to Independence, Missouri, Truman's hometown. There had been a bitter fight between reform forces and the Pendergast political machine which controlled Kansas City for decades. The reformers had finally won, and now they informed Washington that they wanted no part of a large luncheon at which Truman, whose political career had been launched by Pendergast, would be a speaker. Major embarrassment was avoided when Judd suggested a way out to the schedulers in Washington: Explain to Truman that since he was in Kansas City all the time and they had a request from Topeka for that same day, they could put Judd in Kansas City where he was a new face and send Truman to Topeka. Truman readily agreed, and "to the best of my knowledge," said Judd, "never knew the [real] reason why."

Coming together after their separate appearances, the two men drove to their next engagement in Emporia, Kansas, and along the way began discussing Pendergast. Truman said: "I knew Pendergast was a crook. He voted people who had been dead anywhere from six months to 10 years. Year after year, he loaded elections. But he never asked me to do one thing that wasn't honorable. I must say he gave me a start by appointing me to that judgeship [in Jackson County] out of which came my election to the United States Senate and such career as I've had." When Pendergast died in 1945, President Truman attended his funeral despite strong criticism because, as Judd put it, he was determined to pay his respects to an old friend "and loyalty to friends was certainly one of his finest qualities."[6]

One day, when they were scheduled to speak in Hastings, Nebraska, Judd suggested they stop off and have Sunday dinner at his parents' home in Rising City, about seventy-five miles away. It was an old-fashioned country dinner with fried chicken, whipped potatoes, and buttered beets out of the Judd garden, lettuce and tomato salad, hot biscuits, home-canned pickles, fresh peaches, home-baked white cake and cold lemonade. The men took off their coats and "sat down like harvest hands." Truman told Horace Judd that he had not had a meal like that since his mother, who was ninety-one, used to cook for him. The two men, both born on Missouri farms, sat next to each other at the dinner table, and afterwards, Horace Judd told his son, "Well, I'm a Republican, and I don't know about his politics, but I'd trust that fellow with my pocketbook."[7] Truman's ability to win over dyed-in-the-wool Republicans like Horace Judd would serve him well, and confound political experts and pollsters, in 1948 when he ran for president.

In between dining at the White House, touring the country with senators, and maintaining a crowded social schedule (one week in May, he and Miriam dined with Senator Joseph Ball and a prominent Minnesota Republican, over 100 alumnae and husbands of Mount Holyoke, Congresswoman Clare Boothe Luce, and President Quezon of the Philippines as well as old friends from China and India) Judd introduced legislation, attended committee hearings (he was appointed to the Insular Affairs and Education Committees), answered constituent mail, and participated in debates on the House floor where he quickly established himself as a member whose ability to talk faster than anyone else was only exceeded by his understanding of the bill under consideration. From his very first day in Congress, he took the time to study the legislation that came before him, particularly in the area of foreign affairs, so that through the years more and more of his colleagues in both parties looked to him for guidance as to how they should vote on highly technical items like foreign aid and mutual security.

He won widespread respect for his firm command of the arguments for and against a bill, but he was never one of the inner circle that gathered in Sam Rayburn's office in the late afternoon for bourbon and political gossip. He did not accept the Speaker's dictum that if you wanted to get along, you had to go along. Reflecting his mother's New England independence, he did not hesitate to go it alone, if his conscience so dictated. Significantly, a close friend in the House was Christian Herter of Massachusetts, another freshman Republican with a reputation for flinty integrity. Among the Democrats, his closest friend for many years was Brooks Hays of Arkansas, who shared his internationalist convictions. Judd picked his friendships carefully; he always maintained a certain reserve. He did not share the enthusiasm of most of the other members for politics *qua* politics nor their penchant for appraising every vote in terms of whether it would help or hurt their re-election. He was there to help win the war and the peace, and then he intended to return to China and resume his missionary work. Rather than resenting Judd's moralistic approach to politics, most congressmen admired it; they decided that the House of Representatives was diverse enough to include even a man who put principle before party. They also recognized his firsthand knowledge of far-off places and peoples they had only read about. He gave the boys in the cloakroom something to talk about: a physician among lawyers, a missionary among politicians, an internationalist in an isolationist delegation, a man who voted to satisfy his conscience, not his constituents.

In his first year in Congress, Judd's legislative efforts were concentrated on two issues: the House's U.N. resolution, introduced by freshman Democrat J. William Fulbright of Arkansas, and a bill repealing the Chinese Exclusion Acts, historic civil rights legislation which upset reactionaries and racists as civil rights bills invariably do. The Fulbright resolution read: "That the Congress hereby express itself as favoring the creation of appropriate international machinery with power adequate to establish and to maintain a just and lasting peace among the nations of the world, and as favoring participation by the United States therein through its constitutional processes."[8] Given the U.S. rejection of the League of Nations and America's historic isolationism, it was revolutionary legislation.

Judd sought to de-escalate the rhetoric, arguing that America had four choices as she considered the next half-century: First, "we can try to go back to so-called isolationism." He conceded that it once was possible to ignore other nations, but "that day has gone" because of our own inventions like the steamboat and airplane and the "refusal of other nations to ignore us." Second, we could develop "an American imperialism (although of course call it by a milder name)." This course would require gaining control of key islands, critical air bases, main routes of trade, and then building "such a giant air force and navy and army that it will be certain no nation can ever attack us." But, he argued, not even America had the necessary resources to go it alone, and if we tried to "police the world single-handed" the rest of the world would "gang up against us." "Imperialism," he declared, "was always immoral. For America to try it now would be suicidal." Third, we could adopt a philosophy of "world WPAism," where America would try to "buy the world's good-will." But, said the former medical missionary, giving people things instead of helping them get on their feet "so they can develop their own freedom from want" was always self-defeating in the long run. Such an approach "destroys independence and will and initiative and self-reliance." Fourth, the United States could participate in a genuinely cooperative effort with our allies to achieve "an organized security." The world, he said, could not "stand these periodic returns to the jungle"; an international organization, a united nations, was not utopian but necessary. Surely, he said, if we could work with our allies to win the war, we were sufficiently intelligent and wise "to be able to work out with our allies ways by which we can jointly win the peace."[9] In 1943, with the Soviet Union an important ally, the Iron Curtain not yet in place, and the Cold War not yet begun, the House of Representatives believed that such a joint endeavor on behalf of world peace was possible and that the United States should be part of it. It approved the Fulbright Resolution by an overwhelming 360 to 29; the Senate later passed its version by 85 to 5, with six senators absent. The way was cleared for the Dumbarton Oaks Conference to draft an agreement for American participation in the United Nations. As William Manchester has written, "It seemed that Wendell Willkie had chosen precisely the right title for his 1943 book: *One World*."[10]

But Judd learned that not all members of Congress were ready for a world (or to be more precise, an America) in which Chinese were accorded the same rights as everyone else with regard to immigration and citizenship. When gold was discovered in California in 1848 and the economy boomed, company agents brought over thousands of Chinese to build the railroads and cultivate the soil until by 1876 there were about 110,000 Chinese immigrants on the Pacific coast. Economic and social conflicts developed, due to nativist fears that America would be overwhelmed by a flood of Chinese laborers—a progenitor of "the yellow peril." Because there was no quota formula to control and regulate immigration, a series of fifteen laws was passed between 1882 and 1913 by which the United States first "regulated and limited," then "suspended" temporarily, and finally "prohibited" Chinese immigration to the United States. Then, with the Immigration Act of 1924, the quota system was devised. Aliens who were eligible for citizenship, that is, "white persons, persons of African nativity or descent, and descendants of races indigenous to the Western Hemisphere," were put on a quota basis. All aliens not included in these groups and therefore ineligible for citizenship were totally excluded from immigration, with certain limited exceptions for government officials, students, professors, ministers, businessmen, and other temporary visitors. Conspicuously absent from those eligible for citizenship, and therefore immigration, were Chinese and other yellow and brown peoples.

As he asked in House debate, "But is that where Americans want to leave the matter? Do we still want officially to stigmatize as congenitally inferior because their skins happen to be yellow instead of white, black or red, the Chinese people who recognized the nature of this world struggle [against the Axis] and held the line single-handed for 4½ years before we woke up?" He declared that it was time to extend the quota formula, to include the Chinese and put them on a "plane of equality" with America's other allies. He urged Congress to do three things: Repeal the old exclusion acts; amend the nationality laws to make Chinese persons or persons of Chinese descent eligible for naturalization by the same procedures that other immigrants follow; and allot an annual immigration quota to the Chinese based on the established formula which would allow a total of 105 Chinese immigrants a year. Even with so insignificant a number, the old and illogical fear of yellow hordes somehow inundating Anglo-Saxon America was so ingrained that Judd had to reassure his colleagues that there were no loopholes in the legislation by which Chinese born in Hong Kong or Mexico could enter as British or Mexicans: "the one quota of 105 would cover all persons of the Chinese race desiring to immigrate to the United States, regardless of where they were born or of what country they are citizens." He added that because only a very small number of Chinese had been admitted for permanent residence, only a small number of the 40,000 Chinese aliens now in the United States could successfully apply for citizenship. Out of varying motives, congressional opponents responded that if only 105 "Chinamen" were involved, why bother to change the law now? Why couldn't it wait until the war was over and American troops came home? Because, Judd answered, repeal of the Chinese Exclusion Acts involved an important point. "The chief thing is the principle of [the Chinese] being treated as equals." Repeal, he emphasized, would help the war effort because it would send a clear signal to the Chinese that we valued them as allies during the war and would work with them as friends during the peace.[11]

As he always tried to do, he appealed to the realistic as well as the idealistic side of his colleagues. China, he said, represented an enormous opportunity for American goods and services. He argued that the gigantic industrial and agricultural plant that the United States was building to defeat the Axis would need new overseas markets after the war was over, that America alone could not "keep the American farmer and manufacturer and laborer at full employment." China would need U.S. technical assistance, machinery, and equipment "in developing new industries there, railways, highways, and so forth. . . . Expanding trade with a friendly China will make a great many more jobs for Americans both here at home and in China than admitting 105 Chinese a year could possibly take away." Judd put it bluntly: "To prove our intention to treat China as an equal is not starry-eyed idealism or sentimental generosity. It is good hard business sense." Finally, he argued, as he would again and again while debating isolationists, particularly in his own party, the United States needed a friendly China not only to help win the war, but "even more to help establish and maintain a stable peace." America could not alienate the "nation which will inevitably be the strongest in Asia." The alleged risks of doing away with the Chinese Exclusion Acts, he insisted, were microscopic compared with the considerable benefits; repeal was both the right and the expedient thing to do.[12] Judd's appeal to reason, principle and self-interest prevailed in December. Congress repealed the Chinese Exclusion Acts.

There was another and broader benefit from the legislation. As it applied only to citizens of friendly and independent countries, the Chinese were the only people of yellow or brown races who were immediately eligible to apply for immigration. But as soon as Japan became "friendly" after the war, and the scores of Asian and African "colonies" (like India and Nigeria) became independent, then all would-be immigrants would be treated as equal. It was a long hard struggle, but finally in 1952 the Congress removed all discrimination from U.S. immigration laws, the first national civil rights legislation since the Civil War.

The same year that Judd entered Congress, Chiang Kai-shek reached his apogee in international politics at a summit meeting with President Roosevelt and Prime Minister Churchill in Cairo in late November. The joint communiqué between the United States, Great Britain, and China ending the conference elated the Generalissimo for it declared that Japan would have to give up all the territories "stolen from the Chinese, such as Manchuria, Formosa, and the Pescadores" and restore them to the Republic of China. Furthermore, Roosevelt pledged that the United States would support a major land, sea, and air offensive in Burma in the spring of 1944 to break the blockade of China and would arm and train ninety Nationalist divisions. The President also promised to back China against "foreign aggression" after the war by a joint U.S.–Chinese occupation of the Port Arthur-Darien naval complex in Manchuria, a pledge clearly calculated to prevent any Soviet effort to seize Manchuria. For his part, Chiang promised to "settle" the communist problem. Roosevelt, believing as he had since the beginning of the war that the key to victory in Asia and to peace after the war was a friendly and united China, was pleased to make the Cairo pledges to Chiang Kai-shek.

But less than a week later, meeting in Teheran with Stalin and Churchill, Roosevelt did not object when Stalin stated that the Soviet Union had certain political claims in the Far East; both knew that Port Darien and Manchuria were two areas of long-standing interest to the Soviets. Roosevelt's main reason for going along with Stalin was simple: he wanted—and he got—a reaffirmation of the Soviet pledge to enter the war against Japan after the defeat of Germany. As president of the United States and leader of the Allied powers, it was understood that FDR was required to balance the needs and wants of many different nations and leaders. What was not understandable to the Chinese and Americans like Judd concerned about the shape of the postwar world was Roosevelt's insistence that Chiang honor his promise to resolve Nationalist differences with the communists while not insisting that America honor its public promises to Chiang.[13] Roosevelt's reversal at Teheran was, in fact, the beginning of the end of unqualified U.S. support of Nationalist China and of the support of Chiang by his own people. It was a signal to officials in and out of the U.S. government to start campaigning against the Nationalists and for the communists as the wave of the future in China. Publicly, however, Nationalist China remained Roosevelt's trusted ally whose valiant fighting men were locked in mortal battle with the Japanese army.

A great propaganda battle was being waged, however, among Americans as to which political group within China the United States should back during and after the war. As John K. Fairbank wrote in *The Great Chinese Revolution*, "The foreign service officers and commanders like General Stilwell who were on the spot saw the admirable determination and strength of the Communist movement. The home-side China constituency generally retained their image of an earlier day when the Nanking Government had seemed the last word in Chinese progress."[14] Stilwell's dispatches kept harping on the inefficiency and disorder of the KMT's military bureaucracy. Clarence Gauss, the U.S. ambassador in Chungking, continually expressed strong skepticism about Chiang, once dismissing as "rot" the argument that he was energetically directing Chinese resistance to Japan. Laughlin Currie, President Roosevelt's administrative assistant, visited China in 1941 with already formed sympathetic views about the Chinese communists; it was later revealed that Currie was a communist. However, not all American visitors were anti-Nationalist. In October 1942, Wendell Willkie, the former Republican presidential candidate, came to Chungking and was won over by Madame Chiang's charm and intelligence and the Generalissimo's scholarly mien and Christian commitment.[15]

Chiang was not always so fortunate in his meetings with visiting Americans. He told Laughlin Currie that he would like the president to send him a political adviser in whom Roosevelt had personal confidence. Currie arranged for the selection of Owen Lattimore, a well-known Sinologist, as a "special political adviser to the Chinese Government," without the consent of Secretary of State Cordell Hull or Dr. Stanley Hornbeck, political adviser on the Far East to the secretary of state. Lattimore, whose appointment in June 1941 was hailed by both the Nationalists and the communists, initially had only words of praise for China's leader, telling San Francisco members of the Institute of Pacific Relations (IPR) that "Generalissimo Chiang Kai-shek is conspicuous for the fact that he is not only a great leader but a leader who has steadily grown in strength commensurate with that of the country itself."[16] In a very short while, Lattimore radically changed his opinion and led the IPR to adopt an anti-Chiang stance. Nine years later, after China had fallen to the communists, the seven senators on the Senate Internal Security Subcommittee of the Senate Judiciary Committee—four Democrats and three Republicans—concluded after two years of hearings:

> "On the basis of these facts and others, including (but without limitation) Lattimore's editing of *Pacific Affairs;* his recommendations on policy to the State Department . . . his falsifications about his close association with Laughlin Currie: his conference with the Soviet agent Rogoff, and the Soviet Embassy official Gokham; and his subservience to Soviet officials in Moscow in 1936, the Subcommittee can come to no other conclusion but that Lattimore was for some time, beginning in the middle 1930s, a conscious, articulate instrument of the Soviet conspiracy."[17] This conclusion was unanimously approved by all 15 members of the Judiciary Committee.

The most important American to visit China in the spring of 1944 was Vice President Henry Wallace, who was sent by a concerned Roosevelt to get "both sides in China to concentrate on fighting the Japanese instead of each other." Wallace was accompanied by John Carter Vincent, head of the Division of Chinese Affairs of the State Department, and Owen Lattimore, then an official of the Office of War Information.

In four long conversations with Chiang in June, the vice president emphasized the desire of the United States that Chiang make peace with the communists, whom he called "agrarian democrats." The Generalissimo responded that the Chinese communists were not "agrarian reformers"; they followed the orders of the Comintern, and "hoped for the collapse of the Kuomintang prior to the end of the war because such a collapse would enable them to seize power."[18] When Wallace insisted on visiting Yenan, the communist headquarters, Chiang at first resisted and then gave in, unwilling to offend the vice president of a government whose support he needed to continue the war against the Japanese and to prepare for the postwar struggle against the communists. On his return from Yenan, Wallace reported that Mao Tse-tung, Chou En-lai and the others were indeed "agrarian democrats." However, he did agree to endorse Chiang's request for the recall of General Stilwell, who had alienated Chiang with his caustic comments. In his official report to President Roosevelt, authored, it has been speculated, by Lattimore, Wallace referred to Chiang's "hatred of Chinese Communists and distrust of the U.S.S.R." and suggested his days were numbered:

"At this time there seems to be no alternative to support of Chiang. ... We can, however, while supporting Chiang, influence him in every possible way to adopt policies with the guidance of progressive Chinese which will inspire popular support and instill new vitality into China's war effort. At the same time, our attitude should be flexible enough to permit utilization of any other leader or group that might come forward offering greater promise." Then he sounded the death knell:

"Chiang, at best, is a short-term investment. It is not believed that he has the intelligence or political strength to run post-war China. The leaders of post-war China will be brought forward by evolution or revolution, and it now seems more likely the latter."[19]

The Wallace Report, which was read by President Roosevelt with "great interest," was not then released; in fact, its existence was denied when Judd demanded in August 1949 that it be made public. The report did not come to light until January 1950, after China had fallen to the communists, when Sen. Herbert R. O'Connor, a Maryland Democrat, released a copy sent him by Wallace. Nevertheless, the Wallace Report became official U.S. policy after Roosevelt's death in April 1945; then-U.S. Ambassador Patrick Hurley, for example, was instructed to use it as a guide. Even before then, it was the policy of a number of State Department officials in Washington and in China. The procommunist bias of the Wallace Mission and many U.S. diplomats in Chungking was so clear that a concerned U.S. Ambassador Clarence C. Gauss, no fan of Chiang, wrote Secretary of State Hull in August 1944 that the United States should give its "entire support and sympathy" to the Nationalist government and warned that asking it to "meet Communist demands is equivalent to asking China's unconditional surrender to a party known to be under a foreign power's influence [the Soviet Union]."[20] Tragically, his counsel would be ignored.

China needed all the support it could get in 1944 for the Japanese, after five years of general inactivity, resumed their offensive. The war was going badly for Japan in the Pacific, and the Japanese high command was deeply worried about the landing of U.S. troops on the China mainland. It was thought critical to gain control of the entire railway from Peking to Canton, slicing China in half and isolating Chungking. To this end, the Japanese transferred ten divisions from Manchuria to Hunan, a Chinese communist stronghold, in March 1944; despite this serious threat to the nation's very survival, the communists did not challenge the Japanese. Instead, Mao and his associates launched a political offensive against the Nationalists, calling for a coalition government with equal status for the Communist party. Undeterred, the Japanese put nearly two million men in the field against Chiang's troops, many of them ill fed and ill equipped. A string of Japanese victories continued throughout the year, and by late November they controlled Kiangsi province and denied the Chinese air force under General Chennault the use of most of its bases. A desperate Chiang gathered his best troops from all over China, some from as far away as the Yellow River two thousand miles to the north, and made a last-ditch stand at Kweichow, only two hundred air miles from Chungking. There in December 1944, the Nationalist forces stopped the Japanese and drove them back into Kwangsi province: "it was the turning-point of the long war."[21] The crucial Nationalist victory at Kweichow and the communist reluctance to even harass the invader in Hunan proved which side in China consistently resisted the Japanese and helped make it possible for the United States to win the war in the Pacific, an essential point that Judd emphasized in congressional debates on U.S. aid to China after the war.

Chiang was also fighting on another front. His long disagreement with General Stilwell came to a climax in the summer of 1944. Stilwell had been suggesting for some time to his boss and longtime mentor, General George Marshall, that the best way to bring China fully into the war was for Stilwell to replace Chiang as Supreme Commander of all

Chinese and American forces in China. Marshall recommended the change to Roosevelt, who cabled Chiang in July 1944 that Stilwell was the "one individual with the power to co-ordinate all of the Allied military resources in China, including the Communist forces." The directive was a direct insult to Chiang, who accepted it calmly but asked for an intermediary with "full power" to settle any differences between him and Stilwell. Roosevelt quickly appointed Brigadier General Patrick Hurley, former secretary of war under President Hoover; but by the time Hurley arrived in Chungking in September, it was too late for him to repair the breach between Chiang and Stilwell, a brilliant field commander who could not control his tongue or his temper off the battlefield.

Stilwell's diaries are filled with unrestrained personal invective about anyone who disagreed with him about what he conceived to be the best way to fight the war in Asia. Chiang Kai-shek was invariably referred to as "Peanut" and a "little bastard." Stilwell made his feelings clear to everyone, including his commander-in-chief, who was to grow very weary of the bitter Chiang-Stilwell infighting. In May 1943, both Stilwell and Chennault were in Washington to discuss future operations in China and were asked by President Roosevelt for their opinion of Chiang. "He's a vacillating tricky undependable old scoundrel who never keeps his word," Stilwell replied. Chennault, who had worked successfully with Chiang for nearly five years, responded: "Sir, I think the Generalissimo is one of the two or three greatest military and political leaders in the world today. He has never broken a commitment or promise made to me."[22] Roosevelt seemed more inclined to accept Chennault's evaluation.

By the fall of 1944, shortly before he was finally replaced, Stilwell was so frustrated that he wrote in his diary: "What they ought to do is shoot the G-mo [Chiang Kai-shek] and the rest of the gang." He also scorned the British for their emphasis on the European front and for not going all out to retake Burma: "The limies are not interested in the war in the Pacific." He even referred to Roosevelt as "Rubberlegs," after the president supported the British demand for a European invasion first.[23] Like General George S. Patton, Stilwell belonged in the field, not in a conference room. He could not understand, as Roosevelt did, all that confronted Chiang as he tried to lead the most populous country in the world in the middle of a war. Citing a message from Stilwell about the need to get tougher with Chiang, the President explained to General Marshall that this was "just the wrong way." The Generalissimo was chief of state as well as Commander-in-Chief, said Roosevelt, and "one cannot speak sternly to a man like that or exact commitments from him as we might do from the Sultan of Morocco." Chiang had become "undisputed leader of 400,000,000 people ... and had to create in a very short time throughout China what it took us a couple of centuries to attain."[24]

By late 1943, Stilwell depended for his political analysis almost exclusively on foreign service officers like John Paton Davies, John Stewart Service, Raymond Paul Ludden, and John K. Emmerson, who were convinced that the communists represented China's future. Chennault described how Stilwell, in the spring of 1944, sent a group to the Chinese communist headquarters. The American mission in Yenan was hardly established, he said, before Stilwell's staff began "to proclaim loudly the superiority of the Communist regime over the Chungking government." Contents of classified reports from the Yenan mission were freely discussed over Chungking dinner tables by Stilwell's staff. No secret was made of their admiration for the communists, who, they said, were really only "agrarian reformers" and more like "New Dealers than Communists."[25]

Finally, in September 1944, after months of mounting frustration and fury at Chiang's conduct of the war, Stilwell received what he thought was the coup de grace for Chiang, a letter from Roosevelt to Chiang instructing him to place Stilwell "in unrestricted command of all ... forces," along with a not very veiled threat that the United States would withdraw support if Chiang refused. Stilwell resolved to deliver the message in person, although General Hurley cautioned him not to. To Stilwell's great disappointment, Chiang showed little emotion although, as he later noted, "The harpoon hit the little bugger right in the solar plexus and went right through him."

It was a pyrrhic victory for Stilwell, for in his response to Roosevelt Chiang said that while he was willing to place an American in command of all Chinese armies and the air force and to make such changes in staff and personnel as would be necessary to bring harmony with the American field commander, he would not "confer this heavy responsibility upon General Stilwell, and will have to ask for his resignation as Chief of Staff of the China theater and his relief from duty in this area."[26] Stilwell protested, General Marshall and Secretary of State Stimson defended him, and Roosevelt suggested that Stilwell remain in command but only as head of forces in Burma. Chiang was adamant, arguing that "so long as I am Head of State and Supreme Commander in

China, it seems to me that there can be no question as to my right to request the recall of an officer in whom I can no longer repose confidence. . . . I am wholly confident that if the President replaces General Stilwell with a qualified American officer, we can work to reverse the present trend and achieve a vital contribution to victory in China."[27]

In a zero-sum game with Stilwell, Chiang knew he would win. Roosevelt "was not now prepared to impose an American commander against the express wishes of a chief of state. That would be impossible to reconcile with his own part in rescinding the unequal treaties and restoring China's sovereignty," wrote Barbara Tuchman.[28] Stilwell learned on October 19 that he would be recalled and left Chungking within forty-eight hours, but not before ordering John Service to return to Washington to argue the case for opening relations with the Chinese communists. Stubborn to the last, he refused to accept from the Generalissimo the Special Grand Cordon of the Blue Sky and White Sun, the highest Chinese decoration given to a foreigner. On October 21, Stilwell climbed aboard a DC-3 and left China forever. Tuchman said that only General Hurley and T.V. Soong were at the airfield, but another American was there to see him off: Congressman Walter H. Judd. Asked by the Dewey campaign to appraise the situation in China, he had sought approval of his visit from the State Department, only to be told that it could not at this time "encourage traveling by Americans in the China-Burma theater." He tartly reminded State that he was not a tourist but a member of Congress who wanted to investigate firsthand "the rumors coming out of China," and before the November election. Judd was confident that Stilwell would not refuse him permission to enter his theater ("he knows me personally") and that Roosevelt would not object for fear of making it look as though the administration were trying to cover up something.[29] By coincidence he arrived in the Chinese capital just before Stilwell's departure.

They had been friends since the middle 1930s when Stilwell stayed with the medical missionary in Fenchow to get information about the communists in Shensi and Kansu from the camel caravans coming in from those areas. Judd admired Stilwell as a fighter who "wanted to be out with the troops" but felt "he was no good as a [theater] commander." On his final night in Chungking, Stilwell hosted a dinner for his old friend, but was so exhausted that he said very little and fell asleep at the table. The next morning, Judd went down to the island in the Yangtze River that was used as an airfield in the dry fall season. The two men shook hands, and the congressman wished the departing general "good luck." Stilwell started up the few steps into the airplane and then stopped to say, bitterly, "God help my successor." "Those were his last words to me," Judd recalled, "and yet his successor, General Wedemeyer, came in and succeeded brilliantly."[30]

Within a few days, Ambassador Gauss, weary and worn out after more than thirty years of service in China, also departed, to be succeeded by Patrick Hurley. The new team of Hurley and Wedemeyer was anticommunist, pro-Nationalist and hoped to make the U.S. policy of reconciliation between the two sides in China succeed. But they were to discover, as George Marshall did on his year-long mission in 1946, that unity between two implacable foes like Chiang and Mao was impossible. The two Chinese rivals had been waging war since 1927 and were determined to continue until one side or the other won.

Stilwell was a longtime favorite of the American press, and his recall precipitated a bitter attack on the Nationalist government. The *New York Times* declared in a front-page story that Stilwell's departure represented the "political triumph of a moribund anti-democratic regime" and committed the United States to support of a government which had become "increasingly unpopular and distrusted in China." The *Times* article scorned the decision to appoint another American chief of staff to the Generalissimo because it "has the effect of making us acquiesce in an unenlightened cold-hearted autocratic political regime ... unrepresentative of the Chinese people who are good allies." As the anti-Chiang propaganda mounted higher and higher, Judd stated publicly, as President Roosevelt did privately, that "no self-respecting head of state" could have accepted what Stilwell demanded; he argued that the United States "had to back down from an impossible position in which we should never have put ourselves."[31] Nevertheless, opponents of Chiang Kai-shek in and out of the U.S. government made extensive use of the Stilwell episode in their campaign to shift American support from the Nationalists to the communists.

Of the foreign service officers, journalists, and academics who analyzed the two competing factions in China in the decade between the Long March and the coming to power of the communists, it can be said that never before were so many experts so cleareyed about the flaws and failures of one and so nearsighted about the virtues and successes of the other. Chiang and the Nationalists were inept, incompetent, inefficient, undemocratic, corrupt, and reactionary. Mao and the communists were honest, principled, selfless, progressive, and disciplined. The Nationalists were fascists, the communists were agrarian reformers. Chiang was a megalomaniac, Mao was a poet. Chiang rarely fought the Japanese, Mao harassed them night and day. Edgar Snow, Agnes Smedley, Anna Louise Strong, Theodore White, Brooks Atkinson, and other journalists joined with the four "Johns" of the State Department—John Stewart Service, John Carter Vincent, John Paton Davies, and John Emmerson—to create a black-and-white portrait of China in which the Nationalists were devils and the communists were angels. The United States, for these men, had no sensible choice but to help the communists bring about a new day in China. What is the truth about the Nationalists? It will never be known in its entirety until the government of the Republic of China allows scholars to examine the archives kept behind locked doors in Taiwan. But this much can be said with certainty: while Chiang Kai-shek made mistakes as commander-in-chief of the war in China, sometimes at the cost of many lives, surrounded himself with aides and officials who were often inefficient and corrupt, and resisted any effective united front with the communists against the Japanese, he nevertheless kept China in the war for eight years when common sense dictated surrender or at least a truce with Japan. Like Churchill in 1940 when England confronted the Nazi juggernaut all alone, Chiang resolved never to give in to the Japanese. Whatever his deficiencies, and they were considerable, Chiang earned the lasting gratitude of the United States for his steadfast resistance to the powerful war machine of Japan. As Judd summed it up:

> We Americans ought never to forget this one fact, which outweighs every other consideration—namely that when our fleet lay at the bottom of the sea and Japan had carried out in six months the single greatest conquest in the history of warfare, only one thing prevented her from completing and organizing her new empire, and turning all her efforts against us. It was this . . . old, so-called backward, corrupt, undemocratic, inefficient China that refused to yield. Chiang could have had peace on very generous terms and saved his people most of the suffering and the economic dislocations [caused by] . . . the war. Instead he chose to buy for us the precious months and years in which we could rebuild our fleet and capture the islands, one by one, and build the atomic bomb and ultimately bring our superior air power and the bombs to bear upon Japan and give her the final blow. That is a fact that takes precedence over every other in the picture.[32]

This was not how several key American diplomats in Chungking and Yenan, particularly Davies, Vincent, and Service, saw the situation in

China. Brian Crozier, a shrewd observer with impeccable anticommunist credentials, wrote: "A reading of their dispatches ... does not provide proof that they were, in any conscious sense, agents of international communism. It is undeniable, however, that their reporting from China strongly and in the end decisively influenced the United States Government away from Chiang's regime (which it was official American policy to support) and towards Mao Tse-tung's Communist Party."[33]

In their eagerness to influence U.S. policy, the memoranda of foreign service officers in China between 1943 and 1945 consistently used the most laudatory language about the Chinese communists. Service wrote that the communist "revolution has been moderate and democratic," and that the communists have "mass support" because their "governments and armies are genuinely of the people." Davies declared that "the Communists are in China to stay. And China's destiny is not Chiang's but theirs." Of the Nationalists, Service said flatly that their "governmental and military structure is being permeated and demoralized from top to bottom by corruption, unprecedented in scale and openness." Davies counseled that the United States "must limit our involvement with the Kuomintang and must commence some cooperation with the Communists, the force destined to control China." He urged the one thing which he knew Chiang would not accept: "A coalition Chinese Government in which the Communists find a satisfactory place is the solution of this impasse most desirable to us."[34]

John Carter Vincent proposed as early as July 1942 that the United States should promote a liberal postwar regime in China, stating that "Communists would probably cooperate with it." Among his recommendations were the use of American influence in the hope of establishing real "democracy" in China; recognition of the Chinese Communist Army as a participant in the war against Japan, and apportionment to the communists of a share of American supplies sent to China. Service offered a program in mid-1944 that included: stop building up Chiang; invite Madam Sun Yat-sen, a strong supporter of Mao, to the White House; "give publicity on the blockade that Chiang was using to contain the Reds"; and "publicize statements by the United States officials ... such as the Sumner Welles memorandum to [American communist leader] Earl Browder, which was disapproved by the Nationalists."[35] In his *Report No. 40*, dated October 10, 1944, Service went so far as to suggest to General Stilwell that the United States switch its support from Chiang to Mao. A public announcement "that the President's representative had made a visit to the Communist capital at Yenan," wrote Service, "would have significance that no Chinese would miss—least of all the Generalissimo." In late 1945, after angrily resigning his post in China, Hurley testified before the Senate Foreign Relations Committee that Service and "the professional Foreign Service men" in China had sabotaged his efforts as ambassador to China; he singled out *Report No. 40* as proof for his charge.[36]

Report No. 40 was written from Yenan and by the time it arrived in Chungking, Stilwell was about to be replaced by Lt. Gen. Albert C. Wedemeyer. When asked by a Congressional committee in 1951 to discuss the report, Wedemeyer responded:

> These reports were not consonant with my interpretation of my directive or of American policy.... If I had followed the advice I would not have been carrying out my orders.... [The Communists] never launched a concerted attack in coordination with those attacks that I was putting on ... their military operations did not make the contributions so often one reads in the press or hears on the radio.... If we threw over the Kuomintang, it meant we were going to assume support and cooperate with the Communists.... The Communists, in my judgment—and I have tried to be objective, I have tried to find good in Marxist theories—the Communists will cooperate when the advantage accrues to them. At no time will a Communist operate otherwise.... [But] their avowed intention is to destroy capitalism, expressed to me personally.[37]

It is difficult to pinpoint the first public appearance of the beguiling phrase "agrarian reformers," which was used so frequently by Americans to describe the Chinese communists after they visited Yenan, but Raymond P. Ludden of the State Department was among its earliest advocates, commenting after a seven-month stay in China: "The so-called Communists are agrarian reformers of a mild democratic stripe more than anything else."[38] Apparently, it never occurred to all these seasoned diplomats and hard-bitten journalists that the communists might have been putting on an act calculated to win American support in their protracted conflict with the Nationalists. Rev. Raymond J. de Jaegher, a Catholic missionary in China, personally witnessed how the communists prepared their version of a Potemkin village for westerners. One day he was amazed to find the "screaming slogans" against America and Great Britain gone from the walls of his city and "complimentary posters" in English placed everywhere. On inquiring, he learned that an American reporter had been invited by the communists to inspect their anti-Japanese activities. "When he was gone the old signs came up again."[39]

Having studied communism firsthand in the Soviet Union in 1923 and having battled the Chinese communists since 1927, Chiang had no illusions about the true objectives of Mao. He protested that the American government should stop trying to force him into agreement with the communists, who were not interested in democracy but in domination. His warnings were dismissed by Service, Vincent, Davies, and the others as predictable anticommunist rhetoric. Years later, columnist Joseph Alsop, who served in China at the time, summed up the cumulative impact of these diplomats as follows: "Throughout the fateful years in China, the American representatives there actively favored the Chinese Communists. They also contributed to the weakness, both political and military, of the National Government. And in the end they came close to offering China up to the Communists, like a trussed bird on a platter, over four years before the eventual Communist triumph."[40]

Like Chiang, Judd was fully aware of the long-range intentions of the Chinese communists: to "adopt the Russian system internally and base [Chinese] foreign policy on closer relations, not with the democracies . . . but with Russia." One of the greatest decisions of all history, he told a Philadelphia audience in March 1944, "is being made in these critical years—whether China is going to stay united with the western democracies, or is to be driven . . . to tie herself to . . . Russia and Russian ideas."[41] Nineteen forty-four was also an election year, and while Judd believed he had earned the support of the voters of the Fifth Congressional District for another term in Congress, he spent September and October campaigning in Minneapolis. His opponent, Edgar T. Buckley of the Democratic party, talked a lot about who was and was not a liberal, a popular label in the city and state. Judd had a ready answer and outlined his personal philosophy, which changed very little during his twenty years in Congress.

If a "liberal," he said, was someone who "reads only the title and lofty purposes proclaimed in a bill," then he was not a liberal because he insisted "on reading the whole bill so that I can pass independent judgment on what it actually contains." If a liberal was someone who was "liberal" with the public's money, voting for every cause that was labeled a "good cause," then he was not a liberal, because he believed in "protecting religiously the solvency of the United States Treasury." If being liberal meant making progress toward better health, wealth, and progress by turning over "more and more of our lives and activities" to the government, then he was not a liberal.

But if a liberal, he said, was one who believed in and worked toward a society "based on equality of opportunity and the possibility of free development, welfare and justice" for individuals and not "the masses," then he qualified as a liberal. Echoing Jefferson, he said that if a liberal was one who believed profoundly that "those are best governed who are least governed," then he qualified as a liberal. If a liberal meant someone who held to certain eternal truths but who advocated "change in their application when change was necessary," and when change would "result in something better," then he qualified as a liberal. But far better than labels, he said, were principles like the rights of an individual rather than a race or class, and the need for nations, races, classes, and economic groups to work together for the good of all.[42]

As a measure of his rapidly rising status in the Republican party, Judd was selected to deliver a nationwide radio address over CBS on behalf of presidential nominee Thomas E. Dewey, a rare honor for a freshman congressman. He may have surprised Dewey as well as Roosevelt by choosing to criticize the president for, of all things, his universally praised Four Freedoms. While readily conceding that freedom of religion and freedom of speech were "true freedoms . . . basic and indispensable," Judd asserted that freedom from want and freedom from fear were quite different. "They are proper objectives, they are good, they are desirable; but they are not necessarily freedoms."

Using a striking analogy, Judd suggested that a bird flying through the air was free, but "he hasn't freedom from want; he has to dig his own bugs from the bark or snow. He hasn't freedom from fear for the hawk may get him or the hunter may shoot him." However, the bird could find economic and political security in a cage in someone's house. There "he would have freedom from want and freedom from fear—but he would have lost his freedom." What free men needed and wanted, Judd argued, was the opportunity to work, to improve their own condition, with the government providing a floor "below which no citizen will be allowed to fall in any of the emergencies or misfortunes of life." Such a floor, he said, was "a definite responsibility of government," but the government should not provide "a bed on which its citizens may rest, without need or incentive to plan providently and with self-reliance for their own future."[43]

On election day, Roosevelt defeated Dewey because a majority of the American people, despite their concern about a fourth term and the many rumors about the president's health, did not want to change chief executives in the middle of a world war. Judd handily won re-election, defeating Buckley by 81,798 to 62,761 votes.

The year 1945 brought victory to the United States and the other Allied powers in Europe and the Pacific, but it also brought Yalta, a diplomatic disaster from which the Nationalist government of China would not recover. Neither U.S. Ambassador Hurley nor President Chiang nor Secretary of State James F. Byrnes was consulted about the Far East provisions of the Yalta agreement signed in February by an exhausted Roosevelt, a studiously neutral Churchill, and a triumphant Stalin. Under secret clauses disclosed a year later, Stalin agreed to enter the war against Japan "two or three months after Germany has surrendered and the war in Europe has terminated." As compensation, the Soviet Union was to receive Japan's Kurile Islands, hegemony over Outer Mongolia, South Sakhalin, and neighboring islands, and control over port and rail facilities in Manchuria. There was a minor caveat: the provisions regarding Outer Mongolia and Manchuria would require Chiang's "concurrence," which Roosevelt promised he would obtain.

In a brilliant maneuver which gave him effective control over the future of China, Stalin declared his "readiness to conclude with the National Government of China a pact of friendship and alliance . . . to render assistance to China with its armed forces for the purpose of liberating China from the Japanese yoke." Without firing one shot, the Soviet dictator achieved at the Yalta summit Russia's historic objectives—"territorial aggrandisement in the Far East, the crippling of Japan, and the debilitation of China." At Yalta, even more than at Teheran, Roosevelt reversed the solemn pledges he gave Chiang at the Cairo summit. It is not surprising that in a few short years, Republicans would be charging Democrats with betrayal at Yalta. The final humiliation came when Stalin asked Roosevelt to delay informing Chiang of what they had done for fear the details might be leaked to Tokyo by alleged pro-Japanese elements in the Nationalist government. The president agreed, going so far in his March 2 report to Congress about Yalta as to say: "Quite naturally, this conference concerned itself only with the European problems of Europe, and not with the Pacific war."[44] In today's parlance, this would be called a coverup.

CHAPTER NINE

---◆---

Struggle for Power

WHILE WHITE MEN in Yalta discussed how best to divide up Asia, a determined Chiang Kai-shek focused his attention on the postwar struggle in China. He could not accede to the communist demands for a coalition government, regardless of American pressure, because he knew it would lead to defeat as coalitions with communists always did. He had to gain time to be in a winning position when the war actually ended. The next several months were filled with political jockeying by Chiang and Mao. The Nationalist leader announced that a new National Assembly would meet in November, as he had promised it would as soon as the Japanese invaders were gone, to begin the process of constitutional government. The communists denounced the program, but declared themselves ready to reopen negotiations with the Nationalists and even to take part in the political process. After all, said Mao, the Chinese Communist party controlled "liberated areas" with a population of more than ninety-five million people, an assertion that has been accepted by many writers without very close examination. The best estimate, according to the analysts Tang Tsou, Chalmers Johnson, and Crozier, is closer to thirty-five million. Mao also claimed that his Red Army totalled 910,000 men, plus a militia of 2.2 million. If the communists had had this many men and used them as aggressively as they often claimed, they could have tied down the Japanese army of over one million men all by themselves. But the Chinese communists never actively engaged in sustained aggressive actions against Japan's occupation forces after being defeated in two efforts right after Japan started the war in 1937. After their "Hundred Regiments' Offensive" in 1940, as Johnson says, the communists stressed "economic guerrilla warfare" over military activities. Like Chiang, the Chinese communists were expanding and preserving their forces for the postwar struggle for power in China.[1] Increasingly alarmed by the prospect of a bloody civil war, American policy makers pushed "coalition government," a political extension of the united front, as the solution in China. But even as the united front was never realized, so coalition government was doomed to fail: neither the Nationalists nor the communists believed it was possible to share power.

On the floor of the House of Representatives, Judd endeavored to explain what was happening in China to his colleagues and the American people. In March 1945, he delivered an extraordinary speech. It was a political and historical tour de force which if given in the 1980s, characterized by the active participation of the Congress in foreign policy and the dominant role of the news media in publicizing contrasting points of view, would have had an immediate and significant impact on U.S.-China relations. But this was 1945, when foreign policy was still made the old-fashioned way—by a small group of like-minded men in the White House, the State Department and the Senate (the House of Representatives being a very junior partner in foreign policy decision making) who did not brook advice or interference from the outside and certainly not from a second-term congressman from Minnesota, however eloquent and knowledgeable. Judd made the sensible point that Americans ought to judge China, not in relation to conditions in America today, but to conditions as they were in China twenty and two hundred years earlier. China was still in the midst of a great revolution when she was "plunged into this war [against Japan] against her wishes." And revolutions, he pointed out, are almost always long affairs. It took the French 80 years to get through their revolution; it took the United States "90 years, including a great Civil War, before we got straightened out." How could we expect China, in the middle of revolution and war, to be a nation of stability and prosperity?

China was now suffering acutely, he reported, from what Churchill called "the diseases of defeat." She lost "80 percent of her modern industry" in the first three months of the war because it was located on the coast where Japan first struck. She needed help and the United States had given her help. But it was not true that China had received untold quantities of arms and supplies; less than 2 percent of American aid went to East Asia until late 1944 or early 1945, and of that amount only 10 percent went to China. In short, China received "only two-tenths of one percent of all the supplies that we sent abroad to our allies."

He admitted candidly that there was moral deterioration, including "graft, corruption, profiteering, a black market." But, he added, it was not as bad as he expected it to be, and it was important to remember that China had always had the "squeeze" system, by which any Chinese who handles a transaction takes 10 percent. "When the Chinese do it, it is 'graft'; when we do it, it is a 'commission.' But it is the same thing." He suggested that America ought to be slow to criticize "people who are starving and drain some gasoline out of a bomber or a jeep when no one is looking" and sell it in the black market "to keep their families alive." If America, said Judd, were to go through half of what China had gone through, for half as long, and "come through in no worse condition internally, I should be astonished and proud."

Another product of the war was political deterioration. What was surprising, Judd said, was not the opposition to Chiang but that after more than seven years, he still had the "confidence of an overwhelming majority of the Chinese people." The United States ought to be thankful that Chiang and China were still able to divert so much of Japan's strength, instead of complaining because Chiang "has not been able in the midst of all his disasters to carry out a lot of internal reforms, desirable and important as they are." In the wake of political deterioration had come governmental deterioration. Yet, argued Judd, China had been judged against an unreasonably high standard. England had not held an election for almost ten years because of the war, and yet Chiang had been reviled for not scheduling elections in a country which in its four thousand years of history "has never before held an election," half of which was occupied by an enemy and "80 percent of whose people cannot read and write."

Next, Judd took up the question of the Chinese communists and to whom they paid allegiance. "I am increasingly convinced [they] are first Communist and second Chinese. . . . this is a reluctant reversal of the opinion I held some years ago. I, too, was taken in for a time by the talk of their being just agrarian reformers, just Chinese patriots struggling only for the freedom of China and for democracy. I am convinced now the primary allegiance of the Chinese Communists is to Russia. . . . [Therefore] how can the Chinese government be asked to furnish arms

111

to a rebel government whose primary allegiance it has every reason to believe is to a foreign power?"

Carefully and logically, he demolished the argument that Chiang had to cooperate with the communists to create a coalition government. The communists, he said, were not a political party, like the Republicans or the Democrats; they were an "armed rebellion" with their own army and government. He used the example of the American Civil War. "When the slavery faction pulled away . . . and set up a separate government with a separate flag and a separate currency and separate taxes and a separate army under a separate command, did we unify them? . . . No. We fought them for four years in one of the bloodiest wars of all history. We, who fought for four years against our brothers to prevent a splitting of our country, are now in the intolerable position of constantly condemning Chiang Kai-shek because he will not consent to a splitting of his country—and under the name of 'unity.' "

As for the future of China, he said, the two main groups vying for power were the communists, who argued that "in cooperation with Russia, we Chinese can build in Central Asia the greatest industrial bloc in the world, in the midst of the greatest land and population bloc on the earth"; and the Nationalists, who were trying "their best under enormous difficulties to make China a sister republic in Asia." The United States, he asserted, should continue to help the Nationalist government of Chiang Kai-shek because of the key role it played during the war by resisting the Japanese and because of the key role it would play in Asia after the war. "The decision that is being hammered out in Asia these critical days is not one for four years, but one for 40 years or even 400 years. Are the Chinese, the most numerous and incomparably the strongest of the colored peoples, to stay on the side of the democracies, or are they to be driven in despair to the other side? The answer to that is still in our own hands. We must understand what we are up against . . . and stay at it until we get, not just defeat of Japan, but a victory which really frees China and assures all Asia of ultimate freedom as its peoples work and struggle and grow to full nationhood and independence."[2]

It was a magnificent speech, but policy makers in Washington paid it little heed; they were determined to impose coalition government on Chiang.

Events in China moved swiftly and inexorably. In June 1945, Ambassador Hurley formally reported to Chiang the Yalta agreements, including the information that the United States would support the Russians at China's expense. Chiang sent T.V. Soong to Moscow to negotiate with the Soviets, who predictably were not in any mood to give up what they had gained at Yalta. In July, President Truman, inclined to be less conciliatory toward the Soviets than Roosevelt, went to Potsdam for a summit meeting with Stalin. Truman tried to assure China some authority in Manchuria, and asked the Soviet leader to agree that Port Dairen (Port Arthur) should be a "free port." In August, after the United States dropped atomic bombs on Hiroshima and Nagasaki and the Soviet Union declared war on Japan, Soong again traveled to Moscow to conclude a treaty with the Soviet Union. China was in an extremely weak bargaining position, and the resulting treaty reflected her weakness. The Chinese agreed to allow the Soviet Union to use Port Arthur as a naval base and declare Dairen a free port; they allowed the status of Outer Mongolia to be determined by a plebiscite (which the Soviets would administer), and agreed to joint Soviet-Chinese ownership of the Chinese railway in Manchuria. For their part, the Soviets generously pledged to recognize the Nationalist government as the legitimate government of China and not to interfere in its internal affairs. The stage was set for the climactic act of the Nationalist-communist war.

As soon as Japan surrendered in August 1945, the Chinese communists immediately moved across North China, demanding that the Japanese surrender to them. The Nationalists responded by ordering the communists not to advance but to wait for orders, a directive they refused to follow. Also General Marshall pressured Chiang not to block the communists. In Manchuria, the communists received massive amounts of Japanese arms that had been turned over to the Soviet armies. At this time, the Nationalist armies were in South and West China, far from the ports and industrial centers held by the Japanese. In contrast, the communist forces were in the lower Yangtze Valley and near the major centers of North China. The weaker position of the Nationalists was obvious, and the United States, under the direction of General Wedemeyer, moved 53,000 Marines into North China to protect Peking and Tientsin and also transported by rail several Nationalist armies to interdict the communist march to Manchuria and other parts of North China. At the same time, Chiang asked the Soviets, who still occupied Manchuria, to delay their withdrawal. Open skirmishes began to occur between Nationalist and communist forces in Manchuria; the very thing that the U.S. government feared, a civil war in China after the end of World War II, was happening. Ambassador Hurley was ordered by President Truman and Secretary of State Byrnes to continue mediating between the two sides. In August, Chiang and Mao, under Hurley's sponsorship, met in Chungking and two months later agreed upon a set of principles "that would gladden any liberal in the world." The KMT and the Chinese Communist party declared they would participate in a representative assembly, join their armies and guarantee civil liberties for all. The reason for this charade was that "neither side could take a stand against the ideal of peace and cooperation."[3]

For most of 1945, it was official U.S. policy to support the Nationalist government of China, as shown by the above military assistance. In late November, however, Hurley suddenly resigned as ambassador to China, charging that career men in the State Department were sabotaging American policy towards China and siding with the Chinese communists.

Hurley was right about what his staff was doing to undermine the Nationalists and build up the communists in China, but wrong about the relationship between Mao and the Soviets. He accepted Soviet Foreign Minister Molotov's assurances, given him in late 1944 when he passed through the Soviet capital on his way to take up his post in Chungking, that the Chinese communists were not necessarily wedded to communism and would abandon their leftist inclinations when economic conditions improved. As General Wedemeyer put it:

> Whereas many Americans were deluded by clever propaganda into believing that the Chinese Communists were not real Communists but agrarian reformers, Pat Hurley would seem to have fallen for a contrary but equally pernicious myth. To him it seemed that Stalin, Molotov and Co. could be relied upon, or their words believed, and that the villains of the piece were the Chinese Communists and the State Department in the person of the political advisers on my staff whom I had inherited from Stilwell.[4]

In short, during this critical period, American policy makers did not understand the true forces struggling for power in China. Hurley kept insisting that Moscow did not control the Chinese communists. Career diplomats like Davies and Vincent counseled the United States government to transfer backing from Chiang to Mao to be on the winning side. Hurley, consistent with official U.S. policy, kept on supporting Chiang Kai-shek but tried to bring off a reconciliation between the two warring factions. Such an effort was doomed to failure, but Hurley's successor, Gen. George C. Marshall, was told to pursue the same policy.

As Judd stressed, one sentence in President Truman's statement explaining the purposes of Marshall's mission made it impossible for the general to succeed: "As China moves toward peace and unity along the lines described above," announced Truman, "the United States would be prepared to assist the national government in every reasonable way to rehabilitate the country." In other words, Truman was telling the communists that if there were no peace and unity there would be no American aid to the Nationalists and the communists would prevail. If the president had said, "As China moves toward better government, wider civil rights, greater democracy, more efficiency, and less corruption the United States would be prepared to assist," that, argued Judd, would have been a legitimate set of conditions and within the power of the Chinese government to fulfill. "The only way to get unity with the communists anywhere," said Judd, "is to surrender to them."[5]

Nevertheless, a determined Marshall labored from December 1945 through January 1947 to produce an agreement, during which time the communists expanded the territory under their control from sixty to three hundred counties, out of some two thousand in China. They stalled and delayed and even personally attacked Marshall, who at last conceded defeat, blaming it in large measure on the communists who, he said, displayed "an unwillingness to make a fair compromise. It has been impossible even to get them to sit down at a conference table."[6]

Marshall began his mission impressively, persuading Chiang and Mao to sign a cease-fire agreement on January 10, 1946. But even while talks were being held, the communists carried out operations in Hopei, Shansi, Suiyuan, North Kiangsu, and Shantung provinces, tripling the area under their control. Another agreement was signed on February 15, calling for the demobilization of all armies: over the next eighteen months, the Nationalist forces were to be reduced to fifty divisions and the communists to ten divisions. However, the communists rejected a proposal by Chiang that the reductions should be supervised by a tripartite commission including Americans. Discussions were held between both sides for a national assembly and a permanent democratic constitution. Marshall was persuaded by the harmony of the meetings to return to Washington in March 1946 to inform the president that all his objectives had been met, only slightly perturbed by a diplomatic memorandum about the increasingly hostile attitude of the communists in Manchuria. The Soviets picked the time of Marshall's departure for home to begin withdrawing from southern Manchuria; the communists swiftly moved to fill the vacuum. An alarmed Chiang tried to counter by sending in Nationalist troops, but the communists seized several key areas which enabled them to block all land movements by their adversary into Manchuria. On April 15, Chou En-lai broke the truce, declaring a state of "all-out hostilities" in Manchuria. An embarrassed Marshall returned to China a few days later to find his agreements broken and his policy in tatters. As one analyst wrote, "In military terms, the catastrophic defeats of the Nationalist armies in the later stages of the civil war were made inevitable by the events of May and June 1946 in Manchuria."[7]

Despite their initial success, it was clear that the communists could not hold off the superior Nationalist forces. At this critical point, Stalin invited Chiang to Moscow to discuss future Soviet-Chinese relations. General Marshall and President Truman urged Chiang to accept the Soviet dictator's invitation, not wanting Manchuria to become part of the Soviet economy; they also pressured him to move ahead with the formation of a coalition government with the communists. But Chiang understood that agreements with Stalin were always one-sided and coalition with the communists would mean the end of Sun Yat-sen's dream for a Republic of China. He declined Stalin's invitation, asserting his intention to "go it alone, if necessary, in resisting Soviet aggression" and his determination not to accept the neutralization of China through "the establishment of a coalition government."[8] It was a courageous, some said foolhardy, decision, but Chiang was unyielding in his determination not to surrender to communists of either the Soviet or Chinese variety.

Stalin responded by handing over to the Chinese communists in Manchuria what they needed most, massive amounts of arms and ammunition. All this equipment, sufficient for nearly 600,000 Japanese and 75,000 Manchuko soldiers, gave Mao a major military advantage over the Nationalists in Manchuria. The communists were also significantly assisted by several U.S. decisions. These included the public statement by Undersecretary of State Dean Acheson in June 1946 that the United States was "impartial" between the Central Government and the communists and that U.S. economic assistance was intended for a government "full and fairly representative of all important Chinese political elements, including the Chinese Communists";[9] and General Marshall's request for a Nationalist-communist truce the same month. Chiang complied, albeit reluctantly, because he still needed U.S. assistance and dared not reject a request of Truman's personal representative. But the Generalissimo paid a heavy price for his concession, halting his offensive when it was close to destroying a large number of Chinese communist troops in Manchuria. The truce allowed the communists to reorganize and receive more Soviet assistance. An American correspondent reported from Mukden a year later: "[In the summer of 1946] the [Central] government had nine armies here totaling perhaps 200,000 regular troops and including some of the best American-trained and American-equipped units in China. The Communists were no match for them. . . . Most observers think they could easily have taken the Communists' Manchurian capital of Harbin. They were prevented from doing so by the truce imposed during General George C. Marshall's attempt to mediate the civil war."[10]

Marshall's most fateful decision came in late July 1946 when, in an effort to force Chiang Kai-shek to share power with the communists, he ordered an embargo of American arms to China. The embargo, which prevented the Nationalists from even buying ammunition for their U.S.-made weapons, was maintained until late May 1947 and made a communist military victory almost inevitable. The *New York Times* reported in June 1947 that the guns of the Nationalist armies were so worn out that "bullets fell through them to the ground."[11] Admiral Charles Maynard Cooke, who commanded the U.S. Seventh Fleet in Chinese waters in the period 1945–1946, later told a congressional committee that "of course, the Communists were being very well supplied in Manchuria by the Russians from arsenals and from captured Japanese guns and ammunition."[12] Even after the Eightieth Congress, spurred by Judd, appropriated $125 million in April 1948 for aid to the Nationalists, shipments were delayed and the guns delivered were sometimes without bolts. General Chennault testified before a Senate subcommittee that the first shipment of American arms after the embargo was lifted did not reach Shanghai until December 1948, far too late to be of any real use to the anticommunist forces in China.[13]

Marshall insisted that he was never deceived by the communists or their designs. His insistence on a coalition policy, however, favored the communists for the following reasons: the policy gave Mao, Chu Teh and other Chinese communist leaders valuable time to reorganize and strengthen their forces after several serious defeats at the hands of the Nationalists in Manchuria and North China; it required the United States to be evenhanded in its relations with the Nationalists and the communists, thereby seriously weakening Chiang since he depended heavily upon American aid while his communist opponents did not; and its ultimate failure afforded the United States an excuse to withdraw from China and allow the two sides to fight it out. Marshall may have thought he understood the communists, but two former American missionaries to China were far more perceptive. U.S. Ambassador John Leighton Stuart, who succeeded Hurley in July 1946 and worked with Marshall, said: "Whatever their motives, the evidence seemed to me convincing that the Communists wanted a coalition but only on their terms."[14] Judd himself summed up the aims of the communists: "They do not want unity. What they want is all the advantages of appearing to want unity so they can get arms and sympathy and support from abroad, while at the same time having all the advantages of complete independence."[15]

Frustrated by the lack of success and surrounded by Europe-centered advisers, President Truman issued in December a "hands-off" statement of American policy on China. On January 6, 1947, he announced that General Marshall had ended his mission and a day later named him secretary of state. Marshall left China on January 8, deeply disappointed over his failure to effect an agreement, but it had been naive in the extreme for him and the U.S. government to expect they could bring together such contending forces. In a long statement released before his departure, Marshall demonstrated that he still did not understand the Chinese communists, saying they included "liberals as well as radicals" while at the same time complaining about communist propaganda calculated "to mislead the Chinese people and the world and to arouse a bitter hatred of Americans."[16]

It is instructive to compare the opinions of Marshall and Wedemeyer, who were good friends and longtime colleagues, as to the right U.S. policy in China. Quoting from a 1947 memorandum he wrote to Secretary of Defense Forrestal, Wedemeyer later said that General Marshall had "tried to get a quick solution to the China problem." Marshall had apparently been counseled by people who felt that "China would be regenerated by first permitting the destruction of the old order, after which a new and better order would arise." This was actually "Marxist doctrine that had been applied in the Soviet Union." A better solution, said Wedemeyer, "in consonance with American interests and those of the whole free world was to recognize that China would be in trouble for a long time to come; that Soviet Communism would be 'the force moving into the vacuum created by the fall of the Nationalist government'; and that the United States therefore had 'no other resource but to support Chiang Kai-shek and his government.' "[17] No wonder, then, that when Wedemeyer was proposed by Secretary Marshall as the successor to Patrick Hurley as U.S. Ambassador to China (following such a recommendation to him by Judd), the Chinese communists protested so vehemently that Under Secretary of State Dean Acheson informed Wedemeyer his appointment had been cancelled, in effect, by the communists. The end result of Marshall's fifteen-month mission to China was summed up by Chennault: "The trend of a gradually stronger central government was reversed and the military balance shifted again in favor of the Chinese Communists."[18]

Other people have other opinions as to why the communists ultimately prevailed. Echoing the judgment of many academics, John K. Fairbank laid it to Nationalist "stupidity on the battlefield and incompetence behind the lines." The central government, he said, mismanaged the economy, producing "starvation and profiteering"; alienated large segments of the Chinese people by using "the Japanese and their puppet Chinese troops to fight the Communists"; and suppressed the public peace movement, alienating liberals and students who "did not go over to communism but rather gave up hope in the KMT."[19]

Judd had long since rebutted, most cogently perhaps in a November 1947 report to the House Foreign Affairs Committee, following an extended trip to Europe and Asia. Regarding the attitude of Chinese liberals about the Nationalist government, he pointed out that the two parties which "had clamored loudest" for a constitution, the communists and the Democratic League, refused to participate in the constitutional convention called by the KMT. The league's "true liberal elements," including the Young China party and the Social Democrats, withdrew from the organization and "are today participating in the [Nationalist] government." The left wing remained in the Democratic League and "continues to obstruct all efforts to establish China's new democratic constitution."

As for incompetence and mismanagement, Judd declared that with the help of General Wedemeyer and other American officials, the Nationalist government had streamlined the organization of its army, navy, and air force and reduced the number of civilian employees of the Ministry of National Defense from eighty thousand to twenty thousand. Top government officials, he said, were not waxing fat off U.S. aid, but received monthly salaries of thirty to forty dollars a month. He conceded there was corruption in China, as there was in any country, including the United States, but "no party or government that is wholly corrupt and unworthy of support could ever have accomplished what the Kuomintang Party has."

It overthrew the Manchu dynasty after 267 years of despotic control.

It succeeded in eliminating all but one or two of the war-lord governments. It would have had them out, too, if Japan had not attacked.

It united China under a Chinese Government for the first time in almost 300 years.

It succeeded in getting China free from more than a century of imperialistic domination by foreign powers.

It inspired and guided, between the years of 1932 and 1937—the only five years of peace it has had—a program of reconstruction and development, of democratization and modernization, of improvement in education, communication, transportation, and public health that cannot be surpassed by any large nation in history in a comparable period of time.

It saw the nature of totalitarianism of the Japanese Fascist type long before we did, and fought against it for 8 years, alone for 4½ years, long before we had sense enough to recognize its nature and to know that the Chinese were fighting on our side, too.

It saw the nature of totalitarianism of the Communist type 20 years before we did and has resisted it alone, not just since March 1947 [the Truman Doctrine] when our Government finally woke up, but since 1927. It is still resisting, still practically alone.

These seven points constituted the heart of Judd's argument then and in the years to come that Chiang and the Nationalist Chinese warranted the support of the United States. He was concerned about the fate of China for the sake of its 450 million people *and* for the sake of America in the emerging interdependent world. What was the worst thing that could happen in China? "For China to come under the Communists and become another puppet of Russia." Therefore, he said, we should strive to ensure an "independent China," which had been basic U.S. policy for a hundred years. Displaying yet again his uncanny ability to foresee the future, he predicted the following consequences if the Nationalist government collapsed:

1. The resources and manpower of China would come under a "totalitarian Communist government subservient to the Soviet Union." 2. The prestige and influence of the United States would be drastically reduced in Asia, while Soviet influence in Korea, Southeast Asia, India,

and the Philippines would be accelerated. 3. The restoration of trade between Japan and Korea with China would be blocked, although such trade was "absolutely essential if [these nations] are ever to become self-sustaining and secure without receiving hundreds of millions of American dollars every year and being defended for an indefinite period by American soldiers." 4. European countries like Great Britain, France, and Holland would find it difficult if not impossible to resume their prewar trade with Asia, "thereby endangering the success of the Marshall Plan." 5. Russia would gain "security all along her Asiatic front," enabling Moscow "to take bolder and more aggressive action against us in Europe."[20]

Most forecasters, political, meteorological, or any other kind, are delighted with a .500 batting average; Judd batted a thousand with these predictions. Chinese communists, not agrarian reformers, seized control of China, and instituted a ruthless Stalinist regime that eventually took the lives of at least 34 million Chinese. United States prestige was unquestionably reduced in Asia while communist influence spread in Korea, Indonesia, Vietnam, and the Philippines, bringing civil war and insurrection in its wake. Communist China withdrew behind economic barriers which prevented normal trade with Japan and Korea and required additional and prolonged U.S. economic assistance and military protection. If Chiang and not Mao had prevailed in China, there is good reason to believe there would have been no Korean War, for the North Koreans would not have dared to invade the south if the China on its northern border had been anticommunist. The nations of Western Europe were denied access to the China market, placing extra strain on the Marshall Plan's design to revive a moribund continent. With its Asiatic border secure, the Soviet Union under Stalin felt free to secure its western border through the military domination of Eastern Europe and agitation and propaganda in Western Europe. The temperature of the Cold War dropped several degrees as the Chinese communists, from 1947 to 1949, continued to take the measure of the Nationalists.

Throughout the Seventy-ninth Congress, U.S.-China relations remained Judd's major concern, but it did not command all of his attention; no one issue could ever absorb all of his formidable energy. In May 1945, he opposed a back-door increase in congressional salaries that would have increased official expenses, including trips to and from the district, by $2500; he argued that congressmen ought "to tighten our belts a little more and a little longer until this crisis is past, just as so many millions of citizens are doing, either voluntarily or involuntarily."[21]

There was also Minnesota politics: Harold Stassen, among others, was urging Judd to run against incumbent Senator Henrik Shipstead in the Republican primary in 1946; because Shipstead had run and won on the Farmer-Labor ticket in 1928 and 1934, he was understandably not a favorite of regular Republicans. Judd, preferring to remain in the House, told Stassen that he himself ought to challenge Shipstead and predicted that if he did, he would be elected in the fall and would gain a national platform on which to run for president. However, as Judd wryly remarked, Stassen was "one of the two smartest men I ever worked with," except when it came to dealing with his own career where he could not "think straight." He rejected Judd's sound advice, allowing Governor Edward Thye to take on and defeat Shipstead in the Republican primary, and win the Senate seat in November.[22]

In Washington, Judd and other members of Congress were asked to consider a special message from Truman in the fall of 1945 about the "reconversion" of the U.S. economy from a wartime to a peacetime basis. A key provision was "full-employment" legislation which was sent to the House Committee on Expenditures in the Executive Departments, of which Judd was a member. The Minnesota Republican waited until he had heard all the arguments for and against during many days of committee hearings before announcing during House debate that he opposed the bill because it would delude the American people into thinking that "nobody will ever again be unable to find a job if he seeks one"; and its language was too vague and imprecise about critical considerations such as what employment is "useful," "regular" and "full time." He joined with other committee members, mostly but not all Republicans, in offering a substitute bill which spoke of "promoting" but not "assuring" the general welfare, and of working toward full employment within "a free, competitive economy" with government stimulation and assistance only where needed.[23] Here again, he hewed to Jeffersonian principle by opposing a federal program that had no realistic chance of achieving its objective. At the same time, he acknowledged that the federal government had a responsibility to "assure the people of the rights and liberties guaranteed them in the Constitution"; he favored limited but not limitless government.

At some political cost to himself in Minnesota, where organized labor was so powerful an electoral force, he voted for the Federal Mediation

122

Act, denounced by the American Federation of Labor as "anti-labor." Insisting that he would vote against any measure that was honestly antilabor, he pointed out that all the bill would do is to treat both management and labor fairly and equally in a labor dispute. Specific provisions included requiring both sides, once the mediation board offered its services, to maintain the status quo for up to sixty days before any lockout or strike; allowing labor organizations as well as employers to be sued for violations of contracts concluded as a result of collective bargaining; and outlawing of the use of secondary boycotts to force a business not to handle the products of another business. As he explained: "When unions become as big as big business, then it is inescapable that the government, as the agency representing all the people, must exercise regulatory functions in both cases in order to protect the public interest against abuse of power by any business or labor organization which does not conduct itself in a responsible way."[24]

To organized labor and the Democratic-Farmer-Labor party in Minnesota those were fighting words, and Judd found himself in a tough reelection campaign that fall. He took time in June to tell the people of Minneapolis what he had been doing as their representative in Congress, and why. In an address over radio station WCCO, he began with a brief lesson in political theory, explaining that the Founding Fathers expected a member of Congress to "vote according to his judgment as to what is best for the nation as a whole." If his reasons were sound and given frankly and openly to the people, a majority of them would approve his actions. "If events prove that his judgments on the most important issues have not been sound," he said, "then the people properly will replace him with someone who they believe will have greater ability, wisdom and effectiveness." These few words encompassed the most important parts of his approach to representative government. First, a congressman should support or oppose legislation based on whether it is best for the nation; in the end, a congressman represents the United States and not just Minneapolis or New York or Chicago or Los Angeles. Second, a congressman can depend upon the innate wisdom of the people to recognize the soundness of his decisions if they are sound and if he explains them properly; here was the populist strain in Walter Judd. Third, a congressman does not have any divine right to office; he must submit himself and his judgments to the will of the people and be prepared to be replaced by someone they consider more able and effective. Judd always considered Congress a means, never

123

an end. There were many reasons why he wanted to remain a congressman, and as he emphasized in his radio talk, many of them dealt with domestic issues.

As a member of the Committee on Expenditures in the Executive Department, he focused on the problems of converting the U.S. economy to a peacetime basis. One major concern was the intelligent disposal of surplus property amounting to $100 billion, "more than a third of our national debt," so as to get the maximum possible return to the government, reduce inflationary pressures, and avoid "competing with and thereby hindering new production and jobs." Another question was how to regain control of government corporations like the Tennessee Valley Authority, the Export-Import Bank, and others, with resources of more than $25 billion. Another challenge was the long overdue reorganization of the executive branch, which had "22 agencies dealing with housing, 27 with labor relations, 93 with government lending, 37 with foreign trade, 27 with employment and unemployment, 64 dealing with business, 44 with agriculture, and 305 with national defense. ... The more one studies the maze," he remarked, "the more one wonders—not that there is confusion in Washington, but that anything gets done at all." One proposal that his committee supported was the creation of a new combined executive agency, the Department of Health, Education and Welfare, which was finally adopted in 1953 by President Eisenhower. Judd later cosponsored legislation that resulted in the Hoover Commission, which presented extensive recommendations for reorganizing and streamlining the government, a number of which were later adopted.

He told his constituents that he supported the G.I. Bill, and had in fact amended its educational provision so that any veteran who wanted an education or vocational training and could do satisfactory work at an approved institution would be eligible, regardless of his age or length of service. "I believe," he said, "that education for veterans should be considered not so much as a personal reward as a sound investment in the whole nation's future." He opposed a bill which would have given a federal "subsidy" to almost every teacher in America, regardless of his or her salary, because it would lead to "steadily increasing influence by the federal government over the public school system." At the same time, he cosponsored a bill to provide federal assistance to states that were trying to provide a decent education for their children in proportion to state income, tax load, and resources but still fell short of the national average expenditure.

He consistently voted for the extension of price controls, but in the context of taking other necessary steps to curb inflation, such as the reduction of federal expenditures, the balancing of the budget, and the adjustment of price ceilings where necessary "to get maximum production." He had worked for a Fair Employment Practices Commission, opposed compulsory military training in peacetime, worked for a voluntary health insurance program, and supported an appropriation of $400 million for immediate low-cost housing.

The legislative profile is clear: in the area of domestic affairs, Walter Judd was a liberal Republican in a party still opposed to Big Government. He was not a committed welfarist like the liberal Democrats who sought a broad expansion of the New Deal, but he supported federal programs and federal spending where and when it was clear to him that private efforts would not suffice. In the field of foreign affairs, he was a devout internationalist in a party still filled with isolationists who would not acknowledge that World War II had changed the world and the United States permanently. He was often too conservative for liberal Democrats and too liberal for conservative Republicans, but his legislative influence among both parties steadily increased, because of his ability to explain the most complex issue, foreign or domestic, in understandable terms to his colleagues and his facility for offering amendments that invariably improved legislation. He did not always get his way, but as he had learned in China, he sought and often found the golden mean among extremes.

Back in Washington, he delivered a compelling warning about radioactivity during the course of a House debate on the creation of the Atomic Energy Commission. In a very rare personal reference, he mentioned that he had had "considerable personal experience with one form of radioactive energy" (the overexposure to X-rays which caused his recurring facial cancer) and went on to point out that for the first time in his history, man "has discovered how to release radioactive energy artificially." The discovery reversed a process of declining radioactivity which had been going on since the formation of the earth. It meant far more, he said, than the ability to set off "bomb explosions, destructive as they are. If too much radioactive energy is released in an uncontrolled form, what may it do to human life itself; in fact, to all life?" Congressmen from both parties and of varying philosophical persuasions listened to Judd, looked at his cancer-scarred face, and gave the Atomic Energy Commission the authority to control civilian as well as military development of atomic energy.[25]

Congress also moved to revise the legislative budget so that, among other things, each member received a 25 percent increase in salary, from $10,000 to $12,500 a year. Judd opposed the salary increase, arguing that while congressmen had not received a pay hike since 1927, it was the wrong time "when prices have risen sharply, when there are strong pressures by some to start another series of strikes to get further wage increases." However, Congress passed the Legislative Reorganization Act of 1946, including the increase in its salaries.

Partially as a result of such self-serving actions, President Truman and the Democratic party found themselves in serious political trouble. The cost of living was rising rapidly, unions were striking from coast to coast, there were shortages of meat, automobiles, and housing. Capitalizing upon widespread public dissatisfaction, Republicans summed up their 1946 campaign in the succinct phrase, "Had Enough?" Addressing the Minnesota Republican State Convention in September, Judd offered his variation on the theme, asserting that "the election this fall will determine whether we are going to be led further down the road toward statism or whether we are going to reverse the direction and march once more toward a sound government of and by free men and women." He recounted how he had been unable to attend the convention the preceding night because he was filling in temporarily for a "doctor friend" and had delivered a baby. "I couldn't help but wonder," he said, "what kind of an America will there be for this child?" The Democratic party, he stated, was "hopelessly split from top to bottom. . . . The Republican Party can save this nation." He declared that because the 1946 election was "something more than the ordinary political campaign," Republicans had a "solemn obligation" to carry the issues to every corner of the state and the union to bring about "a smashing victory—not for us, but for those great eternal principles by which alone free men can govern themselves well."[26] This was predictable political rhetoric, but Judd elevated his remarks from the mundane to the moving by his utter sincerity and conviction.

Campaigning in October, he sharply attacked "those who don't believe in our system," who would lead the country "toward national regimentation under the guise of liberalism." He appealed to Democrats, and former Democrats like himself, to vote Republican "to save the Democratic Party [from] being taken over by usurpers whose belief that the all-powerful State is the way to make conditions better is the complete opposite of the philosophy of Jefferson, Cleveland, and Wilson." He declared euphorically that the Republican party was "in the process of being reborn."[27]

One week before election day, he used radio station WCCO to ask the people of Minneapolis, "How can we get the kind of government we want?" His answer centered on the need for national unity. And since the Democratic party in the nation and the Democratic-Farmer-Labor party in Minnesota were "so torn within themselves," it remained for the Republican party to explain to the people how it would unite the nation and to what ends.

Republicans stood for individual rights, personal liberty, and "a maximum of self-government," Judd declared, while Democrats have moved toward "regimentation of our society" and the concept of a "political elite" which knows better than the people how best to govern. Republicans supported a system of "free management, free labor, and free exchange of goods with the least possible interference by government." He approvingly quoted William Green, president of the American Federation of Labor, who three weeks before had asked: "Shall our unions be free-formed democratic unions, or government-dominated, government-controlled and government-administered unions?"—a sharp jab at the rival and far more liberal Congress of Industrial Organizations (CIO). Republicans stood, he said, for the right of organized labor "to organize and bargain collectively with employers," but also believed that "governmental machinery to promote peaceful settlement of disputes can be and should be improved." Here was a harbinger of the Taft-Hartley Act, to be passed by the Republican Eightieth Congress.

He called on "regular Democrats" to fight radicalism in their own party by voting Republican and thereby "save the Democratic Party."[28] In keeping with his pledge in his first campaign, he did not ask the residents of Minneapolis to vote for him. Yet he did not hesitate to urge his listeners to vote Republican; in fact, it is the strong partisan tone of his radio address that strikes one most forcefully. There were few qualifications in the charges he leveled at Democrats, who were guilty of "dictatorship," "regimentation," "concentration of power," "bungling," and "reckless expenditures." He referred several times to the attempt by "extreme radical groups" and "left-wing groups" to take over the Democratic party and "make it the instrument of their will and desire." Because the Democrats were so divided, he said, "they simply cannot give the sound and united leadership the country so sorely needs, in both its domestic and its foreign relations." The obvious choice for Americans "determined to take charge once more of the affairs of their own government and to prove that representative government still worked" was the Republican party.

There was more than adequate evidence to substantiate the charges— he pointed out that Eleanor Roosevelt had explained her decision not to attend a CIO-PAC rally in New York City with the simple words, "I am a Democrat"—and there is no question that he was appalled at the leftward swing of his former party. But the basic reason for his fierce criticism of Democrats and his eloquent support of Republicans lay in his deep concern about the American political system which he believed was now out of balance. One party had been in power too long and had inevitably been corrupted; the divisions among the Democrats were a visible sign of their decline. The only way to redress the political imbalance and restore "Constitutional government" was to elect Republicans to the Congress. Judd was unquestionably partisan, but for what he argued were nonpartisan reasons; he was not anti-Democrat but pro-democratic. He saw the election of a Republican Eightieth Congress as the best way to preserve the government and the institutions for which Americans had "fought the greatest war in history." In this, as in all his crusades, Judd gave little quarter and asked for none.

Eric Goldman wrote: "A nation which had quite enough of inflation and the Russians, of strikes, shortages, and the atom bomb, of everlasting maybe's about peace and prosperity, rose up in a hiss of exasperation and elected the first Republican Congress since the far-distant days of Herbert Hoover."[29] Walter Judd easily won re-election over Douglas Hall of the Democratic-Farmer-Labor party. Republicans gained thirteen seats in the Senate and a remarkable fifty-six seats in the House of Representatives. The new Congress consisted of 246 Republicans, 188 Democrats, and 1 independent in the House; and 51 Republicans and 45 Democrats in the Senate. One group of euphoric Republicans, emboldened by the results, proposed to cut ten billion dollars from the budget, lower taxes, and abandon "the philosophy of government interference with business and labor."[30] Led by Senator Robert A. Taft of Ohio, Republicans decided that a strongly partisan line in domestic policy would build on the success of the November returns, accentuate the differences between the two political parties and win them the White House in 1948. However, external events transformed their partisan plans into bipartisan cooperation, at least in the area of foreign policy, although not without prolonged debate and often heated disagreement.

Even Judd, an ardent advocate of bipartisanship, was sorely tempted to wax partisan because of shifting U.S. policy toward China.

Throughout 1946, while General Marshall was in China, Judd generally refrained from expressing public criticism of his attempts to do what the Minnesota congressman deemed impossible—reconcile two irreconcilable parties. But in May, he signed the Manchurian Manifesto, along with fifty-nine other leading Americans, calling on the Soviet Union to observe "punctiliously" the Sino-Soviet pact, stop arming Chinese communists in Manchuria, and halt the stripping of all industrial equipment from that province. The manifesto urged the U.S. government not to abandon the traditional American policy of the "open door" as well as the preservation of the "territorial integrity of China" as the "keystone of American security in the Pacific."[31] That the manifesto represented the mainstream of American thinking at the time was shown by a *New York Times* editorial which suggested that protests about the growing peril to peace in China should be directed "not against [the Nationalist] Government and those who assist it, but against those who oppose it and divide China," that is, the Chinese communists. The *Times* rejected the call, coming "most loudly out of Moscow," for the United States "to get out of China immediately—withdraw its troops, withhold all further aid to the Chinese government and abandon its traditional policy of the open door."[32] As 1946 progressed, Judd became more worried and outspoken about events in China. Writing in August to a Congregational minister, he said, "There never was a chance . . . for General Marshall's mission to succeed. It is not possible to get unity unless both sides in a dispute want unity. The Communists have never wanted unity in China any more than they do in Europe or in any other country where they, when a minority, always pushed for a so-called 'united front' until they could build up strength and seize absolute power."[33]

His comments about the true goal of the Chinese communists and their direct links to Moscow were based in part on an analysis made by the U.S. Military Intelligence Service in July 1945 before the entry of the Soviet Union into World War II. The analysts concluded:

(1) The "democracy" of the Chinese Communists is Soviet democracy.
(2) The Chinese Communist movement is part of the international Communist movement, sponsored and guided by Moscow.
(3) There is reason to believe that Soviet Russia plans to create Russian-dominated areas in Manchuria, Korea and probably North China.

(4) A strong and stable China cannot exist without the natural resources of Manchuria and North China.

It was therefore necessary "for the maintenance of peace in the Far East and for the long range interests of the United States that the Cairo Declaration be implemented without modification."[34] When it was so clear to U.S. military intelligence what the communists were up to and what U.S. policy in China should be, Judd wondered, why was it so difficult for U.S. foreign service officers in China and the State Department to come to the same conclusions? Why could not American policy makers pay more attention to experts like General Wedemeyer, who after working closely and effectively with Chiang Kai-shek and the leaders of the Nationalist government, had declared:

> I can attest to [Chiang's] unselfish devotion to the Chinese people and his earnest desire to provide a democratic way of life within China. I am confident that if he were given the full support of his allies, the support that I feel his loyalty and his unstinting assistance during the war days fully merits, Generalissimo Chiang Kai-shek will evolve a solution to the political and economic problems that confront his country today and he will establish a happy, prosperous, united and democratic China.

Judd and many other Americans, in and out of Congress, were deeply worried as to what would happen to China and the rest of the world if that "full support" were not given.

CHAPTER TEN

◆

Waging the Cold War

THE COLD WAR is usually said to have started because of Soviet military aggression and/or U.S. economic imperialism, but we should not overlook a more prosaic but no less powerful factor—the weather. The combination of one of the worst winters in European history and the economic aftermath of World War II reduced Great Britain in early 1947 to a state of bankruptcy. On February 22, 1947, the British Embassy in Washington delivered two notes to officials at the State Department stating that Britain could no longer meet its traditional responsibilities in Greece and Turkey and would have to pull out by no later than April 1. The import of the notes was clear: since both Greece and Turkey were on the brink of collapse and being pressed by communists, only a firm American commitment could prevent a Soviet takeover of the strategically placed nations. For the first time since its founding, there was no one to protect the United States and its national interests but the United States itself. All the other Western powers—Great Britain, France, Belgium, the Netherlands—were in a seriously weakened condition. A grim, bipolar world suddenly confronted the United States. Joseph Jones, a State Department official who helped draft the Truman Doctrine speech, observed, rather breathlessly, that the British "had within the hour handed the job of world leadership, with all its burdens and all its glory, to the United States."[1] After a weekend of State

Department discussions of the notes, Undersecretary of State Dean Acheson told Secretary of State George Marshall in a memorandum: "This puts up the most [serious] decision with which we have been faced since the war."[2] Marshall and Acheson brought President Truman their recommendation: Greece needed substantial amounts of aid, and quickly. The alternative appeared to be the loss of Greece and the extension of the Iron Curtain across the eastern Mediterranean, Truman recalls in his memoirs. If Greece were lost, Turkey would become an untenable outpost in a "sea of communism." Truman viewed Greece and Turkey as "free countries being challenged by Communist threats from within and without." America, he felt, had no choice but to help them and prevent Soviet expansionism.[3]

The Truman Doctrine has been described in such apocalyptic tones by some writers that it is useful to examine what President Truman said and did not say to a joint session of Congress on March 12, 1947. He began by describing the military and political pressures being applied to Greece and Turkey by terrorists and communists, but did not mention the Soviet Union. He explained that the British government could give no aid beyond March 31. He said that the assistance of the United Nations had been considered but that it was not in a position to extend the help required. He conceded that the Greek government was not perfect, and stated that U.S. aid did not mean condoning extremism on the left or the right. Reaffirming U.S. support for the United Nations' goals of freedom and independence for all its members, Truman insisted that these objectives would not be realized "unless we are willing to help free peoples to maintain their free institutions and their national integrity against aggressive movements that seek to impose upon them totalitarian regimes." He then uttered the key sentence: "This is no more than a frank recognition that totalitarian regimes imposed on free peoples, by direct or indirect aggression, undermine the foundations of international peace and hence the security of the United States." Here was the heart of the Truman Doctrine: international peace and U.S. security were intertwined. America assumed Great Britain's role as keeper of the peace not only in the Near East but around the world.

In response to the totalitarian threat, Truman said, the United States must respond firmly but "primarily through economic and financial aid which is essential to economic stability and orderly political processes." Critics of Truman and his "doctrine" often ignore or minimize this emphasis. His other two key statements were: "I believe that it must be the policy of the United States to support free peoples who are resisting attempted subjugation by armed minorities or by outside pressures"; and "I believe that we must assist free peoples to work out their own destinies in their own way." Truman asked Congress for $400 million in aid to Greece and Turkey, arguing that "the free peoples of the world" looked to the United States to help them maintain their freedom. "If we falter," warned the President, "we may endanger the peace of the world—and we shall surely endanger the welfare of our own nation."[4]

Isolationist and internationalist opponents in both Houses sprang to the attack, sensing the epochal nature of the measure. Senator Harry Byrd (D-Va.) questioned the amount of money that would be involved in implementing the Truman Doctrine all over the world, as well as the wisdom of bypassing the United Nations. Democratic Senators Claude Pepper of Florida and Allen Ellender of Louisiana criticized the President's proposal for being warlike and for passing over the United Nations. Congressman Lawrence H. Smith (R-Kan.) said that the Truman plan "smelled of oil politics." Congressman George H. Bender (R-Ohio), one of the most outspoken opponents of the Truman Doctrine in the House, accused the Greek government of fostering fixed elections, a black market, and concentration camps; he charged Turkey with harboring former Nazis in its army and persecuting political dissidents. Congressman Robert F. Rich of Pennsylvania, another Republican, claimed that the Turkish government outdid Hitler's regime: while the German dictator had permitted elections, however rigged, Turkey's dictators ruled without even the appearance of democracy.[5] Notwithstanding their antipathy toward communism, isolationists like Congressman Ben Jensen (R-Iowa) expressed concern about the financial strain of the Truman Doctrine and quoted the aphorism ascribed to Lenin: "We will force America to spend herself into bankruptcy; then we will take her over." To some members, the real menace was not the communists in Greece or Turkey but those inside the United States. Congressman Paul Shafer (R-Pa.) preferred "ferreting" domestic communists out of the civil service and unions to bolstering a "dissolute king" overseas. Congressman John Rankin (D-Miss.) said: "If we are going to fight communism . . . let us begin in the Library of Congress." Yet for all their wild swings and impractical alternatives, opponents of the Truman Doctrine touched on key points, including the reactionary character of the Greek and Turkish governments, the creation of an emergency atmosphere, and the danger of overcommitting the United States overseas.[6]

The man who provided most of the answers to these and other

questions in the Senate was Arthur Vandenberg of Michigan, chairman of the Senate Foreign Relations Committee. Although Senator Vandenberg was unhappy that he and other congressional leaders had not been consulted earlier, he felt that given the present crisis and the president's urgent request, Congress had little choice but to go along or invite future and more serious Soviet aggression. As he said in a letter: "The overriding fact is that the President has made a long-delayed statement regarding communism on-the-march which must be supported if there is any hope of ever impressing Moscow with the necessity of paying any sort of peaceful attention to us whatever."[7] At the same time, Vandenberg and other Republicans believed that the Truman administration had not kept Congress fully informed, had delayed too long in dealing with the implications of Great Britain's economic decline, and had failed to go directly to Stalin about the deterioration of U.S.-Soviet relations. As Vandenberg put it, Republicans would like to be included "on the policy takeoffs, instead of merely the crash landings."[8]

Although the Truman Doctrine represented a radically new U.S. policy, it was also the logical end to a trend that had begun as early as 1944 when Averell Harriman, U.S. ambassador to the Soviet Union, counseled the White House about the need to be firm with Stalin. By 1946 many U.S. officials, including President Truman, had become disturbed by the Soviet Union's expansion throughout Eastern Europe and its attempted incursions into the Near East. They kept hoping that Stalin would go so far and no farther, but like Hitler, his appetite seemed to grow with each new acquisition of influence and territory. To Truman, Vandenberg, Judd and other makers of foreign policy, the course of action seemed clear: the Soviet Union had to be resisted, not simply in Greece and Turkey, but internationally because of its expressed goal of global domination. It was logical, therefore, that the United States should state publicly that communist gains were a threat to international peace and U.S. security, and should be checked wherever they occurred. The international commitment outlined in the Truman Doctrine, calling for the expenditure of hundreds of millions of dollars, produced another peacetime first: the executive branch needed the active cooperation and support of both Houses of Congress. For the first time in the history of the American republic, the House of Representatives, where money bills originate, became a continuing major player in foreign policy, requiring large adjustments by both the executive and legislative branches. No longer could the Senate presume to speak for all of Congress in the field of foreign relations; the House would be heard, or there might not be funds for all the grand designs. The greatly expanded role of the House of Representatives in foreign policy gave additional prominence to members like Judd, who helped steer the House through the new waters of foreign aid, technical assistance, global markets, and international balance-of-power politics.

Following President Truman's address to the joint session of Congress, the number two Democrat in the House, John McCormack of Massachusetts, rose to endorse the Truman Doctrine on the basis that it was in "the national interest of the United States of America." He took an unequivocal anticommunist line: it was not in the best interests of America for Greece or Turkey or Italy or France or Spain or China to "go under the control of the Communists." Judd commended the former majority leader for his "forthright" statement, particularly with regard to China. When Congressman Thomas A. Jenkins of Ohio suggested that Truman's statement amounted to a "declaration of war," McCormack rejoined that there was a calculated risk in "everything we do." The question before the Congress and the nation, he said, was whether the United States would do nothing and let Greece and Turkey and perhaps all of Europe fall to the communists or follow the recommendations of the president. Seeking to blunt the charge of U.S. intervention made by Jenkins and other isolationists, Judd argued that the United States had not created the crisis but was seeking to defend "the general way of life in which we believe against attacks from others."[9]

There was an unusual somberness in the voice of the congressman from Minnesota; he was mourning the death of his father. Two weeks before, Horace H. Judd, at age eighty-five, had had a heart attack and died shortly thereafter. Walter and Miriam and their three daughters took the long train ride through one of the worst snow storms in years to Chicago and then on to Columbus, Nebraska, where they were met by Jim Judd, who drove them to Rising City to join Gertrude and Myrtle. Horace Judd lay in the study of the home which he had built so many years ago, surrounded by the "masses of flowers that kept pouring in," as Miriam wrote. Neighbors prepared the meals and cleaned up while old friends from town or from all over the state dropped in to "bid goodbye." The minister came to plan the service, the choir director discussed which of "Mr. Judd's" favorite songs should be sung, Myrtle wrote the obituary, the undertakers brought a casket exactly like the one in which Mrs. Judd had been buried, which "particularly pleased Walter," who had been in China when she died in April 1935. Gertrude began playing the songs they had sung as children, and soon everyone, neighbors too, was singing. "It was the kind of evening Mr. Judd would have loved," Miriam wrote, "surrounded by his family and his friends and music, and though it was not untouched by sadness and tears, by memories and loneliness, still there was nothing of hopelessness or despair or fear—more the feeling of a peaceful and gentle ending to a noble story." At the funeral service on Sunday morning, which took the place of the regular worship service in the church, the minister emphasized the esteem in which everyone had held Horace Judd. He recounted how only the week before Walter and Miriam Judd had been at the White House, and when they mentioned that it was Horace Judd's eighty-fifth birthday, the president, remembering his visit in 1943 to the Judd home, responded: "Give my special greetings to your father. He's like my mother, the salt of the earth. They don't make many like that any more." Walter drove Miriam and the girls to the cemetery in Surprise, where all the Judds and Greenslits are buried, talking all the way about his father and his boyhood. There was a brief prayer at the grave, located at the top of a hill, and then everyone returned to their cars while Walter and Jim waited at the gravesite until the casket was lowered into place beside Mrs. Judd.[10]

Returning to Washington, Judd plunged into his work and took on one of the most important responsibilities of his Congressional career. The House Committee on Foreign Affairs, to which he had just been appointed, began public hearings on U.S. aid to Greece and Turkey on March 20. The representatives expressed concerns about the measure similar to those of their colleagues in the upper House, who had already held hearings. What kind of precedent, if any, was being set by aiding Greece and Turkey? Was this the beginning of a new get-tough policy with the Soviet Union? What were the chances of the situation developing into war? Was the United States helping Greece and Turkey, or Great Britain, with its aid? The answers provided by administration witnesses consistently avoided a provocative anti-Soviet or anticommunist line. Invariably, they softened the belligerent language of the congressmen, insisting that aid to Greece and Turkey was just that and no more, and certainly not an ideological crusade against Moscow. It was Congress and not the administration which publicly presented Greek and Turkish aid as essentially an anti-Soviet move. When Congressman Mike Mansfield (D-Mont.) asked if the Truman Doctrine might lead to war, Acting Secretary of State Dean Acheson replied:

"I do not see how it possibly can lead to war. It seems to me that by strengthening the forces of democracy and individual freedom and strengthening the economies of these two countries, you do a great deal to eliminate the sort of situations which would produce friction between the great powers."

In response to the suggestion of Congressman John Vorys (R-Ohio) that the United States was "pulling British chestnuts out of the fire," Acheson responded firmly: "The sole basis for doing this, and the sole reason that we put it forth, is that this is in the interests of the United States of America."[11]

Under the steady hand of Chairman Charles Eaton of New Jersey, the House Committee on Foreign Affairs favorably and quickly reported out the Greek-Turkish aid bill on April 24, with only one member, Lawrence H. Smith (R-Wisc.), dissenting. Floor debate began on May 6 and lasted four days, the House operating as usual under a limited rule. The members were immediately reminded of what Secretary of State George Marshall, returning from a meeting of foreign ministers in Moscow, had said about the situation in the Near East: "The patient is sinking while the doctors deliberate."[12] Eaton argued that the House was confronted with a choice, which he made as stark, as black and white, as he could: "Is the world civilization now in process of creation to be a civilization of freedom or of slavery? Does Americanism or communism hold the key to the future of mankind? There stands the challenge which we must meet. And we must meet it here and now."[13]

The opposition was a disparate group, including ultraliberal Vito Marcantonio of New York, Republican isolationists, and Democratic liberals. They did not have sufficient strength to defeat the bill, but could have weakened it through amendments. However, their cause was doomed through the clumsiness of communist opponents and congressional supporters. American communists sat in the visitor's gallery during the first two days of debate and hissed speakers who urged passage. Many of the communists wore military discharge buttons in their lapels as they lobbied congressmen; they were attending a meeting of communist veterans in Washington, D.C. Congressman Charles Kersten (R-Wisc.) told the House about a group that called on him: "I put the question to them repeatedly, in case of a conflict of interest between the United States and Soviet Russia which government would they support. I had to put it six times, and finally they said they would support the government of Russia in a conflict with the United States!" Kersten's bitter denunciation brought a burst of applause from his colleagues.[14] Then as now, the U.S. Communist party was under the tight control of the Soviet Union; the lobbying could not have occurred without the approval and direction of Moscow, whose clumsy attempt at influencing U.S. legislation badly backfired.

The other strategic moment came during the second day of debate with the introduction of two amendments proposing that the problem be handled by the United Nations rather than through unilateral U.S. aid. At this critical moment, when many members were casting about for a way to express their unhappiness without directly voting against the measure and the president, Eaton, a veteran of many legislative battles, read a telegram from Warren A. Austin, U.S. representative to the United Nations, who assured the House that the bill strengthened rather than weakened the world organization and should be passed. The amendments were shouted down.[15]

It remained for Judd to put the question of Greek-Turkish aid in perspective. He told an attentive House that he supported the bill because the present ideological and political warfare between the United States and the Soviet Union would determine "our own future and that of mankind." He said the two superpowers were competing in four critical geographical areas. The first was Germany with its strategic location, enormous resources, and industrious people. "Almost everybody agrees," he said, "that as Germany goes, so will go Europe." The second area was the Middle East. "If we do not pass this bill," he argued, "every bit of the testimony indicates that Greece as a free nation will go down tomorrow. . . . And if Greece goes down, Turkey is hopelessly flanked." The third area was China: "As China goes so will go Asia." The fourth area "where the struggle between the forces of freedom and of slavery is most crucial is the United States. Which way are we to go?" He declared that it was "precisely because I don't want war with Russia that I beg us not to pursue further the fallacious notion that we can get peace with her by sacrificing our principles and other peoples' territory."[16]

A majority of the House agreed with Judd because of the force of his arguments and because they had a common view of the United States and the world. They were, almost to a man, middle to upper class, college-educated, Protestant, and lawyers. They had been taught that America was the greatest and freest nation in the world and had a manifest obligation to help other nations enjoy the same blessings of political and economic liberty. They were patriotic but not zenophobic, committed to the process of law and rational decision making and pragmatic as to goals and objectives. Legislative compromise was their way of life; and what was bipartisanship, cooperation between a Democratic president and a Republican Congress, but compromise in the realm of foreign affairs? They looked to men like Vandenberg in the Senate and Judd in the House to lead the way in foreign policy as they looked to other experts in taxes, tariffs, labor, and housing when the time came to cast their vote on a piece of legislation about which they might know very little. Besides, it was an article of political faith in those days that elections were won or lost on bread-and-butter domestic issues, not foreign affairs. However, this laissez-faire attitude was to change significantly, especially in the House of Representatives, when the price of foreign policy began to soar into the billions of dollars with the coming of the Marshall Plan in 1948.

On May 9, the House of Representatives overwhelmingly approved U.S. aid to Greece and Turkey by 287 to 107. A conference report adjusted minor differences in the Senate and House versions and was passed by both Houses on May 15. When Truman signed the bill, he said in part: "The act authorizing United States aid to Greece and Turkey ... is an important step in the building of the peace ... The conditions of peace include, among other things, the ability of nations to maintain order and independence, and to support themselves economically."[17] Truman's language was significant for two reasons: It emphasized the economic character of aid to Greece and Turkey, avoiding the anticommunist rhetoric some historians erroneously insist was the key element in the selling of the Truman Doctrine; and it helped prepare the way for the much larger task of economically assisting a sorely distressed Europe.

In June, Judd played a pivotal role in saving the State Department's information program, including a new overseas radio operation, the Voice of America. Critics argued that the dissemination of information about America was better left to private agencies and individuals, and that, furthermore, the people picked to run the government program were liberals and worse. In the House debate, Judd offered examples of the flood of misinformation about the United States that was being distributed by the Soviet Union and its Eastern European allies. He declared that he believed, along with "the great Teacher," that "You shall know the truth and the truth shall make you free." But, he asked, how can the truth "make men free if they do not know it? And how can they know the truth if they do not hear it? And how can they hear it if nobody tells it?" With regard to personnel, he reported that he too had had serious reservations because those operating the war information programs in Europe and Asia had not been "the voice of America" but "mostly the voice of the left wing of the administration in power." But he had carefully studied the operations of the Voice of America in the last six months and had become convinced that its "personnel has been drastically combed and culled out." It was doing a "good job now," he declared, "and there is no reason to doubt that it will do an increasingly good job in the future." The future of the nation and the world, he stated, depended upon the spread of the ideas of the American Constitution and government. "That, in my judgment, is the only way we can ultimately turn back the tide of totalitarianism and tyranny which is sweeping over the earth."[18] The appropriation passed, and the Voice of America was not silenced.

Judd was also concerned about the truth about China, which he felt was not served in books like *Thunder Out of China*, written by Theodore White and Annalee Jacoby. He told the House that the book, which had become a bestseller after selection by the Book of the Month Club and laudatory reviews in the *New York Times* and elsewhere, was not "straight reporting of the facts" but "clever selection and manipulation. . . . Even if all the particular incidents they chose to report were true, the total impression given is grossly false." The basic difficulties in China, he asserted, "were not produced by the present Chinese government; they have been there for thousands of years and are what [the Nationalist] government has been struggling with—and on the whole making incredible progress until Japan struck." Anticipating an argument he would make the following year when he urged aid to China under the Marshall Plan, he said that it was as "short-sighted and dangerous for the United States to have China come now under Communist—which means Moscow's—domination as it would have been to have China come under Japanese militarism's control."[19]

It was not at all impossible that Western Europe would suffer the same fate. As Walter Lippmann wrote in April 1947, "the danger of a European economic collapse" and the possible withdrawal of Great Britain from Germany leaving the United States "isolated in Europe, face to face with the Russians," necessitated extraordinary political and economic measures. Billions of dollars had already been channeled into Europe through the United Nations Relief and Rehabilitation Association, a loan to Britain of $3.75 billion, and Greek-Turkish aid. In late spring, Congress approved a $350 million emergency aid program for Austria, Hungary, Italy, Trieste, China, and Greece, but it was clear that the economic problems left by World War II could not be solved by such emergency stop-and-go relief. A long-range solution aimed at restoring the economic health and vigor of Europe was offered by Secretary of State George Marshall at Harvard's commencement exercises in June. Outlining what came to be called the Marshall Plan, Marshall stressed that the program had to be European in concept and in execution. "The role of [the United States] should consist of friendly aid in the drafting of a European program and of later support of such a program so far as it may be practical for us to do so."[20]

Senator Vandenberg described Marshall's speech at Harvard as a "shot heard round the world," but knew that it fell on many deaf ears in a Republican Congress committed to reducing taxes and cutting government spending. There was strong apprehension in Congress and in the country that American goods would be removed from the domestic market for foreign consumption, and that success of the program would only serve to increase foreign competition for American business. Judd also had his reservations, not the least of them being that Marshall had not mentioned China or any other nation in Asia. When Governor Thomas E. Dewey of New York, a leading contender for the Republican nomination for president, subsequently called for U.S. aid to China, Judd placed his address in the *Congressional Record,* commenting: "It has been most disturbing to have the administration ask us to put some $20 billion into helping the people on the European front withstand the attacks of Communist-led groups and nothing as yet to help those on the Asiatic front. . . . To be successful anywhere we must have a well-rounded and consistent program against this sort of warfare everywhere."[21]

In July, he made another significant contribution to the internationalization of the United States in the post-World War II world when he submitted to the House a report of the Committee on Foreign Affairs, providing for U.S. membership in the World Health Organization (WHO). Formed in 1946 as a special agency of the United Nations, the WHO was already at work establishing a center for the communication of information on diseases, epidemics, and medical knowledge throughout the world. In keeping with the general U.N. formula, the United States would provide 40 percent of WHO's budget, approximately $2 million a year.[22] Approved by Congress that summer, membership in the World Health Organization turned out to be one of the best investments in international relations America ever made.

The Soviet Union and its satellites provided a political response to the Marshall Plan in October when Communist party delegates, meeting in Moscow, announced the establishment of the Communist Information

Bureau (Cominform) and issued an analysis of the world situation which stated that it was the West and not the East which was engaged in imperialism. In the eyes of many congressmen, the birth of the Cominform was the latest in a long list of hostile Soviet acts since the end of World War II which proved Moscow's contempt for mutual understanding and cooperative action, acts which included the failure of the Soviet Union to observe its Yalta commitments.

In November, the Communist parties of France and Italy demonstrated their obedience to Moscow by initiating widespread strikes in an attempt to bring down their governments. In Marseilles, where the red flag was raised over the Palais de Justice, the political committee of the French Communist party praised the "working and democratic population of Marseilles in its struggle against the American Party," i.e., the Ramadier government, which did in fact fall. For days France had no government. About two million workers were idle. Coal was not mined and food deliveries were not made. The communist-dominated Confederation Generale du Travail revealed its true colors by condemning U.S. aid to France. By the end of November, communists in the National Assembly had nearly stopped deliberations through tactics of delay and disorder. However, the new government of Robert Schuman did not waver, and in December strikers began to grow tired of the demands of their communist leaders. When the communists called a strike of the Paris subway on December 8, it failed because workers did not respond. On December 9, the strikes at last ended, and the next day France went back to work. Encouraged by the demonstrated weakness of the communists, the Schuman government moved against the Communist party, closing, for example, the main party newspapers. At the same time, Italian communists were promoting strikes and violence in Italy with the Marshall Plan as a major target. Addressing a meeting of the Italian Communist party in January 1948, its chairman, Palmiro Togliatti, declared that the main goal of the party was to combat "the policy of financial groups and the Marshall Plan."[23] Such open communist activity in Western Europe helped convince the U.S. Congress that the situation was indeed serious enough to warrant so monumental an undertaking as the Marshall Plan.

Judd was able to personally appraise the efforts of the communists as well as the mood of European leaders and citizens when he flew to London in September at the request of the chairman of the House Committee on Foreign Affairs. He had not been certain that he would be able to make the trip because an April operation for skin cancer had revealed a more active malignancy on his lip than his doctors expected. However, there was no immediate regrowth of the tumor, and he gave the go-ahead to the committee clerk. Traveling with Karl Mundt of South Dakota, Senator Carl Hatch of New Mexico and several others, Judd talked with dozens of government leaders, including British Foreign Minister Ernest Bevin. Bevin, he wrote to Miriam, "portrayed an extremely dark picture." The French, he said, were "heavy" and "tired" and the victims of a widespread black market that offered 250 francs to the dollar when the official exchange rate was 110. "I don't see how the French people can make it," he said pessimistically. He was impressed by the spirit of the Finnish people, who were "fully aware of the difficulties of their position next to Russia, desirous of getting along, but determined to be free." He admired the various Parliament buildings he visited which, with the exception of Britain's, made the Capitol look "antiquated, inefficient and inadequate." He especially approved of their electric voting method "where everybody presses a button, aye or no or present, and it's all instantly recorded, saving thirty minutes on each roll call."[24] Some 25 years later, in 1972, the House finally adopted an electronic voting system; the Senate still resists such automation.

He also visited Warsaw, whose desolation, he wrote Miriam, was beyond description: "the awful deadly empty stillness of literally miles and miles and miles of 3 to 10 story buildings ranging from empty shells to the three square miles of ghetto which is one brick pile without a single wall standing." Some 95 percent of the destruction, he pointed out, took place after the surrender of the Bor rebellion in the summer of 1944. The Germans took almost 2 months to destroy with dynamite an area "as big as from Georgetown to the Capitol and the Potomac to Walter Reed Hospital." He praised the Poles for their determination to rebuild Warsaw and not to transfer the capital to Lodz or some other undamaged city. "They . . . are strong people." Why was it "their tragic fate" to have such cruel neighbors on each side? "The whole spectacle makes one almost sick at one's stomach—the dividing line between so called civilization and barbarism is so *very* thin."[25]

Judd's September 1947 trip was only one of many visits he made to Europe, whose problems he spent more time trying to solve in committee and on the House floor than those of China, although the press usually presented him as almost exclusively preoccupied with Asia. As we have seen, he played a key role in House approval of the Truman Doctrine, and would play no less important a role in congressional passage of the Marshall Plan and the United States's first peacetime military alliance, NATO (the North Atlantic Treaty Organization).

Still, China remained one of his central concerns. Again at Eaton's (chairman of the House Committee on Foreign Affairs) request, he took the long flight east in late October and spent several days in Japan conferring with General MacArthur and his staff, in Korea with President Rhee and American officials and with U.S. and Chinese officials in Peking, Nanking, and Shanghai. Writing to a missionary friend in Soochow before he left, he expressed anxiety about the future of the Nationalist government and added that without U.S. aid, it faced disaster. "Unfortunately," he wrote, "it is already so late there is reason for grave doubt that [assistance] can retrieve the situation."[26]

He cut short his tour of Asia because President Truman had asked Congress to reconvene on November 17 to consider a request for $642 million in stopgap aid to Europe. Wasting no time, congressional committees began aid hearings on November 10, with Secretary of State George Marshall, Secretary of Commerce Averell Harriman, and Lewis Douglas, U.S. ambassador to Great Britain and special liaison officer for the Marshall Plan, presenting the case for a specific emergency request of some $600 million to aid France, Italy, and Austria through March 1948. Although the Truman administration differentiated between this interim aid and the Marshall Plan, Marshall told the Senate Foreign Relations Committee that the three countries could not survive beyond January without U.S. help and that without such assistance, the Marshall Plan would be finished before Congress had the opportunity to consider it. Marshall emphasized the Cold War in his presentation, stating that interim aid was necessary to prevent the Iron Curtain from moving west.[27] A major sticking point was the question of aid to China which Vandenberg, at the urging of Judd and others, was determined would be included in the Marshall Plan. Pressed hard and needing the interim aid without delay, Secretary Marshall promised to submit an assistance program to China. The Senate committee unanimously approved interim aid and sent the measure to the full Senate, which overwhelmingly approved the bill on December 1. The next day, the House Foreign Affairs Committee reported out its version of interim aid, which included $60 million for China (a result of Judd's intervention) and a total authorization of $590 million. House opposition to the assistance came from Midwest isolationists and Southern Democrats as well as farm state Republicans who attempted to prohibit the shipment of goods in short domestic supply such as grain, fertilizer, fuel, and farm machinery. However, Europeans were in desperate need of precisely such materials and goods. In floor debate, Judd urged passage on the basis of concern for the national defense of the United States and to give the people of Europe "the opportunity to build up their recuperative forces." John Davis Lodge (R-Conn.) conceded that the aid program could be called intervention but asked, "For what purpose do we intervene? We intervene not to impose our will on others, but to save others from domination. We intervene in the cause of freedom. We intervene in the cause of peace."[28]

The growing frustration of partisan Republicans who cared little about the fate of Europe but a great deal about the future of the Republican party, particularly in 1948, was expressed by majority leader Charlie Halleck of Indiana, who unleashed a bitter attack on the Truman administration's foreign policy, charging: "We would not now be called upon to appropriate huge funds for Western Europe and China three years after the war if New Deal administrations had not made very serious mistakes in our country's foreign relations. . . . Deals made at Yalta and Teheran and elsewhere now plague us . . . having the result of boosting prices and increasing discomfort at home."[29]

Like his fellow Republican Vandenberg in the Senate, Judd did not join in the Democrat-bashing, choosing to help build a bipartisan coalition in support of foreign aid for Western Europe and China because he believed such aid to be in the national interest of the United States. He knew, as did Vandenberg, that humanitarian considerations alone would not persuade a majority of Congress to approve the expenditure of billions of dollars for foreign assistance, no matter how critical the situation in Britain, France or China. He carefully explained his amendment providing $60 million in Chinese aid to skeptical colleagues. He pointed out that the figure was based on an estimate by Marshall that the United States should provide some $300 million over fifteen months to help China "meet her balance of payments, get essential imports and stay further deterioration of her economy." The $60 million was in effect interim aid for China, to be used during the first three months of 1948 "until [the Marshall Plan] is presented by the State Department and approved" by Congress. He conceded that inflation in China was rampant, the government was "crooked" by U.S. standards, the situation was so desperate that it might well be too late, but "the alternative, to abandon China and let it come under the Communists by default, will cost us so much more and will mean such a threat to our security in the Pacific that I believe we have got to take that risk."

His primary concern was not, he insisted, "what will happen to the Chinese if the Communists succeed in capturing the Government, much as I shall suffer with them in their enslavement. . . . they will survive . . . *Within 25 or 50 years, the Chinese people will vomit up communism, I am sure*" (emphasis added). What worried him most was what would happen to the United States if China fell to the communists and Russia had satellites "all along her Asiatic borders" and could "concentrate all her efforts" on "infiltrating and undermining the free governments of Europe." If that were to happen, he warned, the Marshall Plan "could have no hope of success." He concluded, echoing the language that he used when explaining why he was going to China as a missionary: "It is not because I care less for our own country's interests and for free Europe, but because I care more for them that I feel we must make every effort to support the Government and people of China in this dark hour."[30]

In this statement Judd revealed his special abilities as pragmatic politician, prophet (today, some forty years later, China is "vomiting up" Maoism) and strategic analyst (the Korean War began barely six months after Mao Tse-tung came to power). In the heat of the debate and because he spoke so fast, it is unlikely that every member understood fully his prophetic analysis, but they got the basic message: because America now lived in an interdependent world, she had to be as concerned about what happened in Europe and in Asia as she was about events in New Jersey, Ohio, and California. Not everyone accepted his rationale: the *Washington Post,* in an editorial titled "China's Judd," argued that aid to China would "adulterate interim aid to Europe," only one out of ten soldiers in the Chinese communist armies was a communist, the real communist threat was in Europe not Asia, and "the first principle of strategy is to meet the danger where we are most vulnerable."[31]

Congress chose to listen to Walter Judd, not the *Washington Post.* Amendments to limit certain goods and to reduce the authorization by $300 million being defeated, interim aid for Europe and China was approved by the House by voice vote on December 11. A major factor in the rejection of the crippling amendments and final passage was the attitude of the several hundred members of Congress who had visited Europe that summer and had seen how perilous the situation was and how critically needed U.S. aid was. Republicans in this group declined to follow Halleck and stopped their partisanship at the water's edge; in so acting, they saved Western Europe from going under in that terrible winter of 1947–1948 and placed one more nail in the coffin of Republican isolationism. They also made a commitment to helping China, and helped prepare the way for one of the most controversial questions of the post-World War II period: Who lost China?

Amid the sound and fury of the congressional debate about foreign aid, Judd quietly introduced a bill to remove all racial discrimination from America's naturalization and immigration laws; it was a logical extension of his earlier successful effort to remove discriminatory clauses against the Chinese. He explained that his legislation would place "all people in the world on an equal footing in their ability to become citizens of the United States"; it would extend but not change the quota law. He offered the example of Sadeo Munemori, a member of the all-Japanese-American 442nd Regimental Combat Team, who died a hero's death in Italy in World War II and posthumously received the Congressional Medal of Honor. When his mother applied to become an American citizen, she was turned down because under existing law "you and all persons of your race are ineligible for citizenship, no matter what your personal attainments or your demonstrated loyalty and devotion to the United States and its ideals." Judd asked: "What then is the measure of citizenship? What further price must Mrs. Munemori pay to prove her worth?" He said that the United States was engaged in "one of the world's most hopeful projects—that of helping the Japanese people to learn the meaning and the practice of democracy." He argued that the Congress could greatly serve American interests by "removing the stigma contained in our exclusion laws. We have done this for the Chinese, the Filipinos and the people of India. There is but a short distance to go to complete the task once and for all."[32] Coming so soon after the war and with the memory of Pearl Harbor, Bataan, Iwo Jima, and Okinawa still fresh in the minds of many, his bill was not immediately endorsed, but five years later its essential wisdom was accepted with its inclusion in the Immigration and Naturalization Act of 1952.

The congressional hearings on the Marshall Plan were historic in several ways: they were the first full public examination of the principles and practices of U.S. foreign aid; they were the first broad debate over the new role of the United States, defined by the Truman Doctrine, as protector of freedom around the world; they marked the beginning of the last serious attempt of America's isolationists to abort the new internationalist policy of the United States; and they introduced several major elements of future U.S. defense policy, including the establishment of overseas strategic bases and operational activities of the Central Intelligence Agency.

The House Committee on Foreign Affairs began public hearings on January 12, 1948, and before it was through heard 25 spokesmen for the Truman administration and received testimony, most of it oral, from over 150 private citizens, producing an official record of 2,269 pages. "The House Committee," stated executive director Boyd Crawford, "was willing to hear all who wanted to be heard."[33] The hearings turned service on a House committee which had been ignored and scorned into a sought-after assignment and a means to national prominence and influence. The Committee flexed its muscles during the major national debate over U.S. policy toward China. Many members of Congress, not just Walter Judd, were upset by the failure of the Truman administration to submit a program of military and economic aid for Nationalist China, under heavy and continuing attack by the Chinese communists. In February 1948, the White House finally submitted a program of $570 million in economic aid to China, to be disbursed over fifteen months. However, the House Foreign Affairs Committee, led by Judd, decided to earmark $150 million to support a policy of military assistance to China, similar to U.S. policy in Greece. In so doing, the committee deliberately initiated a foreign policy at odds with the executive branch for the first time in its history. It must be added that the committee's action helped establish a precedent for today's often intrusive micromanagement of foreign policy by Congress; the difference is that the Congress of the late 1940s managed foreign policy rarely and prudently; the Congress of the late 1980s managed foreign policy frequently and often recklessly.

Secretary of State Marshall was the first witness before the committee in its Marshall Plan hearings. Before he departed, he and Congressman Judd engaged in a long colloquy about U.S.-China relations, the most telling exchange dealing with the probable future of China if it should not receive U.S. aid.

JUDD: Would you say that without American help there is grave danger of a collapse of the Chinese Government in the next few months or a year or so?

SECRETARY MARSHALL: I would say that deterioration is dangerously rapid now. Unless something is done to halt it, it can rapidly run away and bring about the fall of the Chinese government. . . .

JUDD: If the present Chinese Government were to collapse or disintegrate, China, or large parts of it would almost certainly be taken over and organized by the Communists?

SECRETARY MARSHALL: That would appear to be the case in North China, particularly. . . .

JUDD: If North China and Manchuria should be taken over and organized by the Communists, do you think our position in Korea would long be tenable?

SECRETARY MARSHALL: I think it would not be tenable. . . .

JUDD: Do you think that Japan can ever become self-sufficient or long remain secure, if the continent of East Asia north of the Yangtze is controlled by Communists?

SECRETARY MARSHALL: That would present a great problem, for Japan to take care of herself without help from the outside.

JUDD: We would be faced with withdrawal from Japan and abandonment of the western Pacific or else almost endless subsidies of Japan and military support as well as economic?

SECRETARY MARSHALL: There is no question but what we would be faced with a very serious situation in Japan.[34]

At the political level, Judd was trying (with good results) to get Secretary Marshall to admit that without U.S. aid, the Nationalist government would fall and China would be "taken over" by the communists. On a more fundamental level, he was using his "China is the key to Asia" analogy: for him, China was literally the "middle kingdom," the palm of Asia, from which all other Asian nations—Korea, Japan, the Philippines, Vietnam, Laos, Cambodia, Thailand, Indonesia, Malaya, Burma, even India—extended like fingers. They were so joined, geographically and historically, that the future of all were involved in the future of one—China. If China were at peace and under a government that truly represented the culture, traditions, and interests of the Chinese people, then Korea, Japan, the Philippines, Vietnam, and all the other Asian nations would enjoy peace and security. But if China were at war or under a government that sought to impose an alien imperialist philosophy on the Chinese people, then the rest of Asia would be plunged into war or was in danger of falling victim to the same imperialism. To put it more simply,

Judd believed that if China fell to the communists, much if not all of Asia would suffer the same fate—and that, most assuredly, was not in the national interest of the United States.

Using its new legislative clout, the House Committee on Foreign Affairs insisted on amending the foreign aid bill beyond the lines drawn by the Senate Committee on Foreign Relations. The House Committee reported an omnibus measure of $5.3 billion of economic aid to Europe, $275 million of military aid to Greece and Turkey, $420 million of economic and $150 million of military aid to China, and $60 million for the International Children's Fund. It also limited the authorization for any appropriation to one year and tightened U.S. control over exports to Western European countries that traded with Eastern Europe; members did not want the U.S. taxpayer's money winding up in the pockets of communists behind the Iron Curtain. The stage was set for debate in and between the two Houses about this radically new direction in U.S. foreign policy.

But first the Soviets again demonstrated their contempt for freedom and democracy as well as their indifference to the proceedings of the U.S. Congress by seizing power in Czechoslovakia by means of a military coup. With the Soviet army poised on the border, communist "action committees" roamed the country, suppressing all political opposition. Communist Premier Klement Gottwald formed a new cabinet, and the Czechoslovak Republic, which from its birth at the end of World War I had been a symbol of successful democracy in Central Europe, was transformed overnight into a communist satellite. The Czech coup shocked the west from Paris to London to Washington: it was the first Soviet seizure by force of a free popular government. In the eyes of most westerners, it cast a new and frightening light "upon the power, ferocity and scope of communist aggression," and as much as any other single event, locked the United States and the Soviet Union in a Cold War stretching into the 1980s.[35]

In a pessimistic letter to a constituent shortly before the Czech coup, Judd predicted that Czechoslovakia would shortly "come under the Iron Curtain," based upon his trip to Eastern Europe the previous fall and his reading of current Soviet actions. "At least fifty million people in Eastern Europe," he wrote, "who wanted to be on our side are now having their resources and their labor used to build up [the Soviet Union] which is determined to destroy almost everything that we believe in and stand for." He blamed their fate on U.S. policy at the end of the war and since which maintained "the fiction that the Russian Communists are merely Jeffersonian Democrats and ... men of integrity, instead of the opposite," as they have repeatedly demonstrated. He admitted that he had almost given up hope "until the American people decide at the polls on a change in those who run our foreign policy."[36]

Ironically, the man responsible for U.S. foreign policy shared Judd's deepening concern about Europe. Disturbed by the communist takeover of Czechoslovakia, shaken by a telegram from Gen. Lucius Clay in Berlin about the possibility of war, and eager to capitalize on Senate passage of the Marshall Plan, President Truman addressed a joint session of Congress on March 17, with his primary target the House of Representatives. Truman said that "rapid changes are taking place in Europe which affect our foreign policy and our national security." He asked Congress to restore the draft, approve universal military training, and quickly pass the Economic Cooperation Act of 1948, the official name for the Marshall Plan. As if he had been reading Judd's correspondence, the president accused the Soviet Union and its agents of having "destroyed the independence and democratic character of a whole series of nations in Eastern and Central Europe. It is this ruthless course of action, and the clear design to extend it to the remaining free nations of Europe, that have brought about the critical situation in Europe today." It was tough talk, but at a White House staff meeting the day before, Truman declared that the country would be "sunk" if Congress did not act in the face of Soviet expansion and the spread of communism. He acknowledged that Secretary Marshall feared he might "pull the trigger" by his action, but said, in his typically pugnacious way, that if war was to occur, it was better that the people and the Congress should be warned in advance than that it should break open unexpectedly as it did in 1941.[37]

March 17, 1948, was a doubly important day in the development of the Cold War because Great Britain, France, Belgium, the Netherlands, and Luxembourg signed a fifty-year collective defense treaty in Brussels, preparing the way for NATO. In his speech to Congress, Truman praised the Brussels treaty, saying, "This development deserves our full support. I am confident that the United States will, by appropriate means, extend to the free nations the support which the situation requires. I am sure that the determination of the free countries of Europe to protect themselves will be matched by an equal determination on our part to help them to do so." Several Republican congressmen rejected the president's call "to back the will to peace with the strength for peace." What alarmed them the most was not European economic assistance but the proposed restoration of the draft and the approval of universal military training, measures which conjured up images of World War II—and World War III.[38] Truman's strong anticommunist rhetoric alienated rather than mobilized many members and gave partisan Republicans the opportunity to accuse the president of creating a wartime mood.

It was in this strained atmosphere, filled with crisis and uncertainty, that the House began debate of the Foreign Assistance Act of 1948. John Vorys of Ohio served as floor leader, along with Chris Herter of Massachusetts, Judd's closest friend in Congress. Echoing the president's rhetoric, Herter emphasized the anticommunist thrust of the bill. He argued that the fierce communist opposition to the Economic Recovery Program "indicates clearly the wholesome fear which communism has with respect to its eventual success."[39] Vorys then asked Judd to explain Titles III and IV, which provided $150 million of military aid and $420 million of economic aid to China.

Judd argued that the Marshall Plan was in fact not just one but two sets of calculated risks: first, if the United States did not provide a program of assistance to the nations of Western Europe, they would surely "go down one by one," whereas if the European Recovery Program were implemented, there was "a good chance" that they would be saved and freedom would be preserved. In short, he said, "if we do not give aid, there is no hope. If we do give aid, there is some hope."

The second calculated risk was that "we may not be able to carry out this program without gravely weakening the economy of the United States." Among the pitfalls were "the necessity to export materials and commodities already in short supply, [and] the increase in inflationary pressures that will raise prices and reduce our standard of living." But the long-range gain for the nation's security, he said, was worth the short-run risk to the nation's economy. If the Marshall Plan succeeded in increasing the economic and political strength of Europe's free countries, as it was supposed to, it would "reduce the strain on us for building even greater armaments, and will expand the area with which we can trade in the future."[40]

He was arguing that the Marshall Plan should be approved by the House because it was idealistic *and* realistic, the two essentials of every successful U.S. foreign policy. It was idealistic in declaring that it was America's duty to help its World War II allies, now brought so low; it was realistic in seeing that foreign aid today would help create markets for American goods and services tomorrow. Judd understood that as no other people on earth, Americans liked to do good if it meant they would also do well.

But aid for Europe alone was not sufficient. "The crucial question of the twentieth century will be this: Which way will the people of Asia go?" You could not say, he argued, that saving Europe was more important than saving Asia or the reverse. "We must hold both to hold either. It is the same as when a man has gangrene in both feet. It is not enough to take care of one foot. We have to stop the spread of communist gangrene in the foot in Asia as well as in the foot in Asia. . . . [And] to save Asia, China must be kept free." He quoted from Gen. Douglas MacArthur's telegram to the House Committee on Foreign Affairs:

> I can say without the slightest hesitation that a free, independent, peaceful and friendly China is of profound importance to the peace of the world and to the position of the United States. It is the fundamental keystone to the Pacific arch. Underlying all issues in China is now the military problem. Until it is resolved little progress can be expected toward internal rehabilitation regardless of the extent of outside aid. Once it is resolved, however, there is little doubt but that China's traditional resiliency will provide the basis for rapid recovery to relative stability. . . .[41]

When challenged by Congressman Hugh Scott of Pennsylvania to show how "a combination of economic and military aid can be made workable" (Scott favored the former but not the latter), Judd replied that unless there was U.S. military assistance to help China "push back the Communist threat," U.S. economic aid to China would be "operation rat hole." He pointed out that the United States had provided the Nationalist government with Springfield rifles during and after the war but from July 1946 until "just recently" had refused to send any ammunition for the rifles. This in effect disarmed the Chinese, who could make ammunition only for their old-style rifles. While it was true that some 120 million rounds of ammunition had been approved for delivery in the summer of 1947, they had only been actually released with a presidential order dated March 4, 1948, "after 8 or 9 months of fateful delay. . . . Is it reasonable," asked Judd, "for us to condemn the Chinese because they cannot fight without supplies?"

In conclusion, Judd compared China and Greece, arguing that the situations and the solutions were almost identical. Both Greece and China were keystone nations in their region, both were threatened by communists, and both needed military and economic assistance. "Let us be done," he urged, "with this business of appearing to help, without really helping." The choice, he said, was not between "helping the present government or something better. I wish it were. Our only choice is between helping the present government or allowing it to go down and having China become a Soviet satellite."[42]

With the backing of the chairmen of the House Foreign Affairs Committee and the Senate Foreign Relations Committee, Judd and others who shared his views about the importance of Asia succeeded in obtaining $338 million in economic assistance for China in the final version of the foreign aid bill, with another $125 million to be spent at the president's discretion. However, aid to China was placed under a separate title and was not included with aid to Greece which would have created the impression (which Judd earnestly desired) that the United States was as committed to the defense and rehabilitation of China as it was to Greece. Nevertheless, the legislation did create the Joint Commission on Rural Reconstruction (JCRR) in China, which had responsibility not only for land reform but education, housing, health, and highways, "the whole pattern of development."

The JCRR legislation was the creation of Judd, who drew several of his ideas from Jimmy Yen; he insisted that the commission have three Chinese and two U.S. directors over the objections of several colleagues who wanted an American majority. "The Chinese knew," he explained, "what was needed and the rate at which they could go. Our people knew the rate at which we could give." President Truman telephoned Judd and after complaining about "the goddamn China aid act you put in there," asked him to suggest names for the American commissioners. Judd recommended Raymond Moyer, a distinguished agricultural expert who had lived in China, and John Earl Baker, who had worked with the Chinese government in the 1920s and had administered the building of the first modern rural highway in China. Because it was important that the Chinese appoint men of similar stature, Judd telephoned Madame Chiang from a House committee room, with several other members present, to urge her to name Yen, who enjoyed the support of prominent Americans like Henry Luce and Dewitt Wallace, as well as the most prominent Chinese leader possible as chairman. They settled on Dr. Chiang Mon-lin, president of Southeastern University in Nanking; his appointment "was a ten-strike." The JCRR was based on the principle of horizontal relations between donor and donee—not the vertical relations that characterize so much of U.S. aid.

"Not once," said Judd, in all the years of the JCRR, was there "a major clash" between the two Americans and the three Chinese. Paul Hoffman, the first administrator of the Marshall Plan, later asserted that the communists might not have won in China if the work of the Joint Commission on Rural Reconstruction had been started a year or two earlier on the mainland.[43]

On April 2, both Houses accepted the conference report without change, the House voting 317 to 75 for the European Recovery Program, and the Senate approving the measure on a voice vote. In Judd's words, the Eightieth Congress "turned the United States around," from a predominantly isolationist country to one working as hard to keep the peace as it had to win the war.

By passing the Truman Doctrine, a rite of national passage by which the once-isolationist United States became the leader of the noncommunist world; the Marshall Plan, which committed the United States to a policy of economic and political solidarity with other nations; and the Vandenberg Resolution, which instituted the principle of transoceanic military alliances in peacetime and laid the foundation for the North Atlantic Treaty Organization (NATO), the Eightieth Congress established a record in the field of foreign policy which has never been equaled by any other Congress.

In the late winter of 1947, politics was not the only thing on Walter Judd's mind. Just before House consideration of the Marshall Plan began, he was returning to Washington on a train and idly ran his finger along his upper lip. One little section was numb. "My first reaction," he remembered, "was, 'I've got leprosy.' I'd been exposed to plenty of it in south China, more than 16 years before, and the normal incubation period is 15 to 18 years." But as the numb area grew rapidly into a nodule, he thought by March that it was another and more serious malignancy. "It was so dangerous that one of the doctors at the Mayo Clinic told me, 'When I saw that, I kissed you off.' Luckily, it was on my upper lip. If it had been on my lower lip it would have extended faster and I'd have been a dead duck." The surgeons removed a piece of lip about the size of a Lima bean. There was no cure, only a constant scrutiny that led to the removal of at least six to ten growths from Judd's face every year.[44]

CHAPTER ELEVEN

◆

Politics at Home and Abroad

PRESIDENTIAL POLITICS was what most Republicans were concentrating on in the summer of 1948, and they confidently nominated Governor Thomas Dewey of New York and Governor Earl Warren of California to their 1948 national ticket and settled back to watch a dispirited and divided Democratic party convene in Philadelphia. Judd was not so sanguine about the fall election and had in fact placed in nomination for president a man whom he admired enormously, the former governor of Minnesota, Harold E. Stassen. Stassen was a man of intellect, charisma, and experience, a man who had won Republican primaries in Wisconsin, Nebraska, West Virginia, and Pennsylvania and received more popular votes than Dewey. Although he became a political joke in later years, Stassen was at the peak of his career in 1948, a serious presidential possibility who attracted Judd and other Republicans because he appealed to independents, farmers, veterans, and "the 6 million young men and women who this year are casting their first Presidential ballot." Among a very small number of politicians and pundits, Judd declared that "the 1948 election is not in the bag" and that the sixty million American voters were "reserving their decision."[1] But the GOP delegates were not in a mood for warnings; they were agreed, along with pollster George Gallup, that Dewey and Warren were a sure thing.

Indeed, Democratic prospects were exceedingly dim. Truman's approval rating had sunk to the mid-thirties. Public dissatisfaction with the course of the economy was rising. The Democrats faced rebellion on the left and on the right. Political observers estimated that the Progressive party ticket of Henry Wallace and Senator Glen Taylor would draw several million votes, certainly enough to cost Truman the state of New York. At the Democratic convention, after the Dixiecrats narrowly lost a roll call on a strong civil rights plank, they walked out, signaling a probable loss of the Deep South in November. When Truman stepped to the podium at nearly 2 A.M. on Thursday, July 15 (in these long-ago and faraway times, the political parties and not the television networks controlled the program), a weary and anxious crowd awaited him. Within a few minutes, the combative, confident Truman electrified the convention by predicting that he and vice presidential nominee Alben Barkley would win in November, castigating the Republicans for killing a series of needed domestic programs which he had proposed, and announcing that he was calling Congress back into a special session to give them the opportunity to pass "some of these laws they say they are for in their platform."[2] Editorial comment was highly critical about the special session, but the president's attack focused everyone's attention on the target that he and his advisers had shrewdly chosen—the Eightieth Congress.

The proceedings of the special session exceeded the fondest dreams of the White House, lasting twelve days, six of them in a filibuster conducted by Southern Democrats against Senate consideration of an anti-poll tax. Congress grudgingly passed a $65 million loan to the United Nations for its headquarters building (which Judd supported), a limited curb on consumer credit, and a housing bill that omitted any funds for slum clearance or low-cost public housing. That was all. Senator Robert Taft of Ohio, who dominated Senate Republicans, refused to cooperate any further, declaring that in calling the special session, Truman had abused his powers, and that his shopping list, which included an increase in the minimum wage, extension of Social Security, and inflation control, should be ignored. A concerned Vandenberg tried to reason with the adamant Taft: "Bob, I think we ought to do something. We ought to do whatever we can to show that we are trying to use the two weeks as best we can. Then we have a better case to take before the public." A fellow Republican remembers Taft responding: "No, we're not going to give that fellow anything."[3]

In a letter to a constituent after the special session ended, Judd explained that he opposed expanded public housing, at this time, because of commitments already made to other federal programs such as veterans benefits, national defense, the European Recovery Program, wage increases for postal and federal employees, and an increase in Social Security payments. "Excepting defeat in war," he wrote, "the worst thing that can possibly happen to this country and every one in it is to have runaway inflation and the soundness of our currency endangered. The most urgent need is to put out the fire [of inflation] and it is not possible to do that by pouring gasoline on it, which is what the second half of the President's request [calling for more public housing and federal aid to education] would do." In response to the president's charge that the Eightieth Congress was a "do-nothing" Congress, Judd said: "It is precisely because we do care about those hardships [the people face] that we must have the courage, like any wise and sound physician, to stick to the only kind of remedies which will ultimately remove the causes, not just treat the symptoms. . . . I cannot vote for any measures which I am convinced will not work, and in fact are likely to do grave damage to the country."[4]

A majority of the voters of Minneapolis accepted Judd's prescription and re-elected him to Congress in November. Writing to one of the twelve hundred volunteers who worked in the city's precincts and wards, he lamented the fact that Dewey, who "had as much ammunition as any candidate for President ever had," did not use it because "he was so sure that the election was in the bag." The key to victory, he stated, did not lie in trying to surpass the Democrats "in their kind of program" but in presenting "a sounder program . . . adequately and convincingly."[5] Although his fellow Republicans had not listened, Judd had warned them at their national convention that it was possible to lose the presidential election. Many now remembered and reflected on his advice as well as that of other Republican leaders sorting through the electoral returns for clues as to why they lost. A consensus began to emerge: next time, Republicans would nominate and run a man who had wide public appeal beyond the Republican Party, who was a demonstrated national leader, who could overcome the initial numerical advantage of the Democrats. Political philosophy and ideology would not be as important as one simple question: Could he win the election? The search became an obsession in the next four years and led the Grand Old Party to make new alliances and break old commitments in the pursuit of victory.

For Judd, 1948 was also the year that he became directly involved with Alger Hiss. His experiences in South China in the late 1920s, when

158

he had been a semiprisoner of the Chinese communists and had seen what happened to people under them, had made him an anticommunist. His anticommunism grew deeper and stronger as he witnessed the Soviet Union's calculated efforts in the post-World War II period to spread its sphere of influence across all of Europe. When he learned firsthand of communist attempts at subversion and espionage in the United States, anticommunism became the central crusade of his life. In 1947, the Republican majority set up a subcommittee of the Government Operations Committee to investigate personnel in the State Department. The subcommittee, of which Judd was a member, removed 134 security risks from the department without a single headline or any publicity; all but ten resigned voluntarily when they learned they were being investigated. In the course of the committee's work, Judd ran across Hiss's name and contacted Whittaker Chambers, then with *Time,* who candidly described his years as a communist in the 1930s. Among the communists whom Chambers said he worked with and received information from was Alger Hiss.

On March 1, 1948, Judd wrote a cautionary letter about Hiss to an old friend who was the chairman of the board of the Carnegie Endowment for International Peace, John Foster Dulles; he had first met Dulles in 1944 when he was a special assistant to Secretary of State Cordell Hull. It was widely reported that Hiss was going to be named the new president of the Carnegie Endowment, and Judd felt compelled to counsel his friend and fellow Republican. He recounted the Chambers-Hiss connection, without mentioning Chambers's name, and the existence of an FBI file on Hiss; he added that Adolph Berle had been given the story about Hiss as early as 1939 and would be able to provide more details. However, when Judd saw Dulles soon after in the Capitol, the foundation head said that Hiss had "denied any connection with the Communists." Dulles subsequently wrote Judd that Hiss acknowledged some of his associates in the Department of Agriculture in the 1930s may have been "fellow travelers," and that some labor people whom he worked with when he first came to New York "may have been, or may have become, Communists," but that he "categorically denies any connection with, or sympathy for, Communism."

There the matter rested until early August when Judd came to New York at Dulles's invitation to discuss the Dewey campaign. While talking with John Foster and Allen Dulles in the Roosevelt Hotel, "Foster was called to the telephone in the next room and came back and said to Allen, 'Go out and see what you can find out on that.'" That very morning, Whittaker Chambers had named Alger Hiss as a fellow communist conspirator in the 1930s and Hiss denied it categorically. Judd warned Dulles: "It's going to come down around your ears."[6] Within the week, Hiss appeared before the House Committee on Un-American Activities to deny, under oath, the charges that Chambers had made. Judd was present at the hearing at the suggestion of the acting chairman, Karl Mundt of South Dakota, who had asked him to draft some questions about the United Nations and China to be asked of Hiss. Judd sat next to a young Republican congressman from California, Richard Nixon, and listened attentively as Mundt interrogated the witness: Did Hiss have anything to do with the drafting of the United Nations Charter? Back came the arrogant reply: "Yes, with some modesty, I can say I contributed to or participated in the drafting." Did he have anything to do with the drafting of Article 27 [granting veto power to any member of the Security Council]? Again, he replied, "Yes," adding that the draft had been sent by President Roosevelt to both Soviet Premier Stalin and British Prime Minister Churchill prior to the Yalta Conference and had been adopted, in that form, at Yalta. "The world thought," explained Judd, that the U.N. Charter "was being drafted in San Francisco" in June 1945. "But actually this communist agent had drafted it and then Roosevelt took it and presented it to Stalin, who said, 'Well, if you want it, I'll agree to it.' That's how they got the mechanism that gave them control in the United Nations."[7]

Hiss denied ever having heard the name Whittaker Chambers and said when shown a photograph of him: "He looks like a lot of people. I might even mistake him for the Chairman of this Committee." (Both Mundt and Chambers were middle-aged, jowly, and heavy-set.) But Nixon noted that Hiss was careful never to state without qualification that he did not know Whittaker Chambers; he used phrases like, "to the best of my recollection." Once, when Hiss hesitated in an answer, Nixon turned to Judd and said: "He's squirming. Look at him squirm." The Californian saw a contradiction between Hiss's ease and poise when talking about advising presidents and prime ministers and his equivocation when discussing Chambers. "Nixon's career began that morning," said Judd. "Nixon was smart. He saw the guy was hiding something."[8]

Judd also discovered that Hiss, who had never visited China, had been a key member of the China section of the State Department from 1939 to 1944. In that position, Hiss was able to "make China policy—build up the Communists and build down our ally—by selecting the [information] he passed on to his superiors, such as the reports of Service and Davies which were overwhelmingly favorable to the Communists. . . . Then people wonder why we lost China."[9]

Despite the dramatic nature of such issues as the Marshall Plan and the activities of Alger Hiss, Judd still spent a great deal of his time on domestic matters, often pursuing, for a Republican, a liberal course. For example, the House of Representatives, after "a comprehensive study" of Social Security, had passed two bills strengthening the system, both of which he supported. One bill increased the allotment to the 3.5 million "neediest beneficiaries" but was vetoed by Truman on the grounds that it was not generous enough. A second bill placed 3.5 million new people in the system, mostly state and municipal employees and those working for nonprofit institutions; however, the Senate failed to act on the legislation before adjournment. In contrast, he told a constituent that he "resisted Federal aid to education in any form, great as are the needs for increased financial support of our schools." His reasoning was to the point: "Once the Federal government has authority to say what must *not* happen in the educational system, it has corresponding authority to say what *must* happen." Nevertheless, he did support a program of grants-in-aid to those states, about fifteen, which were making a greater-than-average effort in education but were unable to reach the average level of education expenditures because of "inadequate resources."[10] That was as far as he was willing to go.

Still, throughout the incredibly crowded and challenging year of 1948, China remained uppermost in Judd's mind; and it seemed to him, realist that he was, that its fate was increasingly bleak. Among other things, he was troubled that General Wedemeyer's report about his fact-finding trip to China in July–August 1947 had not been publicly released. During his trip, Wedemeyer had been invited by Chiang Kai-shek to address government officials and military officers, and he spoke candidly of maladministration and corruption, defects of organization, shortcomings of officials, inefficiency, and ineptitude. On his departure from China, Wedemeyer issued a public statement complaining of "apathy and lethargy, abject defeatism" and a lack of "inspirational leadership," a clear reference to Chiang.[11] All of these negatives were widely reported. But when Secretary of State Marshall read Wedemeyer's recommendations for a new program of military and economic aid to China over the next five years, including measures to stabilize the currency and the right of the Nationalists to purchase military equipment, supplies, and ammunition, he immediately suppressed the Wede-

161

meyer Report. The *China White Paper*, a mammoth apologia published in August 1949, states that the Wedemeyer Report was not made public because it contained a recommendation that the United States place Manchuria under a guardianship of five powers, including the Soviet Union, and publication of such a proposal would have been highly offensive to Chinese sensibilities about their sovereignty. But critics argue that the real reason is that the report effectively repudiated the Marshall Mission to China. Wedemeyer later argued:

> I knew that the delay in implementing my recommendations for immediate moral and material support to the Chinese Nationalist Government was serving the purpose of the Communists. The State Department knew as well as I that the situation was deteriorating rapidly, yet the hands-off attitude prevailed. . . . I feel positive today that the publication of my report would not have caused embarrassment to my Government and to the Chinese or the Koreans. If I am wrong, then it would appear that the subsequent publication of my report in the White Paper in 1949 was a serious mistake in diplomacy.[12]

By 1949, of course, it was clear that the communists were going to win, and Wedemeyer's recommendations were academic. Other experts shared his conviction that China could be saved if the United States took certain steps, not including the dispatching of U.S. troops. In his "Report on China" published in *Life* in October 1947, William C. Bullit, former U.S. ambassador to the Soviet Union, recommended the sending of American military advisers in training and operations, the immediate release of stocks of munitions by the United States to be used in Manchuria, and that American military should have direct military control of all supplies to the Nationalists.[13] In February 1948, Leighton Stuart, the U.S. ambassador to China, wrote Marshall that the situation was "definitely one to cause pessimism. [But] if American aid should materialize in adequate measure and palatable form, the tide may turn quickly in our favor." A month later, Stuart wrote, almost beseechingly: "The Chinese people do not want to become Communists yet they see the tide of Communism running irresistibly onward. In the midst of this chaos and inaction the Generalissimo stands out as the only moral force capable of action."[14] But the State Department preferred a course of watching and waiting for the Nationalist government to sink beneath the communist tide. In February 1949, Secretary of State Dean Acheson and Ambassador-at-Large Philip Jessup proposed to President Truman that military supplies then being loaded in ships in Hawaii and San Francisco for the Chiang Kai-shek government be stopped as a move toward world peace. Senator Vandenberg, ranking Republican and former chairman of the Senate Foreign Relations Committee, attended the meeting and pointed out in his diary: "If, at the very moment when Chiang's Nationalists are desperately trying to negotiate some kind of peace with the Communists, we suspend all military shipments to the Nationalists, we certainly shall make any hope of negotiated peace impossible. We shall thus virtually notify the Communists that they can consider the war ended and themselves as victors. . . . We seal China's doom."[15]

In his introduction to the *China White Paper*, Acheson piously washed his hands and laid the loss of China squarely on Chiang and his Nationalist government: "Nothing that this country did or could have done within the reasonable limits of its capabilities could have changed that result; nothing that was left undone by this country has contributed to it. It was the product of internal Chinese forces, forces which this country tried to influence but could not."[16]

Yet, as Judd pointed out, the United States did contribute decisively to the loss of China through the Yalta conference, which gave the Soviets "effective control of Manchuria" after the United States had promised the province to the Chinese at Cairo; the four cease-fires during 1946 which General Marshall forced the Nationalist Chinese to accept, thereby destroying Chinese confidence in us and "weakening decisively the morale of the [Chinese] armed forces"; the 1946–1947 embargo on ammunition for the Springfield rifles which the United States had provided China; and the "deactivation" of about 180 of Chiang's 300 divisions, "throwing their officers and men into the street, in effect leaving them little alternative except to go over to the Communists," with the inevitable demoralizing effect on the remaining divisions.[17] As critical as he was of Marshall, Judd never questioned his patriotism (as some ultraconservatives later did), describing him as "an extremely honorable, patriotic and un-self-seeking American." But he did not hesitate to fault Marshall for "stubbornly adhering" to an unwise and unsuccessful policy. He offered an explanation: "As a wise Chinese once said to me: 'A sage can always admit his mistakes; a hero, never.' "[18]

Fairbank and other supporters of U.S. policy during this critical period do not deny that Secretary Marshall's actions in 1946 and 1947 sealed the fate of China, but argue that Chiang's defeat was inevitable and that Marshall "succeeded in preventing the Americans from going into a super-Vietnam to quell the Chinese Revolution."[19] The suggestion that supporters of Nationalist China were seeking a "super-Vietnam" through which hundreds of thousands if not millions of American soldiers would be sent to China is far off the mark. What Wedemeyer, Judd, Dewey, and others concerned about U.S. interests in China and Asia wanted and urged was adequate U.S. military and economic aid to China, not American forces. They understood full well the impossibility of America winning a land war in Asia, as President Lyndon Johnson later demonstrated he did not.

In the U.S. Congress, although now a member of the minority and without the power or prestige of a subcommittee chairmanship, Judd continued to make a significant difference in the legislative decisions of the House of Representatives, often in areas far removed from U.S.-China relations. For example, in March, the House passed his amendment to the immigration and naturalization law. The amendment removed race as a bar to American citizenship. It affected about 86,000 people, more than 95 percent of them Japanese, who were admitted to the United States prior to 1924 and were denied citizenship by a law passed that year. It also gave immigration quotas to all countries and territories in the world, except those in the western hemisphere which already had no limits on immigration; all those born in a particular area or whose ancestry was at least one-half of a particular nationality were eligible to use the quota for that area—this they could not do under the 1924 law. Judd's legislation also established the principle of equality under a universal formula by quotas but prevented any "flood of immigration." "I do not know," he said on the House floor, "anything else we might do in the field of foreign relations whereby for so little we can accomplish so much."[20]

In August, the House debated the Mutual Defense Assistance Act, creating NATO, and Judd surprised his colleagues by urging Congress to authorize only half the $1.1 billion requested "until the [European] nations involved agree on genuinely unified mutual defense plans." It was the first time that he had ever supported a major cut in foreign aid. He argued that without such an inducement, Western Europe might not move toward the military cooperation "which is absolutely essential if the whole project is to increase their joint defensive strength more than it weakens ours." He had pressed for "maximum economic cooperation" in 1948 when Congress passed the Economic Recovery Program, and believed that similar cooperation was vital in the military sphere as well. His conditional support of the NATO authorization did not mean that he was halfhearted in his approval of the measure's central thrust. He declared that the North Atlantic Treaty served the national interest of the United States because it would act as a partial deterrent to the imperialist designs of the Soviet Union. While the United States' most important deterrent, he asserted, was the atomic bomb, the Russians "will someday have the bomb," and he felt the West should move promptly to strengthen its defenses when it could do so from a position of strength and not weakness. He expressed the hope that NATO would develop the "real teamwork" that would give both Western Europe and the United States security and reduce the need for the military expenditures America would have to make "if we stand alone."[21] The amendment passed the House by 209 to 151.

Meanwhile, as the communists continued to capture major city after major city in China, it was clear that the end was near for the Nationalist government. Nevertheless, Judd continued to insist that it was not too late and that "the free peoples of China now have a chance to do to the Communists what the Communists did to them before," that is, establish themselves in a remote area of the country and provide an alternative of freedom to Mao. To those who suggested that China should be written off and the United States should concentrate on saving the countries on its borders, he replied scornfully: "That is like letting the hub of a wheel be chopped out and imagining that we can save or make anything out of the individual spokes. . . . How are you going to hold the wheel together if the hub is gone?"

It is a tribute to his influence that he was able to persuade the House to approve military assistance for China and Southeast Asia to be used at the discretion of the president. In addition, about a third of the authorized economic aid to China had not been spent when the communists came sweeping down and took all the major cities of China. Let us use that money, Judd suggested in accordance with the policy outlined by Secretary of State Acheson in the *White Paper on China*, which stated: "Our policy will continue to be based upon . . . our traditional support for the Open Door and for Chinese independence and administrative and territorial integrity." Acheson also wrote: "We continue to believe that, however tragic may be the immediate future of China . . . she will throw off the foreign [i.e., Communist] yoke. I consider that we should encourage all developments in China which now and in the future work toward this end." Although the language was obviously self-serving, diplomatically and politically, Judd and other supporters of a free China used the same words in outlining how the proposed aid would be used—to "work toward the end of assisting China to throw off the foreign yoke, to retain her independence, and to regain her administrative and territorial integrity."

Ever farsighted, Judd also pointed out that helping the Nationalist Chinese "maintain an independent legal government" would enable them to keep their seat in the United Nations rather than having the seat go over to the communists, giving them "two out of five permanent seats in the Security Council." It was also important that the Nationalists "retain control of the Chinese embassies and consulates around the world," which otherwise would become centers of "Communist propaganda, intrigue, espionage, and conspiracy" aimed at the United States. His amendment, he argued, would further historic U.S. policy, as reaffirmed by Acheson in the *White Paper,* by encouraging and helping "friendly Chinese to maintain somewhere an independent Chinese Government." Judd's proposal may have seemed quixotic to State Department officials, journalists, and historians convinced that communism would prevail in China and Chiang and the Nationalists were destined for the ash heap of history. But he would not give up the fight for a free China and declared, his words pouring forth inexorably, that he and other proponents were not trying to "throw money away. We simply recognize that Communist conquest of China is a mortal peril to all Asia; and conquest of Asia constitutes a mortal peril to Europe and to the United States."[22] This was not wild rhetoric. On April 4, 1949, three days after the communists and the Nationalists began peace talks in Peking, Mao announced publicly that in the event of a third world war, the Chinese communists would side with Russia against the United States.[23]

Remaining Nationalist resistance was dealt a near-mortal blow in late April when the communists occupied Nanking. In early May, Chiang Kai-shek, who had resigned as president of the Republic of China in January but had traveled to Shanghai and other cities at considerable personal risk to encourage anticommunist opposition, left the mainland of China for Taipei, Taiwan. But he refused to surrender formally. China's greatest city, Shanghai, fell to the communists in late May. In July, Chiang flew to the Philippines. There he and President Elpidio Quirino announced a plan for an anticommunist alliance of all the independent nations in East Asia; the following month, Chiang flew to South Korea where he persuaded President Syngman Rhee to join the alliance and send a joint letter to President Quirino asking him to convene a conference at which interested nations could join the proposed union. However, when Quirino traveled to Washington soon thereafter, Secretary of State Acheson firmly opposed Chiang's anticommunist Asian alliance, and the conference was never held.[24] One may speculate whether, for example, North Korea would have invaded South Korea in 1950 if it had belonged to an Asian alliance for joint defense, like the one that the U.S. government prevented Chiang from forming.

Mao did not wait for the fall of Canton on October 15, but declared the formation of the People's Republic of China on October 1 and designated the northern city of Peking (it had been called "Peiping," or "Northern Peace" under the Nationalists) as the new capital. On October 10, 1949, a defiant Chiang said in his annual Double Ten message (his first from Taiwan) that he would continue to fight communism; in mid-November he flew to Chungking, which had not yet been captured by the communists. His plans for a last stand in the southwest—in Szechwan, Sikang, Yunnan, and Kweichow—collapsed when several top Nationalist generals defected to the communists. On December 8, the Executive Yuan voted to remove the capital of the Republic of China to Taipei.[25] Just who lost China—Chiang Kai-shek and the Chinese Nationalists, the U.S. State Department under Marshall and Acheson, or some combination thereof—immediately became a major issue in American politics and has remained a challenging question for more than forty years.

Judd's initial reaction to the *China White Paper,* which laid most if not all of the blame on the Nationalists, was relatively muted; he noted that the document was almost entirely negative, a list of excuses for "failure in China." He told the House that the American people were entitled to know what the State Department's "plans for success" in China were. He declared that on "the most important issue of this century"—the objectives and methods of the worldwide communist conspiracy—Chinese leaders "understood the nature and . . . insidious threat of that conspiracy. Our leaders did not."[26] He quoted from a *New York Times* editorial, which said that Chiang's "incompetence" was not the sole cause for the "debacle in China"; there were other large factors such as the "foreign-inspired dynamism of the Chinese Communist Party." The *Times* editorial agreed with Judd that "President Chiang's estimate of the [Chinese Communists'] aims was right and that the State Department's estimate was wrong." As for the future, said the *Times,* the United States should strive to implement the basic principles enunciated by Acheson in the *White Paper*: "the development of China as an independent nation" and the safeguarding of "basic rights and liberties in China"; and opposition to "the subjection of China to any regime acting in the interest of a foreign power." But to do that, the *Times* asserted, Acheson would have to acknowledge what the rest of the thousand-page document tried to overlook: "The Chinese Communists are by no means independent and [the] Chinese, as well as nationals of other states, cannot be described as a free people if they are under Communist rule."[27] The forceful language of the *New York Times*, then as now the leading American newspaper in the realm of foreign affairs, shows that Judd was in the middle of the political mainstream with his criticism of Truman-Acheson policy toward China.

Two weeks after the release of the *White Paper*, and after the Truman Administration expressed its opposition to the bipartisan amendment introduced by Judd and others authorizing military aid to China and Southeast Asia, Judd felt obliged to step up his criticism of the *White Paper*, which was used by the State Department as the basis for its rejection of the amendment. After pointing out that the administration had maintained an "iron curtain" on the Wedemeyer Report, he listed several other documents and facts still being withheld, including the 1945 top-secret report on the Chinese communists prepared by the Military Intelligence Service of the U.S. Army, which concluded that "the Chinese Communist movement is part of the international Communist movement, sponsored and guided by Moscow." "We have not tried to win the war in China," he said. "We have tried to end it. But the only way to end a war with communism—anywhere—is to win it."[28]

In October he released a revealing memorandum from John S. Service, while at the Chinese communist headquarters in Yenan, to General Stilwell in Burma. Dated October 10, 1944, the Service memo declared the Kuomintang leadership to be "bankrupt," "reactionary," "traitorous" (for unspecified relations with Japan), "impotent," "antiforeign," "anti-democratic," and "corrupt." Service urged that the United States do in China what it did in Yugoslavia—back the communists: "Public announcement that the President's representative [Stilwell] had made a visit to the Communist capital at Yenan would have significance that no Chinese would miss—least of all the Generalissimo."[29] The bias of the Service memorandum and similar documents angered Judd, who was deeply worried about the future of an

168

Asia in which China was not free and independent but communist and a satellite of the Soviet Union.

Just before Christmas, he wrote to the editor of the *Hartford Times* lamenting the failure of the United States "to understand the imperativeness to our security of having China in the hands of friends instead of enemies." He drew a parallel between the present and the dark days leading up to World War II, and predicted: "Just as I felt sure in the 30s that our failure to oppose effectively Japanese aggression in China was morally wrong and would lead to war, just so I have felt all this decade that our failure to give vigorous and effective moral, material and military support . . . to those resisting Communist subjugation of China will prove morally wrong and will lead to war."[30] Six months and three days later, North Korean soldiers, equipped with Soviet tanks, mortars and howitzers, and with a sympathetic communist China behind them, suddenly invaded South Korea, starting the Korean War, during which U.S. casualties totalled 142,091, including 33,629 dead. Judd was now convinced that the only way to prevent such foreign policy disasters in the future was the "complete removal or transfer of those in our government responsible for the policies of the past."[31] That meant, in turn, the selection of a presidential candidate in 1952 who would win the White House and help produce a Republican majority in the Congress. He didn't care how long the person had been a Republican or whether he had ever held public office as long as he adhered to basic Republican principles of limited government and would carry out a firm policy against America's and the free world's enemy, communism.

Judd first saw and heard Dwight D. Eisenhower up close in October 1945 when General Eisenhower addressed a group of congressmen about the importance of not bringing home "our boys" until the United States had consolidated the positions it had sacrificed so much to win. He pleaded "cogently and convincingly that day," recalled Judd, that U.S. armed forces should remain in Europe and the Pacific until the job of securing the peace was accomplished. But his counsel was not heeded. Public pressure and propaganda "were sufficient" to demobilize "pell mell" and thereby made it inevitable that a "weakened China would go down under the Communists."

The next time Judd saw General Eisenhower firsthand was at the Minnesota State Fair in September 1946, when the war hero delivered the main address to some 100,000 people. Judd sat and talked with

Eisenhower, then army chief of staff, about his future. "My strongest leaning now is toward educational work," Eisenhower said. He pointed out that he had been working with young people all his life, training them in the military, leading them into battle. He was concerned about the confusion he now saw in many of them. "We've saved our country from external enemies," he said, "but we've got to plan constructively for the long-term future against hostile forces here and abroad." He wanted to work in "the educational field" to communicate to the younger generation the values of "our country, the things that are right and good about it, the things we must conserve and strengthen."

Eisenhower was "eloquent and moving," recalled Judd, who told the general how he had given up his medical career to enter public life and further ideas that he felt were important to the future of the country. "From that time on we had a lot of camaraderie. Every time I'd see him, [Ike would] say, 'I often remember that conversation we had out in Minnesota, when I was debating whether or not to go into education.' " In fact, when he resigned from the military in 1948, Eisenhower became president of Columbia University, although still remaining on the active list of the army. That same year, leaders of both parties urged him to become a candidate for president, but he announced that as a military man, he had never belonged to either political party and could not accept the nomination for any political office. "Besides," said Judd, Eisenhower "didn't believe in the New Deal philosophy. He believed in individual self-reliance and resourcefulness."[32] In December 1950, President Truman asked Eisenhower to take over as commander in chief of NATO and to build up the military forces of the Western alliance; he returned to Europe, establishing his headquarters in Paris, but was not sure he could organize an effective NATO response to the growing nuclear and conventional threat of the Soviets.

Having visited many of Western Europe's military installations, Judd shared Eisenhower's skepticism, but he believed that with the proper support, especially from the United States, NATO could be transformed into a credible deterrent to the communists. Such a transformation was unlikely, however, if America had a secretary of state who in Judd's view was erratic and arrogant and did not understand the importance of Asia to U.S. global foreign policy, including Europe; who had a penchant for dramatic gestures when quiet diplomacy would have fared better; and who pledged public loyalty to old friends like Alger Hiss, a red flag to a passionate anticommunist like Judd.

When Acheson declared in January 1950, after Hiss was sentenced to five years in jail for committing perjury in connection with espionage, "I do not intend to turn my back on Alger Hiss," Judd responded that as a private citizen, Acheson had the right to choose as friends whomever he wished but that he was not now just an individual but secretary of state. Remembering Hiss's authorship of the Security Council's veto clause in the U.N. Charter, his presence in the China department of the State Department during World War II, and his lies to John Foster Dulles when under consideration as president of the Carnegie Endowment, Judd bluntly called for Acheson's removal: "If the Secretary of State does not intend to turn his back on ... a man, duly convicted in our courts of perjury regarding the most heinous of crimes, treason, then a responsible Congress and the people of the United States must demand that the President of the United States turn his back on Mr. Dean Acheson as his Secretary of State."[33]

The same month, in House debate about a bill to provide economic aid to the Republic of Korea, Judd again had occasion to refer to Acheson. Judd announced that he intended to vote for assistance although "Korea is not essential to our security" and its position was not tenable "whenever there is any effort by Russia or her satellites to take it." He noted that the previous week Acheson had publicly stated that neither Korea nor Formosa (Taiwan) was essential to U.S. security because they were beyond a line he drew from the Aleutians through Japan and Okinawa to the Philippines. Nevertheless, he said, although Acheson believed that Korea was literally beyond the pale and although Owen Lattimore, former State Department official and continuing adviser on Asia, had suggested that the United States should "let South Korea fall—but not to let it look as though we pushed it," he still favored the bill because the United States was "responsible for the formation of this young Republic, and we are duty bound to give it the best possible chance we can." Besides, he asked, if America walked away from South Korea, "what do you think it will do to the hearts and hopes and confidence in us of the other 700 million human beings in Asia?" Responding to Judd's logic, the House passed the Korea assistance bill. When laying out the reasons why one might oppose the bill, Judd made the following prediction: "As a result of our actions at Yalta and our inaction in China, the odds are against this young Republic and the difficulties we have helped pile up for it may prove beyond its strength—*and I am willing to predict ... that it will be overrun and our money will be lost.*"[34] Concerned about the impact of such a forecast on the struggling young nation, Judd removed it from the official *Congres-*

sional Record, but a transcript of his remarks reveals that he did predict the invasion of South Korea.

Convinced of the strategic importance of the Far East and deeply disturbed by the Truman administration's apparent inability to understand what was happening there and how it critically affected the United States, Judd proposed a China policy whose essential elements became and remained the foundation for U.S.-China relations for the next quarter of a century. Speaking at Constitution Hall on January 30, he declared: "I am not and never have been interested in any persons, groups, or parties in China. I am interested in the security of the United States of America, and in freedom, world order, and peace." He advanced the following policy:

1. The United States should accept the "real nature" of the communist movement in China—that it is not interested in agrarian reform but is "committed to dictatorship and world conquest." America should abandon the State Department line that there is "some hope in the Communists in China, and none in the [Nationalist] Chinese government" and determine "really to help the free Chinese resist those who would enslave them."

2. The United States "should not grant diplomatic recognition to the Communist regime at Peking." Such official recognition, he stated, would be tragically wrong for several reasons. It would "greatly weaken" the will to resist of the Chinese on Formosa as well as the many Chinese communities in all the countries of Southeast Asia. It would "shake the confidence in us of the peoples in Asia still on the fence. . . . If they were to witness official abandonment by the powerful United States of an ally which stood by us during the nightmare period following Pearl Harbor, could they then be expected to have any faith in our present declaration that we will resist the spread of Communist aggression beyond China and help them against Communist threats to their own independence?" In addition, recognition of Peking would put an "avowed enemy" instead of a "proved friend" in the U.N. Security Council and in Chinese embassies, legations, and consulates "all over the world."

3. The United States should "make a forthright statement of support to the Chinese [Nationalist] Government and all other anti-Communist forces in their struggle to remain free." The Chinese, he said, needed moral support, the same sort of support "we have given to the

Greeks, Italians, Turks and others in Europe" resisting being "taken over by Communists and made Soviet satellites."

4. The United States should "extend effective military aid to the defenders of Formosa." The model, he said, was the military assistance program carried out successfully in Greece, which did not include American combat troops. "I do not know anyone who has ever suggested that we should send American combat troops to Formosa or that we should occupy it with American forces, even though the State Department is busily engaged in shooting down that straw man set up by itself." Rather we should help the "Chinese and Formosans hold their island as many of our best military students believe they can do," with a "relatively small amount of munitions, equipment and supplies."

5. The United States should "continue to give economic assistance to the Chinese [Nationalist] Government on Formosa." If the United States provided such commodities as cotton and oil, "exactly as we are helping Korea and Japan," the economy of Formosa will become "reasonably stable."

6. The United States should give "every possible assistance and even leadership in encouraging the free peoples of Southeast Asia to get together in a mutual assistance defense pact, such as we have sponsored in the North Atlantic." Such a Pacific pact, he argued, would prevent the communists from picking off those countries one by one.

In a "jungle world such as ours," he said, "survival depends to no small degree on the capacity to distinguish friend from enemy." In such a situation, what the United States ought to do seemed simple: "We should oppose whatever assists our mortal enemy; we should assist whatever opposes that mortal enemy." Therefore, Judd asserted, "the first requirement of [U.S.] security in the Pacific is not a democratic Chinese Government or even a better Chinese Government, but an independent Chinese Government." European experience has taught us, he concluded, that communist expansion can be stopped only through a regional effort, through assistance to all in a given area, even though some of the governments involved may "not meet with our full approval." If we would keep Asia free, he said, "there must be a program of regional defense there also." Time was short, he warned; the United States must act to help those fighting for their freedom or it would be forced to fight later for its "own survival under the most difficult circumstances possible."[35]

Here was the outline of U.S.-China policy from 1950 until 1972: recognition that communism was the prime enemy; no diplomatic relations with mainland China; support of the Nationalists and other anti-communist governments in Asia; military aid to the Republic of China; continuation of economic assistance to Taiwan; and the creation of a mutual defense assistance pact in Asia. Judd was directly involved in the creation and implementation of every element of this policy. Economic assistance to the Republic of China on Taiwan, for example, was based initially on the work of the Joint Commission on Rural Reconstruction, his brainchild. SEATO (the Southeast Asia Treaty Organization), which was founded in 1954 during the first Eisenhower administration by Secretary of State Dulles, grew out of Judd's suggested Pacific Pact (which he first proposed during the Eightieth Congress). No other member of Congress of either party had more lasting impact on the relations between the most powerful nation in the world and the most populous nation in the world than Walter Judd, a remarkable accomplishment when one considers that he never held the chairmanship of a congressional committee and was a member of the majority for only four of his twenty years in Congress.

In addition to his pivotal role in U.S.-China relations, Judd led the group of Republican congressmen who brought their once-isolationist party into the interdependent postwar world. For example, he consistently supported the Point IV program—technical assistance to and the encouragement of private investment in underdeveloped areas of the world. Bipartisan recognition of his efforts came in May 1950, when he was appointed by Speaker Sam Rayburn to represent the House of Representatives at the World Health Assembly, held in Geneva, Switzerland. In a special radio broadcast to the United States from Geneva, he described the work of the delegations from the sixty-one countries represented, all of whom realized, he said, that "health, like peace, is indivisible and that many problems of public health are no longer merely national." He reported that WHO (World Health Organization) was giving top priority in its field operations to combating malaria, tuberculosis, and venereal diseases, pointing out that malaria "kills about 3 million people a year" and "strikes 300 million more. . . . Yet with DDT and other methods, malaria can be effectively controlled." Tuberculosis was no less a scourge, killing about five million people a year and afflicting another fifty million. In response, "WHO teams in association with International Children's Emergency Fund workers have vaccinated about 10 million children against [TB], mostly in the war-devastated areas of Europe." In the field of venereal disease, the WHO was training people in the use of penicillin and other new drugs. However, the annual WHO budget was only $7.3 million "for the whole world," and its financial problems were made worse by the refusal of the Soviet Union and its satellites to pay their share, cutting the budget by some 15 percent. Judd proposed that in view of the vital work WHO was doing that the funding ceiling of $1.92 million imposed by the Congress be raised to $3 million a year.[36] He successfully fended off attacks and amendments by some of the most skillful budget cutters in Congress, and a majority of the House agreed with him that the money was well invested and approved additional WHO funds.

When North Korean forces invaded South Korea on June 25, 1950, Judd immediately urged the United Nations to condemn "such naked aggression and flagrant violation" of its charter and the United States to make "our full strength available for carrying out [the U.N.'s] decisions." On June 27, President Truman also condemned North Korea's aggression and ordered U.S. air and sea forces to give South Korean troops "cover and support." Acknowledging that communism had added "armed invasion and war" to its tactics "to conquer independent nations," Truman declared that the occupation of Formosa by communist forces would be a "direct threat to the security of the Pacific area and to United States forces." He therefore ordered the Seventh Fleet to "prevent any attack on Formosa," an order that laid the foundation for the subsequent Mutual Defense Treaty between the United States and the Republic of China. At the same time, Truman banned Chiang Kai-shek from attempting any offensive against Communist China with these unequivocal words: "I am calling upon the Chinese Government on Formosa to cease all air and sea operations against the mainland. The Seventh Fleet will see that this is done." From this moment on, any hope that Chiang had of recovering the mainland had to be based on political rather than military efforts. In the same statement, Truman also stepped up military assistance to the French in Indochina and to U.S. forces in the Philippines.

Judd publicly praised Truman's action as "honorable" and having "some chance . . . of stopping this and further Communist aggressions in Asia." But privately he wrote that those presently in charge of our foreign policies "had steadfastly retreated all these years in Asia" and had placed the United States and its allies "down on our own five yard line." As early as 1946, after visiting Korea, he had urged the building up of South Korean forces to match the well-known buildup of communist forces in North Korea by the Soviets. In 1949 and in the first part of 1950, he tried to get the Truman administration to keep a U.S. military presence in South Korea and to "send effective military aid along with economic assistance" to that new nation. Unfortunately, his counsel was not heeded, and the result was "the needless tragedy in which we find ourselves and out of which we must fight."[37]

In the face of communist aggression in Korea and elsewhere, the free world had no choice, as the *New York Times* stated, but to build up its own armed strength to the point "which will enable it both to deter Russia from going to war and to nip in the bud or crush by overwhelming force any aggression by Soviet satellites acting as Moscow's cat's-paws." After President Truman sent a strong message about the Korean conflict to Congress, motivated in large part by the political fear of "losing" Korea so soon after China, Judd rejected partisanship and responded that because the administration was no longer following "negative and defeatist policies," he felt more optimistic about the future than at any time since the fall of 1945. "There is hope," he said, "when we start moving forward, no matter how long and hard the task of retrieving the positions of strength inexcusably abandoned or bartered away. There was no hope as long as we were running backward in half of the world."[38]

But to move in the right direction in the future you had to examine where and how you had gone wrong in the past. And so, during House debate on the Mutual Defense Assistance Act, Walter Judd, physician and scientist, conducted a 15,000-word autopsy of U.S. foreign policy around the world. It is an extraordinary document, sweeping in its theme and specific as to detail. He traced the crisis facing the nation and the possibility of another world war to the same error: "failure to realize how important it is to our own security that the opposite shores of the Pacific as well as of the Atlantic be in the hands of friends instead of enemies."

For more than a century, he said, U.S. policy makers saw that the "best guaranty of our security on our west was to have there an independent China friendly to ourselves" because then neither Japan nor Russia could threaten us. It was a sound policy that worked until in our desire to get the Soviets into the war against Japan, the United States invited the Soviet Union into Manchuria and "set up the situation which has led us in five years to the brink of another world war." He recalled the fateful day of August 8, 1945, when a reporter telephoned him with the news that Russia had just declared war against Japan and Secretary of State James Byrnes had said that Russia's entry would shorten the war and save American lives. "There goes the peace," Judd had remarked. "What do you mean?" inquired the reporter. Judd had responded, "Well, there goes Manchuria, then China, then Asia, then Europe, and then ourselves—unless somewhere along the line we fight."

He knew that without Manchuria, which Russia was effectively given at Yalta, China could not recover economically from the war, any more than Western Europe could recover economically without the Ruhr and West Germany, a simple fact which it took the United States and its Western allies five years to agree on. Knowing Moscow's long-range objective of global conquest and its control over the Chinese communists, he had consistently opposed the Soviet Union's entry into the Pacific war; he had even privately urged President Truman, before he went to Potsdam, to try to keep the Soviets out of the war. Certainly, there was no need to offer any special inducements to them, he argued; they would come in of their own accord because of an "understandable desire to have a major hand in the settlements in that area of the world." He had another and more subtle point: the Soviet Union had a nonaggression pact with Japan, and yet the United States was urging Moscow to break its pledged word. "If it is all right for Russia to break its word in this instance," he asked, "because it is to our advantage, then how can we expect Russia or any other country to keep the new agreements we are entering into, whenever it becomes advantageous to them not to do so? . . . We are cynically violating the international morality on which alone a lasting peace can be built."[39]

"International morality" was not a phrase he idly used, but a concept to which he had been committed since his days with the Student Volunteer Movement in the 1920s. It was one reason why Woodrow Wilson had been one of his heroes until the Treaty of Versailles when Wilson violated his own principle of "open covenants of peace openly arrived at" and accepted Japanese occupation of North China because he did not want to challenge Great Britain's secret agreement with Japan. "International morality" was at the core of the Atlantic Charter, which "the world had rallied around," believing it was a set of solemn principles, "not a propaganda document." Commitment to "international morality" was why he had been among the earliest supporters of the United Nations, which he still considered man's most promising instrument for world peace if it were given the right tools, like its own military force; if debilitating amendments, like the Security Council veto, were removed; and if all its members, particularly the Soviet Union, truly sought to keep the peace.

In his speech, Judd stressed that Asia and specifically China had always been a major Soviet target. He quoted Lenin, who, in 1923, wrote, "In the last analysis, the outcome of the world struggle will be determined by the fact that Russia, India, and China, and so forth, constitute the overwhelming majority of the population of the globe." He quoted from 1937 letters of Mao Tse-tung, Chou En-lai, and Chu Teh, leader of the Chinese Red Army, to Earl Browder, then head of the U.S. Communist party, asking for support from their communist brothers in America. In November 1945, he revealed, William Z. Foster, the new leader of the U.S. Communist party, had told the party's national committee, as reported in the party's official newspaper, the *Daily Worker,* that "on the international scale, the key task . . . is to stop American intervention in China."[40] Why? asked Judd. "Because [the communists] knew . . . that without the right kind of outside assistance the Chinese government could not possibly recover." They knew that with China, the hub of Asia, in communist hands, the eleven spokes stretching out from the hub, Korea, Japan, Formosa, the Philippines, Indonesia, Indochina, Siam, Malaya, Burma, India, and Pakistan, would be vulnerable to communist influence and takeover as well.

Three years before, he reported, he had had a long interview in Japan with General MacArthur, who remarked that he was no longer anxious about Japan per se but was concerned about the situation in China. MacArthur said: "Our failure at the end of the war to help the Government of China effectively with its otherwise insuperable problems, particularly the Communist rebellion, will turn out, I fear, to be the single greatest blunder in the history of the United States. For the first time in our relations with Asia, we confused the paramount strategic interests of the United States with an internal purification problem in China."

Because MacArthur's views were at such variance with the current official U.S. line that communist expansion in China was unimportant, Judd asked him: "Is it possible that our Government has sent you to do a job in Japan and has not consulted you as to what you think is necessary on the continent in order to enable you to succeed in Japan?" The general replied: "That, of course, I cannot answer"—thereby confirming Judd's suspicion that the Truman administration had deliberately bypassed America's most experienced military officer in Asia. How tragic it was, Judd pointed out to the House, that General Mac-Arthur was now called upon to retrieve a situation "in which we would never have been if his counsel and advice had been sought and heeded." How fortunate for Japan and the United States, he added, that Mac-Arthur's plan to retain the emperor and as much of the Japanese political and economic structure as possible had prevailed over the opposition of the State Department, which had announced a policy of "social and economic revolution." "How tragic," Judd said, "that he was not in charge of our affairs in China as well as in Japan."[41]

On the same 1947 trip to Asia, Judd met with Kim Koo, former head of the Korean provisional government, then in exile in China. He asked Kim, who had since been assassinated, what America should do in Korea. Kim replied, "It doesn't make any difference what you do now. There isn't any way to get Korea so that she can be independent and secure and self-sustaining, until you solve the Communist problem across the border in Manchuria." Kim knew, said Judd, that if the communists controlled Manchuria, which was to the immediate north of Korea, they would move to control all of Korea when the United States left the Korean peninsula. "Our boys now have to go over to Korea," said Judd, "to fight and die in an effort to save something out of the smashup there which inevitably followed our refusal to pay attention to the wisdom and foresight of the many men who did understand the problems of Asia."

He insisted that his purpose was not to blame or recriminate but, if possible, "to prevent our government's ever again imagining that we can get good faith with one ally by bad faith with another; that we can buy the good behavior or goodwill of the strong by sacrificing the weak; or that might makes right, even if the might be our might." He emphasized the critical point that just as the "expediencies of Yalta" did not end but rather multiplied U.S. troubles, so America could not extricate herself from the present predicament in Korea "by making another deal at the expense of someone else or of our own principles." That is, America could not and should not bargain away the rights of South Korea or further compromise the principle of "international morality" embodied in the U.N. charter. Both realism and idealism required the United States to fight and hopefully win the conflict in Korea.

Among the several mistakes that the United States made in Korea, he said, the worst was dividing the country along the thirty-eighth parallel "on our initiative without any request or suggestion to that effect from

Russia"; it was a decision made by the War Department in August 1945 without consulting MacArthur, anyone from the State Department, or the Koreans. Although it is an approximate midpoint on the peninsula and is roughly midway between the two largest cities, Pyongyang in the north and Seoul in the south, Judd declared that the thirty-eighth parallel was "just about the worst possible line" that could have been chosen; its selection "made it impossible for either side to survive [economically] without a lot of assistance from the outside." The best agriculture was south of the line; most of the good coal, minerals, water power, and industries were north of it. The factories in the south derived their power and raw materials from the north. United, Korea had a reasonably balanced economy; divided, neither side could survive without outside aid and the outside influence that inevitably accompanied it.[42]

The military mistakes in Korea, he stated, had been numerous, particularly the failure to train and organize the South Korean armed forces while the Soviets were "feverishly developing large forces in North Korea." The United States had the satisfaction of following the terms of the "trusteeship" to the letter; the Soviet Union was satisfied with building a North Korean army and then offering to withdraw its troops by the end of 1948. Although the new Korean national assembly passed a resolution in November 1948 which urged U.S. troops to remain until the armed forces of the Republic of Korea were capable of maintaining national security, the U.S. Army departed within seven months, long before South Korea was ready to "hold [its] own against the northerners known to be backed by the Russians and the Chinese Communists in Manchuria." Judd asserted that he and other members of the House Foreign Affairs Committee "practically begged" the State and Defense departments to keep even one U.S. battalion in Korea for another year or two "as the symbol of American power and determined interest in the security of a republic which in so many respects is our own child and that of the United Nations." They refused on the grounds that it would not be lawful under the terms of the trusteeship agreement, but as Judd argued, "if Korea is important enough to our overriding interests to justify our sending troops back in this June after an attack was well under way, then it could not have been right to pull out last June."[43]

Which brought him to "the biggest error of all"—the announcement by President Truman on January 5, 1950, that the United States would not provide any military aid or advice to Chinese forces on Formosa. Secretary Acheson enlarged upon the president's statement at a news conference, asserting, "We are not going to get involved militarily in any way on the island of Formosa." Those statements, said Judd, "gave public notice to the Kremlin that the door to Formosa was open as far as we were concerned, and they could walk right in."[44] What bothered him most about such open invitations was their essential misunderstanding of the nature of communism, which relied not on the force of ideas but on the force of arms to prevail. "I am completely confident," he said, "that communism will ultimately fail, because of its own immoralities; but it can and will destroy us and our civilization first—unless we are as well organized, determined, and strong." Paradoxically, Judd declared that he was now optimistic about the future because for the first time the policy of containment was to be applied in the East as well as the West. It was not possible to "contain" communism by closing off one end of the barrel in Europe and the Middle East "and leaving the other end of the barrel—Asia—wide open."[45]

He concluded his global analysis by expressing his two greatest fears. The first was that the United States might underestimate "the strength, the determination, the wide infiltration, the cruel ruthlessness of the forces of the Kremlin." The second fear was that "we might fail to understand . . . the size, the strength, the wide distribution, even behind the curtain, of the forces of freedom that are for us." He said that the "cruel attack" on the people of Korea could have an ultimate benefit if it awakened Americans to "communism's crusade for enslavement of the world" and led to a rededication to America's "historic mission"—the "crusade for freedom" of all peoples. The Korean conflict, he suggested, could be "the beginning of the end of the Kremlin's tyranny" if the United States mobilized and organized effectively its "moral, material and military resources" and those of all free peoples. Indeed, he said, we had little choice for "only then can we secure once more the blessings of liberty for ourselves and for our posterity."[46]

No other member of Congress had the intellectual rigor, the historical perspective, or the physical stamina to compose and deliver a 15,000-word address on the Korean invasion, U.S.-China relations over the past hundred years, the origins of World War II, the Nationalist-communist war in China, the goals of the American Communist party, the geostrategic importance of mainland China, the Yalta agreement, U.S. policy in Korea and the Far East after World War II, and to outline what needed to be done to make the policy of containment truly effective. Judd did not persuade by rhetorical tricks but by solid logic. He was not a poet but a scientist. He used plain language and often a medical analogy: he was, for example, the first public official to compare communism to cancer. He spoke with utter conviction. Like St. Paul, whom he admired most of all the apostles, he was committed to the truth as he saw it, regardless of personal gain or loss, convinced that the truth would make all peoples free. He always saw himself as a missionary, once writing: "I would not have left my missionary work to enter politics if I had not been convinced that what I am trying to do here [in Washington] is quite as much a Christian ministry as what I was trying to do in China under the direct sponsorship of the Church."[47] Is it any wonder that many congressmen were shaken loose of their usual moorings by this irrepressible force from Minnesota and wound up voting for things which were admittedly good for the country but might not gain them one single vote for re-election? They became converts to Walter Judd's vision of a world filled with great danger and even greater promise, a world in which the United States, above all other free nations, had the power to decide whether freedom or tyranny would prevail.

In late June, Judd filed for re-election as the representative in Congress from Minnesota's Fifth Congressional District. In September, replying to a League of Women Voters questionnaire, he listed his stands on a number of foreign and domestic issues, revealing, as he had since first running for office in 1942, an internationalist position in foreign policy and an often liberal position in domestic policy. He considered the United Nations an "effective organization" that could prevent aggression and preserve world peace. He supported the Economic Recovery Program in Europe and undeveloped areas, the Mutual Defense Assistance Program, the Voice of America, a "Pacific Pact for common defense," organizations designed to promote "world health, education, better nutrition and labor conditions," the removal of all racial discrimination from U.S. immigration law, and "international control of atomic weapons and genuine disarmament as soon as all are willing to accept inspection to prevent violation." He did not use the phrase "peace through strength," which became popular under President Reagan more than thirty years later, but clearly it was his basic position on negotiations and treaties with the Soviets.

On the domestic side, he supported a balanced federal budget, including "up to $10 billion more a year in taxes toward extraordinary military expenditures"; reduction of all "non-essential" programs; and a freeze of the economy "across the board." He argued that it was better to freeze everything, as Canada did during World War II, and then "to remove commodities or services from controls as soon as possible" than to apply controls selectively. He was not a libertarian or a supply-sider, but a pragmatic liberal who believed that the government should be used when necessary but only then, and as a last, not a first, resort. Asked to list legislative items that he particularly favored, he mentioned those above and added slum clearance and flexible price support programs for "certain agricultural commodities" (i.e., wheat, a key crop in Minnesota). Asked what he especially opposed, he listed "a nationalized government-operated system of medical care" and the "Brannan Plan," a far-reaching and very expensive system of farm subsidies.[48]

In a radio address delivered on election eve (which Miriam typed), he answered charges made by his opponent that he had voted against the interests of the Fifth Congressional District on a wide range of domestic issues. It was not true, he said, that he had voted "to kill the Social Security bill"; he had voted to extend benefits to 1.3 million people not covered by the administration bill and to reduce the increases to those in the highest income brackets "in order to give greater increases to those in the lowest income brackets." Nor had he voted to cut the appropriation for school lunches; he had supported the full amount recommended by the congressional committee "responsible for that program." He had voted against a last minute amendment that would have provided "more money for [the] program than it needs for orderly expansion." He concluded his remarks with stinging criticism of the Democratic administration which posed as the party of peace and prosperity but was the party of war and deficit. "Never has an administration been so convicted by events of incompetence and lack of foresight." However, he said, "we must pull together in order to pull through" the present situation. "That is the first and most urgent reason," declared Judd in his first public endorsement of the man with whom he would work closely for the next decade, "why Dwight Eisenhower must be elected President. Eisenhower can sweep things clean and make the drastic changes in policies and personnel necessary in order to regain the lost confidence of our own people and of people around the world. Only with the kind of skillful, confident and inspiring leadership which he has proved himself capable of giving can we hope to win the desperate war of ideas and of arms in which we are engaged in so much of the world."[49]

Minneapolis liked Judd's "progressive conservatism" and gave him a comfortable margin of victory over Marcella F. Killen, who had first challenged him in 1948. He was grateful for his constituents' vote of confidence, but without taking a vacation he immediately began the urgent business of securing the Republican presidential nomination for Dwight David Eisenhower. The first thing he had to do was to find out if Ike was interested.

Baby Walter, age one.

Young Walter with brother Maurice (Jim) and sister Gertrude.

As a high school graduate,
with elegant tie.

As a World War I
second lieutenant
in the field artillery.

As an intern at the University of Nebraska Hospital in Omaha.

As a medical missionary in Shaowu, South China.

Horace H. Judd,
Walter's father.

Mary E. and Horace H. Judd, Walter's parents.

Miriam Barber, shortly after graduation from Mount Holyoke.

Miriam, Walter and Mary Lou Judd on their way to China in August, 1934.

With his medical team in Fenchow, North China.

Walter and Miriam with the girls (left to right), Mary Lou, Carolyn and Eleanor.

Congressman Judd and Senator Harry S Truman on the road for the United Nations in 1943.

With President Chiang Kai-shek in Taiwan.

Reporting to President Lyndon B. Johnson on his 1967 trip to Vietnam.

With President and Mrs. Richard Nixon as well as former Congressman and Mrs. Brooks Hays at a White House prayer breakfast.

Cutting the cake on his 80th birthday.

With granddaughter Cindy Carpenter.

Walter H. Judd with Gerald Ford in the Oval Office, 1975.

On the 1960 campaign trail: Vice President Richard Nixon, Walter H. Judd, President Dwight D. Eisenhower, and vice presidential nominee Henry Cabot Lodge.

Former President Eisenhower came to Minneapolis in 1962 to campaign for both Governor Elmer Andersen and Walter H. Judd.

Walter H. Judd with Barry Goldwater.

Walter H. Judd with President Chiang Kai-shek (center) in 1967. Also present are Professor David Rower of Yale University and Frederick Chein, Chiang's interpreter and later the ROC's representative to the United States.

Walter H. Judd receiving the Presidential Medal of Freedom from
President Ronald Reagan in 1981.

Walter H. Judd with President Reagan at a White House
reception in 1988.

Walter H. Judd speaking at the Heritage Foundation dinner celebrating his 90th birthday.

CHAPTER TWELVE

◆

I Like Ike

IN JUNE 1951, sixteen congressmen, including Judd and Chris Herter of Massachusetts, visited Europe to consider President Truman's request for eight billion dollars in military and economic assistance to the European community. They were briefed by NATO commander Eisenhower and his staff on the need for "military strength to protect the economic miracle" which had transformed Western Europe from a continent on the brink of economic collapse to one well on the way to economic recovery. The congressional group visited England, France, Norway, Holland, Belgium, Italy, and the French and American zones of occupied Germany, where they saw how much remained to be done to prepare the West for a possible attack from the east. "We saw some equipment," recalled Judd, "that was still unpacked because they hadn't enough organization to get it unpacked. It was a shambles, really, five years after the war. Whether [Eisenhower] could pull them together or not, was touch and go." Nevertheless, the congressmen all agreed that Eisenhower had "done more in five months than was done in the previous 18 months without him. . . . It is . . . due more to their faith in Eisenhower than any other factor that the Europeans are being welded into a reasonably solid team against the Communists." Judd and Herter took advantage of the visit to talk some politics with the general. Both congressmen were convinced that "there had to be a halt to this headlong rush toward government management of almost everything, or else we faced disaster, here at home." In their search for the right candidate, they asked themselves two key questions: First, who was the best man? Second, who was the best man who could get elected? "There is no use having the angel Gabriel as a candidate," said Judd, "if you can't get him elected." Both Judd and Herter believed that "Ike could get elected. But what were his views? Would he be a candidate?" They talked privately with Eisenhower and concluded that while he was not interested in running for the presidency and felt that his first responsibility was to help the situation in Europe, he was a Republican and "believed as we did on basic matters." They told him: "We're not asking you to make a decision now, we're just making up our own minds as to what we're to do."[1] But in fact their minds were all but made up: Eisenhower was their man. The only remaining question was: Would he run?

That fall Judd returned to Europe to participate in the first Consultative Assembly of U.S. and European parliamentarians and political leaders, out of which came the Council of Europe. He and Senator Alexander Smith of New Jersey, a Republican, had pushed through the 80th Congress a resolution endorsing eventual political unification of Europe and, in effect, led the U.S. delegation to the meeting in Strasbourg. Judd took advantage of the trip to stop in Paris and again see Eisenhower, whom he had definitely decided to support for the Republican nomination for president in 1952. "I talked to him outright about it. I wanted to know if he wouldn't give us a lead. . . . What he said, and I wrote it down right then, was: 'Walter, no man who loves his country can refuse the bona fide request of his own political party to be its candidate for the presidency of the United States, but I have not sought it, I do not seek it, and I will not be maneuvered into appearing to seek it.' I said, 'OK, General, that's all I want to know.' "[2]

Upon his return to the United States, he was off and running on a political crusade—the nomination and election of someone who, as he put it in his newsletter to constituents, "is reasonably certain to be able to interrupt the present dynasty which has brought our country's security within six years from its all-time high to its all-time low." His was not a one-man crusade; many other Republicans shared his belief that Eisenhower should be the party's standard-bearer in 1952. Senator Henry Cabot Lodge of Massachusetts, with whom Judd would compete eight years later for the vice presidential nomination, returned from France in early January 1952 to report that the general would accept the

Republican presidential nomination if it were offered. In Paris, the next day, Eisenhower refused to reveal his party identification to reporters but admitted that Lodge had given "an accurate account of the general tenor of my political convictions and of my Republican voting record." But consistent with his response to Judd six months earlier, he insisted that he would not "seek nomination to political office." That was firm but not Shermanesque, and then Eisenhower added, meaningfully, that if he had no choice he would, of course, answer a call to "duty that would transcend my present responsibility."[3] That was all that waiting Republicans needed to hear. Judd immediately responded that "for more than a year I have worked and hoped for this development, because he is the man for the job at this critical period in our history." For those who questioned whether Eisenhower was a "good Republican," he asked, "How many men would give up the Presidency for their convictions? Ike rejects an almost sure thing with the Democrats in order perhaps to be rejected by the Republicans. . . . Yet he refuses to be [the Democratic] candidate because he is so strongly opposed to New Deal ideas, and believes so deeply in basic Republican ideals."[4] Lodge and Governor Sherman Adams of New Hampshire quickly went to work, and on March 11, Ike won the New Hampshire primary, the nation's first, receiving 44,497 votes to Robert A. Taft's 35,820. It was an impressive win, signaling the emergence of a major new force in American politics. The Minnesota results a week later suggested the presence of an irresistible force.

The odds, however, were very long against Eisenhower in Minnesota: former Governor Harold Stassen was on the ballot, Judd and others had to organize a write-in campaign for the general who was not yet a formal candidate, and the primary was much earlier than usual, giving the pro-Eisenhower forces little time to organize. Yet on March 19, Stassen barely won the Minnesota primary with 128,605 votes; Eisenhower received a remarkable 106,946 write-ins. "This was a miracle," said Judd. "Thousands couldn't spell his name. Every combination appeared on the ballots. Some just wrote in 'Ike' . . . Ike later told me that 'if 106,000 Minnesotan Republicans went out in a blizzard to write in my name for the nomination, I could not ignore that, and that's when I decided, all right, if they want me that much, I can't say no.' "[5] Publicly, General Eisenhower said that the New Hampshire and Minnesota results had caused him to "reexamine" his "political position," and the following month, he asked to be relieved of his command in Europe, a request that the White House immediately granted. Judd quickly pointed out that "the people have made Eisenhower a candidate. He did not seek the nomination." He cautioned against assuming that Ike had the nomination locked up, knowing of the strong emotional ties between traditional Republicans and Taft and pointing out that the general would not be able to begin campaigning until after the primaries were over. "From now on, just as heretofore," he said, "the job of winning votes and lining up delegates will have to be done by [us], not by him."[6]

Ike confirmed Judd's judgment of his political philosophy when he opened his formal campaign in June by declaring that the most important issue facing the nation was "liberty versus socialism." As for specifics, he wanted the Senate to have a stronger role in determining foreign policy (as president, Eisenhower would insist on congressional approval of diplomatic and military initiatives in the crises of Quemoy and Matsu in 1955 and the Middle East in 1956–1957) and called for lower taxes, an improved Taft-Hartley law, a "decent armistice" in Korea, abolition of needless federal agencies, continuing membership in NATO and the "rooting out" of "subversive elements."

When Judd committed to Eisenhower for the Republican nomination, he decided in his forthright way to let an old friend whom he greatly respected know that he could not support him. He told Taft face to face, "Bob, I'm going to work for Ike for the nomination." When a disappointed Taft asked why, Judd was direct: "He'll get more votes than you. If anybody ever deserved his party's nomination, you deserve ours. But elections are where we determine what kind of government we're to have for the next period—it isn't a matter of rewarding the deserving or punishing those who have jumped the track in the last election. Conventions are where we choose the best man *who can win*. Now, maybe you'd get enough votes, you believe you would, a lot of people believe you would, but we've got to choose the man surest to win. We've simply got to reverse the trend in this country and that requires gaining power. However many votes you'd get, Ike will get more.... [And] he's fundamentally sound on government. He doesn't know government as well as you do, but he'll be a good chief executive."[7]

It was blunt talk, but Taft took no offense. Both men prided themselves on their rational approach to the often emotional business of politics. Still, Judd did not tell his Senate friend all the reasons why he opposed his nomination. He felt that Taft "was a genuine intellectual, and the intellectual belongs more in the Senate, figuring out legislation." Furthermore, he was not an easy man to work with, "whereas Eisenhower is a master at getting people to work together."[8] And although he never expressed it publicly or privately, Judd must have been concerned about Taft's less than ringing endorsement of the Truman Doctrine, the Marshall Plan, and NATO as well as his general indifference to foreign affairs. Judd wanted a president who would be an active internationalist, who understood that isolationism was no longer possible, who would work to build a better and more peaceful world. Most of all, he wanted a Republican candidate who would win.

Notwithstanding his efforts on behalf of Eisenhower, the requirements of the House Foreign Affairs Committee, and the increasing demands of his constituents, Judd found time to launch and serve as chairman of Aid Refugee Chinese Intellectuals, a major private effort to aid some ten thousand Chinese scholars, scientists, and professionals who had fled China and were mostly living in Hong Kong who were either unemployed or existing on substandard salaries and conditions. The nongovernmental organization sought to resettle as many refugees as possible outside of Hong Kong, if possible in the countries where they had studied, including the United States. At the founding dinner in New York City, Dean Rusk, president of the Rockefeller Foundation and until recently assistant secretary of state for Far Eastern affairs, declared that it was important to preserve "a large body of trained and competent Chinese in communities outside the borders of China who could be available to the Chinese people when freedom returns to that unhappy land."[9] A major part of the program was to help intellectuals, especially teachers, find employment in Taiwan. To provide temporary housing for arriving refugee families, ARCI constructed a relocation center in the suburbs of Taipei which was named "Juddville." Here, between 1952 and 1956, "hundreds of refugee families were comfortably cared for" until suitable positions became available for them.

As Judd reported to ARCI officers and directors in 1970, when the organization was formally dissolved, Aid Refugee Chinese Intellectuals helped an estimated 14,000 Chinese college graduates and their families to settle in Taiwan, brought 2500 refugees to the United States, aided approximately 1000 others to migrate to other parts of the world, and helped more than 15,000 Chinese to find suitable employment in Hong Kong where they chose to remain. Judd was particularly proud of the manifold contributions to American society made by the 2,350 ARCI registrants who entered the United States between 1953 and 1960. "One dramatic index of their industry and integrity," he wrote, "is their voluntary repayment of the travel loans which ARCI advanced to enable them to get to the United States. Of the $241,297 advanced in travel loans, they have to date repaid . . . 96.3 percent."[10]

The first eighteen months of the Eighty-second Congress, from January 1951 to June 1952, were a period of transition during which President Truman fired General MacArthur as supreme commander of the Allied powers, commander in chief of the United Nations command, and commanding general of the U.S. Army in the Far East, for failing to support fully his efforts to negotiate a cease-fire and peace agreements with North Korea. He thus created a political firestorm that, among other things, precluded his seeking re-election. Senator Arthur Vandenberg, the Republican apostle of bipartisanship, died of cancer, leaving a foreign policy vacuum in the Senate that no one was able to fill. Communist China by its direct entry into the Korean War prevented U.S. diplomatic recognition of Peking and ensured the maintenance of U.S. relations with the Republic of China on Taiwan, giving the Nationalist government precious time to initiate economic and political reforms. Senator Joseph R. McCarthy (R-Wisconsin) burst on the national scene with a speech in Wheeling, West Virginia, charging that he had "in his hand" a list of 205 communists "still working and shaping the policy of the State Department."[11] Truman cronies in the White House, the Reconstruction Finance Corporation, and the Internal Revenue Service were caught defrauding the government and lining their pockets at the expense of the public. As a result, the Republican formula for victory in 1952 was created: K^1C^3—Korea, Crime, Communism, Corruption.

While conceding readily that Truman had the authority to remove MacArthur, Judd argued that the president's "unwise action greatly weakens the position of the United States" in Asia and allowed "the Communists there to build up for the expansion of the war which they have long proclaimed as their firm objective." He feared that because of MacArthur's enormous prestige throughout Asia, his dismissal would lead to instability in Japan, Formosa, the Philippines, and other Asian countries. He was also concerned about the increasing volume of "wishful thinkers" who wanted to "negotiate some kind of a deal [with Communist China] and end the war in Korea." He stated that the issue was not the reputation or the place in history of MacArthur but the "peace and security of the United States." The United States, he said, had tried at Teheran, Yalta, and Potsdam "to get good relations with Communists by giving them what they said they wanted. But ... what they [really] want is conquest—most of all conquest of the United States of America because we are all that stands between them and world domination." Any political compromise, he said, would not end the war but "only move the conflict to another country." He opposed Truman's action because he feared it would do the very opposite of what the president claimed it would do—"expand the war in Asia, rather than contain it in Korea."[12]

Was Judd's deep-rooted concern for China affecting his ability to be objective? Surely, MacArthur was not so revered in Japan and throughout Asia—or was he? The Truman administration would not rush to negotiate with the communists and seek an end to the Korean fighting regardless of the terms—or would it, with one eye on the approaching national elections? By now, Secretary Acheson must have understood the central importance of China in Asia and the close interrelationship of the countries of East Asia, as close as that of the nations of Europe. Or did he? Because he could not be sure of the answers, Judd suggested a stark scenario of impending war which might look overdrawn today but was quite believable in the spring of 1951 when no one could be sure what Peking might do next in Asia, or Moscow in Europe. He was certainly no more bleak in his analysis than the famed National Security Council policy paper, *NSC-68* (edited by Paul Nitze), which saw the world as locked in a total struggle between "free society" and the "implacable purpose of the slave state" and recommended "a rapid build-up of political, economic and military strength in the free world," led by the United States. The fall of China and the acquisition of nuclear weapons by the Soviet Union, said *NSC-68,* suggested "a permanent and fundamental alteration in the shape of international relations. ... The issues that face us are momentous, involving the fulfillment or destruction not only of this Republic but of civilization itself."[13] Judd shared with the authors of *NSC-68* the conviction that world domination by Soviet ideology and military power was not only possible but probable unless the United States took appropriate action around the world.

Joseph McCarthy was everything that Walter Judd was not—impetuous, careless with facts, a headline grabber. Long before McCarthy discovered communism, Judd had personally confronted communists in China, and carefully tracked their influence in the United States. He knew about the security risks (not "communists") in the State Department because as we have seen, the Republican Eightieth Congress had set up a subcommittee of the House Committee on Government Operations, of which he was a member, to investigate State Department personnel. They succeeded in removing 134 security risks from the department without a headline. "All but ten of them," he recalled, "when they knew they were being investigated, dropped out voluntarily.... There were about 105 cases still unresolved when the ... Congress adjourned in June of 1948." After Truman and the Democrats won in November and returned to Washington, one of their first acts was to abolish the subcommittee. Judd begged House Majority Leader John McCormack, a good friend, not to do it, saying: "John, you will be the chairman of the committee. You'll have three Democrats and only two of us Republicans. If we didn't do any dirty work, when we were in the majority, we sure can't when we're in the minority. Please don't stop halfway through. Let's finish those 105 cases." The remaining cases were a "hodge-podge," including homosexuals, alcoholics, and those with pro-communist backgrounds. Judd believed that a clerk of the House committee leaked the list to McCarthy, who served on the corresponding Senate committee. He couldn't resist the temptation to refer to "communists" in his speech a couple of weeks later, "and the cause was lost."

It was lost, argued Judd, because the communists were able to divert attention from themselves to McCarthy. They coined the word "McCarthyism," which was quickly picked up by the establishment press; they pointed to the inaccuracies in his statements. McCarthy "was always a few percent inaccurate," said Judd, and "you can't be one-half percent inaccurate when you're dealing with the Communists. If they find one footnote that's wrong out of a thousand, then the whole case is discredited." He pointed to two basic errors in McCarthy's West Virginia speech. First, there were no "names" of State Department employees, only numbers. "All those 134," he explained, "were gotten rid of on the basis of their records," not their names and reputations. "Joe never could produce any names." Second, the remaining cases were not proven communists. Looking back years later, Judd shook his head and commented: "Joe's overstatements allowed the Communists to look like the underdog, and the housecleaning job never was completed."[14]

In June 1952, his hard work of almost ten years was crowned with success when the Senate overrode President Truman's veto of the immigration bill and removed the remaining racial bars from America's immigration and naturalization laws. While conceding that not all inequities had been eliminated, Judd stated that the bill extended the quota principle to all peoples, including the Japanese and the Koreans, who had been excluded by reason of their national origin. The process of extension began during World War II when through his efforts a quota was granted to the Chinese, and was continued in 1946 with regard to persons coming from India and then for Filipinos after they attained their independence. He applauded Congress for recognizing the moral, security, and economic reasons for overriding the president's veto; it was a case, he pointed out, "where what we ought to do because it is right coincides with what we ought to do because of intelligent concern for our long-term well-being."[15]

There was no bipartisan consensus about China, with Republicans charging that the Democrats had "lost" the country to the communists and Democrats accusing the Republicans of belonging to the infamous "China lobby," which put Chinese interests first and American interests second. The China lobby and its alleged influence on U.S. decision makers in and out of government remained an issue for nearly a quarter of a century. Like something out of a spy novel or a Hollywood movie, the China lobby was accused of wielding enormous power in Congress and spending millions of dollars to influence the public. Because Judd was always named as a prominent member of the lobby (Drew Pearson, the muckraking columnist, even suggested that Judd had violated the Logan Act in July 1950 by recommending that Albert Wedemeyer be appointed MacArthur's deputy in Formosa, an absurd charge, even for Pearson), he explained in a 1952 floor speech what it was and what it was not. It *was* a group of Republicans and Democrats, some close to the White House, "who from the moment of the first Japanese attack on China worked steadily and consistently for the right kind of effective help to Nationalist rather than to Red China." The so-called China lobby was *not* those who "have shaped our pro-Russian Asian policy of the last decade," insisting that the Chinese communists were "agrarian reformers," pressuring the Nationalist Chinese to cease fire in 1945–1946 when they "had the upper hand over the Communists," bringing about the "present unhappy stalemate in Korea," urging the French to "turn over all of Indo-China to that camouflaged 'Nationalist,' Ho Chiminh . . . who spent years in Moscow getting trained" for his present revolutionary mission.

As for the money supposedly spent by the Nationalist Chinese to influence American public opinion in their favor, his answer was clear and direct: "I do not know. I never got any and I do not know anyone who did." In fact, Judd had declared as early as August 1949 that if any Americans took Chinese money, they should be exposed and punished. But no action had been taken by a Democratic Congress or administration, and "I suspect none will be taken. It is far more useful and diversionary to spread unsupported charges . . . than to have it revealed in a proper investigation that the so-called China lobby was peanuts compared with the lobbies which other foreign governments have maintained." Unfortunately for America, Judd said, the "so-called China lobby failed. What needs to be investigated is the *anti*-China lobby—for it succeeded. And we are all paying the price."[16]

Far from being a compliant member of a China lobby, Judd never hesitated to criticize, and sharply, the Republic of China on Taiwan when circumstances required. In November 1950, he sent a letter to Chiang Kai-shek about a financial transaction which appeared to be "a misuse of public funds by a high official of the Chinese government." In early 1951, he was informed that the case "was being investigated," but he was not satisfied and in March, he wrote again to Chiang, stating that it would be "very difficult" for him to continue advocating aid for the Republic of China "unless this case is concluded immediately." Firm, prompt action, wrote Judd to Chiang, "will confirm our faith [in you] and demonstrate your high integrity and patriotism."[17] Judd's warning let President Chiang and his government know that they would have to adhere to a higher standard of public integrity on Taiwan than they did on the mainland if they wanted to continue receiving his support. During the war against Japan and the subsequent struggle against the communists, Chiang had been reluctant to take action against graft and corruption among his subordinates, many of them his longtime supporters, refusing to believe that the situation was as serious and widespread as had been charged. But what had been acceptable in the far reaches of the Middle Kingdom could not be tolerated on the small island of Taiwan; besides, Chiang desperately needed U.S. aid to preserve free China as a viable alternative to Communist China and to keep alive his hopes that one day he and the other Nationalists would return to the mainland. Chiang understood full well the import of Judd's warning, immediately dismissed the official, and announced that similar breaches of the public trust would not be tolerated.

The Republican National Convention in Chicago was a fight to the political death between the supporters of Dwight D. Eisenhower and

Robert A. Taft, who claimed on the eve of the convention to have enough delegates to win the presidential nomination. The only chance for the Eisenhower forces lay in challenging delegates accredited to Taft with their own delegates. As television evangelist Pat Robertson did in 1988, Eisenhower partisans packed local and state caucuses with new Republicans who picked delegates to the national convention pledged to Ike. In Texas, they convened in a separate hall from the regular Taft Republicans and selected their own delegates, producing two slates of Texas Republicans that both showed up in Chicago. Demanding "fair play," Senator Lodge and other Eisenhower followers also challenged the Georgia and Louisiana delegations, which heavily favored Taft. As William Manchester said: "The issue was bogus. The Eisenhower delegations were no more representative than the Taft southerners, and the Taftites were at least lifelong Republicans."[18] But Republicans were willing to do almost anything to win the presidency, even play the hypocrite and humiliate a United States senator whom they liked to call "Mr. Republican." The Taft camp played into the hands of the Eisenhower forces by banning cameras and reporters from the credentials hearings and creating the impression they were trying to ramrod their delegates through. When Ohio Congressman Clarence Brown, a Taft manager, offered a compromise amendment to the convention that seemed to suggest that the proceedings had not been fair, it was narrowly defeated 658 to 548, and "by that margin control of the Republican party . . . passed into the hands of Dwight Eisenhower."[19]

Shortly after he was nominated, Eisenhower was visited by a small committee who wanted to know his choice for vice president. He drew from his billfold a short "eligible list," written in longhand, of those he thought were qualified and available. The first name he read was Senator Richard Nixon of California, young, vigorous, articulate and a strong anti-communist. Nixon was enthusiastically approved by the party elders. In his memoirs, Eisenhower explains that Nixon's conduct in the "historic Alger Hiss case" strongly appealed to him, especially "the reputation that Congressman Nixon had achieved for fairness in the investigating process." What the general did not reveal publicly until a decade later was that Nixon was not his only choice, but rather his first choice among five men whom he considered worthy of consideration as vice president. The others, in order, were congressman Charles Halleck, Congressman Walter Judd, Governor Dan Thornton and Governor Arthur Langlie.[20] Eisenhower does not suggest regret in any way about the selection of Nixon, but how different history would have been if the committee had displayed less enthusiasm for the controversial senator from California and more interest in the seasoned congressman from Minnesota. Strangely, all three men, Eisenhower, Nixon and Judd, would be major actors in another vice presidential decision at another Republican convention eight years later.

Meanwhile, the selection of Nixon did little to assuage the unhappy Taft forces. On the last day of the Republican convention, with acrimony heavy in the air, despite a late-night visit by a peace-seeking Eisenhower to an agonized Taft in his hotel suite, Judd addressed the still-restless delegates. He was introduced by the chairman, Joe Martin, as a man "whose public utterances over the last 15 years contain an unbroken chain of prophecy that are unequalled, so far as I know, in modern times." Judd spoke about the future of their party and the nation, urging reconciliation, unity, and realism. A political party, he declared, "does not win elections with the people it keeps out. It wins with the people it gets in. If we want to win . . . we must become the majority party as well as the party of right." He talked about convincing the people of America that the Republican party could lead the nation to victory over "communist imperialism," to achieve a peace based on a "workable world organization with other free peoples," to maintain "our free society here at home." Balance was the key, he stated, echoing James Madison and Thomas Jefferson, balance between the branches of government and "between the major economic groups," because "too great a preponderance of one, which inevitably leads to monopoly, can only be at the expense of others." He disagreed emphatically with those who said that the "explosion" of the presidential nomination fight "would mean the end of our Party. . . . I think it is far more right that the future will regard this 1952 convention as the one that marked a rebirth of the Republican Party and the beginning of a return to soundness and sanity in this beloved country."[21]

Back in Minneapolis, Judd had to answer a number of angry letters from Taft supporters who accused him and other Eisenhower delegates of dirty tactics at the convention and of trying to drive them out of the Republican party. He carefully answered all their charges. He pointed out that Eisenhower forces had not challenged any Taft delegates in Florida or in certain seats in Texas and Louisiana, but only where they felt "the balance was definitely in [Ike's] favor. I cannot see anything improper in that." He insisted that he was not trying to exclude anyone from the Republican party but to bring in as many new people as possible. Anticipating language that Ronald Reagan would use three decades later when he sought to broaden the base of the Republican party, Judd said: "Democrats are not taking over the Party; the Party is taking over former Democrats." He did not understand why anyone would believe that he "would rather have Democrats than real Republicans in our Party. On the contrary, what I have sought to accomplish is to get Democrats to become real Republicans and join us in our Party."[22] It seemed logical to him; after all, he had been a Democrat for the first forty years of his life.

In July, he was invited by the Eisenhower campaign to come to its Denver headquarters in the Brown Palace Hotel where he, along with some thirty other experts, developed campaign positions on everything from agriculture to Western Europe. On the first morning, Ike, the ultimate team organizer, set the tone for the strategy sessions and the ensuing campaign: "We've got a real hard fight ahead of us. We have every reason to believe that if we do it well, we'll prevail. I've been in this campaign business a long time, and there are only two rules we'll lay down. One is, we're going to work together, and second is, we're going to smile." The man with the million-vote smile said: "You have no idea how much can be accomplished . . . by having a good grin, and if there are people that are going to get disagreeable when their position doesn't prevail and they can't play ball with a smile, then they can detach themselves from the team right at the start."[23]

Among the several conferences which Judd had with the presidential nominee the most important, from a historical point of view, was one during which Eisenhower responded to the charge, already made by the Democrats (and later to be repeated by ultraconservatives like Robert Welch, founder of the John Birch Society), that he had "turned Eastern Europe over to the Reds" by withdrawing American troops to the Elbe River instead of letting them continue on east. The general strongly denied the charge and described his firm opposition to the division of Germany. He said that he even went to the White House in early January 1945 and "pled with Mr. Roosevelt, who was then in bed . . . not to divide Germany. And I said if the Russians insist on having this one area, let us keep our part as a unit." But at Yalta, convinced that the participation of Russia in the Pacific war would save American lives, Roosevelt agreed to the division of Germany and conceded a dominant position in Eastern Europe to the Soviets. "I must have got the decision," recalled Eisenhower, "maybe the first of March and from then on, all of my movements, all of my planning, had to take into consideration where we were going to be situated after the war." However, he discovered that no decision had been made about Denmark or Austria, and he prevented the Russians "getting into Denmark by putting a strong force in Lubeck" and got as far south as Linz, thirty miles short of Vienna, although the Russians reached Vienna before "we got there." But in Eastern Germany when he pushed 150 miles "further than my boundaries," he was forced to pull back.

When Churchill urged Eisenhower not to retreat, he replied: "Why, Mr. Prime Minister . . . you and Stalin and the President agreed [to the boundaries]. How can I defy that? I have to go back." Summing up his situation, Ike said, "In the center I was fixed . . . [but I never retreated one foot in those areas where I did not have orders to." Eisenhower emphasized to Judd and the others his abiding concern about what he called the "East-West division of the world" and the aggressive attitude of the Russians. "In talking to Mr. Roosevelt about these things," he revealed, the president "just laughed. 'I can handle Uncle Joe.' That is exactly what he told me." However, Roosevelt was too ill at Yalta to handle himself, let alone the Soviet dictator, and fatal concessions were made, as Judd later said, "with respect to Poland, Czechoslovakia, Germany, Manchuria, the Kurile Islands and Korea."[24]

During the fall campaign, Eisenhower traveled 33,000 miles and delivered over 200 speeches, 40 of them televised; his strategists used television commercials extensively for the first time in a presidential election. But his early appearances were lackluster and disappointed his supporters. Republicans wanted strong conservative rhetoric, but Ike stuck to the middle road. However, after a two-hour meeting in September, Eisenhower and Taft publicly agreed that the basic issue of the campaign was "liberty against creeping socialism." Eisenhower went on to call the Democratic platform "un-American" but allowed Nixon to make the most partisan charges. On a mudslinging scale of one to ten, Nixon earned an eight by calling Governor Adlai Stevenson of Illinois, the Democratic presidential nominee, "Adlai the Appeaser" who had received "a Ph.D. from Dean Acheson's College of Cowardly Communist Containment" in foreign affairs. "Can such a man," Nixon frequently asked, "be trusted to lead our crusade against communism?"[25]

Eisenhower continued to run only narrowly ahead of Stevenson. Finally, in early October, the pro-Eisenhower Scripps-Howard newspaper chain ran a critical editorial on the front page of all nineteen of its papers, charging that "Ike was running like a dry creek" because he was not "coming out swinging."[26] Alarmed by the criticism, Judd sat down next to Eisenhower on the campaign train and talked plainly to the man who he had told Bob Taft and everyone else within the sound of his voice would get more votes than any other Republican in 1952. Ike listened carefully and asked him to write his ideas down, which Judd did that night in his Pullman berth, as the train clicked and clacked its way from Oregon to California.

His concise four-page memorandum, dated October 8, 1952, began by discussing the two major issues on which the public was uncertain as to Eisenhower's position: welfare and Korea. Judd's advice on welfare was to the point—Ike had to show that he cared about people. Democrats, said Judd, were making some headway with their charge that Republicans would "turn the clock back," "put profits ahead of people," and bring another depression. The public, he said, needed to be sure that an Eisenhower administration "will be dedicated to maintaining, strengthening, and extending all measures that are beneficial to human beings and to our common welfare." He counseled the use of specific illustrations—people in slums, catastrophic illness, retired persons with "inadequate benefits reduced to half their value" by the inflation resulting from the current administration's bad management —so that the people would say, "Ike likes me, understands my problem, will not let me down." Eisenhower accepted Judd's advice then and later, creating, among other things, a brand new department to supervise federal welfare programs, the Department of Health, Education and Welfare (also recommended by the Hoover Commission several years earlier).

As for the war in Korea, said Judd, "the people are more anxious about this than any other issue." The task was to "win or get peace in Korea, while keeping the peace elsewhere." Obviously, a president with "vast military experience, close personal contacts and unequaled influence all around the world" was best equipped to "win and keep the peace." The problem with Ike, explained Judd years later, was that he did not want to talk about his military record or capitalize on it; he had been brought up, as Judd had, not to boast about himself. But this was a presidential campaign and the future of the nation and perhaps the world was at stake. "I was pleading with him to take leadership as a military man." It did not happen immediately, but on October 24, acting on the advice of Judd and others, Ike promised to end the war in

Korea if he became president and to go to Korea to achieve that objective. The frontpage headlines trumpeted, "Ike Will Go to Korea," and the campaign was effectively over.

The other seven points of the memorandum ranged from how to handle his opponent ("keep Stevenson everlastingly identified with the present administration") to how to make a public speech ("swallow for four weeks your wholly admirable dislike of playing for effect and read the punch lines a little more slowly and deliberately with rising emphasis on each word toward the end of a key sentence"). When Judd suggested this technique as they were talking on the train, Ike said, "That's corn," to which one of the best public speakers in America responded, "Well, maybe it's corn, but there's nothing wrong with it, nothing immoral or dishonorable . . . and it comes over."[27] The first two points of the Judd memo were the ones that Ike took to heart and used to help transform a campaign "running like a dry creek" into a roaring river that swept him into the White House and gave the Republicans a narrow majority in the House and a disappointing tie in the Senate.

As further evidence of his key role in the Eisenhower campaign, Judd was asked by the *Saturday Evening Post,* one of the nation's most popular magazines, to "make the case for the Republicans." He charged that when America had "an unprecedented opportunity [near the end of World War II] to secure the future peace, the Democrat leadership appeased at Yalta, compromised at Potsdam, wavered at Paris, fumbled in China, [and] permitted the infiltration of key Government agencies by our enemies or their sympathizers." To prove he was not "twisting the facts to fit my diagnosis," he referred to the State Department official (it was Acheson although he did not mention his name) who said in 1949 that even if the communists seized all of China, it would not mean much in the world political picture because "it would take the Communists five decades to develop China into anything that could be a threat to any of its neighbors." As he pointed out, "less than two years later, Chinese communists crossed the Yalu River and gave our forces in Korea as bad a military defeat as any in American history."

Republicans, he said, would not try merely to "contain" communism but would "take the initiative and inaugurate a comprehensive system of encouragement and support for free peoples who seek to oppose communist domination and for enslaved peoples who seek to liberate themselves from the iron grip of the Kremlin." This was a foretelling of the Eisenhower-Dulles doctrine of liberation cum brinksmanship that was applied in Iran, Guatemala, and Quemoy and Matsu. He did not neglect domestic affairs, presenting a generally moderate program of "reasonable safeguards against serious price fluctuations" for farmers; the extension of Social Security coverage; health care for those "who are unable to secure proper care"; and the promotion of civil rights through education, persuasion, and conciliation.

He concluded his case for the Republicans with a long list of Eisenhower's strengths and virtues, several of which were predictable; the very last, however, was a shrewd estimate of the general's fundamental character and appeal: "He will follow the middle course, avoiding the extremists of both sides and pursuing a policy of reconciliation and harmony."[28] That is what Eisenhower tried to do in the area of domestic policy and within the Republican party during his eight years as president. A similar policy of moderation characterized Judd's stance in domestic policy but not in foreign policy; his dedication to freedom would never allow him to compromise with communism, which he always perceived as an implacable enemy.

On election day, notwithstanding the wit, intelligence, and television charisma of Adlai Stevenson, Eisenhower won a landslide victory, receiving 55.4 percent of the popular vote and carrying thirty states with 442 electoral votes. He was the first Republican since Hoover to win in the South, carrying Virginia, Tennessee, Texas, and Florida. Despite his intensive campaigning for Eisenhower outside Minneapolis, Judd easily won re-election, receiving more votes than ever before or ever again, 99,027 to 68,326 for his opponent, Karl F. Rolvaag. For the first time in his campaigns, he used television: a five-minute, three-times-a-week "program," called, "Your Congressman Answers His Mail." Standing in front of a board with dozens of letters addressed to "Walter H. Judd" pasted to it, he answered one letter on each program—why he supported a general for president or his position on taxes—and often used props, like a map of Europe or Asia, or a book from which he read an appropriate passage. Miriam, who made him wear a bow tie once to vary his appearance, echoed a majority opinion when she wrote her parents: "Walter comes over well."[29]

Judd celebrated the twin victories briefly and then set to work preparing for the new administration and the new Congress in which he would have increased political authority, not as the chairman of a committee, but as one who could pick up the phone and talk to the president when necessary. He never abused that privilege, but did not hesitate to call when he had something important on his mind as he did only three days after the election. He telephoned Eisenhower, who was vacationing in Augusta, Georgia. "Ike," he said, "I know that there are some people who either have approached you or will be asking you to appoint me to various positions. I don't think you ought to consider [them] because . . . you're going to need me in Congress more than in an administrative post." Judd then said that he had two suggestions regarding appointments: "The first is John Foster Dulles as Secretary of State." Ike replied, "Well, he's being considered, but there's a lot of opposition to him." "Why?" asked Judd. Eisenhower implied that Dulles was not sympathetic enough to the British. "That's one of the reasons I'm for him," said Judd. "We've had administrations where our State Department was an outpost of the British Foreign Service. . . . It was particularly so under Mr. Acheson. . . . I know that Mr. Dulles is sympathetic toward the British, but he'll have an *American* foreign policy. That is one of the strongest reasons for his appointment, in my opinion."[30]

It is a measure of Judd's commitment to principle over politics that he also recommended Harold Stassen as head of the foreign aid program. Stassen had opposed both Eisenhower and Taft at the national convention, winning few friends or delegates by his stubborn belief that the convention would deadlock and turn to him as a compromise candidate. Judd believed strongly that Stassen would be an eminently capable administrator in the right job, like head of the Economic Cooperation Administration. He always said that Stassen was one of the two ablest men he had ever known, second only to Douglas MacArthur. Ike accepted Judd's recommendation, and Stassen "did wonders" as ECA head until White House fever took hold of him again. Judd also played a key role in the appointment of Walter Robertson, a retired foreign service officer who had negotiated extensively with the Chinese communists, as assistant secretary of state for the Far East. He wrote to Dulles in January and again in February strongly recommending Robertson; he included the former diplomat's 1948 testimony before the House Foreign Affairs Committee, saying that Robertson "saw with complete clarity the nature and objectives of the Communist movement in China and analyzed prophetically the inevitable results of the administration's policies if persisted in." Although he did not know Robertson personally and was aware that he was a Democrat, Dulles appointed him and later told Judd, "Walter, you've done a lot for us in this administration, but the best thing you ever did for me was to recommend Walter Robertson as Assistant Secretary of State for the Far East."[31]

Because of his access to the highest levels of government, his deep knowledge of international relations from China to Europe, and his extraordinary influence in Congress on both sides of the aisle, Walter Judd would play a leading role in shaping the foreign policy of the United States in the crucial decade of the 1950s.

CHAPTER THIRTEEN

◆

The "China Lobby"

THIS IS THE Age of Conspiracy. Concocted by partisans of the far left and the far right, publicized by news media eager to multiply their viewers and readers, and accepted by a public made cynical by a government that lied about the course of the Vietnam war and tried to cover up the Watergate scandal, conspiracy theories are now offered about almost every major event in modern American history, from the assassination of John F. Kennedy to Pearl Harbor to the sinking of the U.S. *Maine* in Havana harbor in 1898. Conspiracy theorists see "reds" under every bed or the CIA behind every fall of government. What they fail to see, or concede, is that the course of human action is more often marked by chance and circumstance than plots and conspiracies. This was so in the case of the formation of the Committee of One Million (Against the Admission of Communist China to the United Nations), the most visible manifestation of what has come to be known as the "China lobby."

What was this mysterious lobby that in the minds of some represented an American front for the "yellow peril"? In his vehemently anti-Chiang work, *The China Lobby in American Politics,* Ross Y. Koen argued that the term originally referred to representatives of the Nationalist Chinese government who were seeking U.S. support for their government and combating pressures from American "leftists" to discredit the Republic of China. How far left these anti-Chiang Kai-shek critics were can be deduced from the fact that in January 1949, the Communist party of New York State called for a congressional investigation into a "Chinese lobby in Washington." In a 1950 congressional hearing, Owen Lattimore, a primary target of Senator Joseph McCarthy and others trying to determine who was responsible for the fall of China to the Communists, charged that McCarthy was a "willing tool" of the "so-called China Lobby." Shortly thereafter, the *New York Times* published a long article headlined, "Is There a China Lobby?" It concluded that rather than a "tight and tangible conspiracy of possible sinister intent," the "China lobby" was more accurately a "loose conglomeration of persons and organizations which for various reasons are interested in China." Furthermore, the "lobby" drew its strength from people "who passionately believe American policy to be wrong; who think that American withdrawal from China has caused a needless and dangerous break in the dike against the spread of communism."[1] In mid-1951, the *Congressional Quarterly* described the "China lobby" as "probably the most variously interpreted term now in the news." Despite his anti-Nationalist bias, even Koen distinguished between Kuomintang "paid agents" and the former missionaries, businessmen, military leaders and congressmen who supported the ROC's cause: "No question concerning the 'loyalty' or 'patriotism' of these Americans need be raised."[2]

The Committee of One Million had a long incubation. On June 15, 1950, three years before its formation, Judd inserted in the *Congressional Record* a Gallup poll showing that the American people opposed U.S. recognition of Peking by a margin of two to one, despite the fact that British Foreign Minister Ernest Bevin was urging that Communist China be given a seat in the United Nations. A month later, Judd spoke on the House floor against the admission of the "Chinese Communist regime" to the United Nations, "where it could only make trouble for the organization and for all peoples who want to work together to prevent further Communist aggression."[3] Earlier that same year, Matthew Woll, president of the Free Trade Union Committee of the American Federation of Labor, wrote a very strong letter to Secretary-General Trygve Lie of the United Nations opposing the expulsion of the Republic of China from the U.N. and its replacement by Communist China. Woll's unequivocal language anticipated that of AFL leaders William Green and George Meany, who helped the Committee for One Million obtain one million signatures in 1953–1954.[4] Neither Judd nor any of the other original congressional members of the Committee's steering committee introduced the first resolution against the U.N. admission of Communist China. That task fell to Senator John L. McClellan (D-Ark.), whose resolution expressing "the sense of the Senate that the Communist Chinese government should not be admitted to membership in the United Nations as the representative of China" was unanimously passed by the Senate on January 23, 1951.[5]

Far from being the first citizens' organization concerned with U.S. policy toward China, the Committee of One Million followed a number of other groups, including the American China Policy Association, founded in 1946 by Alfred Kohlberg; the China Emergency Committee, of whose National Advisory Council Judd was a member; and the Committee to Defend America by Aiding Anti-Communist China, whose chairman pro-tem was Frederick C. McKee.[6] As will be remembered, Judd started Aid Refugee Chinese Intellectuals in 1951 with the help of other prominent Americans upon whom he would later call when launching the Committee of One Million. He was far from the only member of Congress who felt that the fall of China to the communists was a tragedy of the first magnitude. For example, on January 30, 1949, in an address in Salem, Massachusetts, Congressman John F. Kennedy (D-Mass.) declared that it was "of the utmost importance that we search out and spotlight those who must bear the responsibility" for "the disasters befalling China and the United States." Sounding very much like Walter Judd, the young liberal Democrat laid the blame on the policy makers who insisted that "aid would not be forthcoming unless a coalition government with the Communists was formed." So concerned with the "imperfections of the diplomatic system in China" and "the tales of corruption in high places" were "our diplomats and their advisers," said Kennedy, that "they lost sight of our tremendous stake in a non-Communist China." The freedom of China which young Americans had fought to save, concluded the future president with a scathing reference to Truman, "our diplomats and our President have frittered away."[7]

It was to such troubled Democrats that Judd turned when he organized the Committee of One Million, knowing that if it were going to be effective, the committee would have to be bipartisan. The idea of an organization specifically aimed at preventing the admission of Communist China to the United Nations, an organization that Judd had unstintingly supported since 1943 and for which he still had high hopes, was an idea that only needed a little push to become a reality. The push came from Nicholas de Rochefort, a fervent Russian-born anti-communist who had worked with various intelligence agencies. On July 31, 1953, he testified in executive session before the Far East and Pacific Subcommittee (headed by Judd) of the House Committee on Foreign Affairs.

De Rochefort suggested the creation of a "National Committee" financed and coordinated by the federal government to mobilize public opinion in the United States and Western Europe against Communist China. He had in mind an organization of organizations rather than of individuals. He wanted American labor groups to "address French anticommunist trade unions," American Catholics to talk to Irish or French Catholics, American political scientists to contact British academics, and so on. Judd and other congressmen present, including the emphatically liberal Jacob Javits of New York, expressed strong doubt about the wisdom of federal funds being so spent, as well as a preference for activity from the bottom up rather than the top down. Judd suggested several people who might be interested in participating, including Fred McKee, David Dubinsky of the Garment Workers Union, and former State Department official Stanley Hornbeck. But in response to open hints from de Rochefort that he ought to become involved, Judd said: "No one feels more strongly about [the UN admission of Communist China] than I. On the other hand, with all I have to do, how in the world could I take on any more?"[8]

The truth is that de Rochefort initially came to Judd in June 1953, "after the workers' rebellion in East Germany." "What's the matter with you anti-communists in America?" he asked. "What's the matter with the AFL? These [riots] expose the nature of communism better than anything else." Judd recalled saying, "Yes, I know what you mean. In 1925, the year I went to China, there were some workers who protested against British rule, to get rid of foreign concessions, and someone shot and killed a Chinese. They carried a [coffin] up and down the main road in Shanghai, morning and evening, for a year. The Communists were there and helped manage it—it was agitprop." De Rochefort, speaking with considerable passion, responded that "you talk about it but you don't agitate. Why isn't the AFL carrying a casket up and down Pennsylvania Avenue, up and down Fifth Avenue, up and down State Street in Chicago for a year? The workers' revolution? Why don't you expose it? Agitate! Agitate! Agitate!"

Judd agreed that something ought to be done, and he turned to a young man in New York City, Marvin Liebman, who worked for the Harold C. Oram Company, which was raising funds and handling public relations for Aid Chinese Refugee Intellectuals. Liebman, who had been a member of the Young Communist League and the American Communist party, quit communism in 1945 after coming "to see the Soviet Union as a world danger." He worked for the International Rescue Committee in 1951 before coming to New York City to join the Oram company for which he was a senior officer from 1953 through 1958 when he started his own firm, Marvin Liebman Associates. Richard Dudman of the *St. Louis Post-Dispatch* once described Liebman as "the best single action-group organizer on the far right today."[9]

At Judd's direction, Liebman held a meeting with "perhaps five or six people" at the University Club in New York City to discuss the possible formation of a new organization. Judd had stressed two things: first and most importantly, "we have to be bi-partisan"; second, "we have to keep the China issue from Joe McCarthy . . . he will wreck it." As a former communist, Liebman was familiar with the Stockholm "Petition for Peace" instigated by the Soviets in 1950 and suggested a variation of it for their campaign. Geraldine Fitch, an old China hand, and Christopher Emmett, a founder of New York's Liberal Party, were also present at the New York City meeting. The seed money for the Committee came from Governor Edison. Liebman recalled that Harold Oram brought in de Rochefort, who did prepare the first draft of the Committee's petition. Changes were made here and there, but a good part of the petition language was de Rochefort's; the remainder came from Judd's arguments made over the years.[10] Judd was impressed by de Rochefort's eagerness to *do* something. "We raised a little money," recalled Judd, "and sent him to the AFL convention down in Miami and got them committed for a million signatures against Red China in the U.N. De Rochefort also went out to the American Legion [convention], and [eventually] we got a million signatures."[11] But the final names did not come until 1954, by which time de Rochefort was no longer associated with the Committee of One Million. In December 1953, the Committee's steering committee agreed "to discontinue the full-time services of Dr. Nicholas de Rochefort" but expressed its "gratitude" for his "splendid work."[12]

The Committee of One Million prevailed as one of the most successful citizens groups in America for nearly twenty years because it reflected the majority opinion and will of the American people, who did not want a government that played a major role in the Korean War to be admitted to the United Nations, whose members were pledged to keeping the peace. Some politicians and policy makers tried to argue that realism required the admission of Peking, but as long as the memory of

Korea and the Americans who died in that war remained fresh, the U.S. public stood firm against admission of Communist China.

The Committee of One Million was strictly bipartisan, at the insistence of Judd, who understood that if the organization were ever branded as the ideological creature of Republicans, its effectiveness would be severely impaired. The presence of distinguished Democrats like John McCormack and Senator Paul Douglas on the steering committee and advisory board prevented critics from characterizing the Committee as a Republican or Republic of China front. It always had energetic, committed leadership in the person of Walter Judd, who was chairman in all but name for the first decade and officially took that title in the mid-1960s; and in Marvin Liebman, who worked organizational and public relations miracles with an annual budget that never exceeded $100,000 while he was secretary.

The fortunes of the Committee of One Million were tied to the basic American policy of containment, waxing in the 1950s when Eisenhower and Dulles rigorously resisted communism from Guatemala to Lebanon to Quemoy and Matsu, and waning in the 1970s when Nixon and Kissinger ardently pursued détente with Moscow and Peking. Nixon's 1972 visit to the Middle Kingdom, while not "changing the world" as he claimed, certainly changed U.S. attitudes toward a nation previously considered unfit by its own actions for membership in the United Nations and the international community.

The original petition that Judd and the others presented to President Eisenhower in the White House on October 22, 1953, listed 210 very prominent Americans, including Senator John Sparkman of Alabama, chairman of the Senate Foreign Relations Committee; Congressman Robert Chiperfield, chairman of the House Foreign Affairs Committee; Senator William F. Knowland of California, the Senate majority leader (after Robert Taft's death in July 1953); Congressman John W. McCormack of Massachusetts, the House minority whip and future Speaker; Congressman Jacob Javits of New York; and Senator Hubert H. Humphrey of Minnesota. The petition also listed twelve governors; eleven retired generals, including George C. Marshall, whose endorsement was a source of special satisfaction and vindication to Judd; seven retired diplomats, including the last U.S. Ambassador to China, J. Leighton Stuart; four labor leaders, including George Meany, soon to be head of the combined AFL-CIO; eleven retired politicians, including Tom Connally, former chairman of the Senate Foreign Relations Committee; fourteen church leaders; twenty-two scientists and educators, including

Arthur M. Schlesinger of Harvard and Dean Roscoe Pound of Yale; eighteen publishers and journalists, including Norman Chandler of the *Los Angeles Times,* William R. Hearst, Jr., William L. White, the famed Kansas editor, and Frank E. Gannett; and thirty-three executives from business, industry, and finance, including Robert E. Wood, head of Sears Roebuck, Conrad Hilton, J. P. Grace, Jr., and Juan Trippe.[13] These men represented the apotheosis of the American establishment of the 1950s and provided a lasting foundation for the Committee's activities and reputation for years to come.

The petition declared that admission of Communist China to the United Nations would violate the spirit and the law of the U.N.; require the expulsion of a charter member of the United Nations; encourage Asian nations to "make fatal compromises with the Communist bloc"; restore the prestige and authority of the Soviet Union "at a time when Communist dictatorship seems to be badly shaken inside the USSR and in its satellite Empire"; and encourage subversive movements in free nations, increasing "the danger of a new war." The petition stated that Communist China had shown itself unworthy of U.N. membership by "systematically disregarding every human right and violating every freedom" and by "aiding in aggression upon South Korea and making war on the United Nations."[14] The arguments were basically the ones that Judd and others had been making against U.N. admission and U.S. recognition of Communist China and echoed the language of House Concurrent Resolution 129, introduced by Judd on July 21, 1953, opposing the admission of "the Chinese Communists" to the United Nations, a resolution which passed the House 379 to 0.

Eisenhower formally acknowledged receipt of the petition and agreed that "existing international facts" precluded the "seating of the Chinese Communist regime to represent China in the UN." He added that there was "every reason to fear that the Chinese Communist regime in fact now seeks representation in the UN in order to promote the objectives of international Communism."[15] Consistent with his longtime position, Judd responded that the Committee agreed with the president that if and when the Chinese Communist regime convincingly demonstrated its intention to live according to "civilized international rules" and became truly representative of the Chinese people, the United States should reconsider its position.[16] Here again, Judd demonstrated his keen understanding of the political process; some supporters of the Committee, notably Alfred Kohlberg, wanted the organization to take a blood oath that it would never under any conditions endorse the admission of the Chinese communist regime. Ever the realist, Judd endorsed Eisenhower's conditional opposition.

With President Eisenhower's imprimatur and the backing of the AFL, the American Legion, and similar organizations, the Committee set confidently to work collecting signatures, and on July 6, 1954, it sent a telegram to the White House, announcing that it had received its one millionth signature. "The spontaneous and overwhelming success of the Committee's efforts," commented Charles Edison and Judd, who signed the telegram, "convincingly upholds your own view that 95 percent of the American people will support all measures taken to prevent appeasement of communism by rewarding its aggression." In barely nine months and with total expenditures of less than sixty thousand dollars (most of the contributions were for ten or fifteen dollars), the Committee *for* One Million became the Committee *of* One Million. Because the question of U.S. relations with the Republic of China and mainland China persisted as a major issue in Congress and even in presidential campaigns, the Committee continued its educational and lobbying efforts, stepping up activities each year just before the annual U.N. vote on the China seat every fall, and taking advantage of Mao Tse-tung's various experiments in revolution, such as the Great Leap Forward and the Cultural Revolution, to argue that Communist China did not belong in the United Nations or any other international organization respecting law and order.

For some eighteen years, the Committee of One Million acted as the conscience and reflected the mood of the American public regarding U.S. relations with Communist China. For example, in April 1955, the Committee published full-page advertisements in the *New York Times* and the *Los Angeles Examiner* that warned against appeasement, opposed any surrender of Quemoy and Matsu (which had been hit by large-scale Communist Chinese air attacks in January), and congratulated President Eisenhower and Congress on the wording of the Formosa Resolution, which authorized the president to use U.S. armed forces at his discretion to protect Formosa (Taiwan) and the Pescadores Islands, which included Quemoy and Matsu. In 1956, the Committee carried out a successful campaign to include planks opposing the U.N. admission of Communist China in both the Republican and Democratic party platforms; it repeated the process every four years through 1968. In 1957, the Committee expressed its opposition to U.S. trade with Communist China, sending President Eisenhower a statement signed by 176 leading businessmen.[17] When the liberal Americans for Democratic

Action called in 1958 for an immediate start on negotiations toward U.S. recognition of the "People's Republic of China," the Committee distributed widely a statement by liberal Senator Paul Douglas (D-Ill.) opposing closer relations with the mainland; Senator Douglas was a member of the Committee's steering committee as well as a prominent member of Americans for Democratic Action. That same year, a World Order Study Conference of the National Council of Churches passed a unanimous resolution in favor of U.S. recognition of Communist China and its admission to the United Nations; at the suggestion of Judd, the Committee polled Protestant clergymen across the country, reporting in February 1959 that of 9,088 replies received, 7,837 opposed both recognition and admission while only 1,042 favored a change in present U.S. policy.[18]

In 1959, the Committee of One Million helped organize one of the most successful and admirable relief efforts in the postwar period—the American Emergency Committee for Tibetan Refugees. Beginning with their seizure of the mainland in 1949, the Chinese communists began efforts to bring Tibet under military control. For almost a decade the Buddhist rulers of Tibet, using compromise, delaying tactics and military resistance, prevented Peking from gaining control of Tibet and using the Dalai Lama as a pawn. In early 1959, when it became clear that the Chinese communists would soon gain control of the capital city of Lhasa by force, the Dalai Lama escaped into India, where he told the world of the cruelty and lawlessness of the invading communists.

Judd, with the support of B. A. Garside of the American Bureau for Medical Aid to China, made a one-man trip to India at Christmas 1959 to see the Dalai Lama at his refuge in a remote area on the Tibetan border. Judd then interviewed Indian Prime Minister Nehru and offered to provide American help to the spiritual head of Tibet and the Tibetans who had escaped. Nehru thought there were only a few hundred refugees and responded that India needed no help. When the number soon increased to about 10,000, Indian Ambassador Mehta in Washington advised Judd that American help would be welcomed. Judd, Garside, Liebman and others asked Lowell Thomas, the well-known newscaster and author who had frequently traveled to and written about Tibet, to help organize and head the American Emergency Committee for Tibetan Refugees. Thomas promptly accepted and gave effective leadership, inviting prominent citizens in business, education, religion, and social service to join him. With Thomas's help, more than two million dollars was raised over the next two years, a demonstration "of the

American people's sympathy and admiration for a devout and indomitable people."[19] The political impact of Communist China's brutal invasion was considerable in the U.S. Congress and the United Nations, which again voted to postpone consideration of the Chinese question for another year.

In 1961, President John F. Kennedy, who had told the Committee as a presidential candidate that he opposed "the recognition of Communist China under present conditions," accepted a change in strategy regarding Peking's admission to the United Nations: instead of postponing any vote, the United States moved to have China's credentials considered an "important question" under Article 18 of its charter, which required a two-thirds majority. Both Washington and Taipei were confident they could block a two-thirds vote for the foreseeable future.[20] In what Liebman called a clearcut victory for the Committee, the U.N. General Assembly not only voted to declare China's credentials an "important question" but voted 45 to 30 against admitting Communist China without expelling the Republic of China; and defeated a Soviet motion to admit Peking and expel Taipei. A year and a half later, however, Judd wrote to Liebman expressing his concern about a forthcoming "big push" to change China policy; President Kennedy himself stopped admission in 1961, he said, and it would be the president and the Committee who would have to stop it again.[21] Following Kennedy's assassination, the question was: would President Johnson continue his predecessor's anti-Peking policy? In March 1964, Secretary of State Dean Rusk reassured the Committee and its supporters with an unequivocal endorsement of the Republic of China, asserting that "Peping continues to insist upon the surrender of Formosa as the sine qua non of any improvement whatever in relations with the United States. We are loyal to our commitment to the Government of the Republic of China, and we will not abandon the 12 million people of Free China on Taiwan to Communist tyranny."[22] A plank opposing the admission of Communist China to the United Nations was inserted in both the Democratic and Republican platforms in 1964; in the same year more than 300 members of Congress formally endorsed a Committee declaration against admission. Judd traced the bipartisan support to "Communist China's cynical violations of its solemn pledge in the 1962 agreement to support the independence and neutrality of Laos. . . . Without Red China's military assistance to the Pathet Lao and Viet Cong today, their cruel assaults on Laos and South Vietnam, with almost daily killing of Americans, simply could not continue. So it seems clearer than ever that

United States opposition to Red China's aggressive expansionism has been sound, and must be resolutely maintained."[23]

In March 1966, 198 academic members of the Association for Asian Studies urged the U.S. government to drop its opposition to seating the People's Republic of China in the United Nations and to open negotiations toward the establishment of formal diplomatic relations; and in response, the House Committee on Foreign Affairs and Senate Committee on Foreign Relations held hearings on "U.S. policy with regard to Mainland China." Supporters of change like John F. Fairbank of Harvard kept insisting that now was the time for the United States to reach out to mainland China while Judd (no longer a member of Congress) and his colleagues defended the China policy which had been supported by Presidents Truman, Eisenhower, Kennedy, and Johnson. Fairbank and the others fell silent when within a few weeks Mao Tse-tung launched the Great Cultural Revolution, which plunged mainland China into political and economic chaos and suffering for a decade.

With the election of Nixon in 1968, it seemed that the Committee would enjoy a period of continuing influence. After all, Judd and Nixon were political allies of more than twenty years, providing the Committee with direct access to the White House and U.S. policy making. However, Nixon had indicated as early as the summer of 1967 in a *Foreign Affairs* article that he was interested in "improving" relations with the People's Republic of China. The "Communist China lobby" seized the opportunity and began to press harder than ever for a more "realistic" policy of recognizing mainland China without making any moral judgments about its government. Travel and trade regulations were soon relaxed, and in July 1971 Nixon told a surprised nation on national television that he would be the first American president to visit China.

Badly shaken, the Committee urged the president to ask the Chinese communists about the release of American servicemen in China; its role as an "aggressor" in the Korean War; its practice of genocide in Tibet; its responsibility for the death of American soldiers in Vietnam through the supply of arms and ammunition to North Vietnam; and its continuing description of the United States as an "imperialist aggressor" surrounded by "running dogs."[24] The Committee dared not attack Nixon publicly for fear of alienating him and his Republican sponsors in Congress. Just before the fateful UN vote that fall, Judd argued in the Committee's very last newsletter that if the Republic of China could be kept in, Communist China would stay out as Peking had no intention of sharing the China seat with Taipei. But it was not to be: with the announcement that President Nixon was going to mainland China, the Republic of China's position in the United Nations was fatally weakened. The U.S. delegation, led by Amb. George Bush, could keep insisting that the United States was 100 percent behind the Republic of China, but the delegates of the United Nations took their cue from the travel plans of the American president. The Committee enjoyed a long run, far longer than most single-interest political organizations, but finally closed its doors when on October 25, 1971, the United Nations General Assembly voted 76 to 35 to expel the Republic of China and seat the People's Republic of China.

CHAPTER FOURTEEN

◆

Containment and Liberation

WALTER JUDD'S DAILY SCHEDULE in the 1950s reflected his lifelong ability to make use of every possible minute. He awakened at about 7:30 A.M. and went downstairs to have breakfast with Miriam, the girls, Mary Lou, Eleanor and Carolyn, having already gone to school. Breakfast was simple: cereal, fruit and black coffee. He did not read the morning newspapers; in fact, he did not take the *Washington Post,* considering it too liberal, depending on the more moderate *Washington Evening Star.* He drove to Capitol Hill along Rock Creek Parkway, and arrived at the Longworth House Office Building before 9 A.M. He went over the day's schedule with his administrative assistant, made phone calls, prepared for any committee hearing and sometimes had an appointment before making his way to the House Foreign Affairs Committee. Hearings began promptly at 10 A.M. and usually continued until noon, when the House convened.

Judd made it a point to be on the House floor for the chaplain's invocation and to listen to the one-minute speeches of his colleagues about the "hot" issues of the day. Sometimes, he made a mini-speech himself, but he was not comfortable with the time restriction. At least two or three times a week, he had lunch in the House Members Dining Room, perhaps with visiting constituents, or at a large round "common" table, where he "talked with other Republicans about what was coming up on the floor."[1] The Democrats had their own common table, and never did the twain meet. On the other days, he had a cup of Navy bean soup and a sandwich in the cloakroom of the House chamber.

During the afternoon, he remained on the House floor if there was an important debate, particularly on foreign policy, often asking a question or proposing an amendment. This was true legislative work, and he worked hard at it. Sometimes the Foreign Affairs Committee had an afternoon hearing requiring his attendance. Otherwise, he returned to his office to answer correspondence; he insisted that "all letters be answered promptly," even from outside the district.

On a quiet day, he left around 6 P.M., perhaps stopping briefly at an embassy reception to have a gin and tonic before arriving home for dinner with Miriam; by then, the girls would already be doing their homework. But more often, he remained at the office to edit and reedit his remarks on the House floor that day. As he remarked, "I'm a rewriter, not a writer." He was a perfectionist, never satisfied with the text of a speech, whether prepared or not; he constantly changed words, phrases, sentences, paragraphs. Revisions were supposed to be given to the Clerk of the House before midnight. But some nights it took him so long to revise his remarks that he went to the sixth floor of the Government Printing Office (which printed the *Congressional Record*) and finished his editing there, after midnight. It was important, he explained, to get what he said on the House floor "just right." Other nights, he had a speech in a city like Harrisburg, Pa., Richmond, or Indianapolis that could be reached within an hour's flight; and he flew there after the close of House business, made his talk and flew back to Washington late or as early as possible the next morning.

He went to his congressional office every Saturday that Congress was in session. He liked working on the weekend because there were no telephone calls, no hearings, no floor business. "I could sit there with my dictaphone," he recalled, "and answer my letters.... I didn't feel I could just thank them and move on. I had to figure out how to answer them properly."[2] But he never worked on Sunday, always going to church in the morning and often speaking somewhere again in the evening. Whenever he arrived home from the office or from a trip, Miriam would stop whatever she was doing—cooking, reading, helping the girls with their homework—and go to the front door to greet him with a kiss and an embrace. It was a daily act of love that the Judd girls never forgot.

Judd adhered to a tightly structured schedule that allowed little time for casual socializing or the small pleasures of family life. The first Saturday he did not work while in Washington was Mary Lou's wedding day in 1957. "I was brought up that way," he said. "The job, the cause, always came first." Politics was never far away, even at social events. Miriam remembered that Walter and John Carter Vincent of the State Department sat quietly side by side while their daughters played duets at piano recitals, but launched into "vigorous debate" about U.S.-China policy at the intermission.

Time was precious and not to be wasted. One Christmas, Mary Lou, Carolyn and Eleanor wrote and presented a little play for their parents, who were charmed until it went on too long. Their father broke in to ask them to "wrap it up" and then walked out to do some work in the study. Truth had to be served. An excellent musician since his undergraduate days at the University of Nebraska, he once told the girls' music teacher at a piano recital that they were always making mistakes and how could she say they were making "beautiful music"? The teacher replied that he wanted "perfection" while she wanted "love of music."[3]

Yet, for all the New England sternness (he opposed Mary Lou joining a sorority in high school until Miriam remarked, with some asperity, that this was one time when he should let his oldest daughter make up her own mind, which he did, reluctantly), the girls had warm memories of the times they did spend with their father. Carolyn recalled their annual automobile trip from Minnesota to Washington when they played alphabet games, capitals of the states, Twenty Questions and "sang a lot. He has a wonderful voice and a wonderful sense of harmony." Those were "precious times," she said, "when we had Dad as a captive audience."[4]

They admired his honesty and his determination; they marveled that no matter how often he lost, in or out of Congress, he kept fighting. Eleanor recalled that in the summer of 1959, she was in Europe on a student tour when she read that Congress had approved a huge cut in foreign aid. She immediately wrote a letter to her father, saying how badly she felt because she knew how important the program was to him. When she asked her mother, upon her return, whether he had read her letter, Miriam replied, "Yes, but he couldn't understand your concern. He wasn't upset at all about the defeat. You see, he was born to be a crusader."[5]

The girls remembered that when they were sick, it was very often their doctor father who cared for them. Carolyn spoke of "his hands" that had "such healing and goodness in them." Eleanor remembered that as a small child, she had very bad nightmares and her father would come and "hold me and hold me" until the fear went away. "When it really came to a crisis in my life," added Eleanor, "and I've had a few, he always came to help."[6] As they grew older, the girls noticed that unlike the fathers of their schoolmates, their father did not seem to have buddies with whom he played golf or went fishing. He had many acquaintances, and close political allies, but he did not appear to have intimate friends. They felt sorry for him until their mother told them that their father had more friends, more people who respected and admired him, than anyone else she knew. They came to understand that whatever else their father had or did not have, he was blessed with one great friend, protector and mediator—their mother.

In the 1950s, at the end of a long day on the Hill, he usually drove down Independence Avenue past the Washington Monument and the Mall, turned right just before the Potomac River and stopped in front of the Lincoln Memorial. At night, there were only a few lights on, and Lincoln sat there, in partial darkness, looking up the Mall at the Capitol and, so Judd liked to imagine, reflecting on what Congress was doing. He received "more spiritual inspiration" from his nightly visits with Lincoln than almost anything else in Washington. He also often took family and friends at night to visit Lincoln, and standing in the middle of the monument, he would read aloud what was written on the marble walls—"government of the people, by the people, for the people"—his voice carrying far in the silent night.[7]

One of President Eisenhower's first acts when he entered the White House in January 1953 was to order a review of U.S. foreign policy; task forces studied and made recommendations regarding three possible strategies: (1) a continuation of *containment,* the basic policy during the Truman years; (2) a policy of *global deterrence,* in which U.S. commitments would be expanded and communist aggression forcibly met; and (3) a policy of *liberation,* which by political, economic, and paramilitary means would "roll back" the communist empire and liberate the peoples behind the Iron and Bamboo Curtains. The latter two options were favored by Secretary of State John Foster Dulles, who counseled the use of the threat of nuclear weapons to counter Soviet military aggression and who argued that having thus resolved the problem of military defense, the free world could "undertake what has been

219

too long delayed—a political offensive."[8] Such a nonmilitary offensive was precisely what Judd had been stressing for years, as evidenced in his support of the Voice of America, Point IV, the United Nations, and other programs. He believed that the protracted conflict between the United States and the Soviet Union was essentially one of ideas and not of weapons, and would be won by the side which was most effective in marshaling its arguments and not its armaments. Presented with the three options, Eisenhower, an instinctive moderate, rejected "liberation" as too dangerous and containment as too passive, and selected deterrence with its emphasis on air and sea power. But Dulles managed to convey an impression of deterrence "plus" during his six years as secretary of state, as with his January 1954 speech to the Council on Foreign Relations when he announced that the Eisenhower administration was proposing a new American policy—"a maximum deterrent at a bearable cost," in which "local defenses must be reinforced by the further deterrent of massive retaliatory power. . . . The way to deter aggression is for the free community to be willing and able to respond vigorously at places and with means of its own choosing."[9]

The House of Representatives was forced to consider its own defenses on March 1 when four Puerto Rican nationalists, seated in the visitor's gallery, suddenly jumped to their feet and began shooting at the members below them. Judd had just finished a long-distance telephone call in the cloakroom and stepped into the chamber, raising his hand to cast a vote, when he heard a shot and saw the terrorists firing down into the House. When colleagues began diving beneath their desks and one congressman stumbled out of the chamber, bleeding, he realized that the House was under attack. With little thought for his own safety, Judd dashed down the aisle to help Alvin Bentley of Michigan, who was badly wounded, and probably saved Bentley's life. Several colleagues were mistakenly holding up the bleeding man in a sitting rather than a lying position, and Judd could feel no pulse. He immediately put Bentley's head down to get the blood flowing toward his brain and covered him with his own coat. He began rubbing Bentley's legs to help the blood flow and looked again at the deathly pale man. "By golly, there was just a little twitching of his eye, and I knew he was not dead," Judd remembered. If they had kept holding him up for a couple of minutes more, "he probably would have died." When a young doctor arrived, Judd told him where he thought the bullet had entered, about half an inch from his heart, suggested an injection of morphine (the young doctor had apparently never seen a gunshot wound before) and helped carry Bentley out and down to the ambulance. The thirty-five-year-old Republican recovered and went on to serve another three terms in Congress, thanks to the emergency treatment of someone unflustered by guns and bullets, even on the floor of the House of Representatives.[10]

Judd was also required to defend Dulles and Eisenhower—from charges that their foreign policies were inflexible and old-fashioned. Indeed, in later years, some critics asserted that "massive retaliation" was not new at all but a continuation of Truman's containment policy; and that rather than providing flexibility, it locked the U.S. military into a rigid strategy of either using local forces or escalating to nuclear war. Such an assessment ignores the historical facts. Truman-style containment produced the fall of China to the Chinese communists and the stalemated Korean War because it was limited in application to only one continent, Europe. Eisenhower-style containment produced the coming to power of the Shah of Iran, helped overthrow the pro-Marxist regime of Jocobo Arbenz Guzman in Guatemala, helped protect the Nationalist islands of Quemoy and Matsu from Chinese communist seizure, and blocked the intervention of Iraq and/or Syria in Lebanon because it was applied on every continent without exception. Nor was the Eisenhower-Dulles "new look" a policy with only two options, the use of local forces or nuclear threats: marines were used in Lebanon, economic pressures in the Suez crisis, and the U.S. Navy in the Formosa Straits. Furthermore, during the Eisenhower years, the United States completed the construction of a powerful ring of alliances and commitments around the communist empire: NATO in Europe, the Eisenhower Doctrine and the Baghdad Pact in the Middle East, SEATO in Southeast Asia, the Korean and ROC mutual security agreements in East Asia, and the revised Rio Pact with its emphasis against communist subversion in Latin America. As Eisenhower said in his inaugural address on January 20, 1953: "Conceiving the defense of freedom, like freedom itself, to be one and indivisible, we hold all continents and peoples in equal regard and honor. We reject any insinuation that one race or another, one people or another, is in any sense inferior or expendable."[11]

Eisenhower was president at a time, Judd argued, when the world was "filled with confusion," when a third of its people had gained their independence and a third had lost it: "no two such convulsions have ever previously occurred in all of human history." Yet, he said, the Eisenhower years went by so calmly, until the U-2 incident in 1960, that most people "didn't even realize the dangers overcome."[12]

Criticism of Eisenhower's foreign policy came from the left and the right. Conservatives, for example, charged that the Eisenhower administration failed to help the Hungarian freedom fighters against invading Soviet tanks in October 1956. While sharing their disappointment at the failure of the Hungarian revolution, Judd argued that the revolt was not America's to win or lose. The Voice of America did not encourage the students of Hungary, although, he conceded, Radio Free Europe, financed by the U.S. government and run by exiles from Eastern Europe, did give the impression that the West would come to the students' assistance if they revolted. According to Judd, there were three basic reasons why the United States did not act. First, there was a moral reason: "There was no way we could get there without violating the neutrality of Austria. . . . How could we justify violating Austria's neutrality to go to Hungary to repel the Russian violation of Hungary's neutrality?" Although it is not generally known, the United States asked Austria for freedom of passage, but Vienna refused to grant transit by land or even use of its air space. Second, there was a practical reason: the United States had no plan for dealing with an uprising of major proportions behind the Iron Curtain. "I'm sure [we've] got plans for a war with South Africa or a war with Nicaragua or a war with Iceland or a war with Timbuctu." But "apparently no one believed" that something like the Hungarian revolution "might happen." Third, there was a strategic reason: "If we had even one platoon there, it wouldn't have been a defeat of just a bunch of high school students or radical freedom lovers in Hungary, it would have been a defeat of the great United States." As it was, the Hungarian uprising showed that the "whole Communist movement in Eastern Europe was a great deal weaker than we realized." What had been viewed as invincible was exposed as filled with weak spots. "Whatever imprisons people," said Judd, "is not as strong as it looks."[13]

Three weeks later, the Suez crisis revealed that the West too was far weaker than anyone suspected. On October 29, 1956, the Israelis launched an attack against Egypt, led by the anti-western Gamal Nasser. The British and the French vetoed a cease-fire resolution sponsored by the United States and the Soviet Union in the U.N. Security Council, and joined the Israeli assault on October 31. The fighting continued for another five days during which the Soviets crushed the Hungarian revolt, gambling that the West, particularly the United States, would be too preoccupied with Suez to take any action in Hungary. With Dulles ill and in the hospital, Eisenhower took charge personally and applied economic and political pressure on Great Britain in particular to force a cease-fire in their attack on Egypt. Judd, ever the anticolonialist, agreed with the U.S. action, arguing that if Washington had not taken it, "We'd have lost the whole non-white world right then. They never would have believed us again, that we are people of principle and will stand by our commitments including those in the United Nations." They would have said: "Blood is thicker than water. In a showdown the United States always stands with the British." Significantly, for all his disappointments in its performance, Judd still believed in the need for an effective United Nations and would not accept the blatant disregard even by long-standing allies of one of its resolutions.

Contrary to many analysts who have said that Eisenhower coasted through much of his second term, Judd felt that 1958, for example, was a year that showed Ike at his best. The communists tested the West on three fronts simultaneously: to the west, in West Berlin; to the south, in Lebanon; and to the east, in Quemoy and Matsu. Lebanon was important because it was "the bridge across to Africa and key to control of the Suez Canal and the oil on which Western Europe depends to keep its wheels running." Judd recalled that in a forty-eight-hour period such disparate countries as Israel, Turkey, Greece, Egypt, Jordan, and Tunisia told the United States that it had to stabilize Lebanon or the Middle East "would collapse." The Soviets responded that if the United States embarked on a military adventure in Lebanon, there would be "bombs in the streets of the capitals of the West." President Eisenhower made the decision to send in fourteen thousand marines, and told his advisers: "Now, they've made these threats. Everybody understands, doesn't he, that if they do what they say they're going to do, this is the big one?" But when the marines landed, not one shot was fired, not one person was killed on either side, the crisis was resolved, stability was restored, and in a few months, U.S. forces withdrew.

Asked some years later to describe the difference, if any, between U.S. troops in Lebanon and Soviet troops in Hungary, Judd responded: "One, we were invited into Lebanon by the legitimate government and the Russians were not invited into Hungary. Second, nobody got killed in Lebanon, and in the other case [many] were killed. Third, we got out, and the Russians still ... have troops in Budapest. That's a lot of difference."[14]

To the east, the United States stood firm in Quemoy all through the summer and fall of 1958, while the communists threw as many as a thousand shells a day at the island. Columnist Walter Lippmann, among others, wrote that the United States ought to yield, that there must not be a "confrontation" that would lead to all-out war. But, as Judd explained, the struggle was not over Quemoy, "any more than the Civil War was over Fort Sumter. . . . The question [in the Civil War] was whether [the United States] was to be one country or two. And if one, what kind of country was it to be, with or without slavery?" Similarly, the conflict over Quemoy was, "What kind of Asia is there to be?" Would it be with or without freedom? Eisenhower and Dulles stood "firm as a rock" on Quemoy "despite all the pressures here," and when the communists realized the United States was not going to yield, their push "petered out."

In November 1958, the Soviets issued an ultimatum that "this abnormal situation in West Berlin" had to be ended in six months. Judd recalled that he once talked with Eisenhower, who said, "You know, it is kind of abnormal, West Berlin." To which, Judd responded: "Mr. President, if they call West Berlin abnormal, we ought to come back and ask, 'Is it abnormal to be free? The abnormal situation, Mr. Khrushchev, is in East Berlin. When are you going to end that abnormal situation in East Berlin?' " The Soviets hoped that pressure by the American public, especially the churches, would force Eisenhower to concede. But the Soviets did not have the true measure of the president. Just before the six-month ultimatum expired, Eisenhower held a news conference at which a reporter asked (Judd always suspected it was prearranged), in effect: "Mr. President, the ultimatum that [the Soviets] gave us on Berlin expires next week. What if they do what they've been threatening to do?" Eisenhower's reply was only seven words: "It would not be a ground war." "He prevented a war," commented Judd, "with seven words—and the power and the will to use it behind the words."[15]

In 1968, many years before historians began revising their negative appraisals of the Eisenhower presidency, Judd said flatly that "Ike's patient firmness prevented war" many times, as in Lebanon, Quemoy, and Berlin in 1958 and early 1959. "It was not belligerence, he never raised his voice, he didn't call any names, he didn't get into any public brawl. He just stuck by his dedication to human freedom and to commitments the United States had made to its allies." He scoffed at the notion that Eisenhower was not a "great leader" because "he didn't engage in dramatic fireworks. He got crises headed off *before* they got to the fireworks." Responding to critics who said that Eisenhower was not a "strong President," Judd predicted that "history will reveal every year that goes by how much stronger a president he was than was realized. He was one of our really great ones."[16] As they study and consider the two Eisenhower presidential terms, more and more historians are now coming to the same conclusion.

During these same years, Judd reached the apogee of his influence in Congress, by reason of his easy access to the White House and the State Department, his ability to successfully steer the most difficult legislation, especially foreign aid, through Congress, and his adherence to the principle that he was a United States Representative first and the congressman from and for Minneapolis second—a political inversion that first amused and then awed many of his colleagues. His access to the president and the secretary of state gave him political influence; his skill at compromise and the timely "little" amendment on the House floor gave him legislative influence; his commitment to "lost" causes, like the elimination of racial clauses in U.S. immigration law, the fate of refugee Chinese intellectuals, and statehood for Hawaii, which had little appeal to his constituents, gave him moral influence. In a sense, he served as the conscience of the House, exhorting his colleagues, educating them, challenging them to look beyond the halls of Congress to the needs of the nation and the concerns of the world.

In 1953 and 1954, when his party held a majority in the House, Judd led the fight for foreign assistance, fending off the attempts of mostly Republican members to cut if not kill the program; he was equally supportive for the rest of the decade when the Democrats were in the majority. His rationale for foreign aid was simple: "What we are trying to do in this program is to safeguard the security of the United States, period. That means we are striving to build a world of peace and freedom; otherwise we will not long be secure. That means we have to stand with all others who are striving for the same kind of a world." The primary purpose of foreign aid was not "to buy friends," as critics charged, but to help "free peoples stand on their own feet so that they can maintain their independence and keep their land and resources out of the hands of our enemies."[17] He often used various medical analogies, comparing foreign aid to a needed operation on a very ill patient who has not yet completely recovered: "Was the operation a failure? No, look at the alternative. Without it, he would have been in the cemetery. With it, he is alive. He is not yet well, but he has a chance to get well." Similarly, he argued, you could not say that foreign aid has been a failure because of the "bad conditions existing here and there" among its recipients. "Where would they and we be without it?" Foreign aid, in the form of the Marshall Plan, he said, had kept Greece, Turkey, and Western Europe out of communist hands and free. The "patient" was still alive, he declared, and as long as he was, there was hope that measures would be taken to develop "strong resilient governments" in Europe, Asia, and elsewhere.[18]

He rejoiced at the passage of the McCarran-Walter Act of 1952, which removed racial discrimination from U.S. immigration and naturalization laws and fulfilled a vow he had made in 1925 on his way to China as a medical missionary. While in Japan, he saw firsthand the impact of the 1924 Exclusion Act on the Japanese people—"the[ir] numb shock, coming as it did from the western friend which, only a year before, had aided them so promptly and so generously after the great Tokyo-Yokahama earthquake." The act's racial provisions strengthened the hand of the militarists in Japan and furnished "communism with its most powerful propaganda weapon in turning hundreds of millions of people in Asia against us." His bill granting immigration and naturalization to Chinese persons and persons of Chinese descent was passed in 1943, his first year in Congress. His bill to eliminate racial discrimination against all persons of Asian ancestry was considered but not acted upon in succeeding Congresses, until it was finally incorporated into the McCarran-Walter Act, which was passed by both Houses, vetoed by President Truman, and then passed over his veto. Judd's provisions were "the only civil rights legislation enacted" in decades, an accomplishment of which he was proud and which made the later attacks on his allegedly "poor" civil rights record both puzzling and painful.[19]

It was this same concern for civil and human rights that motivated his strong support of statehood for Hawaii when other congressmen were suggesting that Hawaiians would not be loyal citizens because of their mostly Asian origin. There were references to "sabotage" at Pearl Harbor, which brought a quick rebuttal from Judd that the FBI and the intelligence agencies of the army and navy did not find "a single case of sabotage in Hawaii by any persons of nonwhite ancestry." Cognizant that it was the Hawaiians' Japanese origins that disturbed his colleagues the most, he emphasized the demonstrated bravery of Japanese-American soldiers in World War II. When a Texas congressman joined the chorus of insinuation, Judd recalled that in the fall of 1944, a battalion of the "Remember the Alamo" regiment of the Thirty-sixth Texas Division was cut off and surrounded by Germans on the Vosges Mountains. Many attempts to rescue them were made but failed. At last, the 442d Regimental Combat Team volunteered and finally reached the 211 survivors of the lost Texas battalion, at a cost of more than 2,000 casualties, including almost 200 killed. In appreciation, the state of Texas gave honorary citizenship to every member of the Regimental Combat Team, "made up wholly ... of Japanese-American volunteers, mostly born in Hawaii." The congressman from Texas fell silent.

Judd went on to discuss his reasons why statehood should be granted to Hawaii: "How can we ... talk about people having the right to governments of their own choosing, for example in Eastern Europe, unless we show by our deeds that we believe in it in the Pacific as well?" In the ongoing struggle between democracy and communism, the United States would give "new validity and life" to the appeal of the democratic system, particularly in Asia, by extending statehood to the people of Hawaii who "have proved [themselves] in every reasonable sense."[20] But even with the backing of the Eisenhower administration, statehood would not be granted to Hawaii (along with Alaska) until two years later, when charges by Southern Democrats of communist infiltration and an overly large "non-Caucasian" population in Hawaii were disregarded by a political coalition of Democrats, who saw Alaska as helping their party, and Republicans, who believed Hawaii would advance their cause.

In the fall of 1953, four members of the House Foreign Affairs Committee, with Judd as chairman, flew more than 30,000 miles in the Far East and Southeast Asia, visiting fourteen countries. Their report urged continued opposition to U.S. recognition and U.N. admission of Communist China; the formation of a "Pacific Pact" of Asian nations, similar to NATO in Europe; U.S. support of Asian nationalism and independence; increased U.S. economic and technical assistance which had so far totaled about six billion dollars; "maximum use ... of Vietnamese forces" in Indochina; and flexibility regarding the evolution of democracy in the region. The reference to the use of Vietnamese forces was significant, in light of the subsequent Americanization of the Vietnam War. Judd consistently resisted sending American troops to Vietnam, taking his lead from Eisenhower and MacArthur, both of whom viewed involvement of U.S. troops in an Asian land war as dangerous and unnecessary. As he wrote a constituent, if an "armed struggle" became necessary "sending ground troops into Indochina. . . . would be the least effective way to do it."[21] The plea for American flexibility in regard to Asian governments in the 1950s ("The Asian nations must work out their own political pattern in the light of their own background and experience") echoed his criticism of the inflexibility of foreign missionaries in China in the 1920s and 1930s. The four congressmen concluded that they saw no immediate danger of a third world war in the region, but stated that American policies must be directed against local violence and subversion and the "constant attempts to sow dissension among our allies."[22] It was to counter such communist attempts at dividing and conquering that Judd kept pushing for a Pacific Pact, which to be effective, he argued, had to include Japan and the Republic of China. It is a measure of the many nationalist, linguistic, and cultural divisions in Asia that such a Pacific Pact has yet to become a reality.

When President Eisenhower asked Congress in January 1955 for the authority to "employ the armed forces of the United States for protecting the security of Formosa, the Pescadores and related positions and territories of that area," in response to Chinese communist attacks on the islands of Quemoy and Matsu, Judd urged adoption of the enabling resolution, not "just to save one island and some outposts but to help keep free over one-third of the human beings in the world [in Asia] and keep the world balance of power from being turned overwhelmingly against us." Firmness of action and will, he said, would "prevent war in the Far East with Communist China." Dulles used much the same language in 1958 when Quemoy and Matsu were again under Communist Chinese attack.[23] In 1955 and again in 1958, Dulles and Eisenhower let it be known that the use of nuclear weapons was under consideration. Both times, Communist China backed down.

But U.S. foreign policy during the Eisenhower years did not depend solely on the nuclear "stick," as some critics later charged. The mutual security program, which provided military and economic assistance to America's allies, was a key ingredient of the strategy against communist expansion. And a key player in obtaining congressional approval of mutual security each year, regardless of which party controlled the House, was Judd, who always took the time to place the program in a global context. In June 1956, for example, he pointed out that following a series of setbacks, the Kremlin was shifting its target areas from west and east to south, and moving tactically from power and threats to deception and tricks. In the previous decade, he said, the Soviets tried to seize Greece but failed; tested the West with the Berlin blockade but lifted it when the West refused to be intimidated; threatened the West if it did not abandon NATO but then backed off; promised dire consequences if West Germany were given her independence and allowed to rearm, but then proposed a conference to settle the status of Austria. The communists, he said, were more successful to the east, gaining control of Manchuria, North Korea, mainland China, and North Vietnam. Their next targets were the natural resources of Southeast Asia (oil, iron, copper, rubber) and the industry of Japan. "But there was one major obstacle standing in the way," said Judd: the island of Formosa with its army and airbases. President Eisenhower said at a press conference that if the communists tried to take Formosa, "they will first have to run over the 7th Fleet." Communist China did not try.

So, Judd said, the communists were now looking southward, at the Middle East and South Asia, which were filled with "awful weakness, division and disunity." He mentioned the dispute between Greece and Turkey over Cyprus, the Arab-Israeli conflict, and the struggle between France and its North African colonies. In South Asia, the weak spots included Indonesia and the new nations of Malaya, Burma, and Ceylon. There were strong points in South Asia as well, nations like Korea, Formosa, and Pakistan, and in the Middle East, Turkey, all of whom had been preserved and strengthened by U.S. military and economic assistance. Such aid gave these and other nations "the capacity to fight for themselves, to defend their own freedom," and thereby to serve U.S. interests. He readily conceded the last: "There is no reason why we should refuse to help a friend just because it also helps ourselves. In fact," he said, "it is my conviction that whenever we do what is right for others, it will turn out to be beneficial to ourselves too."

The amount of foreign aid was substantial, he admitted, some four billion dollars, with one-third of the three billion in military assistance scheduled to go to Korea, Taiwan, Pakistan, and Turkey. He mentioned that he often received letters asking, "Why send all this aid abroad? Why not use the money to build highways, hospitals, schools, and give better old-age assistance to needy Americans, or to reduce our taxes here at home?" His colleagues listened carefully, for they received the same kind of letters. Such writers, he said, believed that "if we do not spend this money for our defenses abroad, we will have that much more to spend on ourselves here at home. Unfortunately, it is a false belief." Cutting assistance to Korea or Formosa or other U.S. allies, he said, would only mean that the United States would have to fill the gap with its own armed forces, and that would require more money than was presently being spent on mutual security.

He conceded that the mutual security program had not been as successful as had been hoped, that it had not yet achieved the security and unity of the world and that it could certainly be improved. He urged the program's administrators to simplify their approach, to focus on basics and not try to do too much in a country: "In our enthusiasm to help [nations]," he said, "we almost take them over. [The vice president of Burma] told us in 1953: 'You Americans are so aggressively friendly.' " A basic flaw in the program was that it was conducted most of the time on "a crash basis. . . . We would do better and have more accomplished at the end of a year if we devoted more time and effort to training our personnel so that they know more about the people and the language and the history and the overall needs of the country to which they are going." That was how he had been trained as a medical missionary; he remembered how he had wanted to rush off into the interior of China when he first arrived in 1925, but had spent a year in Nanking, learning the language and the history and the customs of the Chinese.

Despite the determined efforts of the communists, he said, "most of the world is still free—and it would not have been free without this mutual security program." Furthermore, the program had saved the United States money by not requiring us to expand greatly "our own armed forces." The program, he stated, was not a test of U.S. strength or resources of which we had an abundance, but "of our maturity, our decisiveness, our steadfastness. . . . We must make it clear to all that those who stand by us will never be let down." It was not enough to supply things like food, guns, and dollars because men, he said, "do not live by bread alone—or guns or dollars. We have not paid enough attention to the things of the spirit." But he was confident that once America set herself to winning the hearts and minds of men, "we can and will succeed with [that] too."[24]

No other congressman would have ended a rationale for foreign aid with an appeal to the spirit. No other congressman had the historical and global perspective to range from Lenin to Stalin to Khrushchev, from Greece to Pakistan to Indonesia. No other congressman could talk so convincingly about the importance of taking the time to understand a nation before undertaking to help it. Of all the assignments that Judd undertook for the Eisenhower administration, none was more important to the cause of world peace, more difficult of success in an often hostile Congress, and more dangerous politically in his own district than his annual shepherding of the mutual security program through Congress. Quite simply, there would have been no foreign aid program through the 1950s, at least in its final size and scope, without the determined and sustained efforts of Walter Judd. Eisenhower frequently and warmly expressed his appreciation of Judd's key role, as in an October 1956 letter when he wrote, "I prize your friendship."[25]

For all his preoccupation with issues, foreign and domestic, Judd always found time for politicking. He strongly backed the renomination of Richard Nixon for vice president in 1956 when some Republicans were concerned about President Eisenhower's health (he had had a serious heart attack in September 1955 and an operation for ileitis, an intestinal condition, in June 1956) and were suggesting other names, including Christian Herter and Harold Stassen. Judd stated publicly that if Eisenhower were unable to be a candidate, he favored Herter "as the best qualified person all around to take Ike's place"; but if Eisenhower was able to run, replacing Nixon with Herter would lose more Republican votes than it would gain Democratic or independent votes. On August 5, before the Republican convention, he said emphatically that an effort "to dump Dick Nixon at this stage of a campaign would make millions of Republicans so angry that they simply would not vote at all." Nixon immediately wrote that "the name of Walter Judd carries a real 'wallop' around the country and I am deeply grateful for your action and for the fact that you are in my corner."[26]

He comfortably won re-election to Congress through the rest of the decade, defeating Anders Thompson in 1954; Joseph Robbie in 1956, and Robbie again in 1958. Although he won by a solid 56 percent in 1956, he described the campaign as "the meanest" in his career, filled with misrepresentation and charges of bad faith. He warned his supporters that "we must carry on a program of more effective education to undercut in advance such distortions as were the sole bill of fare this time."[27] The distortions centered on his supposed support of "big corporations" and his alleged lack of interest in the people and problems of Minneapolis. The Judd campaign organization successfully countered Robbie's charges in 1956 and 1958 (Robbie subsequently moved to Florida and bought the Miami Dolphins football team), but a pattern of "negative advertising" emerged which was to reach its apex in his 1962 re-election campaign.

One major reason for his political success in Minneapolis was his legislative staff in Washington, which included only four people in the late 1950s (compared with four times that number in the average congressional office of the 1980s). Dorothy Bageant, who came to work for Judd in 1958 (and stayed with him after his retirement for fourteen years) remembered the efficiency and dedication of the staff: "It was very infectious working for him. Even if you did not agree with him at the start, you found yourself committed to his causes." Judd was on the go every day, sometimes starting with a breakfast meeting prior to coming to the office between eight and nine, attending committee hearings from ten to noon, and then proceeding to the House floor before returning to his office to sign the mail in the late afternoon. As a member of the House Foreign Affairs Committee, he was invited to many embassy and other social functions, but regardless of his schedule, there were always one or two dictation discs at Dorothy's desk the next morning, waiting to be transcribed. "We never knew when he did them. But they were always there." He was a stickler for detail, directing his staff "to look it up in the dictionary" if they had a question about the right word to use and not to guess. Bageant recalled that Republicans often came into the office to ask his opinion about an issue or bill and to learn how he was going to vote. "I remember that once I walked with him from the office to the floor and what is about a five-minute walk took us 30 minutes because everybody wanted to talk with Dr. Judd." When he was scheduled to speak, other members made a point of showing up to hear, a rare accolade in what has been called the "House of winds." He never complained, despite the crowded schedule and constant demands. He never criticized anyone personally with one exception: Soviet Foreign Minister Mikoyan, whom he refused to dine with. He was proud to be a congressman, but when he was once asked whether he preferred to be addressed as "The Honorable" or "Doctor," he replied, "Doctor, I earned that."[28]

Because he never saw the Cold War as one that could be won strictly through military containment, Judd consistently supported and often initiated economic, political, and information measures not readily accepted by a Congress and a nation that thought the United States would always have sufficient military power to dictate what it wanted in the world. The Soviets launching of Sputnik in October 1957 jarred the nation badly; Khrushchev moved quickly to gain political advantage from the Soviet Union's demonstrated ability in the field of long-range missiles. Despite all the heated talk about a "missile gap" (later proven to be nonexistent), Eisenhower refused to take "heroic measures" to increase the number of U.S. long-range missiles, but did propose the National Defense Education Act (which Judd supported) to increase the number of American students in science through a program of loans. For his part, Judd introduced legislation to create a Freedom Academy "for the training and development of leaders in a total political war." As he explained, the State Department's Foreign Service Institute prepared people "to be traditional diplomats" while the Freedom Academy would develop "systematic knowledge" about communism, develop a program of "counteraction" consistent with democratic methods and values, educate and train private citizens about communism and the "science of counteraction," and do the same for government officials. In his forthright way, Judd was saying that the United States was engaged in a global war with international communism and ought to take appropriate steps to meet the enemy on all fronts, and in the open.

As early as 1953, he proposed a Joint Congressional Oversight Committee on Intelligence. In the 1970s, it was revealed that for more than twenty years, the CIA had been secretly funding a large number of private individuals and organizations in anticommunist activities all over the world. Judd believed that it would have been far better to conduct the bulk of such operations publicly to help the American people understand the magnitude of the threat and to prevent the excesses that inevitably occur under total secrecy. Congress finally saw the wisdom of such oversight and created Senate and House committees on intelligence in 1976 and 1977. Clearly, there would not have been so many rogue CIA operations if there had been the check and balance of a Congressional oversight committee. Former Congresswoman Edna Kelly of New York, who co-sponsored oversight legislation with Judd, went so far as to assert: "[I am] sure there never would have been a Watergate . . . had we succeeded in 1953."[29]

As the decade drew to a close, Judd became more and more concerned with the many changes taking place in the United States and around the world. For nearly fifteen years, America had enjoyed unchallenged economic and military superiority; now she was struggling with economic recession and facing a more aggressive Soviet Union, emboldened by the success of Sputnik. U.S. leadership was changing as well: his longtime friend John Foster Dulles was ill and would soon die of cancer. President Eisenhower's second term was coming to an end; perhaps he would be replaced by Vice President Nixon, whom Judd had known since 1946 when the young Californian entered Congress. Chris Herter was the new secretary of state; he greatly respected Herter's intelligence and integrity, but did not care for the rumors about an impending visit of Soviet Premier Nikita Khrushchev to the United States. Khrushchev had been responsible for the death of millions in the Ukraine in the 1930s; such a man did not deserve the usual welcome accorded a foreign leader. There might be state visits, summit meetings, and treaties, but the "hard fact" was that the United States was engaged in a Cold War. That was one thing that had not changed. Since the Cold War would not and could not go away, he insisted, America must seek to win it by confronting the communists with "such unity and sustained firmness and strength—military strength, economic strength and moral strength— . . . [that the] disintegrating forces that are plainly at work behind the Iron Curtain so weaken them at home" that they abandon their goal of world conquest.[30] He urged the Eisenhower administration not to rush to a summit, to stand "firm in support of our principles, in support of our honorable commitments, in support of our allies, and in support of the efforts of peoples everywhere to retain their freedom or to regain it."[31]

For the first time, the future of freedom in the Western hemisphere came into question. In January 1959, two weeks after Fidel Castro came to power in Cuba and one week after the United States recognized the new Cuban government, Judd discussed the possibility of the United States' extending economic aid to Cuba. He stated that any assistance and cooperation should be given on the usual conditions that they would be used "to improve the lot of the people" and to further better relations "with the rest of the world." He added that he did not have any special information about the new government, but he noted that "there have been reports for months that Communists may have achieved a dominant position in the Castro movement." He was so far unwilling to accept such reports, "but I must say that this pattern of wholesale executions follows consistently the pattern the Communists have uniformly followed in other countries where they have gained power." In prophetic words that echo down to us today, he said: "I hope and pray that the new regime in Cuba does not come under the control of the Communists, who understandably are trying to capture it; because if it does come under Red control, it bodes ill for Cuba and everybody else in the hemisphere."[32] When securely in power, Castro boasted that he had been a Communist all along.

He deeply mourned the death of John Foster Dulles in May 1959, lauding Dulles's conviction that "there is in the world a moral order. There are such things as right and wrong. . . . There are such things as good and evil. Men can live in harmony with these principles or men can live against them, but the principles endure. You and I can violate the principles; but we cannot break them. In the end if we violate the principles, they break us." Judd revealed much of himself while talking about his old friend and colleague. Like John Foster Dulles, he saw the world as one in which people were constantly choosing between good and evil. Like Dulles, he had faith that there would be peace on earth if man gave "glory to God in the highest," that is, if he sought God's kingdom first. Communists stated there was no God and therefore no moral order, but they were terribly wrong. "Our task," he said, "is to . . . adhere to [the truth] patiently and persistently, as we strive to apply the eternal principles in our everyday living—as individuals, as families, as communities, as nations and as one humanity." In a final eulogy of Dulles, he said: "I do not know when again we will be privileged to know and work with a man who so deeply understood these principles and so well exemplified them in his faith at work, and who, therefore, was so almost indispensable to a world which today is floundering because of loss of faith in or adherence to these essential truths."[33]

He was concerned that without Dulles at the helm of the State Department and as a counterbalance to the eagerness of White House aides to project Eisenhower as the great peacemaker, the administration might forget there was still a Cold War going on. It was no coincidence that only three days after Dulles's death, Judd delivered a major address on the House floor entitled, "On the Erosion of America's Will to Win." He rejected the policy of containment as too defensive, and a policy of convergence as unrealistic, declaring that the West must "accept the unpleasant reality that we are in an all-out struggle with the Communist bloc. One side is going to win; the other will be destroyed. More containment will not win." Student exchanges were not the answer nor was increased trade. We needed, he said, "an activist program in the Western tradition." It was vital, he declared, that "American voters . . . not let the Congress or the executive branch go on hoping wishfully for a compromise or modus videndi with the Soviet bloc." He called for a rededication to a belief in "America's high purpose and ultimate destiny," especially among her youth who must not go forth into public life, "as many are today, ashamed of their country's wealth, convinced that we have already passed our historical prime, believing that nothing is important enough to fight for, and unwilling to make the sacrifices which will be required to defeat world communism."[34] History, he liked to say, was the story of the rise and fall of nations, and although the United States was far from falling, he saw disturbing signs of uncertainty and weakness, like the invitations which were in fact extended to Soviet Foreign Minister Anastas Mikoyan and Premier Nikita Khrushchev to visit the United States.

When he and Mrs. Judd were invited by Eric Johnston of the Motion Picture Association to have dinner with Mikoyan in early January 1959, he tendered their regrets, explaining that they would not be present for the same reasons they "would not attend a social function honoring Hitler, Himmler, Nero, or Genghis Khan: [the] ghosts of too many enslaved, tortured and murdered human beings will be looking down on the dinner." Why not, he suggested, "first give a dinner for [the] martyrs of Hungary and invite Mikoyan?"[35] In response to the Khrushchev visit, he said flatly that it strengthened "the dictator and weaken[ed] his opponents. If the strong [like the United States] accept the tyrant, how much longer can the weak resist him?" He joined the ad hoc Committee for Freedom of All Peoples to send a message to the Soviet premier and to all peoples behind the Iron Curtain "that our politeness to a visitor does not mean any softening of our will or diminution of our concern for those whom Mr. Khrushchev holds today in enslavement."[36] He insisted that he was not being emotional but realistic in his opposition to initiatives that built up America's enemies and hurt her friends. He could not, he would not compromise with certain basic principles, regardless of the political criticism and consequences.

Lecturing at the National War College in July 1959, he recounted how an old friend had described all the things the Soviet Union was doing to "raise" the Iron Curtain and finally said: "Walter, you are just playing the same old tune I have heard you play for 20 years. Why don't you change the tune? We ought to give them the benefit of the doubt, believe the best of them, have faith in them, trust them." To which, Judd responded: "How much is two times two?" "Four." "Why don't you change that answer? . . . There are some things in arithmetic you can't argue about. And there are some things in communism you can't argue about . . . [it] is based on two things: power and deception." He therefore had no choice but to keep saying, at forums like the National War College, or the House floor, on radio and on television, that communism remained the preeminent enemy of mankind but could be defeated if the West "mobilized and released in the world the truly revolutionary forces of freedom."

He told the assembled military officers that such an offensive would include: (1) maintaining West Berlin as "an escape hatch from slavery to freedom"; (2) not extending U.S. recognition or U.N. admission to Communist China, which was experiencing serious internal problems (Mao's "Great Leap Forward" had just flopped); (3) not accepting the permanent enslavement of the peoples of Eastern Europe, "our best ally"; (4) studying the enemy far more thoroughly through institutions like the proposed Freedom Academy; (5) standing by our principles and our pledges "so that free men everywhere will know that we won't let them down."[37]

Some people called such remarks "Cold War rhetoric," but he called them realistic. He was prepared, as he had been since his first campaign, to let the voters of Minneapolis decide whether they wanted him to continue as their representative in Congress. In truth, he was growing a little weary of the congressional grind, of the constant constituent demands that took him away from his duties as a legislator. He had not intended to be a congressman forever. His days never seemed to stop; he often worked past midnight answering letters from constituents. He was caught up in an endless cycle of appointments, meetings, hearings, trips, speeches. He kept up his daily prayers, but he remembered the young friend back in medical school who had stunned him one evening by saying, "Walter, you are not as good a Christian as you once were." What would she say about him today?

There were compensations. One of the most satisfying was his work as a U.S. delegate to the Twelfth General Assembly of the United Nations, from September through December 1957. Two members of Congress served on the U.S. delegation every year; in election years, two senators not up for re-election were appointed; in off-election years, two representatives were named by the president. As one of the U.N.'s original congressional supporters in 1943 and one who endorsed its central mission of furthering international peace and understanding Judd happily accepted the appointment. He demonstrated his special talent for solving "impossible" problems by promoting a multimillion dollar technical assistance program for underdeveloped countries that was accepted by the General Assembly, after eight years of impasse. Since 1949, the Soviet Union and its supporters had been proposing a gigantic United Nations capital investment fund, SUNFED, which the United States and other Western countries opposed because (1) no one, including the United States, could put up the three to five hundred million dollars needed for such a fund; and (2) most Third World countries did not have the necessary infrastructure, trained personnel, and understanding of the role of private capital for the effective use of the fund. SUNFED would have delayed the more fundamental steps of development which ought to be taken first; it would have created "structure without substance."

In its place, Judd, speaking for the United States, proposed that U.N. technical assistance be increased from thirty to a hundred million dollars a year, with half set aside for the establishment of a Special Projects Fund (SPUR) for natural resources surveys, industrial and agricultural research, and the training of technical personnel and public administrators and statisticians. SPUR was a variation on two earlier Judd programs, Point IV and the Joint Commission on Rural Reconstruction on Taiwan, which had proven so effective. As a further inducement, he declared his willingness to go before Congress and urge it to raise the U.S. contribution for technical assistance from 33.3 percent to 40 percent. The Judd plan, along with a promise to consider a capital development fund at some future date, was approved without opposition by the U.N.'s Economic Committee. The *New York Times* called the vote "a triumph for the United States." U.S. diplomats called the negotiations among "the most grueling of their experience." The U.S. Chamber of Commerce pointed out that Judd was the right man to lead them, since he was "at once an idealist and a realist." The State Department publicly commended him for his "outstanding negotiating job."[38] The next year, as he promised, Judd went before committees of both the House and the Senate and persuaded them to authorize increased U.S. support for United Nations technical assistance, including SPUR. One wonders what other intractable problems he would have solved if he had been given the opportunity to serve as the U.S. ambassador to the United Nations under President Nixon in the late 1960s.

In his arguments for foreign aid, Judd always mentioned the remarkable and unmatched success of the U.S. economic assistance program for Taiwan, which received some $800 million from July 1950 through December 1958. With the stimulus of U.S. aid, Taiwan's gross national product expanded 85 percent, agricultural production rose 45 percent, and manufacturing went up 160 percent. At the same time, the price index went up only 2 percent in 1958 after rising some 80 percent since 1950. The International Cooperation Administration, which administered American foreign aid, asserted that "one of the most successful ventures" was the JCRR, "a singularly effective organization," which had supported nearly 3,000 projects in cooperation with local groups. One of the most important was the land reform program which benefited about three-quarters of Taiwan's farm families and earned the Republic of China government's "worldwide acclaim for this progressive and forward-looking experiment in rural democracy." Speaking on the House floor, Judd speculated on why Taiwan, whose government had been pictured as "hopelessly inept, incompetent, inefficient, corrupt and reactionary," had been so successful? He suggested several reasons: the more manageable problems on Taiwan, with a population of less than 10 million compared with more than 400 million on the mainland; the freedom on Taiwan "from the drains and dislocations of civil war"; the security provided by 100 miles of water so that the government and the people could concentrate on solving their economic problems; a better government than had existed on the mainland due in part to the fact that the "best elements" not "the worst" had left China for exile on the island of Taiwan; "effective assistance" from the United States as well as moral support instead of previous "vilification." He suggested that the United States should work to bring about the same combination of national independence, dedicated able leadership, and effective support in other countries around the world. With his usual reluctance to blow his own horn, he did not add that the "effective support" for the Republic of China would not have been forthcoming from the United States without his help and commitment.[39]

Notwithstanding his preoccupation with foreign affairs, he also strove to obtain appropriate federal assistance for Minneapolis, although his political opponents charged otherwise every two years. Since his first year in Congress he had worked for the economically important

Upper Harbor Development Project, creating a clear channel between the Mississippi River and the upper part of the Minneapolis Harbor. Republican Senator Joseph Ball had pushed through the first appropriation in the Republican Eightieth Congress. Senator Edward Thye, another Republican, and Judd had kept the project going with annual appropriations for the necessary dredging by the U.S. Engineers, who requested $4 million in fiscal year 1960. When President Eisenhower recommended only $2.44 million in his 1960 budget, Democratic Gov. Orville Freeman asked Judd to try to raise the amount to $3.2 million. Judd responded that he shared Freeman's disappointment at the "slow progress" of the project, but speaking realistically, Congress was in a budget-cutting mood and "not likely" to increase any White House budget recommendation. Most politicians would have stopped there, but not Judd: "I feel strongly," he added, "that a line on spending must be held this year and in the years just ahead and our particular projects must bear their share."[40] This was not what Freeman wanted to hear, but he could not have been very surprised; it was consistent with Judd's oft-stated conviction that the nation's security required fiscal responsibility on the part of all Americans, including his own constituents.

It was this philosophy of prudence and balance which led him to propose that the four-year scholarships in the National Defense Education Act of 1958 should be in the forms of loans, not grants (his amendment passed the House); to oppose a federal aid for school construction bill in 1960 because it allocated funds to all states on the basis of school-age population, and not to those states where the need was greatest. But he was not insensitive to those in true need; he supported federal-state assistance for senior citizens who "do not have sufficient means to pay their medical bills when illness occurs or continues"; and urged an increase from $1,200 to $1,800 a year for the amount that a person on Social Security could earn without losing benefits (his amendment to increase the ceiling from $900 to $1,200 had been adopted in 1954).[41]

After all the U.S. foreign policy successes of the 1950s—ending the Korean War, saving Taiwan from a Chinese Communist takeover, reconstructing Japan economically, preventing communist dictatorships in Guatemala and Iran, sending the marines into Lebanon, creating a strong ring of agreements and alliances around the Soviet empire, integrating West Germany into Western Europe, transforming NATO into an effective defensive military force—1960 was a painful year for

Judd and the Eisenhower administration because of the shooting down of the U.S. U-2 "spy plane" and the growing realization that Fidel Castro intended to turn Cuba into a communist beachhead in the hemisphere.

The U-2 was a one-man, single turbo-jet engine airplane that flew at an altitude of 65,000 feet and had been taking incredibly detailed photographs of the Soviet Union since 1956. It carried no guns, only sensitive infrared cameras that photographed huge slices of the earth's surface 125 miles wide and 3,000 miles long. The detail was so good that CIA analysts (the U-2 flights were a CIA operation) could read a newspaper headline nine miles below the aircraft. It was thought that the U-2 flew so high that Soviet radar could not detect it.[42] On May 1, some two weeks before President Eisenhower and Premier Khrushchev were to meet in Paris with leaders of Great Britain and France, a U-2 plane piloted by Francis Gary Powers was shot down by a Soviet rocket deep within the Soviet Union. Khrushchev publicly charged the United States with "aggressive acts"; the State Department stated there was no "deliberate intention" to violate Soviet air space; Khrushchev revealed that Powers had made a complete confession, and released photos of the downed plane; and Secretary of State Herter said that Eisenhower had approved the program but not specific flights which would continue.

Counterpunching with devastating effect, Khrushchev warned that Soviet rockets would attack countries that allowed U.S. spy planes to use their territory and stated that Powers would be tried. The Soviet premier declared that he would not participate in a summit unless the United States ended all U-2 flights, apologized for its "aggressions" and punished those responsible for the flights. Eisenhower, still hoping to go to Moscow for a summit meeting with Khrushchev after the Paris meeting, announced that the U-2 flights had been suspended and would not be resumed. In Paris, an angry Khrushchev accused Eisenhower of "treachery" and "bandit" acts, and canceled his invitation to the president to visit the Soviet Union. A grim Eisenhower reiterated that the U-2 would fly no more, but declared that Khrushchev's "ultimatum" regarding apologies and punishment was unacceptable to the United States. Khrushchev walked out of the Elysee Palace in Paris, and returned to Moscow where he announced that the Soviet Union would solve the Berlin problem by signing a separate treaty with East Germany, a move he had wished to make for some time.[43] With his hopes for détente with the Soviets shattered, Eisenhower tried to repair his image by traveling to Asia and visiting Japan, America's strongest ally in the Far East. However, Japan was known to be the Asian base for the U-2 flights, and Japanese leftists, encouraged by communists, began rioting so violently that the Japanese cabinet, meeting in emergency session, asked Eisenhower not to come for his own safety.

In later years, Judd stressed the hypocrisy of Khrushchev and the other Soviet leaders who had been aware of the U-2 flights for years. The United States knew that they knew, he explained, because the U-2 planes also had very sensitive tape recorders that monitored the radio conversations of Soviet ground crews. "We have the recording of these ground crews," said Judd, "talking about their efforts to shoot down the planes. They couldn't reach them; they were frantic." So Khrushchev knew about the "spy" flights when he visited the United States in 1959, but "he never said a word in protest. . . . He couldn't denounce [them] without confessing to his own people that he couldn't shoot down our planes, [without] admitting how far behind [they were]." Judd argued that the president was badly served by his advisers. Instead of initially denying the U-2 flights, the United States should have admitted them without apology and without embarrassment, and then added: "Is there any difference between spying from the air and spying on the ground? How many spies does the Soviet Union have in the United States and every other country too?" The aerial reconnaissance was necessary because the Soviet Union was "a closed society" that did not allow "our officials" to travel outside a very limited area. We should have stated, Judd suggested, that the United States would "continue to spy in whatever ways we can . . . until [the Soviets] opened their society and agreed to genuine disarmament with inspection."[44]

If Eisenhower was deeply disappointed in the collapse of the Paris meeting and the cancellation of the Moscow summit, he was also increasingly worried about the actions of Fidel Castro in Cuba. After helping Castro come to power by denying support to Fulgencio Batista, and then offering U.S. economic assistance to the new government, the State Department watched in dismay as Castro admitted that he had been a communist all along and began setting up a communist dictatorship in Cuba. In the spring of 1960, Judd recalled, Eisenhower "instructed the Pentagon and the CIA to draw up some plans for the liberation of the Cubans." The President was not yet committed to any particular plan, but he was prepared to act to implement the Monroe Doctrine and protect the western hemisphere. By November, the Bay of Pigs plan was almost complete, and Eisenhower expected it would be carried out by a victorious President Nixon. When John F. Kennedy won, Eisenhower promptly told the president-elect about the situation and said: "We got into this mess under my administration. I'm prepared to go ahead and take action right now in these remaining two months of my term and clean this thing up down there in Cuba." Kennedy rejected the offer, saying: "No, the people have spoken. They have chosen me as president. Any decision on this must be left for me in my administration. We'll hope to find some other way." Eisenhower later declared, said Judd, that one of the greatest mistakes he ever made was not carrying out the Bay of Pigs operation against Castro. "If he had done it, Cuba would have been free."[45] Throughout 1960, Judd was privately critical of the "extreme patience" of the U.S. government, particularly the State Department, which kept hoping that Castro "would moderate his actions, and that persons within Cuba would have enough influence to halt the turn toward communism." He was not impressed by the Cuban leader's populist rhetoric and actions, writing: "The fact that Castro did 'good things for the [Cuban] people' . . . by giving them other people's property does not mean his is a good or decent regime. So did Mussolini, Hitler, Lenin, and Mao. Only by giving 'good things' can a tyrant get to power and be able to do his bad things. Castro follows this regular rule. And Uncle Sam generally plays the sucker role."[46]

However, in the summer of 1960, Judd and other Republicans were not as worried about the future of Cuba as they were about the future of their party. Despite eight years of peace and prosperity under Ike, the American people clearly had reservations about the man who had served loyally and effectively as his vice president for eight years and who was undoubtedly going to be nominated for president at the national convention in Chicago. The Democratic nominee, Senator John Kennedy of Massachusetts, led Nixon by fifty-five to forty-five in one of the Gallup polls. Republican uneasiness manifested itself in different ways. Governor Nelson Rockefeller of New York was demanding that planks about civil rights and national defense be inserted in the party platform. Conservatives led by Senator Barry Goldwater of Arizona watched the maneuverings between Nixon and Rockefeller with rising suspicion; they would forgive the man who exposed Alger Hiss almost anything except a political deal with the symbol of the Eastern liberal establishment. And then there was the question of the vice presidency: Whom would Nixon pick? There was considerable speculation about Henry Cabot Lodge, the tall, elegant ambassador to the United Nations who had gained a national reputation by standing up to the Russians in U.N. debate. The Massachusetts-born Lodge would certainly add geographical balance, but there were rumors about his distaste for campaigning. Was there anyone who might work harder and more effectively in what everyone knew was going to be an exceedingly close race?

CHAPTER FIFTEEN

Nearly Vice President

AMERICA CHANGED DRAMATICALLY during the seemingly tranquil Eisenhower years. Americans moved from the farms and the cities to the
suburbs; two-thirds of the remarkable twenty-eight million increase in
population occurred in suburbia. As Theodore White wrote: "For the
first time in American history, the number of white-collar Americans
(professional, managerial, clerical, and sales people) had become
greater than the number of those who held blue-collar jobs (productive
or operative)." Emboldened by the Supreme Court decision of 1954 and
reinforced by the success of sit-ins from Atlanta to New York City,
black Americans were insisting on equal opportunity and equal consideration from national political leaders. Catholics who had been drifting
away from the Democratic party now had a good reason to come home
in the person of a young Irishman named John Fitzgerald Kennedy. The
Catholic vote was crucial to Democratic success in 1960: there were
fourteen key states with a Catholic population of 20 percent or more,
including New York (40 percent), Pennsylvania (29 percent), Illinois
(30 percent), Michigan (24 percent) and Ohio (20 percent).[1] Kennedy
also had to convince Protestants, who had united against a Catholic
candidate for president in 1928, that his election would not breach the
historic division between church and state.

The presidential candidates were preeminent symbols of the nation's

245

transition from the old to the new. Both were World War II veterans, college graduates, and experienced politicians. But Kennedy was Boston, Harvard University, and Hyannisport, the son of one of America's richest men. Nixon was Yorba Linda, California, Whittier College, and San Clemente, the son of a gas station owner. Kennedy was Eastern, big-city politics, and Irish-beguiling. Nixon was Western, suburban politics, and Quaker-quiet. Kennedy saw a nation in decline and adrift at home and abroad. He was a modern liberal who believed that government should unhesitatingly use its power to solve problems; his promises to the people were in the 1960 Democratic platform that offered an "economic bill of rights" including the "right" to a job, a "decent home," "recreation" and "adequate medical care," as well as a pledge to the cities to "clear their slums, dispose of their sewage, educate their children, transport suburban commuters . . . and combat juvenile delinquency."[2] Nixon saw a nation emerging from a decade of peace and prosperity. He was a classic liberal who believed that government had an important role to play in the lives of people but who also believed in federalism with its division of rights and responsibilities between Washington and the states. As with so many U.S. elections, the 1960 presidential campaign was a national referendum on continuity (Nixon) versus change (Kennedy). The Gallup opinion polls gave first one candidate and then the other a narrow lead, suggesting that the American people weren't sure which man they wanted in the White House.

For Judd, the choice was easy: he had served in Congress with both men and Nixon was the one. As he explained to a Rockefeller supporter who wrote him, although he had known Nelson Rockefeller longer (they had worked together for the United Nations and other foreign policy issues as early as 1945), he did not consider the New York governor to be as well qualified for the presidency or "fundamentally as sound and strong a man as is the Vice President." Based on fourteen years of close association and observation, he was prepared to say that Nixon was "the best equipped and best prepared, and incomparably the best tested and proved, candidate the American people have had a chance to vote for the Presidency since George Washington."[3] One is inclined to dismiss so sweeping an endorsement, but Judd had chosen his words carefully: the operative one is "candidate." As he pointed out, "most of the candidates who have been elected have turned out to be fine Presidents, but at the time they were elected, the people had to vote more in faith, and hope than in certainty. This was true even of Lincoln.

But in the case of Mr. Nixon, there is no question as to his qualifications. . . . he is . . . courageous, experienced, and exceedingly able."[4] Judd also liked Nixon's ability to balance the idealistic and the pragmatic in his politics and policies. The roots of Nixon's idealism lay in his Quaker faith, which was deep and abiding. Nixon's pragmatism was evident from his ability while vice president for eight years to work with Taft as well as Eisenhower Republicans and his skillful knitting together of the liberal and conservative wings of the Republican party at the 1960 convention. Liberals liked the strong civil rights plank that Rockefeller insisted must be in the platform; conservatives liked the tough anticommunist and balanced budget planks drafted by Congressman Mel Laird of Wisconsin, the platform committee chairman. Both liberals and conservatives liked Nixon's choice to deliver the keynote address: Walter Judd of Minnesota, whom the *New York Times* described "as a liberal who is trusted by the conservatives."[5]

In a sense, Judd epitomized the Republican party of 1960: generally moderate, sometimes liberal on domestic issues; staunchly conservative, i.e., anticommunist, in foreign affairs; Middle West, middle class, middle of the road; patriotic, Christian, and white. The one area where he did not exactly match the Republican profile lay in his views of how to deal with America's communist enemies: he was among the hardest of the hard. It was significant that Nixon would pick as his keynoter a man who refused to dine with Mikoyan and helped found the Committee for Freedom for All Peoples to turn Khrushchev's U.S. visit into an occasion for "national mourning" for communism's victims.

In 1960, before the mass media, particularly television, nearly eliminated the role of national political parties in the nomination process, the national party convention still served as a time and a place to resolve differences between candidates and factions. It was a time for public officials, politicians, journalists, lobbyists, financial supporters and plain citizens to come together to renew old friendships and make new ones, exchange information and gossip, and get a feel for the state of the party and the nation. The national convention was a seminar in practical politics, a platform for policies and programs, a stage for candidates, and a celebration that never stopped for four days and nights. A national convention was and still is as enduring an American political ritual as the primary, election day and the inaugural.

Judd took his keynote address seriously, thinking about it and working on it for a month in his Capitol Hill office and at home, revising parts by longhand more than a dozen times, and finally finishing it in his Chicago hotel room the night before he was scheduled to deliver it. He called himself a rewriter, not a writer; only minutes before he stepped to the podium and in front of the television cameras that would send him and his message into the living rooms of twenty million Americans, he suddenly changed his speech once again, converting a series of assertions about the Democratic record into rhetorical questions that stimulated a roaring response from the delegates. It was a memorable keynote speech and spawned an enthusiastic Judd-for-Vice-President movement, forced Nixon to place Judd near the top of his list of vice presidential possibilities, and stung the Democrats so badly that some, particularly Robert F. Kennedy, never forgot nor forgave him.

His remarks were entitled, "We Must Develop a Strategy for Victory—To Save Freedom—Freedom Everywhere." Some of the words were familiar to those who knew Walter Judd, and certainly the ideas were not new, but he spoke with a singular passion and conviction about the problems facing the nation and the world.

He listed what the Republican party, under President Eisenhower, had done to preserve freedom around the world. He mentioned the end of the fighting in Korea, how other threats had been prevented from developing into war in Iran, Guatemala, Formosa, Suez, Lebanon, Quemoy, and West Berlin. How was this accomplished? "Not by sacrificing our principles in secret deals under the table but by steady patient firmness and strength in support of principles"; by "keeping our word" and through "steadfast support of friends and allies," and "wholehearted support of the United Nations." He talked about the importance of military strength to back up those principles and repudiated the unfounded Democratic charge of a "missile gap." Like a boxer intensifying his attack, Judd next took on the Democratic charge that Eisenhower had failed to "take the initiative" in the Cold War and should have done "something different" to prevent Khrushchev's breakup of the Paris conference. What, he asked sarcastically, did the Democrats want the president to do? "Apologize and hand over West Berlin? Blow up and start a war?" Khrushchev, not the United States, killed the hopes for peace by "scuttling" the Paris conference. The communists ordered their apparatus into action to prevent Eisenhower's visit to Tokyo because they did not "dare let Ike chalk up another tremendous triumph with millions of people . . . in a key country like Japan."

As for the charge that no previous president ever suffered such insults abroad, Judd responded that communists had not previously faced a president who would "not be taken in or intimidated or tricked into any concessions . . . that would weaken the free world." There was another reason: no previous president had faced a "Communist conspiracy that was strong and arrogant enough to take such action as Mr. Khrushchev took." And how did communism become so strong and arrogant? It was the answer to that question that brought the delegates to their feet and almost made Walter Judd the Republican party's nominee for vice president. He said that he would rather not go over the mistakes of the past, but if Republicans were to be charged "with inability to deal with the forces of aggression," then it was necessary to look at the record to determine who helped build up those forces. He asked ten rhetorical questions and skillfully timed them so that each time the response became louder and louder until the amphitheater rocked.

Was it Republicans who recognized the Soviet Union in 1933 and gave it acceptance into our country and world society as if it were a respectable and dependable member thereof? [A slightly hesitant "No."]

Was it Republicans, who, at Teheran, against the urgent advice of Mr. Churchill, agreed to give the Russians a free hand in the Balkans? [More certain now, "No."]

Was it Republicans who secretly divided Poland and gave half of it to the Soviet Union? [A confident "No."]

Was it Republicans who agreed to the Communist takeover of a hundred million people in Eastern Europe who are not Russian? [A shouted "No."]

Was it a Republican administration which at Potsdam gave the Soviet Union East Germany and left West Berlin cut off from the rest of the free world? [A more emphatic "No!"]

Was it a Republican administration that publicly announced that Manchuria would go back to its rightful owners, the Chinese, and then secretly at Yalta gave control of Manchuria to the Russians? ["NO!"]

Was it a Republican administration that divided Korea and gave control of North Korea to the Communists? ["NO!"]

Was it a Republican administration that gave to the Soviet Union the Kurile Islands which had never been anybody's except Japan's, thereby endangering both Japan's and our security in the North Pacific? ["NO!"]

Was it a Republican administration that rightly put its hand to the plow in Korea, and then when victory was in sight turned back, allowing the Reds to recover so they can make still more trouble for us in the future? ["NO!"]

Was it a Republican administration that fell for the Communist offer of a truce in Korea without requiring that the North Korean aggressors lay down their arms and the Chinese Communists get out of Korea where they had no business to be?

At last, Judd tried to answer his own question, but he was drowned out by the delegates who by now would have shouted "NO!" if he had asked them if they wanted an income tax cut.

The questions were partisan and pointed, and intended to be painful for Democrats. After all, Judd was delivering the keynote speech at the Republican National Convention, not the commencement address at Harvard. Still, they were historically accurate. Judd declined to point out that a Democratic administration had been responsible, with necessary cooperation from a Republican Congress, for the initiation of the Truman Doctrine, the Marshall Plan, and NATO. After all, he was not offering a scholarly analysis of post-World War II foreign policy, but a view of the world through Republican eyes. On the other hand, there was one question he did not ask which a more demagogic orator would not have hesitated to pose: "Was it Republicans who lost China by refusing to help our longtime friends and allies, the Nationalist Chinese, at a critical time in their war with the Chinese communists?"

With the shouts of the delegates still echoing in the hall, Judd declared that in the face of the communist challenge, America had no alternative but to "win this Cold War," not by military might but by "our strongest weapons, the values and virtues of [our] system of government. . . . We must let loose in the world the dynamic forces of freedom in our day as our forefathers did in theirs, causing people everywhere to look toward the American dream."[6]

It was a political speech, a history lesson, a sermon, a philosophical discourse, an exhortation. It was anticommunist in foreign policy and middle-of-the-road in domestic policy. It was intended to fire up loyal Republicans and to sway the millions of Americans watching the first gavel-to-gavel coverage of national conventions by the television networks. At the convention itself, scores of demonstrators immediately began waving huge photos of Judd. Richard Nixon's choice of his running mate now became more complicated. The vice president had settled on Henry Cabot Lodge sometime before; Lodge had already begun working on his acceptance speech before he arrived in Chicago. But Nixon could not ignore the Judd signs that sprang up all over the convention floor, the enthusiastic comments of the delegates (one Young Republican commented next day in the *Chicago Daily News,* "The keynoter just might have talked himself into the vice-presidency") and the editorial comments of such solidly Republican newspapers as the *Omaha World-Herald,* which called the speech a "masterpiece" and "a beacon of truth in a dark and uncertain sea."[7]

The next forty-eight hours for Judd were like operating nonstop in a hospital emergency room, but instead of treating patients, he was called upon to talk to state caucuses. There was the same unrelenting need to display skill and steadiness, to make no mistakes, although not of the scapel but of the tongue. There was much the same feeling that life and death were at stake; many delegates felt that not only the future of the Republican party and the nation but of the world depended on whether the right man shared the ticket with Nixon. Judd was realistic about his chances to be selected and ambivalent about his fitness for the job. He told one reporter: "I just have a strong feeling a younger man ought to be vice president."[8] Now sixty-one, he had been working up to eighteen hours a day during his years as the congressman from Minneapolis, besides speaking coast to coast before political and civic audiences and traveling abroad to expand his knowledge of foreign affairs. He was tired, but more importantly he was concerned about politics becoming an end as well as a means in his life. He was finding it increasingly difficult as a congressman to balance the demands of his political life and his Christian life. How much more difficult would it be as vice president? He had been thinking more and more about getting out of politics, and here he was being pushed into running for the vice presidential nomination. He didn't want to disappoint or let down his friends or supporters, but they should understand by now that for him, the cause always came first.[9] Was his nomination for the vice presidency *that* essential?

The convention push for Judd continued, fueled by delegates who had been deeply moved by his keynote address, anticommunist conservatives who did not like the way Nixon was kowtowing to Rockefeller, and by midwestern leaders who thought that Judd could draw votes and help their states in November. By Wednesday night, when the nominations for president were scheduled to be made, he had moved from a long-shot possibility to a high place on a very short list of names for vice president. At 11 P.M., while the delegates were voting to nominate Richard Nixon for president, Judd was called from the International Amphitheater to the Blackstone Hotel, where Nixon told Judd that "the question of the vice presidency is down to two persons. The press speculates about four—Cabot, you, Jerry Ford and Thruston Morton —but it is really down to Lodge and yourself." Judd responded: "I assumed it is already down to one, Lodge, because I understand he has his acceptance speech already written." He had received this political intelligence from his longtime friend, and brother of Cabot, Congressman John Davis Lodge of Connecticut. Nixon replied: "But it's not so far gone in his favor that it couldn't be reversed if we decided that it is the best thing to do." Did Nixon mean it, or was he making Judd an offer he knew would be refused? Judd thought that Nixon revealed his true preference for vice president by adding: "Would you be willing to give [Lodge's] nominating speech?"

That meant, said Judd in a memorandum that he immediately wrote after meeting with Nixon, that "he was not offering me the nomination, but only offering me a chance to show him how I would be a better *candidate* than Lodge—which I wasn't honestly sure I could do." Judd was acutely aware of his cancer-scarred face and worried about the negative impact it would almost surely have on television.

> I told [Nixon] I felt I was qualified for the position and I knew I would bring the ticket a great deal of strength, particularly in the Midwest and South, because I had spoken to so many and such a variety of audiences there. But I recognized that he, Nixon, was weakest in the Northeast and that Lodge *ought* to be able to bring more support there because of its being his own base, because of his years of exposure on television at the United Nations where he had done an excellent job, and because of what I thought would be an exceptional appeal he probably had to women voters. I added that, of course, I would be glad to nominate Lodge if he, Nixon, wanted me to.[10]

It was a typical response for Judd, analytical, objective, and scrupulous in avoiding any trace of self-promotion. He had never asked anyone to vote for him while campaigning for Congress. How could he now sell himself to Nixon as his best possible running mate? Judd's motives were noble and high-spirited; but they were also unrealistic, a little sanctimonious, and certainly ill timed for the fall election, as he later admitted.

"My great error," he said, "was that I overestimated Lodge's vote-getting capacity, and underestimated my own. It was the greatest mistake of my life from the standpoint of the country. If I had made a real effort myself and given the green light to a good many key people who were wanting to put on a real drive for my nomination ... we could have gotten the delegates to nominate me, the ticket would have gotten a great many more votes in key places, Nixon would have been elected, and the whole course of history in these United States and the world would have been vastly different." Nixon admitted as much a couple of years later when both men were no longer in office, saying to Judd: "Walter, if I had chosen you instead of Cabot, we would both still be in Washington."[11]

As Theodore White and many others commented, if only 4,500 voters in Illinois and 28,000 voters in Texas had changed their minds, those 32,500 votes would have moved those states with their 51 electoral votes into the Nixon column in the general election, giving him an electoral majority of two. Judd was a popular and well-known speaker in Illinois and Texas and might well have made the difference in one or both states. Furthermore, Nixon narrowly lost Minnesota to Kennedy, by only 22,000 votes out of 1.5 million cast; one can state that in all likelihood if Walter Judd had been on the ticket, Minnesota and its eleven electoral votes would have wound up in the Republican column.

Years later, Judd provided further information about the process by which the 1960 Republican vice presidential nominee was selected as well as insights into Nixon's character and personality. During their conversation in the Blackstone Hotel, Judd got the impression that President Eisenhower also would like to have Lodge as vice president. Eisenhower, it seemed, still felt badly that while working so hard in 1952 for his nomination and election as president, Lodge had lost his Massachusetts Senate seat unexpectedly to Kennedy. Nixon did not say that Ike was "pushing" Lodge, but the president felt Lodge would be a good candidate and had, in a sense, earned it by neglecting his own campaign in his efforts for Ike. Judd's response to Nixon was: "Well, Dick, I think you ought to choose whichever one of us you're convinced will bring you the most votes."

That Nixon would give such weight to Eisenhower's opinion in the selection of his vice president reinforced Judd's analysis of Nixon's greatest strength and at the same time his greatest weakness—loyalty. "His loyalty to Eisenhower and his feeling that he had to go along with him [regarding the vice presidency] was a major mistake from the standpoint of his own career."

Nixon made another major mistake in the campaign due to loyalty, this time to the Republican party. When Nixon came to Minneapolis several weeks later, Judd met him at the airport, and as he walked along the fence shaking hands, the former medical missionary noticed that the vice president was limping. When they arrived at the hotel and went up to Nixon's suite, Judd asked, "What are you limping about?" Nixon replied: "Well, I got a little infection or something when I bumped my knee." "Let me see it," said Judd, who watched with alarm as the vice president removed his pants to reveal a red streak going up from his knee to his groin. "You've got a streptococcus infection, Dick." Judd didn't have a thermometer, but he took the candidate's pulse and said, "You've got a little fever." He suggested that Nixon cancel his speech and instead see a doctor. "Oh, no," said Nixon quickly, "I can't call it off." "Don't monkey around with streptococcus infections," warned Judd, "they are serious." Nixon insisted on going ahead with his speech, so Judd took hot towels and put them around the knee and thigh for a half hour, reducing the redness. He knew that such treatment was only a palliative and before going downstairs, he offered his old friend some sound advice: "Whenever the tire goes down, you have to stop, no matter if you're on your way to your wedding. And your tire's gone down, Dick. Let me call a good doctor and he'll testify to that." But out of a sense of loyalty to the party and the people who were depending upon him, Nixon did not pay sufficient attention to the infection until it developed into serious blood poisoning, forcing him into the hospital just a few days later. "He could have died, he would have died," said Judd, "without antibiotics." The antibiotics saved his life, but they helped him lose the first TV debate with Kennedy because at the time he was still taking "enormous doses," about 3000 milligrams a day, three times the normal amount, and the medication slowed him up enough to enable Kennedy to take the initiative and help win the debate.

Judd felt that Nixon was also too loyal to his California friends and associates in 1962 when they begged him to run for governor. Early in the year, Judd and several other congressional Republicans were invited by the state's political leaders to a breakfast at the Sheraton Carlton

Hotel in Washington; everyone took turns telling Nixon why it was his duty to run. Nixon replied: "I don't want to run for governor. I'm not interested, primarily, in the state of California and its politics. I'm most interested in national and international politics." They went around the room, soliciting comments, and when they came to Judd, he said bluntly: "If he doesn't want to run, then you don't have any right to ask him to do it. His heart isn't in it, and he shouldn't go against his own judgment."[12] It was good advice, but Nixon finally agreed to run for governor of California out of loyalty to the party and his state. After being bloodied in the Republican primary by conservative Joe Shell, he narrowly lost to Brown in the general election. Judd would later make the same reluctant decision to run for re-election in 1962, and suffer the same fate.

Years later, as president, Nixon was guilty of too much loyalty to his White House staff which resulted in the Watergate disgrace. "He stood by Haldeman and Erlichman," said Judd, which was praiseworthy in a way. But if he had said publicly, "I'm sorry about this. Mistakes were made," Judd argued that the people would have forgiven him as they did John Kennedy after he admitted he had made a mistake with the Bay of Pigs.

Judd remembered Nixon's loyalty to and love for his wife Pat and their two daughters, Julie and Tricia. He never forgot an overnight train ride through Texas, and how from his Pullman berth, he watched Nixon put the girls (they were about seven and four) to bed; "He was so tender with them, his devotion was so clear." Nixon's deep devotion to his mother, a very devout Quaker, instilled in him a "passion for peace," which was commendable, said Judd. But his loyalty to her and her unqualified commitment to peace led him to make "mistakes in order to get peace," as in his negotiations with mainland China. "Peace is the easiest thing in the world to get," said Judd. "All you have to do is give in. [But] the first objective is to get freedom."

Nixon, summed up Judd, "is a Dr. Jekyll and Mr. Hyde as much as anybody I've ever known." His loyalty, his intelligence, his willingness to make sacrifices are Jekyll-like qualities. But "he was a loner. He looked inward. He consulted himself. . . . He made up his mind on his own. . . . He couldn't develop a personal response to people the way Reagan does. That was his [greatest] weakness."[13]

Nixon's desire for peace, Judd argued, led to his "greatest success," as Nixon himself understood it, and his greatest "mistake and failure" from Judd's standpoint—failing to block admission of Communist China to the United Nations, visiting Communist China, engineering the rapprochement with Peking "on *its* terms." Nixon went to China in 1972, said Judd, for two main foreign policy reasons. One was to practice some *realpolitik* with regard to the Soviet Union and mainland China. When you have two such enemies, Nixon reasoned, it was sensible to try to divide them by helping the weaker (China) become more independent and thereby force the stronger to "pay more attention" to the weaker than to Western Europe and the free world. As a result of Nixon's playing the China card, Moscow did in fact concentrate more on China's actions and Asia, and less on Europe. The second reason was to reduce China's aid to North Vietnam and help bring the Vietnam war to an end. "Nixon thought," said Judd, "that by making friends with the Chinese Communists, they would lower the level of their assistance, but once he had given them what they wanted [political recognition, economic assistance, and assurances that the United States would reduce its commitment to Taiwan] they not only continued their aid [to Hanoi], but in fact increased it a little." Nixon was so carried away by what he called "the week that changed the world" that *realpolitik* became *naivepolitik*. Judd admitted that he had not tried to see Nixon after the admission of Communist China to the United Nations and before he traveled to China. "No, I never did, and I should have. If I had called him, he would have seen me. It is a weakness on my part that I don't push myself."[14]

He did push hard to elect Nixon as president in 1960. He began by nominating Henry Cabot Lodge for vice president, and preventing any possible convention backlash against his not being selected. Judd was generous in his praise of America's representative in the United Nations, calling Lodge a man who had been "tested and proved in the fires of today's world—and found completely worthy—and trustworthy." In the fall, he campaigned across the country for the Nixon-Lodge ticket, convinced that the foreign and domestic policies that would be implemented by a Democratic administration under John Kennedy and Lyndon Johnson would be dangerous for the country and the world. In the closing days of the campaign, he helped focus attention on a relevant issue: the health of the two presidential candidates. He challenged Kennedy to follow Nixon's lead in making full disclosure of his "true physical condition." Unless this were done, said Judd, "I can only conclude that a cover-up job is being done to hide the dulling side effects regularly associated with long-standing Addison's Disease." There had been stories as far back as 1954 about Kennedy having Addison's Disease (a failure of the adrenal glands); James MacGregor Burns in his sympathetic biography admitted that Kennedy's "adrenal insufficiency might well be diagnosed by some doctors as a mild case of Addison's Disease [but] ... can be fully controlled by medication taken by the mouth."[15]

Judd was not satisfied with such rationales and pointed out that "medication for Addison's Disease can have all sorts of side effects which I, for one, would consider dangerous beyond calculation in a President of the United States." He said that the Kennedy campaign ought to answer the rumors in medical circles that Case Number Three reported in the American Medical Association's Archives of Surgery, Volume 71, related to Kennedy. Case Number Three described a young man who had suffered for many years from Addison's Disease and who also suffered from a back injury which caused much pain and required surgical correction and relief. "Doctors know," said Judd, "that Addison's Disease is the result of the adrenal insufficiencies that are disturbing to physical and mental health. If drugs of the large dosage indicated [in the case history] were required some years ago, it is not unreasonable to suppose that more massive and more critical dosages are required today. This is the sort of fact voters are entitled to have, and to have now."[16] But "full disclosure" was not made before election day, and indeed was never made during Kennedy's presidency.

Although he almost spent more time campaigning for Nixon than for himself, Judd easily won re-election to Congress over his DFL opponent, George W. Matthews. But he was bitterly disappointed by Nixon's narrow loss which, as he brooded about it through November and December, seemed to him to be the result of deceptive campaigning and voting. For Walter Judd, two plus two always equaled four; once he had carefully examined all the facts and had come to a certain conclusion, he was duty-bound to report his findings, no matter how disturbing they might be. After his narrow loss, and the many newspaper stories about voting irregularities in Chicago and elsewhere, Nixon had been urged by Senator Dirksen of Illinois and others to demand a recount. Aware that such a process might take as long as six months, seriously affecting America's foreign relations, and knowing that the charges, if proven untrue, would "remove any possibility of a further political career," Nixon sent Kennedy a telegram conceding the election.[17] But Judd felt compelled to speak out. In late January, after John Kennedy had been inaugurated as president, Judd went public, charging in a speech to the Women's National Republican Club in New York City that Nixon had lost the presidential election through "chicanery." As always, he chose his words carefully: chicanery does not mean fraud or deceit, as some accused him of saying, but, rather, "adroit but dishonest maneuvering or scheming." He declared: "In my opinion there is not the slightest doubt that the majority of the voters in this country who voted legitimately and whose votes were counted honestly voted for both Nixon and Lodge for the White House."[18]

Pressed by a reporter for examples of "chicanery," he said he had been telephoned the morning after the election by a Roman Catholic priest who formerly had a parish in Chicago, and had been told by him that registering a voter in several different districts was the way that elections were rigged in Chicago. He also charged that in Amarillo, Texas, some 6,000 votes for Nixon had been thrown out because of a little-known requirement that a voter must cross out the name of a candidate for whom he did not wish to vote. In response to letters of protest from constituents, some of them offended Catholics, Judd insisted that he had not charged "fraud and deceit" in the 1960 campaign but rather "sharp practices." What else, he asked, would you call the television commercials that through splicing of the campaign debates made it appear that Nixon said "I agree." where he did not say that? What about the Kennedy interview in which the Democratic candidate referred to an "old man who supposedly had had to pay high bills for medical and hospital care of a broken hip, when in fact the bills were almost entirely paid by Blue Cross and Blue Shield"? He also referred to an article in *Look* magazine which described how big city political machines "steal" elections. "If it is argued," he said, "that the Republican machines are just as bad as the Democratic machines, that does not prove false the statement I made—because there are no large cities today controlled by Republican machines."

He noted that the Republican National Committee had received more than 135,000 letters and telegrams reporting "widespread [voting] irregularities." However, he said, "so many of the officials of my own Party were so disorganized after the election that they did not bring concrete charges in some states until three weeks later, by which time most of the basic evidence had been destroyed and ballot boxes when opened were found empty." He had raised the issue, he explained, not to embarrass the new president, but to safeguard the electoral process: "If the people of the country become disillusioned ... and come to believe that their will as expressed at the ballot box can be thwarted, then deterioration in public confidence and interest results that could be devastating to our very survival as a good and great nation."[19] In the wake of the questions raised and the charges leveled by Judd and others, the Republican party initiated a national ballot security program in 1964 which, combined with increased news media scrutiny, virtually eliminated such voting "irregularities" in future presidential campaigns. In truth, Judd was both partisan and patriotic in raising the issue; the two are not necessarily always in conflict.

As Congress and the new president began dealing with the pressing problems of taxes, welfare, U.S.-Soviet relations, and foreign aid, Judd noted that Kennedy seemed determined to distance himself from his predecessor. Conscious of being the youngest elected president in U.S. history, and of succeeding the oldest elected president (until Ronald Reagan), Kennedy declared in his inaugural address that "the torch has been passed to a new generation of Americans" and offered a "new" approach to national security, "flexible response." Judd was not certain how Kennedy's brave rhetoric would be translated into effective action, and he still rankled at the campaign results, but he was, of course, willing to work with the new president during the traditional honeymoon period. In April, albeit with some reservations about previous misuse of funds, he endorsed the administration's request for $600 million in assistance to Latin America and urged House approval, commenting: "The probable risks and possible losses for America are less in passing it than the very grave and certain risks, definite and inescapable risks, we would be assuming if we were to refuse to act favorably upon it."[20]

In May, he praised President Kennedy for publicly acknowledging that the United States was engaged in "a war" with the Soviet Union and suggested that the president should develop and proclaim a new global doctrine, comparable to the Monroe Doctrine for the Western hemisphere or the Truman Doctrine for Europe to the effect that "the United States was born in freedom and wherever and whenever man's freedom is denied and jeopardized, the United States must be free to give effective support to people who are giving their lives to retain their liberty or to regain it." Asked if the doctrine he was advocating would not amount to intervention in the internal affairs of another sovereign country, Judd offered a medical analogy and a variation of Mill's ultilitarian principle: "If someone is lawlessly pouring typhoid organisms into the water supply of this city, we have to intervene to stop him and we do. When we have somebody pouring poison into our whole hemisphere, the United States has got to find ways to stop it. The greater obligations must take precedence over the smaller ones."[21] Kennedy did not respond, but twenty years later, President Reagan initiated the Reagan Doctrine, by which the United States supported anti-communist forces around the world, from Afghanistan to Angola to Nicaragua.

Consistent with his belief in a bipartisan foreign policy, Judd strongly supported such Kennedy initiatives as the Peace Corps and the Arms Control and Disarmament Agency, but also criticized the Kennedy administration for its "flabby" response to the Soviet erection of the Berlin Wall. He applauded the president's call for a buildup of conventional forces so that the United States would have "a wider choice than between humiliation or all-out nuclear action." In the spirit of avoiding such extremes, he suggested that the Western powers should threaten to impose various diplomatic and economic sanctions against the Soviet Union and its satellites if Khrushchev moved to carry out his threat to sign a separate peace treaty with East Germany. In addition, Judd said, "We should state that any hostile act of blockading Berlin would engender counteractions of blockade by us. . . . Surely what is fair for one side is fair for the other. No longer should one side have a 'privileged sanctuary' to take offensive action, without expecting to be met by action in kind." Judd conceded the risks attached to the course he was proposing, but "to allow the Soviet Union to advance, step by step in their nibbling technique, involves greater risk of war than trying to stop them where they are. . . . to 'wait and see' in dealing with a malignantly spreading process is not 'playing safe' as it may seem; it is the most dangerous course one can follow."[22]

In the closing days of the first session of the Eighty-seventh Congress, Judd disagreed sharply with the Kennedy administration on an issue that had long concerned him—U.S. trade with communist countries. He pointed out that under Kennedy an "entirely new atmosphere" had been created in which goods from ball bearings to surplus farm commodities to aircraft spare parts were now allowed to be exported to the Soviet Union and Eastern Europe. Judd considered trade an important weapon in the Cold War, which should be used to elicit concessions from or prevent aggression by the communists; it should not be employed in some vague, do-good way to "ease world tensions," as one

Kennedy aide put it. The veteran congressman was becoming increasingly disappointed by the steadily growing disparity between the president's words and deeds in foreign policy.[23]

Because of his absolute integrity and oratorical skill, Judd received an extraordinary commendation from his colleagues. In 1961, *Redbook* magazine asked two questions of members of Congress: "Who (leaving aside the Vice President, the Speaker and the majority and minority leaders) are the three most influential members of your chamber?" and "Which member of your chamber do you most admire?" Approximately one-third of the Congress responded and among the ten "most influential" senators and congressmen there was only one Republican: Walter Judd. The magazine wrote that Judd "derives his influence from force of personality and effective articulation of conservative views." As to their "most admired" colleague, House Republicans picked Walter Judd by a wide margin; he was the choice of 32 percent with Tom Curtis of Missouri a distant second with 8.2 percent.[24] Judd was deeply moved by the honor tendered him by his peers; he said it was the most appreciated honor he ever received because it was from fellow congressmen who knew what they were talking about. It seemed a fitting climax to his career in Congress, a "well done" from the men and women with whom he had worked so closely for nearly twenty years. In early January 1962, he privately told old friends of his intention not to seek re-election. The occasion was the annual retreat of Washington members of the International Christian Fellowship, which he had helped to found. Several of them objected strongly, pointing out that "you have enormous influence now." Judd replied that he believed he might have more influence outside the Congress explaining issues and developing public support or opposition to the policies needed in today's complicated and dangerous world. Now, he was so busy from morning to midnight handling constituent grievances, overseeing benefit programs, attending committee meetings, and debating on the floor, that "I don't have time to think. And I don't have time to consider the basic things." Although "they jumped all over me," he was convinced that his course of action was "right, not only for myself but . . . for [all] Members of Congress."[25]

Many congressmen found themselves in a Catch 22 situation: They came to Washington to be legislators but wound up spending most of their time providing government benefits to their constituents. Most rationalized that if they didn't, they would not be reelected and would not be able to serve the nation or help their constituents. Such a quid pro quo was not why Judd had ever run for Congress, and it was why, in large measure, he decided he would not run again. He hoped to make his last year as a congressman a fruitful one: He had noticed that often the "people who announced they weren't going to [seek re-election] were the best members." All that remained was for him to formally announce his decision back in Minneapolis. He knew that some people would be disappointed, but he believed they would understand and accept his decision. Or so he told himself.

♦

CHAPTER SIXTEEN

A Last Hurrah

THERE WERE SOUND political reasons for Judd's decision not to run: the Minnesota legislature, meeting in a special December 1961 session, had passed a redistricting plan which cut the state's congressional districts from nine to eight and created a new Fifth District that included all of the city of Minneapolis, bringing in thousands of Democratic Farm-Labor voters, few of whom would endorse Judd's implacable anti-communism. The old Fifth covered Republican-dominated south Minneapolis; the new district added DFL-dominated north Minneapolis. Judd had urged Republican Governor Elmer Andersen to insist that the state legislature make two congressional districts out of Hennepin County that would each contain both urban and suburban areas. Thus each area would have two congressmen instead of one working for its interests. "Whichever party put up the best candidate and the best campaign in their district" would win, Judd argued. But neither political party was willing to gamble. Instead, Andersen, believing that Judd could not lose, accepted and signed a redistricting law that made the Fifth District essentially DFL and the Third District Republican. Andersen believed the compromise would gain him DFL support in his own re-election bid; it is one of the ironies of the 1962 Minnesota campaign that the governor lost by only 91 votes statewide, running some 22,000 votes behind Judd in the wards of his old district in Minneapolis.[1]

On April 9, Judd told a stunned and disbelieving Republican Fifth District convention in Minneapolis that he did not plan to run for an eleventh term as their congressman. He said that he was "sort of regretful, yet I feel this is the right decision at this time of my life." At a brief news conference before his speech, he explained that there were two reasons for his decision: the international situation, about which he wanted to speak out more forcefully, and redistricting. "I don't know that you can get elected in the present situation," he said, "unless you are willing to work day and night for it. I am not. I never did." However, he revealed an ambivalence about leaving Congress which encouraged those who thought they might be able to change his mind: "I tell you frankly that I sort of hoped I could have gotten the consent of my mind to reverse the original plan [not to run]." He then acknowledged that "nothing's ever final, but this is my intention." Following his public declaration, many in the audience waved their "I'm for Judd" signs and shouted, "We want Judd!" Governor Andersen walked to the podium and said while "we respect the integrity of Dr. Judd," there should now be a "great outpouring" to draft Judd and persuade him that "the United States [Congress] needs him."[2]

Why did not Judd make a more Shermanesque statement? (In 1884, General William Tecumseh Sherman, the Civil War hero, told the Republican National Convention: "I will not accept if nominated, and will not serve if elected."[3]) In Washington the next day, Judd explained that he had learned as a doctor "not to say anything is certain. . . . There's nothing certain but death or taxes. But as far as anything I can see, this is final." He hoped "very much" that there would be no move to "draft" him or otherwise attempt to persuade him to change his mind about retiring from Congress. Not unexpectedly, Minneapolis Democrats called the Judd announcement part of "a political maneuver whose ultimate aim is to create the illusion of a 'reluctant candidate' who might reverse his decision if shown a 'popular demonstration of support.' "[4] Judd was no Machiavellian; he was sincere in wanting to retire. But like many other elected officials, he was discovering that it was far easier said than done. The life of a congressman is exciting and rewarding, whether you are interested in self-aggrandizement or furthering a cause; it is filled with perquisites and power and is almost perpetual. Furthermore, Judd knew that only he had any realistic chance of holding the seat for Republicans; if he did not run, the almost certain winner in the new district would be Democratic State Senator Donald M. Fraser, an unabashed liberal. It was in this uncertain state of mind that

Judd became the target of an unprecedented state and national campaign calculated to make him run for Congress one more time.

Congressman Charles A. Halleck of Indiana, the House Republican leader, called Judd "one of the ablest, efficient, hard-working members we have" and said the Congress and the nation would particularly miss his services in foreign affairs. Congressman Albert Quie, chairman of the state's Republican delegation (and later governor of Minnesota), declared that Judd's announced retirement was "a terrific blow to us here in Congress. Walter Judd is one of the greatest men who ever served in Congress. News of his retirement was a shock and I hope he changes his mind." WTCN Television and Radio in Minneapolis broadcast an unusual editorial urging its viewers and listeners to contact Congressman Walter Judd urging him to change his decision to "retire from public life."[5]

Prominent Republicans across the country entreated him to reconsider. A telegram from Dwight Eisenhower read in part: "How great would be the loss to the Republican party and to the country if you no longer were able to bring your articulate voice and balanced judgement to bear on problems concerning the Foreign Relations Committee in particular and indeed on all questions confronting our country. I do hope that you will find it possible to continue to serve." Old comrades in diplomacy such as Walter S. Robertson and Joseph C. Grew wrote Judd, Robertson calling him "an irreplaceable public leader . . . [in] the world's struggle against international communism." Leading conservatives like William F. Buckley, Jr. and Eddie Rickenbacker asked him to reconsider. DeWitt Wallace of *Reader's Digest* and Roy W. Howard of Scripps-Howard Newspapers urged him to run again; Wallace asked whether he realized "the intensity of the discouraging impact such a decision leaves in its wake." Even Democratic colleagues wrote him: Morris K. Udall of Arizona asserted that "the Congress and the country would be a lot stronger if you were returning." Richard Nixon, who had been strongly encouraged by Eisenhower and other Republican leaders to run for governor of California and was now embroiled in a fractious GOP primary, eschewed partisanship for sympathy, restricting himself to saying that "America needs you speaking out and in her service— whether it be in the House of Representatives or in some other capacity." Radio commentator Paul Harvey wrote a newspaper column of which Judd said, "He understood why—better than almost any other." Harvey described how members of Congress, once legislators, have become protectors of the interests of their individual constituents, from farm loans to veterans' checks to federal encroachments on private property. While conceding that it was "right and proper" for congressmen to assume such a role since "nobody [else] does," Harvey asked: "But when the conscientious Congressman is ultimately overwhelmed by this avalanche of tedium, where does he get the time or the energy to make wise decisions?" In all, Judd received five thousand letters, telegrams, and cards urging him to seek re-election in the fall. Perhaps the one that finally persuaded him to change his mind was a second communication from Eisenhower, who on May 11 wrote, almost as a commanding general to his subordinate: "By no means do I want to appear to be nagging, but I do believe that it is very important for us to make a maximum showing of good candidates this coming fall. We must stop some of the trends that seem to me to be alarming."[6] That Eisenhower, two years out of the White House and supposedly in bucolic retirement in Gettysburg, would so trouble himself with the electoral future of one Republican congressman suggests that he was not as disinterested in GOP politics as some historians have written.

There was even evidence that high-ranking members of the Kennedy administration wanted Judd to remain in Congress. The *St. Paul Sunday Pioneer Press* reported on May 6 that Secretary of Labor Arthur Goldberg had asked the veteran Republican to stay on in the House while Secretary of State Dean Rusk had written his old friend expressing his regrets that he was retiring. In explanation, the newspaper pointed out that "Judd has proved to be an important administration ally in the field of foreign affairs," influencing as many as sixty votes "and possibly more." (Other political observers have put the number of congressmen who followed Judd's lead on foreign issues at one hundred and twenty, about 75 Republicans and 45 Democrats.) The *Pioneer Press* mentioned, for example, that Judd had supported the Peace Corps, a key Kennedy effort, when "any other Republican would have been hooted from the floor or strung up in effigy by the John Birch Society. Since then it is Republican policy to speak kindly of it."[7]

When the article, headlined "Rusk Asks Judd Not to Retire," was called to his attention, Rusk informed Kenneth O'Donnell, assistant to the president, that he had "not been in communication with Walter Judd on this subject in any way, shape or form." He admitted that he had telephoned Sen. Hubert Humphrey about using Judd in the administration "in some appropriate way" in view of his experience and bipartisan help over the years. They agreed that no initiative should be taken until "it was quite clear that Judd was irrevocably out of politics."[8] However, the secretary was being a little disingenuous. Shortly thereafter, Rusk allowed Frederick G. Dutton, the State Department's chief congressional lobbyist, to memo Lawrence O'Brien at the White House that the secretary of state had in fact telephoned Walter Judd to commend him for his long service in the Congress and to express the hope that he "would continue actively on foreign policy problems." But he had not asked him not to retire. Why, then, had Rusk telephoned Judd and risked the danger of misinterpretation? Because he, and the administration, badly needed Judd's help in a Congress that although Democratic did not rubberstamp each and every Kennedy proposal. Wrote Dutton flatly: "Judd is of critical importance in the Foreign Affairs Committee for the balance of this session on the foreign aid bill, UN bonds, and other matters." Therefore, Dutton hoped that any attempt to "knock down" the story would not involve "Secretary Rusk, who is most anxious to keep out of partisan politics from either direction."[9]

While trying to determine who said what and whether any White House response should be made, O'Donnell received a petulant letter from the Democrat who wanted to succeed Judd—Donald Fraser. After describing several ways in which Judd had been "a harsh critic of the President" in foreign and domestic affairs (Judd had said, for example, that Kennedy lacks "the will to win" as illustrated in his failure to bring down the Berlin Wall) and citing his association with "rightwingers" like Dr. Fred Schwarz and Young Americans for Freedom, Fraser remarked, somewhat like an aggrieved schoolboy: "If despite this record you want to keep Judd in Congress, I would appreciate being advised of this fact directly rather than through a newspaper story." In fact, he said, "if you want Judd back in Congress I am perfectly willing and in fact would be happy to spend my summer in more constructive ways. We have a nice summer cottage and five young children and I am prepared to serve the wishes of the administration in whatever way seems appropriate." But he didn't really mean it: he badly wanted to run and to defeat Judd, whom he considered and would portray as a "leading opponent" of the Kennedy administration. He asked for "an early response" because he was convinced that "Judd is getting prepared to run again."[10] There may have been a placating telephone call to Fraser from the White House, but there is no written response in the Kennedy Library files: Rusk's request to be kept out of any public explanation almost certainly prevented a formal communication. Fraser's political intuition about what Judd might decide to do was proved correct.

On May 31, less than six weeks after announcing his retirement from Congress, sixty-three-year-old Walter Judd declared over Minneapolis television that he would indeed be a candidate for an eleventh term in the enlarged Fifth District, confessing that he "had not recognized or properly evaluated certain factors which have now compelled me to change my mind." He mentioned that among the 5,000 letters he received urging him to reconsider were ones from former Presidents Dwight Eisenhower and Herbert Hoover. He had felt that if he retired from Congress, he could devote full-time to the "larger issues," including lecturing at colleges and universities. But Eisenhower told him that he "could have more influence on the course of the nation" devoting 15 percent of his time as a congressman to foreign affairs than giving 100 percent of his time outside Congress. State Senator Donald Fraser, the DFL candidate, who had publicly lamented the lost opportunity to "debate the issues" with Judd, indicated the elevated level of the debate he sought by immediately attacking as a "myth" the notion that Judd has "been a kind of liberal."[11]

Judd had few illusions about his chances of winning or the guilt-by-association campaign that Fraser would conduct. But he couldn't say no to all the people, especially the Minneapolis women, who had worked so hard for him all those years and were now saying, "Please, don't desert us." There was only one possible answer, he later said, to that plea: "I'd rather lose, trying to be faithful, than avoid [defeat] by walking out on my friends."[12] On July 13, he formally filed for re-election, and stated that the issues in the coming campaign were the same as in previous campaigns—peace abroad and prosperity at home. A "lasting peace," he said, "cannot be secured by yielding more countries and more people to Communist control. Attempts to placate Communist imperialists lead to Koreas, in which our sons are trapped and sacrificed." He also pointed out that he had helped to bring about some "great things" in the Fifth District, including Lower Loop Development, the Upper Harbor, new facilities at Wold-Chamberlain Airport, "the creation of new jobs, the raising of living standards, and continued progress in human rights." But the major issue and "my main effort in life" was to understand and win the conflict between communism and freedom. It was, he said, his deep conviction that continued service in the Congress could be "the period of my greatest usefulness to our country and to the people of our city and state."[13]

There are five basic elements of every political campaign: money, organization, the candidate, issues and the media. There is a sixth element which is particularly important in a primary campaign, where fewer votes are cast and voter turnout is critical: intensity of support. The candidate who has a higher IQ, or intensity quotient, will usually win a primary, all other factors being equal, and may gain an important if narrow advantage in a general campaign.

In the 1962 campaign against Fraser, the Judd team ranked high in money, expending some $105,000, compared with only $6,000 in the first campaign in 1942. The Judd organization looked good on paper but functioned so erratically that in the last eight weeks, State Senator Douglas Head was brought in as campaign manager. Head, who was later elected Attorney General of Minnesota, succeeded, with the help of volunteer chairman Robert Bjorklund, in disseminating the real Judd record (not the Fraser version) and getting out the vote on election day. Judd, of course, was a excellent candidate when he was in Minneapolis, but to be there was the problem. Congressional business, especially the work of the House Foreign Affairs Committee, kept him in Washington while Fraser was able to spend night and day campaigning in Minneapolis and declaring that the Fifth District needed a congressman who spent more time on the problems of Minnesota and less on the problems of the world. After twenty years, everyone knew where Judd stood on the issues, and many people were pleased to have someone of national reputation as their representative. However, his positions did not sit well with the new union-dominated voters in the new wards of the Fifth District who favored a more activist role for the federal government and a less confrontational attitude toward the Soviet Union. An overwhelming majority of the voters agreed on one thing: they liked President Kennedy very much; anyone who went out of his way to criticize Kennedy would feel their displeasure. Judd knew of the president's popularity in his district, but was determined as ever to speak out where and when he thought it necessary, regardless of who was involved and of the political price that might be paid.

One clear advantage he had over Fraser, a young (only 38 years old) state senator, was that he was far better known. He did not intend to help publicize his opponent by debating or appearing with him. As he told one organization who invited him: "These joint appearances generally turn into more of a contest between two persons, rather than a hard-headed consideration of the issues involved. Everybody will turn out for a prizefight or any other gladiatorial combat. I want to concentrate on ideas and policies, not on personal results. . . . I shall try to get my story across in my way. Let Mr. Fraser get his story across in his way."[14] It was a sensible position normally taken by an incumbent. Certainly there was ample precedent: President Eisenhower did not debate Stevenson in 1956; in later years, President Johnson refused to debate Barry Goldwater in 1964, and President Nixon declined to appear opposite George McGovern in 1972. But in 1962, Judd was confronted by a very aggressive challenger who did not hesitate to raise questions about the state of the incumbent's health (Was it true he had cancer and that was why he had initially said he would retire?), his association with alleged "right-wingers" like Fred Schwarz, his "failure" to work for the interests of Minneapolis, and his "indifference" to the cause of civil rights. Judd responded to Fraser's charges when he could and when he thought it necessary, but he was so busy with crucial votes in Washington that often he made no response at all. In effect, he gave his opponent an almost open field (except on the weekends) for much of July, August and September. In a debate, he would have been able to answer the charges directly and effectively.

One of Fraser's most persistent and effective tactics was to link Judd to Dr. Fred Schwarz of the Christian Anti-Communism Crusade. Judd gladly confirmed that he had spoken before some of the Crusade's seminars whose purpose was "to get people to study communism as doctors study diseases." He often referred to and quoted from a book written by Schwarz, *You Can Trust the Communists (To Be Communists)*. Born in Australia and trained as a physician, Schwarz used scientific analysis and passionate rhetoric, much like Judd, to become one of America's best-known anticommunists in the 1950s and 1960s. But there were significant differences in style and substance between the two men: Schwarz often attacked the United Nations while Judd continued to defend the organization, arguing that "it's done better than we've had a right to expect." Schwarz declined to criticize the John Birch Society, while Judd disavowed association with a group "whose leader has made such irresponsible statements."[15]

During a 10-day House recess in late August, an exasperated Judd expended valuable campaign time in Minneapolis answering Fraser's charges about Schwarz when he would have preferred to talk about what he considered the "real" issues in the campaign. It was a new experience for the veteran legislator who nevertheless decided that, no matter how unfounded an allegation, he had to set the record straight. It was an understandable reaction in one who took justifiable pride in his reputation, but the strategy helped keep the accusations alive as the newspapers and other media dutifully reported charge and counter-charge. Despite the increasing ugliness of the campaign, he retained a sense of humor, once suggesting that since he was accused "of playing footsie" with the John Birch Society, which he had criticized privately and publicly for years, he was a victim of "guilt by non-association." Although some advisers counseled otherwise, he insisted on praising the personal character and conduct of Fred Schwarz, whom he described as "perhaps the most thorough student of Communism as a disease of human behavior."

A lesser man and more ambitious politician would have quickly severed all ties with Schwarz. But Judd would not sacrifice someone whom he respected for political gain. "Just what is wrong with Dr. Schwarz?" he asked. "Does vigorous opposition to Communism make a man a far-rightist?" In the minds of Donald Fraser and the DFL, it did, and Judd paid a heavy price for his loyalty to Schwarz as well as his own vigorous opposition to communism.[16]

In mid-September, he received some encouraging news from Robert A. Forsythe, chairman of the Minnesota Republican campaign: A just-completed poll gave him a clear lead over Fraser, 54 percent to 32 percent with 14 percent undecided. Forsythe also reported that "the issue which people seem to be talking most about is that of Cuba. [They] are worried and apprehensive." How the candidates handled the growing Cuban crisis (at this point, Kennedy had not gone public about the Soviet missiles) would obviously have a major impact on the election.[17]

Another key issue was the minimum wage. Fraser charged that Judd had recently voted against an increase to $1.25 an hour. In fact, Judd had voted for four increases in the minimum wage, in 1949, 1955, 1960, and 1961. However, when a House-Senate conference committee in 1961 provided for an increase to $1.25, to go into effect in September 1963, Judd voted against it, arguing that the next congress, not the present Congress, should act on the basis of the economic situation at that time. "Is it wise," he asked, "for a doctor to prescribe for a patient two years ahead of time? . . . My record proves that I will support in the future as I have in the past just as rapid increases as economic conditions will permit. To go faster forces employers to lay off workers and create unemployment."[18] Judd was consistent in his votes on the minimum wage and logical in his explanation for his actions, but Fraser had an emotional issue ("Judd Votes Against Minimum Wage") that he stressed at every opportunity. What Fraser did not say, is that Judd's consistent votes in favor of a higher minimum wage were at direct variance with the label of "far-right conservative" which he and the DFL were attempting to affix to the incumbent congressman. An examination of Judd's domestic voting record reveals that he voted for a $1.5 billion program of grants and loans to institutions of higher learning, for increased Social Security benefits, and for expanded veterans benefits. He also opposed the Kennedy administration's multi-billion dollar farm bill (for its "unworkable" new controls), a cabinet-rank Department of Urban Affairs (for needlessly concentrating more power in Washington), and the King-Anderson bill to provide health insurance benefits for the aged under Social Security ("unfair in its benefits and too limited in the help it gives"); he preferred the Kerr-Mills Act which would have established a cooperative program between the states and the federal government. He took a consistently moderate (liberal, for a Republican) position on the role of government in the area of welfare, supporting it when federal support was demonstrably essential but opposing when it was not. Nevertheless, the perception spread, assisted by Fraser's propaganda, that Judd had shifted to the right since first coming to Congress.

Another charge leveled against Judd was that he was soft on civil rights. This allegation was especially painful for someone who had led the way in removing all racial discrimination clauses from U.S. immigration and naturalization laws. Nor had he overlooked racial problems at home, receiving a statement from the NAACP in 1958, for example, that he had voted correctly on fourteen of fifteen issues it considered significant in the field of racial and civil rights legislation. More recently, he had voted for the extension of the Civil Rights Commission; an amendment insuring voting rights for all citizens; the Powell amendment against segregation in schools receiving federal funds; and the aboliton of the poll tax as a requirement for voting in federal elections. In October 1962, he received a cordial letter from the Washington Home Rule Committee, thanking him for signing the Home Rule Discharge Petition (the Democratic chairman of the House Rules Committee adamantly refused to allow the measure to come to the House floor for debate and voting) and for "all your efforts in behalf of a sane solution to the problem of disenfranchisement of the citizens of the District," three-fourths of whom were black.[19] But in keeping with his oft-stated principles, he did not trumpet his pro-civil rights record or use the issue to political advantage. For example, as longtime NAACP members, he and Miriam once attended a banquet of the Minneapolis chapter, paying for their own tickets and quietly sitting at a table in the back of the room. He was not recognized from the dais (as was Hubert Humphrey, who arrived late and shook his way through the crowd) because no one realized Judd was present until friends saw him as they were leaving. It is difficult to imagine a present-day congressman being so reticent under similar circumstances.

Judd was ready for Fraser's charge that he was more interested in solving the problems of the people of Formosa than the people of Minneapolis, pointing to his almost twenty-year, successful campaign to obtain funding for the city's Upper Harbor project. In August 1962, he announced an appropriation of $4 million, the sixteenth and final one, for the two dams and locks at St. Anthony Falls, the head of navigation on the Mississippi, in the center of Minneapolis. The Upper Harbor project had been a "great satisfaction" to him, said Judd, for he had been able to help convert a great natural resource "into a magnificent development to benefit a great city and a greater area and their people for decades to come."[20]

As for criticism that he had rarely if ever supported President Kennedy (an important issue with the new DFL voters in the Fifth District), he responded that he had voted for five of the seven "most important domestic actions" of the Eighty-seventh Congress, cited by Kennedy himself in a campaign speech. In fact, he had supported the president more often than many congressmen in the president's own party, voting with the president on 72 percent of all roll call votes, and on 89 percent of the foreign policy roll call votes in the last session of Congress. Still, President Kennedy traveled to Minneapolis in early October to attend the annual DFL "bean feed" at the state fairgrounds and to call for the election of Karl Rolvaag as governor and six DFL congressional candidates, including Donald Fraser. Judd was not disturbed by the president's endorsement of his opponent ("You have to root for your own team."), only his timing: while Kennedy was in Minneapolis, Judd was in Washington, helping to pass the president's foreign aid package. In his remarks at the DFL "bean feed," Kennedy was careful not to mention the name of the Republican whose support had been so important in the passage of foreign aid and other key parts of his foreign policy program. But the message was clear: the charismatic young president, so popular in Minneapolis, although he had bested Minnesota's own

Hubert Humphrey for the Democratic presidential nomination, wanted a new face to represent the Fifth Congressional District. The Kennedy visit came at a critical time for Fraser; according to a *Minneapolis Tribune* poll, he still trailed Judd by nine points, 43–52, with a month to go.[21]

Judd was not without resources: he too had presidents he could call on. Dwight D. Eisenhower, still one of the most admired men in America, came to Minneapolis a few days later to campaign for his old friend, whom after all he had urged to run. As many people turned out for Ike as for Kennedy, and they heard a ringing endorsement of their congressman: "Walter Judd for twenty years . . . has been a hero . . . when there was involved the honor, the firmness, the readiness of America to stand up as a leader in the free world. Walter Judd is the kind of man we can't afford to be without—we must not be without."[22]

Judd and his organization did everything that a congressman and his campaign team should do to win re-election: they spent their money wisely, and after an uncertain beginning, they organized well. One of their most effective devices (introduced to Minneapolis by the Judd team) was the lawn sign that read: "Keep Judd Working for You." Robert B. Bjorklund, long-time volunteer manager of campaign volunteers, remembered that the Fraser forces kept removing or destroying them late at night and people kept calling up and saying, "I've got to have another lawn sign."[23] The Judd campaign addressed the issues that mattered most to the voters of Minneapolis; they made intelligent use of their candidate's considerable campaigning abilities although hampered by his continued presence in Washington, D.C. (the Congress not adjourning until late in October after the Cuban missile crisis was resolved) and they efficiently worked the news media, television, radio and newspaper, even obtaining an editorial endorsement from the *Minneapolis Star*.

They failed in only one way: they could not get Walter Judd, once he got wound up, to stop talking. Campaign manager Douglas Head recalled that Judd once asked for help. "Come to my speeches," he said to Head. "Sit in the back of the room. After 35 minutes, stand up and I'll see you and start bringing things to a close. If I don't stop after 40 minutes, hold your hand up. If I go 45 minutes, start waving both your arms, and you'll get me to quit." Although he felt it was unwise for a campaign manager to engage in such public signaling with his candidate, Head agreed. Soon thereafter, Judd addressed a business group, and Head dutifully stationed himself in the rear. After thirty-five minutes, Head stood up, and Judd nodded in acknowledgment. At forty minutes, Head held his hand up, but the candidate kept talking. At forty-five minutes, the manager began waving both arms, but the candidate was in full flight. After fifty-five minutes, and in the middle of a sentence, an inspired Judd interrupted himself to say: "And I am beset with people that don't understand, that don't understand the problems. Why, my own campaign manager is even in the back of the room trying to shut me up. But I won't be shut up—I'm going to finish this speech!"[24]

One issue that affected the outcome more than any other was the Cuban missile crisis. Republicans had been criticizing administration policy toward Cuba for months, demanding that Kennedy do something about the Soviet program of increased arms aid to Cuba. Led by Senators Kenneth Keating of New York (who had access to disturbing reports from Cuban exiles), Barry Goldwater of Arizona, and Homer Capehart of Indiana, Republicans called variously for a blockade, an invasion, or simply "action." Kennedy met the political challenge head-on; at a news conference on August 29, he attacked as "irresponsible" calls for an invasion of Cuba but promised to "watch what happens in Cuba with the closest attention." Less than a week later, he denied any provocative Soviet action in Cuba. On September 13, he condemned "loose talk" calling for an invasion of Cuba. On October 13, the day before photographs by a U-2 flight discovered the Soviet missiles in Cuba, Kennedy campaigned in Indiana against those "self-appointed generals and admirals who want to send someone else's sons to war."[25]

Judd, who had access to some of the same Cuban exile reports as Senator Keating, did not want war; he wanted the United States to take firm decisive action so that there would be no war. In a televised campaign address on September 12, he stressed the gravity of the situation, declaring that "for the first time in the history of our Republic, we have an enemy base [Cuba] controlled by one of the most powerful nations the world has ever known." He asserted that "Soviet Russia is and always has been at war with us. . . . we must do whatever is necessary to win this war." He then sounded a strong bipartisan note, stating that it was a time for "Americans to unite" and support the president in adopting the policies "that offer the best hope of coming through this great crisis. . . . We don't want Mr. Kennedy to fail," he underscored, because "if he fails, every one of us fails."[26] Although he had been sorely disappointed by Kennedy's failure to provide sufficient U.S. support for the Bay of Pigs invasion, his decision to support a coalition (i.e., procommunist) government in Laos, and his feeble response to the erection of the Berlin Wall, he hoped that the president would now act with decisiveness in a crisis only ninety miles from U.S. shores.

When the president continued to temporize and began making legalistic distinctions between defensive and offensive weapons, promising to act only if the latter were introduced into Cuba, Judd did not hesitate to sharpen his criticism, despite Kennedy's enormous popularity in Minneapolis. He declared that the Kennedy administration's "wavering stand against world wide communism" had led to the Soviet military buildup in Cuba and brought "renewed pressure in Berlin." He said that the United States must find a way "to eliminate the Soviet military base in Cuba." He was not suggesting unilateral action, he emphasized, but unified hemispheric action against a common enemy. "I believe this can be done," he said, "if we are patient and firm. But if not, the United States itself must find new ways to help the Cuban people return to freedom."[27]

As he alternated between weekdays in Washington, filled with rumors about Soviet offensive missiles in Cuba, and weekends in Minneapolis, filled with growing apprehension about the possibility of war between the United States and the Soviet Union, Judd fluctuated between criticism and support of the president. The Kremlin, he said in late September, was "testing the will of this administration. . . . If we are willing to stand by and permit the Soviets to turn this island . . . into an advanced base for Soviet Communist aggression, the Soviets are bound to conclude that our response to any Communist adventures in Central Europe will be equally indecisive." Fraser, who did not have the same access to information as Judd, preferred to treat the Cuban missile crisis as a political rather than a foreign policy issue. He suggested that the "current preoccupation with Cuba is a calculated effort to divert attention from domestic issues." Everyone was agreed on opposing Castro, Fraser said, but "we are disagreed on medical care, decent wages, education, housing and all those issues on which the present Congressman has taken a consistently negative and obstructionist position for years."[28] The DFL candidate's stance appealed to the voters who were more interested in domestic issues like wages and medical care and inclined to let the president whom they admired so much handle the nation's security.

On October 19, only three days before Kennedy publicly announced the presence of Soviet offensive missiles in Cuba and the imposition of a

U.S. blockade, and two weeks before election day, an impatient Judd escalated his language: "Cuba represents a clear and present danger to the security of this hemisphere. Hesitancy and efforts to belittle the threat have already resulted in an increase in that danger. Continued indecision will increase it even more. The United States must resolve to take affirmative action. There are now no easy ways, but there are still ways whenever there is the will."[29] He did not have access to U-2 photos or CIA intelligence reports, but it was obvious to any aware person that a serious crisis had developed with regard to Cuba. Why was the Kennedy administration taking so long to deal with it? Judd had no way of knowing that the first hard photographic evidence of offensive missiles in Cuba had been given to Kennedy only three days before. Would the president falter? Judd believed that if the United States acted to protect its own interests, the Soviet Union would not retaliate. But to some citizens of Minneapolis, it seemed that he was being unnecessarily critical of the president and using the crisis mainly to help win re-election.

On the morning of October 22, upon hearing rumors that the president would address the nation that evening, Judd expressed skepticism about the intentions of the White House: "Unfortunately it is not [yet] possible to be sure whether the administration really means business this time or is engaging in showmanship." He insisted that his criticism and that of others had not been partisan or "disloyal" but had been based on what the Kennedy administration "has not been doing to deal effectively with the threat to our very survival."[30] His disclaimer was dismissed by most DFL voters, who recalled that he had denounced Kennedy as "a weaker person than we realized." When the president announced the U.S. blockade of Cuba that evening, Judd immediately sent a telegram commending Kennedy for his decision; he also released a statement that "as in the past, firmness and strength in support of our principles, our commitments and our security offer the *best,* perhaps the *only* hope of peace and freedom in our world. All Americans will support the President wholeheartedly in his decision."[31] It was an unequivocal declaration, but shortly thereafter, in a campaign appearance, he hinted that Kennedy's action may have been politically motivated, inviting charges that he was not as supportive of the president as he should have been in a time of crisis. Polls showed almost unanimous approval of Kennedy by the citizens of Minneapolis, who were eager to rally around the president.

Judd was not moved by what the polls said. Campaign manager Douglas Head recalled that at a heavily attended news conference in the middle of the missile crisis, Judd said that he would stand "foursquare" behind the president if he stood strong against the Soviets. But, he added, if Kennedy "pulled his technique of standing firm publicly and then privately negotiating away his position," he would not support him. "I agreed in principle with what he said," said Head, "but politically I didn't feel it was right."[32] Head's misgivings were justified: the press played up Judd's implicit criticism of Kennedy when Kennedy's popularity in Minneapolis was soaring. Ironically, Judd was correct in his skepticism about the president: Kennedy pledged to Khrushchev that in exchange for his withdrawing Soviet missiles, the United States would not invade Cuba and that other nations of the Western hemisphere "were prepared to give similar assurances."[33]

On November 6, Donald M. Fraser narrowly defeated Walter H. Judd by 52–48 percent, receiving 87,002 votes to Judd's 80,865 votes. In his old Fifth Congressional district, Judd led Fraser by 10,860, about his usual majority there; but in the added wards, he trailed his DFL opponent by 16,997. He had expected to lose by 25,000 or more. The new wards in the district had not even had a Republican ward or precinct chairman they were so dominated by the DFL. Some advocates of good government in the city asked themselves: "If a man like Walter Judd can not be re-elected to Congress, what hope is there for the nation?" Norman Carpenter, a top campaign strategist, remarked: "He was elected as a liberal and defeated as a conservative but didn't change at all." Walter Judd conceded gracefully, while many of his workers wept, wished his opponent well and quoted his mother's counsel that when "some doors are closed, others are opened." But in private he did not hide the fact that his defeat, or rather the manner of it, angered him. As he wrote one out-of-state acquaintance: "We put on the hardest and best-organized and financed campaign we have ever had, but we could not undo in four weeks what an able and unscrupulous opponent had been able to do with scuril[l]ous half-truths and charges in eleven months of campaigning around the clock."[34] For his part, Fraser declared that he would urge the Kennedy administration to appoint Judd to a high position so that his "special talents and abilities in international affairs" would continue to be used.

The letters of regret and consolation poured in. Nelson Rockefeller expressed his "deep distress" at the results; Thomas E. Dewey wrote that "you have been one of the most important, useful and constructive public servants of our times and the voters of your district did the country a tragic disservice." Sen. Jacob Javits of New York, who had campaigned for him in Minneapolis, took a more optimistic view: "We are dismayed but not disheartened. You have many years of fruitful service to give for us all and I expect to continue working with you in friendship and accord." Dwight Eisenhower acknowledged his key role in persuading him to run, and expressed his "deep regret" at his loss. Ike then added, rather formally and somewhat in the form of a benediction, "You will long be respected and admired by those who have shared with you [the] burdens of government and also, from that experience, have come to appreciate your integrity, wisdom and talents." A young Texas congressman named Jim Wright wrote unreservedly that "your perceptive understanding of the international situation and the leadership you have provided have on more than one occasion meant the difference between success and failure for those necessary activities which make up an enlightened and effective foreign policy. Unfortunately, there is no other person in the Congress who can fill your shoes."

Two ranking officials of the State Department agreed with Wright: W. Averell Harriman, assistant secretary of state, said that "I will especially miss your counsel on our Far East problems, particularly now that the Chicoms are on the march in India." U. Alexis Johnson, deputy undersecretary of state, emphasized that "I will sorely miss your always wise counsel and informed views. To those of us who knew you there was never any doubt that you placed the welfare of our country above all other considerations." Even as no man is a hero to his valet, no member of Congress is a paragon to his personal staff or the staff of the committees on which he serves. Even so, Carl Marcy, executive director of the Senate Foreign Relations Committee, wrote Judd that while sometimes staff members believed "they know more about most issues than Members of Congress. . . . at least once a year when the AID bill was in conference everyone of our staff people knew positively that this was not the case because you always knew more about the subject than any of us. Your absence will be felt very deeply." One of the most moving letters came from Ting Chung Kan, a Chinese student at the University of Minnesota, who recalled that Judd had used precious campaign time to talk with him at the campus union although Kan was not an American citizen and could not vote. "I still can not help weeping every time when I think of you, your personality, and that the United

States has lost such a talented ideologist and dignified representative as you. . . . I would wish that Americans in this city know that the friends which you have won in China for this country far exceeded the 6,200 [by which you lost]. I shall pray for you and may God richly bless you."[35]

Two days after his defeat, an important door appeared to open when Rusk telephoned Judd to say, "Walter, we're all sorry here in the Department [about your loss] because you've given us such valuable aid on Capitol Hill. You'll probably have opportunities. Don't you take any position or appointment or anything until you hear from us." Judd did not know what Rusk had in mind, but he had worked with him as far back as the Truman administration. He respected the soft-spoken, tough-minded secretary of state and believed that he could help him and the country, perhaps in the area of U.S.-China relations or foreign aid. But he never received a second call. Nearly twenty years later, he and Rusk were attending a ceremony in Michigan establishing a center for former President Gerald Ford's papers. He decided to try to clear up the mystery of the call that never came. "Dean," he asked, "do you recall calling me up right after the 1962 election and telling me not to take any other job until I heard from you?" "Sure, I do," Rusk replied, half-smiling. "Well, I never heard from you," said Judd, "and I know that somebody in the administration must have blocked it. I'm just curious as to who it might have been. Was it Hubert [Humphrey]?" Rusk paused and then uttered one word, "Bobby."[36] So Judd learned, two decades after the fact, that Bobby Kennedy, attorney general of the United States and the president's closest political adviser, insured that he would not be politically resurrected through a position in the Kennedy administration.

A philosophical Judd told campaign workers and supporters in December that it would have been an upset if he had won. In addition to the redistricting, he noted ironically, there was "the handicap of my lifelong and incurable concern with performance rather than with publicity; [I put] the legislative job first, everything else second." For example, in all his years in Congress, he never had a press secretary or a speechwriter. Today, every senator has at least one press aide and often as many as three, while almost all congressmen have someone who handles the news media. Judd recalled that *Time* had asked: "Can such a man be re-elected?" The "most surprising thing was not that I lost this time," he said, "but that I was re-elected nine times previously." Perhaps, he reflected, he could have won if he had been willing "to attack and promise" but that he had never done "and would not do." From his first day in Congress, he had tried to follow the counsel of George Washington during a dark day of the Constitutional Convention: "If to please the people, we offer what we ourselves disapprove, how can we afterwards defend our work? Let us raise a standard to which the wise and honest can repair. The event is in the hands of God." He thanked everyone for their loyal support and promised that he and Miriam would continue working for the basic American values and traditions they shared "in whatever opportunities lie ahead for service to our country and our world. We shall do our best to justify your faith."[37]

CHAPTER SEVENTEEN

Still a Missionary

ALMOST BEFORE HE HAD TIME to clean out his congressional desk in Washington, Judd found himself in the middle of an intense debate about the Republican presidential nomination in 1964. Partisans of Barry Goldwater and Nelson Rockefeller were not so slowly tearing the Minnesota Republican party apart. Conservatives insisted that Goldwater would arouse the silent majority across the country and bring victory to the Grand Old Party. Liberals countered that the Rockefeller record and name afforded Republicans their best chance in 1964. Conservatives, led by political strategist F. Clifton White, had been working since 1962 to win the Republican nomination for Goldwater, and they were determined not to be denied victory as they felt they had been in 1952 with the defeat of Taft by Eisenhower. Recognizing they did not have the grassroots strength to directly challenge the Goldwater forces, Minnesota liberals settled on a favorite-son strategy by which they hoped to deny Goldwater a first-ballot victory and prepare the way for a Rockefeller triumph on a later ballot. Who had the necessary prestige and would be willing to run as a favorite son? There was only one possible answer: Walter Judd. While the Rockefeller partisans were plotting, uncommitted Minnesota Republicans viewed the growing Goldwater-Rockefeller clash with alarm. These regular Republicans, moderate in their philosophy and politics, did not favor either Goldwater or Rockefeller; they wanted someone who had a chance of winning the presidency and helping Minnesota Republicans regain lost ground. They too opted for Judd as a favorite son. There was no doubt that he was the most respected and admired Republican in the state: some 2,800 people, paying a hundred dollars a plate, had filled the Minneapolis Auditorium in January 1963 to honor him. But would he do it?

Judd had no interest in running for any public office; at a July 1963 news conference in Minneapolis, he spiked talk about his running for the U.S. Senate in 1964 against incumbent Democrat Eugene J. McCarthy. But at the same conference, he said that he would be willing to be Minnesota's "favorite son" candidate at the 1964 Republican National Convention, as had been suggested by some, if that would hold Republicans together in Minnesota. He called the Republican presidential contest "as uncertain a situation as I've seen a year before the convention." It was this uncertainty and the developing divisiveness in his party which persuaded him to allow people to put together a Judd for President committee. It was more important at this point, he said, to decide "whether we're going to act as a team" than to pick a presidential candidate. "There isn't any Republican who can win," he warned, "unless we have more teamwork than we have had in recent months."[1] For the next year, until the convention was held in San Francisco in July 1964, he worked with the Judd for President committee to prevent the Minnesota Republican party from splitting into Goldwater and Rockefeller factions. Along the way, he denied repeated charges from Goldwater supporters that he was a "front" for Rockefeller, was part of an "anti-Goldwater movement," and would "deliver" Minnesota's delegation to still another candidate. Nor did he agree that voting for a favorite son was "throwing your vote away." He was trying to unite the party behind the presidential candidate who had the best chance of winning whether that was Goldwater, Rockefeller or even someone else.[2] His pragmatism belied once again the charge, made by Fraser and others, that he was a neanderthal right-winger. The motives of the organizers of his favorite son candidacy were more mixed. Some were genuinely interested in uniting the party, others were hoping to use Judd to block Goldwater and help Rockefeller, others hoped to secure the vice presidential nomination for Judd, and still others just could not abide the notion of a conservative like Goldwater leading their party.

Judd arrived at the convention in San Francisco with eighteen of Minnesota's twenty-six delegates pledged to him, but had scant impact on the outcome: nothing short of an earthquake could have deterred the assembled delegates from nominating their conservative hero, Barry Goldwater, who easily won on the first ballot. However, Walter Judd's name was placed in nomination by Republican state chairman Robert Forsythe and seconded by Mrs. George S. (Sally) Pillsbury, vice chairwoman for Hennepin County. Almost without dropping a beat, the Minnesota delegation began promoting Judd as Goldwater's running mate. Following a midnight caucus, seven leading Minnesotans visited Goldwater headquarters at the Mark Hopkins Hotel to learn if the former congressman was still in the running. There they were told by Richard Kleindienst, co-director of the Goldwater campaign, that while "Barry has the highest admiration for Walter Judd.... it just would not be fair to involve him at his age [he was 66] in such a rigorous campaign as this one is going to be."[3] Goldwater's choice for vice president was Congressman William E. Miller of New York, who spent most of the 1964 campaign playing cards with the reporters who covered him and speaking in half-filled auditoriums in small cities in electorally insignificant states, a less rigorous schedule than the one Judd had been following since leaving Congress. In the end, his favorite son candidacy had one important and desired effect: it enabled Minnesota Republicans, alone among Republicans outside the Deep South, to hold their party together and survive the resounding Goldwater defeat in November. Not one Republican from Minnesota lost his seat in the U.S. Congress while conservatives of both parties retained their control of the state senate and lost almost no ground in the lower house of the state legislature.

Although they were not consulted by Goldwater's inner circle of advisers, senior Republicans like Arthur Summerfield, who had served as Eisenhower's postmaster general, and Senator Carl Curtis of Nebraska believed that with Judd as the vice presidential nominee, the party would have been able to "hold most of the Republican states in line" and "LBJ could never have claimed a mandate" for his Great Society.[4]

Within a few short months, Judd would be given the largest national platform of his life and the opportunity to help the American public understand critical issues like the Vietnam War and the Great Society. His benefactor was a razor blade magnate, Patrick J. Frawley, Jr. Frawley was a conservative, an anticommunist, an early Goldwater backer, and the president and major shareholder of Schick Safety Razor Company, number two to the giant Gillette. He lived only minutes from

Hollywood and had gained a considerable fortune through shrewd advertising and aggressive public relations. Among other enterprises, he underwrote the work of counterrevolutionary Ed Butler, who argued that the best answer to the Timothy O'Leary-Abbie Hoffman psychedelic culture was a "square" world that promoted basic virtues and traditions like patriotism and religious faith. When John Fisher, president of the influential American Security Council, approached the California business executive about sponsoring a daily five-minute radio commentary about world affairs and national security, featuring Walter Judd, Frawley quickly agreed, familiar as he was with Judd's way with words and the ability of radio to convey a message to millions for relatively little cost. He provided a public service grant of $200,000 a year to the Council to cover all production, distribution, and talent costs. The program first aired in September 1964, and over the next six years, the American Security Council's "Washington Report" became "the largest public affairs, public service program in the history of American broadcasting," reaching a peak of over 1,100 stations. Many stations, including Washington's top-rated WMAL, carried the program during the evening rush hour; several broadcast "Washington Report" twice a day. Three years after he left Congress, Judd found himself more widely known than ever before.

The program reflected his rectitude—he stuck to the issues and avoided partisan criticism of people—and his anticommunist views. Veteran broadcaster John Fulton Lewis, who served as program producer for several years, marveled at Judd's unflagging energy and communications skills. "He was one of the great all-time natural speakers. He had the same gift as Billy Graham, of picking a theme, and riding it for all it was worth. The audience always understood what he was saying and where he was going." He was a stickler for facts, Lewis remarked, and a semanticist who argued fiercely over the meaning of a single word. He was intensely self-absorbed, given to shutting out the concerns of other people, even of his family, if they interfered with his work. "He was generous to a fault," said Lewis, donating as much as half of his annual income to scores of different groups and organizations; but he was not so giving of his personal attention. He once conceded to Lewis, after mentioning the marital difficulties one of his daughters was going through, "Maybe I didn't listen enough."[5]

Typical of his "Washington Reports" was a broadcast in January 1966 when he talked about Vietnam, calling it the "test case" as "Korea was in 1950 and Quemoy in 1958." A communist victory in South

Vietnam, he said, "would lead almost certainly to disintegration of effective resistance in much of Asia." He emphasized a favorite theme: the danger of compromise with communists. The situation in South Vietnam, he asserted, was possible because of a "so-called compromise we forced on Laos in 1962." The communist threat in Laos became "possible only because of a compromise on North Vietnam at Geneva in 1954." The communists' strength in North Vietnam which produced that compromise was possible only because of "efforts to get a compromise instead of victory in Korea in 1951." And the communist attack on South Korea in 1950 was possible only because the communist victory in China was "assisted so decisively by America's efforts to compel the free Chinese to accept a coalition government with the communists." Rather than containing, compromises of this kind with communists "actually expanded ... the struggle." These, he concluded, "are the facts of history."[6] Such broadcasts made sober listening, but Judd, realist, scientist, missionary, was not interested in broadcasting "happy talk" or sugarcoated news but in reporting the facts as he saw and understood them. People were interested, for the number of stations and listeners continued to grow.

In March 1966, he made one of the most important congressional appearances in his life when he testified before the Senate Foreign Relations Committee, J. William Fulbright presiding, on "United States Policy Toward China." The hearings had been heavily stacked for days with pro-Peking witnesses who argued that since the communist regime on the mainland was clearly in command and the Chinese people had obviously accepted communism, the United States should be practical and extend diplomatic recognition to the People's Republic of China and support its admission to the United Nations. Through the last-minute intervention of Senator Bourke Hickenlooper of Iowa, the ranking Republican member of the committee, three opponents of such a drastic change in U.S. policy were given one day to testify; Judd was one of them.

His statement was an urgent plea for continued nonrecognition and nonadmission of Peking and a staunch defense of containment of Communist China as a policy which had enabled much of Asia to enjoy peace and achieve a growing prosperity. He pointed out that twenty-seven years earlier he had been given the opportunity to testify before the committee on essentially the same subject: "how to get and keep freedom and peace in Asia and thus security and peace for the United States." He had then urged that America stop giving Japan's military the sinews of war and do all "we properly could to strengthen and help the free peoples resisting" Japan. His recommendation had been rejected because it was perceived as "too dangerous and costly" and because it was feared that "a confrontation with Japan might lead to war." The U.S. government, he reminded the senators, "was persuaded, until it was too late, to try to placate the aggressor.... The policy did not lead to peace, it led to Pearl Harbor." Now, he said, the same "general approach to aggression in Asia" was being advocated and it should be rejected, or otherwise the United States and the world would suffer terribly as they did once before.

He next examined the changes in U.S. policy proposed by the witnesses who had preceded him. It seemed to him that their recommendations were based on certain assumptions that were not justified. One such assumption was that the communist regime in control of the Chinese mainland was "here to stay." But the same assertion had been made with regard to Hitler, Khrushchev, Sukarno, and Nkrumah. Despots, he stated, "generally appear invincible until the last five minutes." Another false assumption was that the United States was isolating Communist China and was therefore responsible for "its hostility and belligerence." It was Peking, not Washington, however, that had taken military action against India, had practiced genocide in Tibet, and was supporting North Vietnam in its aggression against South Vietnam.

What would be the gains and losses, he asked, if the United States should recognize Communist China? Would the mainland "moderate" and "evolve," as some proponents vaguely suggested? Consider the case of India, he suggested, which was one of the first countries in the world to recognize Peking. It was Communist China's "chief apologist and advocate" in the United Nations and elsewhere throughout the 1950s, and yet, Communist China did not hesitate to invade India in 1962. In contrast to the possible gains, he said, there was no uncertainty about the certain losses that would result from a weakening of American policy. Such a step would "pull the rug out from under our loyal allies on Taiwan.... 12 million Chinese [on Taiwan] could hardly maintain indefinitely the will or the capacity to resist 700 million." "Our Pacific island chain of defenses would be breached.... It is doubtful that the Philippines could long resist Communist pressures and blandishments." The fifteen million overseas Chinese in Vietnam, Malaysia, Thailand, Burma, Indonesia, and the Philippines "would be shaken" as would be the governments of these smaller and weaker countries. U.S. allies in Europe and around the world would wonder if they could depend upon

America: "Why should any country anywhere stand by us if it is not sure we will stand by it?" It would signal the neutral and uncommitted nations they "were right all along and . . . might as well give in to the winning [Communist] side at once." It would tell the 7 hundred million people on the China mainland that "we are accepting their subjugation." The last loss was the worst of all in his estimation because it meant that in a mindless pursuit of peace, the United States was more willing to come to terms with the oppressor than to "stand steadfastly with . . . the oppressed."[7]

Before the end of summer, Mao Tse-tung launched the Great Proletarian Cultural Revolution, which convulsed China for ten years, silenced those "Asia experts" who argued that now was the time to change U.S. policy toward Peking, and again revealed Judd as a man of rare insight and foresight. His compelling twenty-six-page testimony, prepared over a weekend, helped delay the admission of Communist China to the United Nations for five years and gave the Republic of China on Taiwan the opportunity to further demonstrate "its accomplishments and merit." Judd regarded his March 1966 appearance before the Senate Foreign Relations Committee as "one of the most beneficial services I was ever able to render to the Chinese *people* and to better chances for peace for ourselves and the world."[8]

Equally useful—and timely for today—were the suggestions he made in April 1967 to the House Subcommittee on Asian and Pacific Affairs on how to improve America's foreign aid program, with which he had so long been associated. First, it was necessary to determine our primary objective in any country. This was not to make it love us, but to establish a partnership that "will be mutually beneficial." Second, the program needed to be streamlined, confined "to the essentials," that is, food, health, education, transportation, and security. The United States was trying to do too much in too many places, thereby scattering our efforts, complicating our operations and confusing the people we were trying to help. Third, the United States needed a longer range program because we were faced with "a long-range problem." Both the president and the Congress had to state publicly that the United States was making an open-ended commitment to help peoples and nations become self-sustaining so that they could do without our help. Fourth, personnel had to have better preparation and training and to be stationed in an area for longer than two years. He estimated that it took the average American twelve months to get acclimated and learn his job in an overseas post, after which he did good work for about nine months, until he spent the last three months of his assignment preparing to go home. Fifth, there should be more decentralization of authority so that people in the field could make decisions there without always having to check first with Washington. "We have some of the best people in the world in these missions abroad," he said. "So often they are handicapped by the impediments which Washington . . . puts in their way." His counsel was based on the philosophy he practiced as a missionary in China: work *with* people, not do things *for* them. Do not assume that the American way is the only way. As he told his former colleagues, while Americans believe that democracy means popular elections "of the sort we have here," in a true sense, "democracy means governments that the people respect and led by persons from their own ranks."[9]

Since the early 1950s, the fate of Vietnam had concerned Judd. He first visited it in April 1953 as part of a congressional study mission, which issued a report urging the U.S. government to give at least some assistance directly to the Vietnamese rather than channeling all aid (some four billion dollars) through the French, who continued to delay granting full and genuine independence to Vietnam. Late that same year, his Asian subcommittee visited Vietnam and concluded that "until political independence has been achieved, an effective fighting force from the Associated States [of Vietnam] cannot be expected." Judd wrote to President Eisenhower in June 1954 that "division and indecision on the part of the free world [have] left the Vietnamese with complete uncertainty as to whether they could count on it." He was referring to the French decision to negotiate directly with the communist Vietminh at Geneva and British Prime Minister Churchill's announcement that he was coming to the United States to talk over some "family matters" in Asia. We must make it clear, said Judd, "that we are *for* the British and French in Europe, not because they are British and French, or because they are white, but because we support their effort to remain free. Likewise, in Asia we are on the side of those who are striving to obtain or to preserve their freedom from any kind of imperialism."[10]

The Geneva Accords of July 1954, which partitioned Vietnam along the seventeenth parallel and permitted the regrouping of military forces on both sides, disturbed him greatly. Eisenhower and Dulles both stressed the positive aspects of the agreements, asserting that they would enable the United States to build up noncommunist forces in the south, and that they ensured "the truly independent status" of Laos and

Cambodia. But Judd considered the yielding of North Vietnam to the communists as a "smashing defeat for the free world."[11] In a private memorandum which he did not send to the White House, he referred to the Geneva accords as an "Indochina Munich" and predicted it would not bring peace but made war "more likely." In Indochina, he said, the French and the British accepted a truce instead of victory because they "had refused for years to do the things necessary for victory"—grant genuine independence, provide military training to the Vietnamese, and support the formation of a Pacific Pact as urged by the House of Representatives, led by Judd, since 1949.[12]

In 1961, he opposed the coalition government that President Kennedy forced on the then pro-Western, anticommunist government of Laos, predicting that it would lead to a communist Laos (which it did in the 1970s). He similarly protested when the Kennedy administration engineered the 1963 overthrow of the government of President Ngo Dinh Diem of South Vietnam; the U.S. action resulted in Diem's murder and "two years of chaos" in Vietnam "which we were able to overcome only" through the expenditure of American lives and money.[13] In 1965 and 1966, he wrote supportive letters to President Johnson about the "effectiveness of your basic actions in Vietnam,"[14] and in a major address in February 1967, outlined several steps which he felt had to be taken to win the war. First, President Johnson had to unify his own party and the American people by telling them "the full truth" about the critical importance of Vietnam. "We are gaining ground in Vietnam but losing it in America," he said. Second, the United States should allow South Vietnam to start a "true 'liberation front' in the north," drawing on the million people who fled Ho Chi Minh's rule to live in the south. "They want to go back as guerrillas to disrupt things in their native areas as the Vietcong do in the south," Judd insisted. Third, the United States should "conduct more effective bombing of more important targets." He suggested notifying Hanoi publicly of "10 or 20 or 50 military targets that we are going to destroy" so that civilians could be moved away. "We don't want to kill North Vietnamese, but we must reduce [their] capacity to kill South Vietnamese—and to kill Americans."[15] The Johnson administration had failed to take more offensive action, in large part, because of fear that the "masses" of Red China would intervene. Judd said flatly that such an action by Mao Tse-tung, deeply concerned about U.S. retaliation against China's nuclear facilities and forced to use the Red Army to control the Cultural Revolution in China, was most improbable. Regarding the administration's concern that confrontation would "inevitably lead to an escalation," he asserted that the post–World War II record was clear: in twelve confrontations with the communists over the last twenty years (ranging from the Truman Doctrine to the Cuban missile crisis), U.S. firmness in the face of communist threats "led without exception to de-escalation." As he had said so many times while in Congress, he stated that it was because he did not want all-out war that he now urged "steady firmness and strength as the quickest and surest way to a livable peace."[16]

The Johnson administration gratefully accepted even such qualified support as opposition to the Vietnam war sprouted on all sides. Senator Fulbright conducted a series of nationally televised hearings, featuring public critics of President Johnson's policies. Thousands of young Americans used legal loopholes to evade the draft; many others fled to Canada or served jail sentences rather than go to Vietnam. Rallies and demonstrations increased significantly in 1966 and 1967 with participants becoming more and more outspoken. The most dramatic single act of protest came on October 21, 1967, when 50,000 opponents of the war demonstrated in front of the Pentagon, the headquarters of "American militarism."[17] In this intensely antiwar atmosphere, and at his own expense, Judd traveled to Vietnam (his seventh visit to Southeast Asia since 1953), visiting Saigon, Danang, and Hoi An. From October 1 to 5, he talked with a wide spectrum of people, including U.S. Ambassador Ellsworth Bunker, General William Westmoreland, top Vietnamese officials, and journalists, businessmen, and missionaries. He sent a detailed report about military, economic, and political conditions in Vietnam to William P. Bundy, assistant secretary of state for East Asian and Pacific affairs, who was so impressed that he asked him to summarize it personally for the president.

Meeting with Johnson in the Oval Office on October 16, Judd listed his major findings: First, U.S. forces were well led and had a clear understanding of the "nature of the enemy and [the] seriousness of his threat." Second, South Vietnamese forces were better trained, more united and more aggressive than on his last trip in 1964. Third, South Vietnam was doing better politically, having conducted four elections in the last year and reduced the threat of Buddhist militants to a manageable level. Fourth, the South Vietnamese economy was improving, with inflation down in the last several months and "pilfering and corruption" less than in Korea in 1953 or China in 1946, although worse than under Diem. Fifth, South Vietnamese morale was up with citizens telling him something like, "I think we're going to make it." With regard to the

Vietcong, he said it was weakening militarily and had not won a major battle in more than a year; "losses in men from casualties, disease, and desertions were greater each month than replacements by volunteering, impressments, and infiltration from the north." Politically, the Vietcong did not control "as many rice areas" as in the past so it was compelled to raise taxes in order to buy rice which produced "greater hostility among the people."

The North Vietnamese, he reported, were having problems. They were less able to supply men and equipment to the south than formerly except to DMZ (demilitarized zone) areas "where their lines are shorter and not subject to countermoves by U.S. ground forces." Missionaries told him that more and more of the North Vietnamese regular forces were "not communists, not even patriots, just weary and discouraged conscripts."[18]

The "tide definitely has been turned against the enemy," he asserted, due in large measure to "more effective bombing of more important targets" in the north. In fact, he said, the "Communists cannot win in Vietnam," but they refused to negotiate because "they think our side may lose." Their hopes lay in the "divisions and doubts in the United States. . . . The critical front now is not in Vietnam. *It is here at home.*" He strongly recommended that the administration give the American people a complete and candid accounting of the war: "Speeches and exhortations will not do the job. The people must be given the more detailed facts that convinced you and me. These facts will also convince them." He urged a nationally televised, in-depth briefing by Ambassador Bunker and General Westmoreland, predicting that "not only their presentations but their convictions and enthusiasm as to the rightness of this cause and the importance and necessity of our Southeast Asia effort will be convincing to our people. It might be more effective if we have this taped in Vietnam." He argued that the American people should be "trusted with most of what our government knows, as the British were trusted by Churchill in their toughest trial" in 1940, while acknowledging a significant difference between the situation then and now. That was a declared war; this was an undeclared war. He wondered whether a free society like the United States "can successfully fight a long, hard war on a peace-time basis" with no "propaganda agency" to "build up pride in and support of our fighting men," with "no restrictions on the press" and with the battlefield on television. All wars, he said, were "bloody, cruel, mixed-up, with blunders and mistaken killing of civilians or our own forces. The men participating know these things and push ahead. But never before did their wives and mothers also 'participate' [in the gore of the battlefield] via their TV screens every morning and night." "I think," he said somberly, "that no nation ever has" won a war under such circumstances.

He urged the administration to "keep the door open to genuine negotiations [but] closed to tricks [and] stalling." Responding to charges that the Vietnam war had become an American war, he said: "Let the South Vietnamese take the lead in negotiations. . . . We are in a stronger position, morally and tactically, when we are merely advising and assisting." But based upon his long experience with communists, he said that a time limit should be set and the United States should "let Hanoi and Moscow know privately that we intend to use strong measures if Ho stalls. This is the way President Eisenhower got the killing stopped in Korea. *It offers the best hope of peace now.*"[19]

Vietnam remains America's most controversial war, and the debate about its origins, management, and end will continue for many years. Judd's advice might or might not have made a telling difference if it had been adopted by President Johnson in late 1967. But objective historians like George Herring have stated that the infusion of American forces had staved off "what appeared to be certain defeat in 1965" and given the South Vietnamese government a chance to survive.[20] However, enormous problems still confronted the Thieu-Ky regime, including the presence of 500,000 American troops and the expenditure of tens of billions of dollars in assistance. Drawing on his experience as an American missionary in an Asian country, Judd addressed the danger of "too great a [U.S.] military buildup" in his testimony before the House Foreign Affairs Committee in April of that same year. Invited to discuss "rural development in Asia" by his old friend and chairman of the Committee, Clement Zablocki of Wisconsin, Judd expressed his deep concern about the unprecedented American use of men and materials in the Vietnam conflict and uttered these prophetic words: "[Vietnam] is too small to stand it indefinitely. It can be drowned, choked, overwhelmed. Its culture would become hybrid. If this goes on too long a disintegration is bound to take place in Vietnam itself. It could be the old story of a successful operation, perhaps, but a dead patient."[21]

His reflections about the critical impact of the mass media, particularly television, on the war came several months before American television converted the Tet offensive of the North Vietnamese and the Viet Cong from a costly communist defeat into a decisive victory. Early wire service reports exaggerated the success of North Vietnamese attacks on Saigon, including the U.S. Embassy. Televised accounts of the bloody fighting in Saigon and Hue mocked optimistic U.S. reports. Humorist Art Buchwald parodied General Westmoreland's claims of victory by having Custer say at the Little Big Horn: "We have the Sioux on the run." Candid photographs and TV footage of the police chief of Saigon holding a pistol to the head of a Vietcong prisoner—and then firing—"starkly symbolized," one commentator wrote, "the way in which violence had triumphed over morality and law."[22] No one explained that the Vietcong soldier had just murdered a group of innocent Saigon civilians. It was not reported that the North Vietnamese and Vietcong were unable to establish any firm positions in the urban areas in the south, and that the South Vietnamese people did not rise up to welcome the invaders as "liberators." Enemy battle deaths have been estimated as high as forty thousand. The regular units of the Vietcong, who did most of the fighting, were decimated and never completely recovered. But in the United States, the media, led by CBS's Walter Cronkite, declared that the war was no longer winnable, with Cronkite, "the most admired man in America," asserting that "we are mired in stalemate."[23]

The day before Judd reported on his Vietnam trip to President Johnson, two prominent Republicans and potential presidential aspirants, Ronald Reagan and George Romney, criticized the Johnson administration's handling of the war. Reagan charged that Johnson was withholding good news on Vietnam to use in the 1968 presidential election while Romney declared that the war was going badly and the American people were being misled. In rebuttal, George Christian, the President's press secretary, set up a White House press briefing featuring Walter Judd, who told reporters that "unquestionably the corner has been turned out there—the tide has been turned."[24] The failure of the Tet offensive confirmed his judgment, although to this day most Americans think that Tet was a military defeat for the United States and South Vietnam because of the way it was presented on American television. Judd believed that if Johnson had arranged for a televised presentation in Vietnam by Westmoreland, Bunker and experts in the field, including AID and pacification officials, the American people would have been convinced of "the essentiality" of the effort in Vietnam and TV's negative impact would have materially lessened. Much later, in August 1972, Judd set down, in unusually concentrated, spare language, what he called "some painful lessons to be learned from the Vietnam experience—some mistakes free peoples must never make again." First, he said, "no nation should ever enter a war unless it intends to win, and is prepared to exert its utmost to do so." The U.S. decision not to "win" in Vietnam was "of course a decision to lose." A no-win war was the worst of all policies: "it has all the disadvantages of a war-to-win, produces as much fatigue and even more frustration, invites just as much criticism; but it has none of the advantages. What incentive is there for the adversary to negotiate an end to it?" A nation, he said, can justify not entering a war at all or using its power effectively if it does enter a war. But "no one can justify" sending men to fight and to give all they have while at the same time leaving unattacked the enemy's bases and factories and food supply, that is, the capability to take the lives of the enemy. He quoted Douglas MacArthur: "A great nation which voluntarily enters a war and does not see it through to victory eventually suffers all the consequences of defeat."

Second, it was impossible, he argued, to successfully fight a war with communists, especially a long, drawn-out war, "without some censorship to match the total blackout on the Communist side." He favored a government agency, such as the Office of War Information that operated during World War II and explained why the United States could not allow Hitler to gain control of Europe or Japan to dominate the strategic bases, resources, and manpower of Asia. He used a sports analogy: "Who would hope to build a successful football season without ever holding a rally or having a single cheerleader?" It was just impossible, he concluded, to "fight a long war on TV."[25]

Third, the communists in North Vietnam were not interested only in South Vietnam. "Why should Hanoi stop with South Vietnam," he asked, "if it has a chance to humiliate the United States" and advance its aims in Indochina and beyond? Communists are not nationalists, he said, "they intend to win the *world*."[26] Subsequent events in the 1970s proved him right. After the Paris agreements of January 1973 that left several hundred thousand North Vietnamese troops in South Vietnam, Hanoi bided its time, but launched a major offensive in early 1975 that quickly placed the out-manned South Vietnamese on the run. Without U.S. support (Nixon was gone and President Ford was blocked by Congress from sending anything but "humanitarian" aid), South Vietnam collapsed, and Ho Chi Minh proclaimed victory in a war that had begun a quarter of a century before. Cambodia fell to the Communist Khmer Rouge before South Vietnam surrendered, and Communist insurgents triumphed in Laos shortly thereafter. In Africa, Marxist governments took over in Angola and Mozambique while Soviet-supported regimes came to power in Ethiopia and South Yemen. In Central America, the Marxist Sandinistas, with guidance from Havana and Moscow, replaced the authoritarian Somoza government of Nicaragua. And on Christmas Day, 1979, the Soviets invaded Afghanistan, using military force for the first time since the end of World War II to seize control of a non-contiguous country. There is little dispute that defeat in Vietnam paralyzed America's willingness to resist Soviet expansionism. The 1960s were a bad decade for anticommunists like Judd, who worried deeply about the future of his country and of old allies, like the Republic of China on Taiwan.

Paradoxically, he found reassurance when on his trip to Asia in the fall of 1967, he paid a courtesy call on President Chiang Kai-shek in Taipei. He began by congratulating the eighty-one-year-old Chinese leader for what he and the other Nationalists had been able to accomplish on Taiwan, despite the defeat on the mainland, its isolation from the rest of the world, the nonrecognition policy of many Western countries. "I got about that far," he recalled, "when the Generalissimo interrupted me. He looked up at the ceiling and said:

"Well, maybe it had to be, that we didn't succeed on the mainland. We had had eight years of war against an external enemy. We had twenty years of struggle against an internal enemy. We were exhausted. Our economy was disrupted. Because of this disaster, this failure, we are now here on Taiwan. The problem was too great on the mainland. . . . Our society was disintegrating. But here we have a smaller problem and a hundred miles of water—and your Seventh Fleet—between us and [the mainland]. Here we could concentrate on how to preserve the essentials of the old that gave us our long and good civilization and how to put with it, how to integrate with it, the best of the new, such as science, technology, efficiency, and productivity of the west.

"We were able to work it out here and to produce a living standard, a per capita income, ten times what it is on the mainland. This is the pattern that we've established for the development of the mainland when the liberation comes. And this is the pattern for the almost 100 newly independent countries that can enable them to build good societies and to have the high productivity that we have here.' " He added: " 'The Communists always talk of revolution; our concern is for renaissance.' "

Judd sat in awe. Here was Chiang Kai-shek, "inept, incompetent, inefficient, undemocratic, corrupt, and reactionary" (the six adjectives unfailingly used by critics), and yet he had the vision of combining the old and the new, of East and West, and of sticking to it until the Republic of China became an economic model for the developing world.[27]

Notwithstanding Chiang's equanimity, Judd remained concerned about U.S.-ROC relations. Some members of the Committee of One Million cheered the election of Richard Nixon in 1968, believing that the new president would pursue as hard a line against Red China as he had in the past. Nixon pledged during his campaign that as president he would use the U.S. veto if necessary to keep Communist China out of the United Nations.[28] But Judd had read and remembered Nixon's 1967 article in *Foreign Affairs,* in which he wrote: "Taking the long view, we simply cannot afford to leave China forever outside the family of nations, there to nurture its fantasies, cherish its hates, and threaten its neighbors. There is no place on this small planet for a billion of its potentially most able people to live in angry isolation."[29] Judd had been saying much the same thing for nearly twenty years since Mao came to power in 1949. He had always insisted that once Peking renounced revolution and violence and agreed to abide by the terms of the U.N. Charter, it would deserve to be admitted to membership and to receive our assistance. He knew, better than most Americans, of the great potential of the Chinese people, who if they were represented by a government that truly reflected their history, their character and their culture could do great things for their country and the world. For Judd, the central question was: how should mainland China's isolation be ended—on its terms or the free world's?

Despite public statements to the contrary, Nixon had privately made up his mind early in his presidency to change U.S. policy toward the mainland. He sent a memo to his national security adviser, Henry Kissinger, that stated: "I think we should give every encouragement to the attitude that this Administration is exploring possibilities of rapprochement with the Chinese. This, of course, should be done privately and should under no circumstances get into the public print from this direction."[30] Unaware of the memorandum, Judd blamed Washington rumors that began to surface about a pending change in U.S. policy toward Communist China on the State Department and a "palace guard" in the White House. He counseled conservatives who were alarmed about some of Nixon's "liberal" appointments and actions to let the president know about their displeasure privately rather than publicly. He acknowledged that Nixon was projecting a "different image" than he had in the past but stated: "I must believe that there has been no change in the basic views and positions of our new President on these issues."[31] There was a practical reason for his forbearance: any public criticism of Nixon would eliminate the possibility that he might be asked to serve in the administration. In a letter to columnist John Chamberlain, seventy-year-old Judd expressed the hope that the Nixon administration "will use some of us who can perhaps qualify as 'Elder Statesmen'—in the same way that some previous Administrations called on men like Baruch, McCloy, Acheson (on the Bay of Pigs episode), General Marshall (on his missions to China), etc." Such an "expert," he suggested dryly, should be chosen for having "a record of having been essentially right in his analyses and judgments" and not for having "religiously read" other "experts' " books.[32]

But despite more than twenty years of political friendship and association with the president, Judd was never invited to participate in a single project for the Nixon administration. Sometimes, even his telephone calls were not returned. He admitted to former Minnesota Governor Elmer Andersen that in the first month after Nixon's inauguration, he had tried three times to arrange to see the president, but had received no response. "I must assume," he said, charitable as always, "that for some reason or other, the requests did not get to his personal attention during those weeks when his staff was not yet really well-organized. I don't believe, however," he added optimistically, "there will be difficulty on this point from now on."[33] Why did Nixon, Kissinger, and Secretary of State William Rogers not utilize Judd's wisdom and experience as a member of their administration? Because they knew that he would raise objections, valid and persuasive, to the China policy they were intent on pursuing. It was troublesome enough hearing him on the radio every day, as moderator of the American Security Council program, or reading one of his statements as chairman of the Committee of One Million. They did not want to subject themselves personally and directly to Judd's merciless logic and implacable will. It was better by far to keep him at arm's length and go quietly about the business of building a bridge to the PRC while partially dismantling one to the ROC.

For nearly two years, Nixon and Kissinger sent and received confidential messages to Peking, usually through Pakistan and Romania, touching on the prospects for U.S.-China trade, the Vietnam War, Taiwan, and a possible Nixon trip to the Middle Kingdom. In mid-April of 1971, Premier Chou En-lai sent an unmistakable signal when he publicly received an American ping-pong team in Peking. Nixon responded, through a message delivered by President Yahya of Pakistan, that he was prepared to accept Chou's invitation to visit Peking and proposed that Kissinger undertake a secret visit to arrange an agenda and begin a preliminary exchange of views. Following Kissinger's secret mission, Nixon surprised the world by announcing on national television that he would visit China. He then sent a personal letter to President Chiang Kai-shek, reiterating that the U.S. government would continue to honor all its military commitments as formally expressed by treaty. One reason that the 15 million people on Taiwan reacted so calmly to the Nixon announcement, despite its gravity, was a prescient statement a few months earlier by Chiang, who promised his countrymen that "if all of us stand firm in our conviction of what is right and just in accordance with our principles, we shall have peace of mind and find solace. . . . Moreover, danger and doubt will give us opportunity to manifest our convictions of righteousness and justice, and anxiety and pain will provide our nation with opportunity for rebirth."[34] Chiang's serene words would have meant little if he and his Nationalist government had not led the people of Taiwan, in little more than 20 years, from the lowest ranks of the underdeveloped world to the brink of becoming a newly industrialized country; if the per capita income of the average Chinese on Taiwan was not 10 times that of the average Chinese on the mainland; and if there had not been impressive improvements in education, health, and welfare.

While many conservatives engaged in *ad hominem* attacks on Nixon, Judd attempted to point out the flaws in the emerging U.S. policy. Invited to address the American Bar Association meeting in London, Judd noted that the President gave as the main reason for his "pilgrimage to Peking" that "there can be no stable and enduring peace without the participation of the People's Republic of China and its 750 million people." He challenged Nixon's assertion on two counts. One, the basic problem for the U.N. was not the non-participation of the Communist regime in Peking, "but its lawlessness"; and two, there was little in Communist China's words and deeds to suggest that bringing Peking into the community of nations would "encourage improvement in its international attitudes and behavior." He declared that he would have agreed with Nixon wholeheartedly if he had said, "There can be no stable and enduring peace as long as the 750 million Chinese are under the tyrannical and wholly un-Chinese dictatorship presently in control in Peking—whether it is in or out of the U.N." He was not playing with words. To use an old saw, Judd always meant what he said and said what he meant: when and if there was ever a regime, a government, in Peking that was not un-Chinese but Chinese, not tyrannical and expansionist but democratic and peaceful, then such a government warranted membership in the United Nations. It was, after all, Mao Tse-tung, not Americans, who insisted that "power grows out of the barrel of a gun," that world events were to be determined by "revolutionary violence" rather than civilized negotiation. It was not true, Judd told the assembled lawyers, that the U.N. was intended to have universal membership; members had to abide by its rules and Communist China still stood condemned by the U.N. as an aggressor in Korea. As for the argument that one had to be realistic and acknowledge that Communist China did in fact exist, he countered that "gangsters are a fact in some of our big cities. [But] we do not argue, in the name of realism, that the peacekeeping agencies should therefore take the gangsters in. Realism demands that the gangsters be kept out of the forces responsible for maintaining law and order."[35]

Reflecting on the announced Nixon trip, Judd quoted an Asian friend who remarked: "The United States spends billions to go to the moon. Mao just waits—and the moon comes to him." Why did President Nixon want so badly to go to mainland China? In his *Memoirs*, Nixon refers blandly to "mutually advantageous interests," but then reveals his fixation with his place in history. He recounted how he and Kissinger shared a brandy in the small family kitchen in the White House after receiving word from Chou En-lai, early in June 1971, that Kissinger would be welcome to come to China and arrange for a Nixon visit with Chairman Mao. "Let us drink," said Nixon, "to generations to come who may have a better chance to live in peace because of what we have done."[36] Kissinger was more earthbound in *White House Years*, explaining that because of growing Soviet strength and declining U.S. will, caused by the continuing Vietnam war, the United States was obliged to practice "triangular diplomacy," which was not, he agreed laconically, "appreciated at once by everyone." "Equilibrium" was the objective: "We did not seek to join China in a provocative confrontation with the Soviet Union. But we agreed on the necessity to curb Moscow's geopolitical objectives."[37] Implicit in Kissinger's evaluation was the assumption that if in maintaining that balance between major powers, a small country like the Republic of China was bruised and hurt, it was an acceptable price to pay.

It must be added that Nixon, never secure emotionally in any public office he ever held, had his eye on his reelection in 1972 as well as his place in history. In mid-1971, neither was assured. Although it is generally forgotten because of his subsequent landslide victory over McGovern, President Nixon then trailed his chief Democratic rival, Senator Edmund Muskie, by 39 to 47 percent. In fact, Nixon's popularity had fallen to a lower level, according to the Gallup Poll, than "that of any President since Harry Truman," at a comparable point in his administration.[38] A presidential visit to China, with all the attendant publicity and worldwide television coverage, while it might lose him some votes on the right, would gain him far more votes in the center. American political history offers no instance of a conservative who ever lost a presidential election moving to his left.

A number of Democratic and Republican senators, including Fritz Hollings of South Carolina, John Tower of Texas, James Buckley of New York, and Peter Dominick of Colorado, strongly criticized the president's pending trip to Peking. Dominick pointed out that "other presidents have tried this kind of personal diplomacy. President Roosevelt did and he ended up with Yalta. . . . President Kennedy did, and he ended up with the Rose Garden in Vienna and subsequently the Berlin Wall and Cuban crisis. I, for one, hope we won't fall into similar quagmires as a result of the President's move."[39] Despite such vocal opposition, Congress failed in 1971 for the first time in twenty years to pass a resolution against the seating of Peking in the United Nations; such an omission probably would not have occurred if Walter Judd had still been one of its members.

Withal, Judd's central concern that fall was not Nixon's re-election or the effectiveness of triangular diplomacy, but the fate of the Chinese people still held captive by a communist regime that did not represent "their history, heritage, culture or their desires for freedom and an opportunity to develop and modernize in their own way." As evidence of the yawning gap between regime and people, he pointed out in the Committee of One Million's newsletter that the preceding November "more Chinese attempted to escape by swimming the dangerous channel to Hong Kong, than all the East Germans who have ever attempted to scale or penetrate the Berlin Wall in the ten years since it was erected."[40] Confronted by an eager president, a shifting Congress and an increasingly indifferent public, Judd tenaciously fought U.N. admission of Communist China down to the very last moment. In its last year, the Committee raised and spent more money than ever before in its eighteen-year history, over $300,000; collected nearly half a million signatures against admission; commissioned a six-state opinion survey (in the key electoral states of California, Florida, Illinois, New Jersey, Ohio and Texas) which showed strong public opposition to the seating of Communist China in the United Nations; and produced a provocative hour-long documentary film, *U.S.-China Policy: Danger at the Crossroads,* narrated by William F. Buckley, Jr., which was intended for national television but was rejected by all three networks on the grounds that it had not been produced by their own news organizations.[41]

The Committee faced an almost impossible task. In April, a special presidential commission formally recommended that Communist China join "Nationalist China" as a full-fledged member of the United Nations—an official endorsement of a "two Chinas" policy, which was, in fact, opposed by both Chinas. Privately, Judd had urged the Taiwan government to consider just such a diplomatic course of action, but Taipei adamantly refused wedded to the KMT's dream of one day reuniting all of China under the Nationalist banner and Sun Yat-sen's Three Principles of the People. In August, Secretary of State Rogers announced that the United States would favor the seating of the Chinese Communists in the General Assembly in the fall, but would oppose any move to expel the Republic of China. Rogers avoided taking a position on the question of the "China seat" in the Security Council, saying that "we ... are prepared to have this question resolved on the basis of a decision of members of the United Nations." Rogers stressed that in dropping twenty years of American opposition to Communist Chinese membership, the United States was "thinking to accommodate our role to the realities of the world today."[42] The Nixon administration explained that it would keep the Republic of China in the U.N. by making the expulsion of Nationalist China an "important question," requiring two-thirds support of those members present and voting. That is, the United States needed only one-third of the General Assembly, plus one, to block Taiwan's forced removal. But noting Nixon's impending visit to China and the dropping of a twenty-year-old policy by the United States, U.N. members began asking themselves: How "important" a question is the membership of the Republic of China? If the United States, the Nationalists' principal sponsor, seemed so ambivalent about Taiwan, why should other members care what happened to it?

The end came on October 25, 1971, after eight hours of intense debate, when the General Assembly voted overwhelmingly to admit the People's Republic of China and expel the Republic of China. The expulsion of Taiwan was denounced by U.S. Ambassador Bush as a "moment of infamy." The vote was actually anticlimactic, for the assembly had earlier voted to reject the American resolution making expulsion of a charter member an "important question." Among the abstentions on the key procedural vote were eight nations, including NATO members Belgium, the Netherlands, Italy, and Turkey, who had been considered to be leaning toward the U.S. position. If only half of the abstainers had voted with the United States, the "important question" resolution would have been adopted and the later Albanian resolution to admit Peking and expel Taipei would have been rejected. The Nixon administration fatally undercut the valiant efforts of Ambassador Bush and his team by sending Kissinger to Peking to finalize arrangements for Nixon's visit at the very moment when the United Nations was debating the China question; many U.N. members understandably took their cue from the Kissinger trip as they thought they were supposed to.

Kissinger defended the timing by saying that his visit could not have been delayed "if the President's trip was to take place in the early part of 1972"; the trip demonstrated that "it was possible to have businesslike relations with Peking while opposing Taiwan's expulsion from the UN."[43] But that is diplomatic disingenuousness; Chou En-lai was far more candid in a December interview when he admitted that China had not expected to be admitted to the United Nations in 1971. But President Nixon's announced plan to visit the China mainland changed the vote in Peking's favor. "People say," remarked Chou, "since Nixon will go to China, why can't we too?" He pointed out that among the fifty-nine countries that opposed the "important question" resolution of the United States, ten had no diplomatic relations with China.[44]

The Committee of One Million quietly dissolved, after eighteen years as one of the most effective grassroots lobbies in Washington, D.C., and with almost anyone else, that would have been that. But Judd could not and would not quit his efforts for a free and orderly world. "If the people of the world are free," he said, "you'll get along. If they're controlled by a totalitarian regime, like [that of] Hitler or Stalin, you won't."[45] On February 15, 1972, on the eve of President Nixon's departure for China, he announced the formation of the Committee for a Free China, along with Senator Barry Goldwater, Senator Strom

Thurmond, and Clement Zablocki, future chairman of the House Foreign Affairs Committee, explaining that it would distribute the facts about the Chinese Communist government which he characterized as a "self-selected, self-imposed, self-perpetuating tyranny over the Chinese people." At age seventy-three, but bearing the years lightly, he said that the group would also strengthen President Nixon's hand when he conferred with Mao and Chou by symbolizing U.S. resistance to any Chinese-American "deal" that might jeopardize U.S. allies in Asia.[46]

Aside from the televised pictures of a smiling Nixon conversing with Mao, toasting Chou in the Great Hall of the People, posing on top of the Great Wall of China, warmly applauding the anti-Nationalist "Red Detachment of Women" ballet, touring the carefully preserved city of Hangchow with its painted pagodas and floating lotus blossoms, and briefly visiting the ten-million-person metropolis of Shanghai (all of which earned remarkable television ratings and gave Nixon a significant boost in the polls as calculated), the single diplomatic accomplishment of the president's trip was the 1,800-word Shanghai Communiqué. The key issue, everyone agreed, was the future of Taiwan, about which the Chinese part of the communiqué boldly declared: "The government of the People's Republic of China is the sole legal government of China; Taiwan is a province of China. . . . the liberation of Taiwan is China's internal affair in which no other country has the right to interfere; and all U.S. forces and military installations must be withdrawn from Taiwan. . . ." To which the American part weakly responded: "The United States acknowledges that all Chinese on either side of the Taiwan Strait maintain there is but one China and that Taiwan is a part of China. The United States Government does not challenge that position. It reaffirms its interest in a peaceful settlement of the Taiwan question by the Chinese themselves. With this prospect in mind, it affirms the ultimate objective of the withdrawal of all U.S. forces and military installations from Taiwan. In the meantime, it will progressively reduce its forces and military installations on Taiwan as the tension in the area diminishes."[47]

Surprisingly, the initial press reaction to the Shanghai Communiqué was negative and even hostile. The *Washington Post* commented, "Weighing the concessions made by the President, many observers [in Peking] feel that the Chinese got the better of the bargain." One television commentator concluded that China had won "a giant step and given away little." The *Detroit Free Press* quoted an observer as saying: "They got Taiwan; we got egg rolls." *Newsday* headlined: "Consensus —US Paid High Toll for Diplomatic Bridge to China." A disturbed Kissinger speculated that the reporters writing these stories were mostly "liberal" and were "perhaps convinced in their hearts that nothing good could possibly come of a Nixon initiative," but that in any event the negative press stories were overwhelmed by the "visual impact" of the visit. "For once," he said, "a White House public relations strategy succeeded, and performed a diplomatic function as well."[48]

Interestingly, Judd was less disturbed by the Shanghai Communiqué than much of the press and most conservatives. He pointed out that it was not a legal document and was never submitted to the Senate for advice and consent. With regard to the legitimate government of Taiwan, all the United States said was that it "does not challenge" the position of either the PRC or the ROC. "That's Kissinger's smart ambiguity," said Judd approvingly. "We don't agree with [the position stated]; we don't disagree with it; we don't approve it; we don't disapprove it; we just don't challenge it. So there's no commitment."[49] The communiqué never mentioned the 1954 mutual defense treaty between the United States and the Republic of China, which therefore was not affected. The only commitment in the communiqué was that the United States "would progressively withdraw its forces and military installations on Taiwan, as the tension in the area diminishes." Even there, the reservation about diminishing "tension" placed the onus on mainland China to seek a peaceful resolution of its dispute with Taiwan; in fact, there has been no military confrontation between Peking and Taipei since the Shanghai Communiqué. Judd wished that one more phrase had been added to the sentence, "The United States acknowledges that all Chinese maintain there is but one China and that Taiwan is a part of China"—to wit: "and that the mainland is also a part of China."[50] That addition would have let all Chinese know that the United States intended to pursue a two-China policy, not a one and a half China policy, as some deduced from the Shanghai Communiqué. Both Nixon and Kissinger later reiterated, publicly and privately to conservative leaders like Barry Goldwater and Ronald Reagan, that America had not abandoned its commitments to the Republic of China on Taiwan. Jimmy Carter, a future U.S. president, did not interpret the language the same way, and later used the Shanghai Communiqué as a reason to sever diplomatic relations with Taiwan, an act that Judd was to call "shameful." Taiwan reacted to the communiqué with its customary ingenuity, opening trade or cultural centers in place of newly vacated embassies. For example, after Spain switched recognition to Peking, Taiwan opened a "Sun Yat-sen Center" in Madrid while Spain opened a "Cervantes Center" in Taipei.[51]

Like the bamboo tree, the Republic of China knew how to bend but not break under the typhoon winds of change that continued to blow. Three years later, on April 5, 1975, its people donned white robes of mourning for the death of the only man they had ever known as their president, Chiang Kai-shek, who conquered the warlords in the 1920s, routed the Chinese communists in the 1930s, fought the Japanese to a standstill in the 1940s, lost control of the people and the country after World War II, and took up exile on Taiwan where he created a model nation for the developing world in the 1950s and 1960s. Chiang's funeral attracted more than three hundred foreign dignitaries, including a U.S. delegation led by Vice President Nelson Rockefeller and including Barry Goldwater and Walter Judd. Eleven years later, addressing a World Chinese Christian Conference in Taipei, Judd offered an assessment of Chiang, calling him a "giant," using the laudatory Chinese expression, "a man of the age." He said that it was Chiang's faith, his spiritual values, first Confucian, then Christian, which largely influenced what he said and did as a soldier, statesman, and world leader. His mentor, Sun Yat-sen, to whose teachings he was so dedicated was a devout Christian. When in December 1927, Chiang married Soong Mei-ling, her mother presented him with a Bible, saying it was the most valuable and important present she could give. Invited to become a Christian, Chiang replied that he had just finished reading the New Testament for the second time, and was now going to read the Old Testament. "I want to learn more about this Christian faith," he said, "before I publicly accept Jesus Christ as my Savior." It was not until 1930 that he was baptized. Six years later, when Chiang was seized and held captive in Sian for two weeks under threat of death, he refused to yield to his captors' demands that he end the fight against the communist rebellion. Chiang asked his captors for only one thing, a Bible, which along with prayer and meditation enabled him to "overcome temptation and to uphold righteousness."

When Chiang defeated the warlords and united most of China, Judd pointed out, he did not execute any of these powerful local adversaries but asked them to join in building a new China. In the only period of relative peace, from 1932 to 1937, before the Japanese attack, Chiang "inspired and led" a program of modernization in economic development, education, communication, transportation, and public health that "has never been surpassed" by any nation of comparable size in a comparable period of time. Railway lines were extended, highways were expanded, the number of universities and colleges grew rapidly, agricultural societies increased.[52] The new republic, declared Judd, "even had a balanced budget!" He wished the U.S. government would do as well. Chiang kept fighting the Japanese, after they invaded China in 1937, despite repeated offers of peace on the most generous terms. He could have "saved his own people most of the suffering and economic bleeding of the rest of the war" but instead "chose to stand loyally by his allies," tying down a million and a quarter Japanese soldiers on the mainland "who would otherwise have been killing Americans." At the end of the war, Chiang demanded no reparations or reprisals against Japan, as the United States and other combatants did, only its cooperation in "building a new day of peace and prosperity for Asia and the world," an act of benevolence that Japan has never forgotten. In his will, Chiang said simply of his life: "I did only what I should do." That is, said Judd, Chiang wanted the main actions of his life to be in "essential accord with what Jesus had taught and exemplified. . . . He had wanted his deeds to be in harmony with Jesus' words." Judd could have been describing his own life. Because of Chiang Kai-shek's leadership, he said, the Republic of China was a "spectacular demonstration of what the Chinese people can and will do for themselves when they are free and with leaders and a government that represent *their true character* and *their* interests." Judd conceded that Chiang had had failures and that there were "as yet unattained goals" in the Republic of China, but defeats in a "great and noble cause are no disgrace. Default would be. Chiang Kai-shek did not default!"[53]

The Republic of China suffered another shock on December 15, 1978, when, with Congress not in session and unable to protest or take action, President Carter announced that the United States was recognizing the People's Republic of China and derecognizing the Republic of China on Taiwan. Giving diplomatic recognition to mainland China, Judd conceded, may be "recognizing simple reality," but derecognition of the government in power in Taiwan can only be called "*denying* simple reality." Was the president suggesting, he asked, that the government of some seventeen million people on Taiwan—"more human beings than in two-thirds of the world's countries"—did not exist? Were they now to be considered "un-persons" or "non-persons"? He was especially offended by Carter's attempt to link his unilateral action with Christmas, "this season of peace." The attempted association, said Judd sharply, "makes a mockery of the spirit and meaning of Christmas."[54]

In a letter to the editor never published by the *Washington Post*, he argued that Carter's executive decision to derecognize Taiwan was wrong in every imaginable way. It was morally wrong given "the long-standing, friendly relations America has had with the Republic of China since its founding in 1912." It was politically wrong because other allies and friends would rightly question "how dependable are our commitments to them." It was diplomatically wrong because mainland China would not accept such an arrangement as final. It was militarily wrong because Taiwan remained an important part of "the free world's line of defense in the Western Pacific," an observation with increasing relevance as the United States and the Philippines continue to debate the future of Clark Air Force Base and Subic Bay Naval Base in the 1990s. It was strategically wrong because it was interpreted by the Soviets as "excessive U.S. 'tilting' toward the Chinese Communists." It was tactically wrong because of the "obvious uncertainties and instabilities in mainland China. . . . just who is it we are establishing relations with?" And it was economically wrong because it jeopardized "America's present two-way trade with Taiwan which is more than 10 times our trade with mainland China."[55]

The American people agreed with Judd's harsh criticism of derecognition by 45 percent to 27 percent, according to a *New York Times*-CBS survey, and in April 1979, Congress, although predominantly Democratic in both Houses, passed the Taiwan Relations Act, which pledged the U.S. government to preserve and promote "extensive, close and friendly commercial and cultural contacts" with Taiwan. The United States was also required to make available such weapons as to enable Taiwan to "maintain a sufficient self-defense capability." Furthermore, the president was obligated to promptly inform Congress "of any threat to the security or the social or economic system" of Taiwan, and, should that happen, to take "appropriate action" in response to "any such danger."[56] The unequivocal language of the act went far beyond anything that the White House or the State Department thought necessary, but Congress was determined to right the undeserved wrong of an old friend, long-time ally and present partner. Passage of the Taiwan Relations Act by Congress was a public rebuke of Carter and his State Department, which confirmed Judd's characterization of U.S. derecognition as "shameful." He noted that Carter had signed the act without a "word to the press" and might not carry it out to the fullest extent possible. That being the case, said the eighty-year-old Judd, "we may have to work for a change in the White House."[57]

CHAPTER EIGHTEEN

◆

In "Retirement"

WALTER JUDD NEVER LIMITED HIMSELF to doing just one thing or being concerned about just one cause at a time. He was blessed with seemingly boundless energy and a disciplined mind able to compartmentalize widely different problems and solutions. Convinced that he had no right to say no to a worthy endeavor, he presided over, started up, straightened out, and assisted dozens of organizations after retiring from Congress. For example, he was a member and then chairman of the prestigious Judicial Council of the American Medical Association (its "Supreme Court" on medical ethics) from 1963 to 1973. The Judicial Council decrees how physicians must conduct their practice in terms of the ultimate consequences for their conduct toward their patients and society as a whole. During Judd's tenure, the council reaffirmed that a physician should not allow his name or his professional status "to be used in the promotion of commercial enterprises"; declared that a physician may not discuss his patient's health "with the press or the public without the patient's consent or in the event of his incapacity the family's consent"; and stated that it was unethical for a physician to be influenced in the prescribing of drugs or devices "by his direct or indirect financial interest in a pharmaceutical firm or other supplier."[1] For his lifelong services to the medical profession, he was awarded the American Medical Association's Distinguished Service Medal in 1961.

He was a contributing editor of *Reader's Digest* from 1963 to 1976, writing on a broad range of political, economic, and strategic subjects. His last article, published in February 1976, was entitled, "Everyone Wants Economy—Without the *Me!*" and summed up a major problem of wasteful federal spending: "Politicians and citizens alike invariably claim that government spending must be restrained—except where the restraints cut off federal dollars flowing into *their* cities, *their* businesses or *their* pocketbooks." He argued that unless legislators and their constituents agreed that economy had to begin at home, federal deficits and debts would continue. He remarked that the 1947 dollar was worth less than forty-five cents. He quoted British historian Alexander Tytler, who warned nearly 200 years earlier that democracy could not exist as a permanent form of government because the "majority always votes for the candidate promising the most benefits from the public treasury— with the result that democracy collapses over a loose fiscal policy, always to be followed by a dictatorship."[2]

In 1969, Judd and Brooks Hays, a retired Arkansas congressman and close friend, began talking about a possible "alumni association" of former members of Congress. They invited six former colleagues to discuss the possible formation of ex-members of Congress in a non-political, nonpartisan organization. They all agreed that former members were an "underutilized resource" of considerable potential value to government and academe. They circulated a questionnaire to former congressmen and senators, and received an enthusiastic response. In February 1970, fifty-two former members met to elect officers and adopt a statement of purpose. By the end of the year, 325 congressional "alumni" had joined. Judd, who oversaw most of the organizational detail for the first decade, was not interested in an "old boys club" that met once or twice a year to swap campaign stories, but a working organization that recorded the oral histories of former members, sponsored talks on college campuses, and sought to establish a center for the study of the legislative process. He and other officers had their greatest successes with the oral histories project, in cooperation with the Library of Congress, and in promoting membership: the current roster of Former Members of Congress contains more than six hundred names. As Judd joked at a White House event, the organization has "a guaranteed clientele . . . with a new group of persons eligible for membership every two years."[3]

He learned through Former Members of Congress how much others shared his concern about the escalating and conflicting demands on

311

congressmen. He recalled that while in Congress, a Republican businessman who normally decried deficit spending berated him for voting against a bill which would have brought several million dollars into Minneapolis. Judd's response had been: "Where do you think federal funds for Minneapolis come from—people in St. Paul?" Demands like these led him to argue in the 1980s that Congress had changed the meaning of the Constitution: no longer does the federal government "promote the general welfare," now it was called on to "provide individual welfare." He agreed that Washington had to help in emergencies, like war, floods, earthquakes and depressions, but it seemed to him that "now the main job of the federal government is to provide benefits for me and every other citizen." He praised Ronald Reagan for his efforts to bring down expenditures and criticized Congress for often "forcing the president to go in the other direction." One solution, he suggested, was to limit the number of years that a member of Congress could serve to a maximum of eighteen—three terms in the Senate and nine terms in the House.[4] The Founding Fathers intended members of Congress to be part-time citizen representatives, he argued not full-time professional politicians.

More than sixty years after he heard "Dad" Elliott speak at a high school YMCA conference in Lincoln, Nebraska, and accepted Jesus Christ as his savior, he was addressing church groups, national and international, about the principal task of Christians in the world. In 1977, he spoke before the International Christian Fellowship meeting in London, about the two seemingly conflicting views of Christian action: one, to change persons so that they will make society good; the other, to change society so that it will be possible for persons to become good. Those who held the first view, he said, emphasized the "personal" Gospel, worship of God. Those who held the second view emphasized the "social" Gospel, service to man. One stressed faith, "what you believe," like St. Paul; the other emphasized works, "what you do," like St. James. But, he asked, were the two views really in conflict and separate, or were they "inseparable parts of one process?" He suggested that it was not a matter of Christian faith or Christian work but Christian faith *and* Christian work, or, better yet, "Christian faith *at* Christian work."

The Gospel, it seemed to him, was quite clear: "If we love God with all our heart, we must *care*. If we love God with all our soul, we must *commit*. If we love God with all our mind, we must *think*." And if we love God with all our strength, "we must work." Christians, he said, "must always be where the action is, and life-changing is where the action begins."[5]

He always paid particular attention to youth organizations, especially Campus Crusade for Christ, whose members he addressed in the United States and around the world. He held a special affection for the Charles Edison Memorial Youth Fund, named after the former New Jersey governor and secretary of the navy, with whom he worked closely on many anticommunist projects. The Edison Fund emerged in the late 1960s, at the height of the anti-Vietnam War movement, out of Governor Edison's concern over the growing disillusionment and cynicism of young Americans about their government. In time, more than 200 college students came each summer to Washington, attending the Institute on Comparative Political and Economic Systems and the Institute on Political Journalism, which provided classes at Georgetown University in economics, politics, and ethics in the morning; internships at government, congressional, and news media offices in the afternoon; and lectures by politicians, diplomats, and media "stars" in the evening. He lectured every summer before the students, who came from Ivy League schools, state universities, and community colleges. Each summer, he was warmly applauded at the end of his remarks. His topic was always the same: "The story of history is the rise and the fall of nations." He told the young men and women that the United States of America was the "greatest experiment in self-government by free men, voluntarily entered into, that the world has ever seen; but it is an *uncompleted* experiment." The next chapter, he said, would be written by them. He challenged them "not to drop out in frustration and defeatism ... but to launch out with enthusiasm and devotion to *use* and to *improve* this political system," so as to secure the blessings of liberty for themselves and "*their* posterity."[6]

Inevitably, he accumulated almost as many awards as years, receiving honorary doctorate degrees from twenty-eight universities and colleges, including his own University of Minnesota; the National Layman of the Year award from Religious Heritage of America; the Great Living American award from the U.S. Chamber of Commerce; the Silver Buffalo award from the Boy Scouts of America; five George Washington Honor Medals from Freedoms Foundation; the Grand Cordon of the Order of Brilliant Star from the Republic of China and the highest civilian decorations from the governments of Greece and the Republic of Korea; and the Man of the Year Award from Former Members of Congress. In October 1981, at age eighty-three, he received the Presidential Medal of Freedom, the nation's highest civilian award, from President Reagan. He was particularly pleased, he said, that it was called the Presidential Medal of *Freedom* because working for that "most precious of all our blessings in America" had been central to most of his life's efforts: first as medical missionary in China, then as a "political missionary" in the Congress, and for the last nineteen years as "missionary-at-large" to the nation, especially to colleges and high schools, urging "a deeper understanding of what freedom makes possible and what freedom requires." He said that when his "batteries" sometimes ran down, and they did, he liked to visit the Jefferson Memorial, where in giant letters on the corona over his head was the former president's personal declaration: "I have sworn upon the altar of God eternal hostility against every form of tyranny over the mind of man."[7]

His unswerving commitment to freedom led him into disagreement with the very man who had honored him. Early the following year, as chairman of the Committee for a Free China, he privately wrote President Reagan about his forthcoming visit to China. He expressed concern about rumors in the press that the United States intended to make certain concessions to the PRC which would affect the level of U.S. military support for the Republic of China. He invited all five living former U.S. ambassadors to the ROC, Karl L. Rankin, Everett Drumright, Jerauld Wright, Walter P. McConaughy, and Leonard Unger, to also write the president, which they did. The president immediately responded, assuring Judd that: "I have not and will not change my position on our long time friend Taiwan. It is true there are those in certain circles who think we must trade one China for another, but I don't subscribe to that. I'll be tactful and try to improve and maintain the relations with the People's Republic of China started by President Nixon, but there will be no lessening of our relationship with our friends on Taiwan."[8]

That seemed firm enough. But when the U.S.-China communiqué was released on August 17, 1982, at the end of Reagan's trip to the mainland, it read in part: "The United States government states that it does not seek to carry out a long-term policy of arms sales to Taiwan . . . and that it intends to reduce gradually its sales of arms to Taiwan, leading over a period of time to a final resolution."[9] When the news media reported that the Reagan administration had made significant concessions to the PRC, and conservative critics declared that the communiqué contradicted the Taiwan Relations Act, which ensured that the United States would sell arms to Taiwan as long as they were needed for self-defense, President Reagan became so disturbed that he personally phoned Dan Rather to protest there had been no giveaway. Reagan also called Judd at his Washington home to assert that "we didn't yield an inch." Judd politely disagreed. Publicly, he noted with approval that the U.S. government had since informed the ROC government that the United States: "has not agreed to set a date" for ending arms sales to the ROC; "has not agreed to hold prior consultation" with the Chinese communists on arms sales to the ROC; "will not play any mediation role between Taipei and Peking"; "has not agreed" to revise the Taiwan Relations Act; "has not altered" its position regarding sovereignty over Taiwan; and "will not exert pressure on the Republic of China" to enter into negotiations with the Chinese communists. Unfortunately, he pointed out, the communiqué itself did not include these important provisions, but stated that the United States intended "to reduce gradually its sale of arms to Taiwan" leading to "a final resolution." This language, so similar to Hitler's infamous phrase, "the final solution," jolted the Chinese on Taiwan and their friends in America and elsewhere.

He acknowledged that the objectives proclaimed in the communiqué were laudable: "to bring about healthy development of United States-China relations" and a "peaceful resolution of the Taiwan question." But the PRC government insisted that in order to have peaceful and beneficial relations with Peking, the United States must stop selling defensive arms to Taiwan. Thus was plainly revealed, said Judd, Peking's formula for "peaceful resolution of the Taiwan question"—to "isolate and weaken Taiwan until it must 'peacefully' surrender." Describing the communique as "unwise," he pointed out that Peking had tried for thirty-three years, since coming to power in 1949, to persuade every U.S. administration to break entirely with Taiwan, so that the ROC would have no alternative but to surrender. "Fortunately," he said, "Presidents Truman, Eisenhower, Kennedy and Johnson never wavered in their unyielding support for the Republic of China on Taiwan." Nixon unfortunately accepted "ambiguous language" in the Shanghai communique but subsequently "denied" that the United States was agreeing to Peking's claim of sovereignty over Taiwan as part of Communist China. Carter tried to solve the problem by derecognizing "Free China," adopting the "farcical pretense" that henceforth the United States would deal only with "the people of Taiwan," as though, Judd said scornfully, the ROC government "ceased to exist" when Washington withdrew diplomatic recognition. The Reagan communiqué, he felt, only further confused matters made ambiguous by the events of recent years, threatening to weaken the long-standing relations between two old friends and wartime allies. "The American people," he said, sounding the call as he had so often, "and the Congress must, right now, register their determined opposition to any further retreats on so vital an issue as loyalty to friends and to freedom."[10] The phrase, "loyalty to friends and freedom," summed up in large measure Walter Judd's life and career.

In early 1987, at the height of the Iran-contra controversy, Judd attempted to reach the President with a suggestion: he wished to advise Reagan to publicly admit that he had made a mistake, as FDR did with the 1937 Supreme Court-packing scheme which backfired and Kennedy did with the Bay of Pigs failure. He recalled for a top White House aide that Roosevelt had gone on national radio and said something like: "You all know that no man gets a hit every time he comes to bat." Everybody knew, said Judd, that he was saying, "We struck out on this one; it was a mistake. But look at all our hits, and yes, our homeruns." The American people, even most critics, promptly forgave Roosevelt and renewed their confidence in and support of him.[11] The same thing happened in 1961, said Judd, when President Kennedy publicly told the story of the Bay of Pigs debacle. He was confident that the people would similarly forgive Reagan if he followed the FDR-JFK example.[12] It was good advice that, given the abiding affection of the American people for Reagan, would probably have worked. But the president was not given to public confessions, and decided to weather the widespread criticism. He concentrated on negotiating an arms control agreement with General Secretary Gorbachev of the Soviet Union, again triggering a reaction from Judd.

In late 1987, when he read that Gorbachev was coming to Washington for a summit meeting, he telephoned but did not reach the president. He wanted to urge Reagan in preparation for the summit to study his favorite sport, football, because the communists "use precisely the same tactics, power and deception: power plays when they can get just downs that way, trick plays when not."[13] The communists used power when they could, in Hungary, Czechoslovakia, and Afghanistan, and deception when possible, at summit meetings and through trade agreements and disinformation. They came to power by deception, as in Russia, China, and Cuba, promising land, bread, and peace, and then defended their position by force, as the many millions who died in the Soviet Union and Communist China proved. The history of the twentieth century afforded one inescapable conclusion: you could "trust" communists only to be communists.

He felt strongly that the United States should continue to develop and deploy the Strategic Defense Initiative. It was the one thing above all others that the Soviets were scared of because it had the potential to reduce greatly the threat of their long-range missiles, and yet it did not threaten the life of one single Soviet citizen. "Why," he asked, "should anyone be against a weapon that can't kill anyone? All it can do is knock down weapons that would otherwise kill. That's so darn simple there isn't [anyone] that can't understand that."[14]

He acknowledged the skill of Gorbachev and other communist leaders in the art of propaganda, particularly in describing the United States in the most negative way possible. He noted that Gorbachev frequently referred to the "imperialist objectives of militarist America," which might be accepted in some parts of the Third World but ought to be quickly dismissed in the West, and certainly in the United States. "You can demolish the word 'imperialist' because we started decolonization after World War II. America had two great Fourths of July: one was in 1776, the other in 1946, when we gave the Philippines their independence." That latter act started a process which started the end of the old colonial empires and ultimately brought into the United Nations "almost 100 newly independent countries." As for the term "militarist," the United States "could almost have taken over the world by telephone at the end of the war," he said. Instead, we reduced our army by more than 80 percent, put half of our navy in mothballs, and grounded our air force. "In 1947 and 1948, we didn't have one squadron able to get into the air." In response, the Soviets started the Berlin blockade, "thinking we couldn't do anything." But we "dragged out the old C-47s" and sent in food and medicine and other supplies twenty-four hours a day for eleven months until "the Russians gave in."[15]

During his congressional career, Judd had observed with increasing concern the unrestricted authority of the unelected branch of government, the judiciary. Now, in the 1980s, quoting Thomas Jefferson, he said, "The great object of my fear is the Federal judiciary." In a five to four Supreme Court decision, he argued, one man has more power than Congress and the president. He recalled two cases considered by the

Supreme Court: in one case, a man had been convicted of seven crimes and sentenced to life imprisonment "because he was obviously an incurable criminal." The Court, by a five to four decision, upheld the lower court. Two years later, a similar decision, involving a man convicted of eight crimes and also given life, came up before the Court on appeal. One justice changed his mind, and the Supreme Court, by a 5–4 decision, overturned the decision and the sentence of the lower court. "So much power," he declared, "scares me." He had a solution for those occasions when the Supreme Court was considering legislation that had been passed by the Congress and signed by the president: the Court would have to vote by a two-thirds majority (six to three) to overturn it, just as Congress needed a two-thirds majority to override a presidential veto. After all, he pointed out, Great Britain's supreme court could not overturn an act of Parliament; "that's better democracy than we have." During his last term in Congress, he had introduced legislation requiring a two-thirds majority by the Supreme Court to overturn acts of Congress, but judicial activism was then chic, and he failed to win enough support even to hold hearings: "everybody thought I was denouncing God." Rather, he was challenging an institution that often acted as though it were God. As he insisted, "The Constitution starts out, 'We the people,' not 'We the justices.' "[16]

As he approached his ninetieth year, he at last began to slow down, resigning from most of the organizations and committees with which he had associated (but not the Committee for a Free China), making arrangements to send his voluminous personal papers to the Hoover Library at Stanford University and to the Minnesota Historical Society in St. Paul, spending more time with Miriam and their three daughters and seven grandchildren. After decades of very modest living on a missionary's and then a congressman's salary, he found himself a man of some means, as the result of speaking and writing fees, a congressional pension that now exceeded his salary when he served in Congress, and a home worth many times what he paid for it as a result of inflating real estate values in northwest Washington. Characteristically, he increased his donations to charitable and political organizations, giving approximately 50 percent of his income to causes ranging from the Congregational Church to the Bush for President Committee. In 1988, he and Miriam sold the house on Ordway Street in northwest Washington they had lived in since 1947 and moved into a total-care village run by the Episcopalian Church and located in the Maryland suburbs. Aside from the twice-a-year treatment of the skin cancers that developed on his face, he remained in good health, looking and sounding a decade or two younger, although he often complained he could not remember names and dates and found it difficult to stick to one subject while talking. As he put it: "Everything from my neck down works fine; I can't say as much for what is above it." He had to wear a hearing aid, and his eyesight continued to fail.

He also demonstrated that once a physician, always a physician. He and Miriam befriended Timothy Cofer, who served as music librarian and brass instructor for the District of Columbia Youth Orchestra program. One day the young man telephoned the Judds but was barely able to talk, struggling for words. Well over six feet tall, the thirty-two-year-old musician had accidently cracked his head against a sharp steel beam at a concert. Thirty days later, he began having terrible headaches, blurred vision, even a personality change. Five more weeks passed during which ten doctors examined him, including a psychiatrist, but could only conclude that he was suffering from a post-concussion syndrome. The pain, accompanied by some long-range memory loss, continued. Finally, in desperation, Cofer called Judd, who he thought was still practicing medicine. "I'm not crazy," he said, "but I just can't manage [certain] things now." Judd sat and listened while the young man described his symptoms. He suspected that Cofer had probably sustained a tiny fracture on the side of his skull, perhaps breaking the middle meningel artery that goes to the center of the brain, an injury similar to the skull fracture that had caused the childhood death of his brother Russell eight decades before. He urged him to go to the opthalmology department at Johns Hopkins Hospital, one of the best in the nation, and have them "send you through the whole department." Some time later, Tim Cofer called Miriam and said: "I'll always be grateful to Dr. Judd—he saved my life. They really worked at it and found I had hairline fractures which had caused bleeding and clots and pressure on the brain and produced my symptoms." Said Judd: "I knew there had to be something. . . . Old Doctor Charlie [Mayo] used to tell us, 'Boys, the patient will almost always tell you what's wrong with him if you'll just listen.' "[17]

In these twilight years, he sometimes felt that he had been a patron of so many "lost" causes, like opposition to the admission of Communist China to the United Nations, and had so often sounded the tocsin about the dangers of communism, that few people in power listened when he counseled caution about Soviet leader Gorbachev whom he called "the best leader they've had since Lenin himself." He had read all the articles and had heard all the speeches about how different Gorbachev was from dictators like Stalin and super-apparatchiks like Brezhnev. He suggested a simple test of Gorbachev's desire for true *glasnost* and *perestroika:* Let the Soviets pull their troops out of eastern Europe, and allow the Soviet people to vote for a government of their choice. If that happened, then he would agree that they had finally changed and perhaps "you could work constructively with them." At home, he was profoundly worried about the economic future of America, about the ultimate impact of its unbalanced budgets and profligate spending. "I'm not pessimistic," he said, "but I'm anxious." In four of the five criteria that Edward Gibbon listed in *The History of the Decline and Fall of the Roman Empire,* "the United States is running wild. [Gibbon] called it bread and circuses. I call it benefits and excitement." He admitted that he might be seen as negative, "but that is partly my medical training. A patient comes in and you spend your time finding out what's wrong. . . . That's been my basic approach in medicine and politics and religion— to find out the things that are not basically sound and to try to cure or remove them."[18]

Because that meant an unremitting opposition to communists and communism, some liberals never forgave Walter Judd, including some at the *Washington Post,* which in its January 24, 1988 Sunday magazine published an article whose introduction was filled with such snide statements as "His vocabulary still rings with 1950s red-baiting rhetoric" and "The truth is, nobody pays much attention to Walter Judd anymore." The article also said, "A cavalry charge of invective from Walter Judd was something to fear." The accompanying photos, which used lurid yellow lighting, portrayed the eighty-nine-year-old Judd as a wild-eyed Elmer Gantry.[19] A careful writer who checked the record would not have used the word "invective" with regard to Judd, who scrupulously avoided personal attacks against even his most resolute opponents. A less ideological writer would have been able to make the distinction between "red-baiting" and reasoned anticommunism. As for the assertion that people no longer listened to Judd, China specialists, former members of Congress, retired diplomats, and other citizens of varying interests and backgrounds continued to seek his advice and counsel. The chief historian of the United States Capitol Historical Society, Donald R. Kennon, wrote the *Post* (which did not print his letter) that its characterization of Judd as "the one-time power behind the China Lobby" was "inaccurate and slanderous." Indeed, he "was an open, visible, and honest member of the lobby, not some mysterious power broker conniving behind the scenes." In a token demonstration of fairness, the *Post* published a letter to the editor from Sheldon Z. Kaplan, a staff consultant to the House Foreign Affairs Committee from 1949 to 1957, which dismissed the article's "distorted and limited picture of a great man." Kaplan recalled Judd's "concrete contributions" in the broad field of foreign affairs, "many of them still . . . on the statute books." Walter Judd, he summed up, was not a member of a "China Lobby" or any other lobby but a "great legislator and statesman."[20]

Those who had worked with him and campaigned for him, like Douglas Head, agreed. Judd's greatest success, said the man who managed his last campaign, was that he left "in the hearts and minds of countless people around the country an appreciation of a life well-spent," a model that they could follow and recount to their children. He was vivid proof that "people can live a life of principle and be effective and do the right thing and make it work."[21]

On September 28, 1988, some three hundred friends, young and old, Oriental and Occidental, famous and obscure, gathered in black tie and long dress at the Willard Hotel in Washington, D.C. to celebrate Walter Judd's ninetieth birthday. It was not a typical Washington evening although there were congressmen, senators, governors, and cabinet members present, because the speeches mentioned God more than Gorbachev and the honoree did not try to speak longer than anyone else. There were congratulatory messages from Richard Nixon, Gerald Ford, and Ronald Reagan of the United States, and President Lee Teng-hui of the Republic of China. Nixon remarked of the 1960 election that "it is no reflection whatever on Cabot, incidently, that had you gone on the ticket we might have won." Senator Robert Dole of Kansas, who had tried and failed to win the Republican nomination for president earlier in the year, spoke warmly of the years when he served with Judd in the House of Representatives. Glancing at his old friend, he said, "Walter, if I look as good as you do at 90, I may make it to the White House yet." There were letters from former Chief Justice Warren Burger and William F. Buckley, Jr.; prayers by the chaplains of the House and the Senate; a glowing tribute from a representative of the Fund for American Studies, who described Dr. Judd's special qualities as a teacher; conservative words by Edwin J. Feulner, Jr., president of the Heritage Foundation, which hosted the affair; along with liberal words by James M. Quigley, a Democrat and former president of Former Members of Congress, and non-partisan remarks by former congressman Ed Derwinski, former governor Albert Quie of Minnesota, and Ambassador Mou-shih Ding of the Republic of China. In response, Judd was uncharacteristically brief (there were bets among his assembled children and grandchildren as to whether he would go sixty minutes), pointing out that they had all heard him many times before and contenting himself with quoting Shakespeare, "I can no other answer make but thanks—and thanks—and ever thanks." Those thanks were meant in particular for the person who delivered the most moving tribute of the evening, Miriam Judd, his wife and partner of more than fifty-six years, who read a poem she had composed for the occasion.

To Walter at Ninety
It is enough of honor for one lifetime
To have known you better than the rest have known:
The shadows and the brightness of your voice,
The searching mind, the stubborn will, like stone;

The passionate words grown out of strong conviction
And love of God; your bearing the whole world's pain;
Protest, nor conflict, nor no man fearing;
No sense of time, or self, no thought of gain.

Quick laughter, and strict honor, dogged persistence,
Deep pride in family, friends; fierce love of life.
These among others will I hold forever within my heart,
Your always grateful wife.

The following week, he was off to talk to college students in Oklahoma about the meaning of history and the rise and fall of nations, about communism and how not one important communist in the world, including Gorbachev, "has yet renounced the goal of a communist world," and about their responsibility to develop and preserve freedom in America and around the world. Was the Cold War truly over? the students and others asked. Perhaps, he replied, when the Soviets pulled out of countries like Poland and East Germany and allowed the people, including the Soviet people, to vote for a government that reflected their wishes and interests. Clearly, the policy of containment, begun under Truman, reinforced by Eisenhower and refined by Reagan, had succeeded. Communism was in retreat, socialism was discredited, democracy and free enterprise in all their forms were stronger on every continent. Now was no time to abandon a policy of principled firmness

322

that had worked for forty years: "we used to say that the person who held on for the last five minutes prevails."[22]

Confirmation of the abject failure of communism as an acceptable form of government in China came the following spring when on June 3 and 4, 1989, armed units of the People's Liberation Army massacred hundreds of Chinese, many of them students, who had been holding pro-democracy demonstrations in Peking's Tiananmen Square. Rarely before had communism's inherent fear of a government of, by and for the people, rather than the party, been so graphically revealed. Unlike many other Western observers who, caught up in early euphoria, had predicted that the students might well bring about a fundamental change in China, Judd had been cautious and even fearful about the reaction of Deng Tsiao-ping and other aging hardliners. He knew they would not surrender power peacefully. Speaking in mid-May at a Washington seminar on "China in Transition," he cautioned those in the audience and watching over C-SPAN television, that if the demonstrations kept growing, "tanks [could] start rolling over people. . . . there would be . . . violence that I think would be almost unbelievable. I hold my breath during these tragic days."[23]

Two months later, Judd startled another Washington audience of student leaders when he described the Tiananmen Square massacre as "one of the most encouraging things that's happened in China" in a long time. It was "encouraging," he declared, because "it proves that communism . . . has failed" to satisfy the wishes and wants of the people. The Chinese communists have "exposed themselves until even the blindest can see that they are barbarians; they're not true Chinese." He predicted that there would be other rebellions in China and that they too would probably be crushed for a while longer. But, nevertheless, he felt that an end to communism's control was in sight. "I've said all along that I hope this awful [tyranny] can be brought to an end by the close of this century. I [now] think it may even be earlier." Chinese communism was doomed to failure, he argued, because of the advanced age of hardliners like Deng who would be gone within a very few years, the long-range determination of the Chinese students, and the sweep of history which was working against communism and for freedom around the world. "Tyrants," he said, "have almost always looked invincible until the last five minutes and then all of a sudden they fell apart."

The old missionary paused and then finished his 75-minute talk by telling his young audience with that fervor and conviction that had always been his trademark: "I wish I were at your stage with that one life to live, to work in this kind of crucial period of history, to save what's the best in the past and move on to a better life than any of us have ever known before."[24] Spontaneously, the students stood, as people of all ages, religions, cultures and political parties had through the years, and gave Walter Judd an ovation (the only one of the summer by these bright sophisticated leaders of tomorrow) for his eloquence, his wisdom and his challenge to them.

Postscript

SOME FORTY YEARS AGO, six famous writers—Arthur Koestler, Richard Wright, Ignazio Silone, Stephen Spender, Andre Gide, and Louis Fischer—explained why they became communists and then anticommunists in a book aptly titled, *The God That Failed*. The one link between these very different men was that all of them chose communism because they had lost faith in Western democracy. They all subsequently rejected communism because they learned that "peace" and "freedom" were mere catchwords for communists and the things for which they had joined the Communist party were most endangered by the party.

Today, millions of Chinese, East Germans, Czechs, Hungarians, Russians and other nationalities have declared, in their streets and in their parliaments, that communism has failed and that they prefer Western democracy and economic freedom. One by one, communist governments are falling like dominoes, toppled not by tanks and cannons but by people yearning to be free. Without the "glue" of ideology, the communist facade of power and authority collapsed in Eastern Europe and the people's desire to determine their own future, dammed up for more than forty years, burst forth.

For Walter Judd, and those like him, who predicted that communism would ultimately fall and freedom prevail, it is a time of jubilation and thanksgiving. Their faith has become fact: man's natural right to be free cannot be forever suppressed. However, they understand that the struggle is not over: communists, like all totalitarians, do not go gently into the dark night. Barriers beside the Berlin Wall remain; political barriers to free elections and a free press, economic barriers to a market economy and the right to work at a job of your own choosing. But in the end, however long it will take, however many more Tiananmen Squares may be necessary, they are confident that freedom will triumph.

Notes

CHAPTER ONE

1. WHJ to George Judd, May 18, 1971, Private Papers of WHJ.
2. Interview with WHJ, February 10, 1988, Washington, D.C.
3. Walter Lee Greenslit, "Thomas Greenslade," Christmas 1972, privately published, WHJ Private Papers.
4. Ibid.
5. Interview with WHJ, February 10, 1988.
6. Ibid.
7. Ibid.
8. Ibid.
9. Ibid.
10. Ibid.
11. Jerry N. Hess interview with WHJ, April 13, 1970, Harry S. Truman Library, Independence, Missouri.
12. Ibid.
13. Glenn Clark, *Touchdowns for the Lord: The Story of "Dad" A.J. Elliott* (St. Paul: Macalester Park Publishing Co., 1947), pp. 48–53.
14. Interview with WHJ, December 30, 1987, Washington D.C.
15. Victor Cohn, "The Congressman's Scars of Courage," *Coronet,* July 1960, pp. 31–32.
16. Interview with WHJ, December 30, 1987.

CHAPTER TWO

1. Interview with WHJ, December 30, 1987.
2. Ibid.
3. Frank L. Reed to WHJ, July 7, 1978, Private Papers of WHJ.

4. Interview with WHJ, December 30, 1987.
5. *Indianapolis News,* December 29, 1923.
6. Interview with Miriam Judd, October 23, 1986, Washington, D.C.
7. WHJ, "Why Leave Non-Christian America for the Orient?" Student Volunteer Movement for Foreign Missions, 1926. Reprinted from the January and February 1926 issues of the *Student Volunteer Movement Bulletin,* pp. 5–7, 11–14.
8. Ibid., pp. 8–9, 20.

Chapter Three

1. John K. Fairbank, *The Great Chinese Revolution 1800–1985* (New York: Harper & Row, 1986), p. 170.
2. George Botjer, *A Short History of Nationalist China 1919–1949* (New York: G.P. Putnam's Sons, 1979), p. 13.
3. Fairbank, *The Great Chinese Revolution,* p. 182.
4. Botjer, *A Short History of Nationalist China,* p. 17.
5. Ibid., p. 22.
6. O. Edmund Clubb, *Twentieth Century China* (New York: Columbia University Press, 1964), p. 119.
7. Brian Crozier, *The Man Who Lost China* (New York: Charles Scribner's Sons, 1976), p. 64.
8. Botjer, *A Short History of Nationalist China,* pp. 37–38; Crozier, *The Man Who Lost China,* pp. 68–70; Fairbank, *The Great Chinese Revolution,* p. 153.
9. Fairbank, p. 213.
10. WHJ, "On Becoming a Missionary," *The Student Volunteer Movement Bulletin,* vol. 7, no. 4 (January 1927), p. 98.
11. Ibid., p. 100.
12. Columba Cary-Elwes, *China and the Cross* (New York: P.J. Kenedy & Sons, 1957), p. 213.
13. Fairbank, *The Great Chinese Revolution,* pp. 137–138; Cary-Elwes, *China and the Cross,* pp. 223–224.
14. Cary-Elwes, pp. 262–265, 294–295.
15. WHJ, "On Becoming a Missionary," *Bulletin,* January 1927, p. 100.
16. Ibid., p. 102.
17. Interview with WHJ, September 11, 1987, Washington, D.C.
18. Ibid.
19. Botjer, *A Short History of Nationalist China,* p. 47.
20. WHJ to his parents, December 25, 1926, WHJ Private Papers.
21. WHJ, "A Philosophy of Life That Works," Student Volunteer Movement pamphlet (January 1932), pp. 21–22.
22. WHJ to Rev. William E. Strong, March 24, 1927, WHJ Private Papers.

23. WHJ, "A Philosophy of Life That Works," pp. 22–23.
24. Ibid., pp. 11–13.
25. Ibid., pp. 13–14.
26. Ibid., pp. 16–17.
27. Ibid., pp. 19–20.
28. Charles Hirshberg, "Walter Judd Never Met a Communist He Trusted," *Washington Post Magazine,* January 24, 1988, p. 28.
29. *Shanghai Times,* July 12, 1930.
30. WHJ, "Personal Report for 1927," Shaowu, Fukien, WHJ Private Papers.
31. WHJ, "A Philosophy of Life," pp. 23–24.
32. Ibid., p. 25.
33. WHJ, letter of resignation to the Executive Committee, North Fukien Synod of the Church of Christ in China, January 21, 1931; letter to the Shaowu missionaries in Foochow, January 1, 1931; WHJ Private Papers.
34. Interview with WHJ, January 12, 1988, February 10, 1988; WHJ, "How Can We Win in the Pacific?" *Congressional Record* (hereafter cited as CR), February 25, 1943, pp. 1342–1347.
35. Botjer, *A Short History of Nationalist China,* pp. 120–123.
36. WHJ letter to Jesse Wilson, Thanksgiving Day, 1931, WHJ Private Papers.
37. Richard B. Morris, ed., *Encyclopedia of American History* (New York: Harper & Row, 1976), p. 443.

CHAPTER FOUR

1. Interview with Miriam Judd, October 23, 1986.
2. *Minneapolis Tribune,* November 8, 1942.
3. WHJ, "A Philosophy of Life That Works," p. 3.
4. Ibid., pp. 28–30.
5. Interview with WHJ, January 12, 1988.
6. Fairbank, *The Great Chinese Revolution,* p. 219.
7. Botjer, *A Short History of Nationalist China,* pp. 135, 141, 152, 159.
8. Fairbank, p. 220.
9. WHJ to Wynn C. Fairfield, Easter Day, April 1934, WHJ Private Papers.
10. Interview with WHJ, January 12, 1988.

CHAPTER FIVE

1. WHJ, *The Fenchow,* December 1934, published by the Fenchow Station of the North China Mission of the American Board.

2. Interview with Miriam Judd, October 23, 1986.
3. Letter, June 18, 1936, Peitaiho Beach, China, WHJ Private Papers.
4. Crozier, *The Man Who Lost China*, p. 189.
5. Clubb, *Twentieth Century China*, p. 214.
6. Fairbank, *The Great Chinese Revolution*, p. 239.
7. WHJ, "Report on the War of Ideas in Europe and Asia," CR, June 19, 1948, pp. A4555–4562.
8. Theodore H. White and Annalee Jacoby, *Thunder Out of China* (New York: William Sloane Associates, 1946), pp. 209–210.
9. Interview with Miriam Judd, October 23, 1986.
10. *New York World Telegram*, February 6, 1940.
11. Interview with Miriam Judd, Oct. 23, 1986.
12. *New York World Telegram*, February 8, 1940.
13. Interview with WHJ, January 12, 1988.
14. *New York World Telegram*, February 6, 1940.
15. WHJ to Rowland Cross, February 25, 1938, WHJ Private Papers.
16. Interview with WHJ, January 12, 1988. [Fifty years later, Judd refused to divulge the name of the Japanese general, in order to spare his family any embarrassment or loss of face.]
17. Ibid.

CHAPTER SIX

1. *New York World Telegram*, February 9, 1940.
2. WHJ, "America's Stake in the Far East," September 1938, WHJ Private Papers.
3. Promotional brochure about WHJ published in 1939 by the American Committee for Non-Participation in Japanese Aggression, New York, N.Y.
4. "America Supports Japanese Aggression," pamphlet published by the American Committee for Non-Participation in Japanese Aggression, 1940.
5. House Committee on Foreign Affairs, *American Neutrality Policy*, April 20, 1939, pp. 332–337.
6. Ibid., pp. 343–354.
7. Nancy Bernkopf Tucker, *Patterns in the Dust: Chinese-American Relations and the Recognition Controversy, 1949–1950* (New York: Columbia University Press, 1983), p. 89.
8. Samual Eliot Morison, *The Oxford History of the American People*, vol. 3 (New York: New American Library, 1972), p. 346.
9. Adm. Harry E. Yarnell, Town Meeting of the Air, *Town Meeting Bulletin* (Dec. 14, 1939).
10. Botjer, *A Short History of Nationalist China*, p. 194.

11. Crozier, *The Man Who Lost China*, p. 211.
12. Ibid., p. 210.
13. Botjer, pp. 197–198.
14. Interview with Miriam Judd, October 23, 1986.
15. WHJ, "Let's Stop Arming Japan!" *Reader's Digest*, February 1940, p. 44.
16. *New York World Telegram*, February 5, 9, 1940.
17. Morison, *Oxford History*, p. 349.

CHAPTER SEVEN

1. Edward J. Rozek, ed., *Walter H. Judd: Chronicles of a Statesman* (Denver: Grier & Company, 1980), pp. 12–13.
2. Miriam Judd to Mr. and Mrs. B.R. Barber, March 5, 1941, Miriam Judd Private Papers.
3. Memorandum of Gideon Seymour, editor, *Minneapolis Star*, to Stanley High, *Reader's Digest*, January 27, 1947, Judd Papers, Hoover Library, Stanford University.
4. Interview with Miriam Judd, October 23, 1986.
5. Miriam Judd to Mr. and Mrs. B.R. Barber, February 5, 1942, Miriam Judd Private Papers.
6. Seymour memo, p. 3.
7. Interview with Miriam Judd, October 23, 1986.
8. "Statement by Walter H. Judd," about July 1, 1942, WHJ Private Papers.
9. Seymour memo, p. 5.
10. Miriam Judd to Mr. and Mrs. B.R. Barber, September 6, 1942, Miriam Judd Private Papers.
11. WHJ, radio address over WCCO Minneapolis, September 7, 1942, WHJ Private Papers.
12. Seymour memo, p. 8.
13. Interview with Miriam Judd, October 23, 1986.
14. Interview with WHJ, May 22, 1985, Washington, D.C.
15. WHJ, "Representative vs. Delegate," statement during the 1942 campaign, WHJ Private Papers.

CHAPTER EIGHT

1. David Brinkley, *Washington Goes to War* (New York: Alfred A. Knopf, 1988), frontispiece.
2. Miriam Judd to B.R. Barber, November 20, 1942, Miriam Judd Private Papers.

3. WHJ, "How Can We Win in the Pacific?" CR, February 25, 1943, pp. 1342–1347.
4. WHJ to Horace H. Judd, January 15, 1943, Judd Papers, Minnesota Historical Society, St. Paul.
5. Robert A. Devine, *Second Chance: The Triumph of Internationalism in America During World War II* (New York: Atheneum, 1967), p. 128.
6. Interview with WHJ, November 7, 1981, Washington, D.C.; Jerry N. Hess interview with WHJ, April 13, 1970, Harry S. Truman Library, Independence, Missouri.
7. Horace H. Judd to his children, August 3, 1943, Judd Papers, Hoover Library, Stanford University.
8. WHJ, "How Achieve Security for America?" CR, September 21, 1943, p. 7726.
9. WHJ, "After Victory—What?" speech before St. Louis Chamber of Commerce, August 11, 1942, WHJ Private Papers.
10. William Manchester, *The Glory and the Dream: A Narrative History of America 1932–1972*, Vol 1 (Boston: Little, Brown & Company, 1973), p. 357.
11. CR, October 20, 1943, pp. 8588–8593.
12. Ibid.
13. Crozier, *The Man Who Lost China*, pp. 249–250; Tang Tsou, *America's Failure in China 1941–50* (Chicago: University of Chicago Press, 1963), p. 242.
14. Fairbank, *The Great Chinese Revolution*, p. 259.
15. Crozier, pp. 252–253.
16. Anthony Kubek, *How the Far East Was Lost* (Chicago: Henry Regnery Company, 1963), p. 265.
17. Senate Internal Security Subcommittee, Judiciary Committee, *Institute of Pacific Relations Hearings*, 82nd Cong., 1st sess. (Washington, D.C.: Government Printing Office, 1951) Final Report, p. 224.
18. Kubek, p. 249; Crozier, p. 254.
19. Kubek, p. 251.
20. Ibid., p. 253.
21. Crozier, pp. 254–258.
22. Barbara W. Tuchman, *Stilwell and the American Experience in China, 1911–45* (New York: The Macmillan Company, 1970), p. 371.
23. Kubek, pp. 205–208.
24. Tuchman, p. 360.
25. Claire Chennault, *Way of a Fighter* (New York: G. P. Putnam's Sons, 1949), p. 317.
26. Kubek, p. 217.
27. Ibid., p. 219.
28. Tuchman, p. 498.

29. WHJ to Horace H. Judd, September 2, 1944, Judd Papers, Minnesota Historical Society, St. Paul.
30. Interview with WHJ, February 19, 1988.
31. Tuchman, pp. 505–506.
32. CR, June 19, 1948, p. A4560.
33. Crozier, p. 265.
34. *United States Relations With China: With Special Reference to the Period 1944–1949* [The White Paper] (Washington, D.C.: Government Printing Office, 1949), pp. 566–574.
35. Kubek, pp. 224, 228.
36. Ibid., pp. 233–234.
37. *Institute of Pacific Relations Hearings,* vol. 3, pp. 779–783.
38. *Philadelphia Inquirer,* March 25, 1945.
39. Kubek, p. 229.
40. *Saturday Evening Post,* January 7, 1950, p. 17.
41. WHJ, remarks at 54th annual meeting of Pennsylvania Scotch-Irish Society, March 3, 1944, WHJ Private Papers.
42. "What Is a Liberal?" October 1944, WHJ Private Papers.
43. NBC Broadcast, November 5, 1944, WHJ Private Papers.
44. Crozier, pp. 268–269.

Chapter Nine

1. Tsou, *America's Failure in China,* pp. 301–302; Chalmers A. Johnson, *Peasant Nationalism and Communist Power* (Stanford: Stanford University Press, 1962), pp. 73–74; Crozier, pp. 270–272.
2. CR, March 15, 1945, pp. 2294–2302.
3. Fairbank, p. 260.
4. Albert C. Wedemeyer, *Wedemeyer Reports!* (New York: Henry Holt & Company, 1958), pp. 311–312.
5. CR, June 19, 1948, p. A4559.
6. Ibid.
7. Crozier, pp. 289–290.
8. Ibid., p. 291.
9. Ibid., p. 292.
10. *New York Herald Tribune,* June 13, 1947.
11. *New York Times,* June 22, 1947.
12. Testimony of Adm. Charles Maynard Cooke, October 19, 1951, *Institute of Pacific Relations Hearings,* Part 5, p. 1496.
13. Kubek, p. 339.
14. "How the Communists Got China," *U.S. News & World Report,* October 1, 1954, p. 44.
15. *Institute of Pacific Relations, Hearings,* Part 7a, p. 2397.

16. *U.S. Relations With China,* p. 687.
17. Wedemeyer, p. 368.
18. Chennault, p. xii.
19. Fairbank, pp. 262–264.
20. CR, June 19, 1948, pp. A4555.
21. Ibid., May 9, 1945, p. 4357.
22. Interview with WHJ, November 7, 1981.
23. CR, December 13, 1945, pp. 12009–12011.
24. Ibid., May 29, 1946, pp. 5926 et seq.
25. Ibid., July 18, 1946, p. 9361.
26. WHJ, speech to Minnesota Republican State Convention, September 14, 1946, WHJ Private Papers.
27. WHJ, talk over KSTP Minneapolis, October 18, 1946, WHJ Private Papers.
28. WHJ, address over WCCO Minneapolis, October 29, 1946, WHJ Private Papers.
29. William Safire, *Safire's Political Dictionary* (New York: Random House, 1978), p. 286.
30. Manchester, *The Glory and the Dream,* p. 509.
31. CR, May 17, 1946, pp. A2763–2764.
32. *New York Times,* July 24, 1946.
33. WHJ to Rev. Merrell H. Brammer, August 9, 1946, Judd Papers, Hoover Library, Stanford University.
34. *The Chinese Communist Movement,* U.S. Military Intelligence Service, July 3, 1945, WHJ Private Papers.
35. Lt. General Albert C. Wedemeyer, address, Double Ten Celebration, October 10, 1946, New York City, Judd Papers, Hoover Library, Stanford University.

CHAPTER TEN

1. Jones, *The Fifteen Weeks* (New York: The Viking Press, 1955), p. 7.
2. Robert Donovan, *Conflict and Crisis: The Presidency of Harry S. Truman, 1945–1948* (New York: W.W. Norton & Company, 1977), p. 278.
3. Harry S. Truman, *Memoirs, Vol. 2, Years of Trial and Hope* (Garden City, N.Y.: Doubleday & Company, 1956), pp. 99–101.
4. Jones, pp. 269–274.
5. Byrd, Pepper and Ellender in Jones, *The Fifteen Weeks,* p. 175; Smith, Bender and Rich in Justus D. Doenecke, *Not to the Swift: The Old Isolationists in the Cold War Era* (Lewisburg, Pa.: Bucknell University Press, 1979), pp. 74–77.
6. Doenecke, pp. 80–84.

NOTES

7. Author Vandenberg, Jr., ed., *The Private Papers of Senator Vandenberg* (Boston: Houghton Mifflin Company, 1952), p. 342.
8. *New York Times,* March 14, 1947.
9. CR, March 12, 1947, pp. 1984–1985.
10. Miriam Judd to Mr. and Mrs. B.R. Barber, March 2, 1947, Miriam Judd Private Papers.
11. House Committee on Foreign Affairs, *Assistance to Greece and Turkey,* 80th Congress, 1st sess. pp. 24, 43.
12. *New York Times,* April 29, 1947.
13. CR, May 6, 1947, pp. 4616–4617.
14. Frank McNaughton to Don Berlingham, *Time,* May 9, 1947, Papers of Frank McNaughton, Harry S. Truman Library, Independence, Missouri.
15. Ibid.
16. CR, May 7, 1947, pp. 4704–4706.
17. Jones, p. 198.
18. CR, May 27, 1947, p. A2496; January 6, 1947, pp. 6553–6554; June 24, 1947, p. 7615.
19. Ibid., July 26, 1947, pp. A3962.
20. Jones, pp. 283–284.
21. CR, November 25, 1947, p. 10856.
22. House Committee on Foreign Affairs, *Providing for Membership and Participation by the United States in the World Health Organization,* July 17, 1947.
23. Louis J. Halle, *The Cold War as History* (New York: Harper Torchbooks, 1975), pp. 140–141.
24. WHJ from Paris, September 11, 1947; Brussels, September 13, 1947; Stockholm, September 18, 1947; WHJ Papers, Hoover Library, Stanford University.
25. WHJ to Miriam Judd, September 21, 1947, Miriam Judd Private Papers.
26. WHJ to Rev. John P. Minter, November 4, 1947, WHJ Papers, Hoover Library, Stanford University.
27. Susan M. Hartmann, *Truman and the 80th Congress* (Columbia, Missouri: University of Missouri Press, 1971), p. 116.
28. CR, December 4, 1947, p. 11037 (Judd); December 5, 1947, p. 11097 (Lodge).
29. Ibid., December 11, 1947, p. 11283.
30. Ibid., December 5, 1947, pp. 11106–11109.
31. *The Washington Post,* November 29, 1947.
32. CR, December 19, 1947, p. 11747.
33. Henry Bayard Price, *The Marshall Plan and Its Meaning* (Ithaca, N.Y.: Cornell University Press, 1955), p. 61.

34. House Committee on Foreign Affairs, *Foreign Policy for a Post-War Recovery Program*, February 20, 1948, p. 1566.
35. Walter Millis, ed., *The Forrestal Diaries* (New York: The Viking Press, 1951), p. 382.
36. WHJ to J. Emmet Hannon, February 21, 1948, WHJ Papers, Hoover Library, Stanford University.
37. Donovan, *Conflict and Crisis*, pp. 357, 360.
38. CR, March 17, 1948, pp. 2996–2998.
39. Ibid., March 23, 1948, pp. 3311–3312.
40. Ibid., pp. 3327–3328.
41. Ibid., p. 3329.
42. Ibid., pp. 3330–3333.
43. Interview with WHJ, November 7, 1981, Washington, D.C.
44. Victor Cohn, *Coronet*, July 1960, pp. 32–33.

Chapter Eleven

1. CR, July 26, 1948, pp. A4618–4619.
2. Cabell Phillips, *The Truman Presidency: The History of a Triumphant Succession* (New York: The Macmillan Company, 1966), pp. 219–223; Manchester, *The Glory and the Dream*, pp. 556–558.
3. Manchester, p. 562.
4. WHJ to Mrs. Philip J. Cox, August 10, 1948, WHJ Papers, Hoover Library, Stanford University.
5. WHJ to Roy E. Dunn, December 17, 1948, WHJ Papers, Hoover Library, Stanford University.
6. Rozek, *Chronicles of a Statesman*, pp. 345–346.
7. Interview with WHJ, May 30, 1987; WHJ interview for John Foster Dulles Oral History Project, Princeton University Library, December 11, 1965.
8. Interview with WHJ, May 30, 1987; Stephen E. Ambrose, *Nixon: The Education of a Politician 1913–1962* (New York: Simon & Schuster, 1987), pp. 170–172.
9. WHJ interview, Dulles Oral History, Princeton University, December 11, 1965.
10. WHJ letters to Ben Gray, August 11, 1948; J.F. Corbett, December 23, 1948; T.B. Allen, December 10, 1948; Robert M. Herhold, May 24, 1948; Mrs. George Engel, September 14, 1948; Mr. and Mrs. Frederic D. Calhoun, April 1, 1948; Mrs. Gertrude Dahl, April 28, 1948; and Mrs. Joseph F. Kepple, April 22, 1948, WHJ Papers, Hoover Library, Stanford University.
11. Wedemeyer, *Wedemeyer Reports*, pp. 387–390.
12. Ibid., pp. 398–399.

13. William C. Bullit, "A Report to the American People on China," *Life,* October 13, 1947, pp. 152–154.
14. Ambassador Stuart to Secretary Marshall, February 5, 1948, and March 31, 1948 in *U.S. Relations With China,* pp. 842–843, 845.
15. Vandenberg, *The Private Papers of Senator Vandenberg,* p. 531.
16. *U.S. Relations with China,* p. xvi.
17. Kubek, *How the Far East Was Lost,* pp. 406–407.
18. WHJ to Merril V. Reed, December 28, 1948, WHJ Papers, Hoover Library, Stanford University.
19. Fairbank, *The Great Chinese Revolution,* p. 269.
20. CR, March 1, 1949, pp. 1678–1691.
21. Ibid., August 17, 1949, pp. 11676–11677.
22. Ibid., August 18, 1949, pp. 11787–11788.
23. Crozier, *The Man Who Lost China,* p. 332.
24. Ibid., pp. 334–340.
25. Ibid., pp. 345–346.
26. CR, August 5, 1947, p. 10875.
27. Ibid., August 8, 1949, p. A5189.
28. Ibid., August 19, 1949, pp. 11881–11882.
29. Ibid., October 19, 1949, pp. 15091–15093.
30. WHJ to C.C. Hemenway, December 22, 1949, WHJ Papers, Hoover Library, Stanford University.
31. WHJ to Dr. Carl Heathkopf, December 23, 1949, WHJ Papers, Hoover Library, Stanford University.
32. Paul Hopper interview with WHJ, August 29, 1968, Washington, D.C.
33. CR, January 26, 1950, p. 975.
34. Ibid., January 19, 1950, p. 651.
35. Ibid., February 6, 1950, pp. A934–935.
36. WHJ, radio broadcast May 23, 1950, Geneva, Switzerland, WHJ Papers, Hoover Library, Stanford University.
37. CR, June 27, 1950, p. A4828; June 29, 1950, p. A4893; statement by the president, June 27, 1950; WHJ to D.D. Streator, July 1, 1950; WHJ Papers, Hoover Library, Stanford University.
38. *New York Times,* July 17, 1950; WHJ statement, July 19, 1950, WHJ Papers, Hoover Library, Stanford University.
39. CR, July 18, 1950, p. 10551.
40. Ibid., p. 10552.
41. Ibid., p. 10554.
42. Ibid., p. 10556.
43. Ibid., p. 10557.
44. Ibid., p. 10558.
45. Ibid., p. 10559.
46. Ibid., pp. 10559–10560.

47. WHJ to Norman Backstrom, February 6, 1950, WHJ Papers, Hoover Library, Stanford University.
48. League of Women Voters Questionnaire, September 30, 1950, WHJ Private Papers.
49. WHJ, "When Will We Have Peace?" radio broadcast, November 6, 1950, WHJ Private Papers.

CHAPTER TWELVE

1. Hopper interview, August 29, 1968; WHJ report to the Minneapolis Fifth Congressional District, July 1, 1951, WHJ Papers, Hoover Library, Stanford University.
2. Hopper interview.
3. WHJ newsletter, "Just Between Us," October 1951, WHJ Papers, Hoover Library, Stanford University; Manchester, *The Glory and the Dream*, p. 746.
4. WHJ statement, January 7, 1951; WHJ newsletter, "Just Between Us," January 1952, WHJ Papers, Hoover Library, Stanford University.
5. Hopper interview.
6. WHJ statement, April 10, 1952, WHJ Papers, Hoover Library, Stanford University.
7. Hopper interview.
8. Ibid.; WHJ to H.L. Prestholdt, February 5, 1952, WHJ Papers, Hoover Library, Stanford University.
9. CR, May 6, 1952, p. A2889.
10. B.A. Garside, *Within the Four Seas: The Memoirs of B.A. Garside* (New York: Frederic C. Beil, 1985), p. 120.
11. Manchester, *The Glory and the Dream*, p. 639.
12. CR, April 11, 1951, pp. 3684–3685.
13. James A. Nathan and James K. Oliver, *United States Foreign Policy and World Order*, 2nd ed. (Boston: Little, Brown and Company, 1981), pp. 106–110.
14. Philip A. Crowl interview with WHJ for Dulles Oral History, Princeton University, December 11, 1965.
15. House and Senate Judiciary Committees, Subcommittees on Immigration and Naturalization, March 7, 1951; CR, June 27, 1952, p. 8347.
16. Drew Pearson column, *Minneapolis Star,* May 23, 1952; "What About the China Lobby," CR, May 6, 1952, pp. A3056–3057.
17. WHJ to Chiang Kai-shek, March 20, 1951, WHJ Papers, Hoover Library, Stanford University.
18. Manchester, *The Glory and the Dream*, pp. 754–755.
19. Ibid., p. 756.

20. Dwight D. Eisenhower, *Mandate for Change: 1953–1956* (Garden City, N.Y.: Doubleday & Co., 1963), p. 46.
21. WHJ, remarks at Republican National Convention, July 10, 1952, Chicago, Illinois, WHJ Papers, Minnesota Historical Society, St. Paul.
22. WHJ to John A. Thompson, July 30, 1952, WHJ Papers, Minnesota Historical Society, St. Paul.
23. Hopper interview.
24. WHJ meeting with Dwight D. Eisenhower, Brown Palace Hotel, Denver, July 29, 1952; WHJ memorandum to Governor Sherman Adams, Denver, August 11, 1952, WHJ Papers, Hoover Library, Stanford University.
25. Paul F. Boller, Jr., *Presidential Campaigns* (New York: Oxford University Press, 1984), pp. 282–284.
26. Manchester, p. 765.
27. WHJ memorandum to General Eisenhower, October 8, 1952, WHJ Papers, Hoover Library, Stanford University; Hopper interview.
28. *The Saturday Evening Post*, October 11, 1952.
29. Miriam Judd to Mr. and Mrs. B.R. Barber, October 19, 1952, Miriam Judd Private Papers.
30. Philip A. Crowl interview with WHJ, December 11, 1965, Dulles Oral History, Princeton University.
31. Ibid.

CHAPTER THIRTEEN

1. Ross Y. Koen, *The China Lobby in American Politics* (New York: Harper & Row, 1974), pp. 27 et seq.; Stanley D. Bachrack, *The Committee of One Million: "China Lobby" Politics, 1953–1971* (New York: Columbia University Press, 1976), pp. 4–6.
2. Koen, p. 31.
3. CR, June 15, 1950, p. A4506; July 17, 1950, p. 10463.
4. Ibid., April 3, 1950, pp. A2488–2489.
5. Forrest Davis and Robert A. Hunter, *The Red China Lobby* (New York: Fleet Publishing Corp., 1963), pp. 71–72.
6. Bachrack, pp. 31–34.
7. Joseph Keeley, *The China Lobby Man: The Story of Alfred Kohlberg* (New Rochelle, N.Y.: Arlington House, 1969), pp. 406–410.
8. House Subcommittee on the Far East and the Pacific, *Admission of Red China to the United Nations,* July 31, 1953, p. 326, vol. 18, Historical Series, House Committee on Foreign Affairs, Washington, D.C., 1980.
9. Interview with WHJ, February 22, 1987; Bachrack, pp. 61–62.
10. Interview with Marvin Liebman, October 11, 1988, Washington, D.C.

11. Interview with WHJ, February 22, 1987.
12. Bachrack, pp. 54–55.
13. Ibid., pp. 65–69.
14. Ibid., pp. 62–63.
15. CR, July 21, 1953, pp. 9405–9406; Eisenhower to WHJ, October 24, 1953, WHJ Papers, Hoover Library, Stanford University.
16. Bachrack, p. 63.
17. *New York Herald Tribune,* July 16, 1957.
18. Bachrack, p. 148.
19. Garside, *Within the Four Seas,* pp. 126–127.
20. John F. Kennedy to Marvin Liebman, March 16, 1960, WHJ Papers, Hoover Library, Stanford University; Bachrack, pp. 196–197.
21. Bachrack, p. 199.
22. Ibid., p. 211.
23. WHJ, Committee of One Million letter, May 28, 1964, WHJ Papers, Hoover Library, Stanford University.
24. Bachrack, pp. 268–269.

CHAPTER FOURTEEN

1. Interview with WHJ, July 26, 1989, Mitchellville, Maryland.
2. Ibid.
3. Ibid.
4. Interview with Carolyn Judd, September 30, 1989.
5. Interview with Eleanor Quinn, October 2, 1989.
6. Ibid.
7. Ibid.
8. Nathan and Oliver, *United States Foreign Policy and World Order,* p. 176.
9. Ibid., p. 178.
10. Interview with WHJ, April 13, 1988, Washington, D.C.
11. John Lewis Gaddis, *Strategies of Containment: A Critical Appraisal of Postwar American National Security Policy* (Oxford: Oxford University Press, 1982), p. 129.
12. Hopper interview with WHJ, August 29, 1968.
13. Ibid.
14. Ibid.
15. Ibid.
16. Ibid.
17. CR, June 30, 1955, p. 9620.
18. Ibid., June 18, 1953, pp. 6860–6861.
19. Ibid., January 19, 1953, pp. A219–220.

20. Ibid., March 10, 1953, pp. 1803–1826.
21. WHJ to Martin Selender, May 31, 1954, WHJ Papers, Hoover Library, Stanford University.
22. CR, March 3, 1954, pp. 2623–2624.
23. Gaddis, *Strategies of Containment*, pp. 169–170.
24. CR, June 6, 1956, pp. 9687–9692.
25. President Eisenhower to WHJ, October 30, 1956, WHJ Papers, Hoover Library, Stanford University.
26. WHJ to Paul Ravenscraft, August 11, 1956; Vice President Richard Nixon to WHJ, August 11, 1956, WHJ Papers, Hoover Library, Stanford University.
27. WHJ, post-campaign letter, November 21, 1956, WHJ Papers, Hoover Library, Stanford University.
28. Interview with Dorothy Bageant, March 3, 1989, Alexandria, Virginia.
29. Edna F. Kelly to WHJ, July 1978, WHJ Private Papers.
30. CR, May 13, 1958, p. 8595.
31. Ibid., March 5, 1959, p. 3424.
32. Ibid., January 25, 1959, pp. 719–721.
33. Ibid., May 25, 1959, pp. 8992–8993.
34. Ibid., May 28, 1959, pp. 9363–9365.
35. WHJ telegram to Eric Johnston, January 2, 1959, WHJ Papers, Hoover Library, Stanford University.
36. WHJ, statement, August 3, 1959; broadcast, Mutual Broadcasting System, August 1959, WHJ Papers, Hoover Library, Stanford University.
37. CR, September 14, 1959, pp. 20012–20020.
38. William B. Macomber, Jr. to Boyd Crawford, January 8, 1958; *New York Times*, December 13, 1957; U.S. Chamber of Commerce, *United Nations Report*, March 1, 1958; Senate Foreign Relations Committee, April 1, 1958, WHJ Private Papers.
39. CR, March 25, 1959, pp. A2713–2715.
40. WHJ to Orville L. Freeman, April 10, 1959, WHJ Papers, Hoover Library, Stanford University.
41. CR, August 8, 1958, p. 16734; May 26, 1960, p. 11252; June 22, 1960, pp. 13838–13839.
42. Manchester, *The Glory and the Dream*, pp. 1061–1071.
43. Ibid.
44. Hopper interview, August 29, 1968.
45. Ibid.
46. WHJ to Dean Brenner, December 20, 1960, WHJ Papers, Hoover Library, Stanford University.

Chapter Fifteen

1. Theodore White, *The Making of the President 1960* (New York: Atheneum Publishers, 1961), pp. 216–217, 240–241.
2. Victor Lasky, *J.F.K.: The Man and the Myth* (New Rochelle: Arlington House, 1966), p. 409.
3. WHJ to Mrs. C.C. Lammers, July 7, 1960, WHJ Papers, Hoover Library, Stanford University.
4. Ibid.
5. *New York Times,* July 25, 1960.
6. CR, August 29, 1960, pp. 18253–18257.
7. *Chicago Daily News,* July 26, 1960; *Omaha World-Herald,* July 27, 1960.
8. *St. Paul Press,* July 28, 1960.
9. Ibid.
10. WHJ, memorandum, July 1960, WHJ Papers, Hoover Library, Stanford University.
11. Interview with WHJ, May 20, 1987, Washington, D.C.
12. Ibid.
13. Ibid.
14. Ibid.
15. Lasky, *J.F.K.: The Man and the Myth,* p. 376.
16. Ibid., pp. 377–378.
17. Richard Nixon, *RN: The Memoirs of Richard Nixon* (New York: Grosset & Dunlap, 1978), p. 224.
18. *New York Times,* January 29, 1961.
19. WHJ to William L. Hedrick, February 21, 1961, WHJ Papers, Hoover Library, Stanford University.
20. CR, April 25, 1961, pp. 6667–6668.
21. Ibid., May 1, 1961, pp. 6986–6987.
22. Ibid., September 23, 1961, pp. 20956–20959.
23. Ibid., September 27, 1961, p. A8263.
24. "How Congressmen Make Up Their Minds," *Redbook,* February 1962, pp. 56 et seq.
25. Interview with WHJ, January 12, 1988.

Chapter Sixteen

1. WHJ to John A. Buxton, January 2, 1962, WHJ Papers, Hoover Library, Stanford University.
2. *Minneapolis Star,* April 10, 1962.
3. Safire, *Safire's Political Dictionary,* p. 643.
4. *Minneapolis Tribune,* April 11, 1962.

5. *St. Paul Pioneer Press,* April 11, 1962; Editorial, WTCN Television and Radio, April 20, 1962.

6. Eisenhower telegram, April 17, 1962; letters from Grew, April 17, 1962; Robertson, April 16, 1962; Buckley, April 21, 1962; Udall, April 16, 1962; Rickenbacker, April 16, 1962; Wallace, April 26, 1962; Howard, April 14, 1962; Nixon, April 20, 1962; and Eisenhower, May 11, 1962; Paul Harvey column, April 16, 1962, WHJ Private Papers.

7. *St. Paul Sunday Pioneer Press,* May 6, 1962.

8. Dean Rusk memorandum to Kenneth O'Donnell, May 12, 1962, White House Central Subject File, John Fitzgerald Kennedy Library, Boston, Massachusetts.

9. Frederick G. Dutton memorandum to Lawrence O'Brien, May 16, 1962, White House Central Subject File, John Fitzgerald Kennedy Library, Boston, Massachusetts.

10. Donald Fraser to Kenneth O'Donnell, May 7, 1962, White House Central Subject File, John Fitzgerald Kennedy Library, Boston, Massachusetts.

11. News release of Walter Judd for Congress Committee, May 31, 1962; Religious New Service, June 4, 1962, WHJ Private Papers.

12. Interview with WHJ, December 30, 1987, Washington, D.C.

13. News release, July 13, 1962, WHJ Private Papers.

14. WHJ to John W. Johnson, June 19, 1962, WHJ Private Papers.

15. *Minneapolis Star,* August 28, 1962.

16. WHJ, statement, August 29, 1962, WHJ Private Papers.

17. Robert A. Forsythe to WHJ, September 18, 1962, WHJ Private Papers.

18. WHJ, statement, September 4, 1962, WHJ Private Papers.

19. Campaign statement re WHJ voting record, October 1962; George C. Pendleton to WHJ, October 3, 1962, WHJ Private Papers.

20. CR, August 16, 1962, p. 16747.

21. *Minneapolis Sunday Tribune,* October 7, 1962.

22. Campaign newspaper of Judd for Congress Committee, October 1962, WHJ Papers, Hoover Library, Stanford University.

23. Interview with Robert Bjorklund, June 23, 1988, Minneapolis.

24. Interview with Douglas Head, June 24, 1988, Minneapolis.

25. Graham Allison, *Essence of Decision: Explaining the Cuban Missile Crisis* (Boston: Little, Brown and Company, 1971), pp. 188–189.

26. WHJ news release, September 12, 1962, WHJ Private Papers.

27. WHJ news release, September 20, 1962, WHJ Private Papers.

28. WHJ, *Minneapolis Tribune,* September 29, 1962; Fraser, *Minneapolis Star,* October 15, 1962.

29. WHJ statement, October 19, 1962, WHJ Papers, Hoover Library, Stanford University.

30. WHJ statement, October 22, 1962, WHJ Papers, Hoover Library, Stanford University.
31. WHJ to President Kennedy, October 22, 1962, WHJ Private Papers; WHJ statement, October 22, 1962, WHJ Papers, Hoover Library, Stanford University.
32. Interview with Douglas Head, June 25, 1988.
33. Robert Kennedy, *Thirteen Days: A Memoir of the Cuban Missile Crisis* (New York: W.W. Norton & Company, 1969), pp. 202–203.
34. WHJ to Ethan H. Campbell, November 8, 1962, WHJ Papers, Hoover Library, Stanford University.
35. Letters to WHJ from Nelson Rockefeller, November 9, 1962; Thomas E. Dewey, November 27, 1962; Jacob Javits, November 8, 1962; D.D. Eisenhower, no date; Jim Wright, November 14, 1962; W. Averell Harriman, November 8, 1962; U. Alexis Johnson, November 14, 1962; Carl Marcy, November 9, 1962; Ting Chung Kan, November 7, 1962, WHJ Private Papers.
36. Interview with WHJ, March 19, 1988, Washington, D.C.
37. WHJ "Letter to Friends," December 1962, WHJ Papers, Hoover Library, Stanford University.

CHAPTER SEVENTEEN

1. *Minneapolis Tribune,* July 19, 1963.
2. WHJ to Benjamin Berger, August 11, 1964, WHJ Papers, Hoover Library, Stanford University.
3. *Minneapolis Star,* July 16, 1964.
4. Carl Curtis to WHJ, July 20, 1978, WHJ Private Papers.
5. Interview with John Fulton Lewis, February 15, 1989, Washington, D.C.
6. American Security Council, *Washington Report,* January 11, 1966, WHJ Papers, Hoover Library, Stanford University.
7. WHJ statement, March 28, 1966, WHJ Private Papers.
8. Ibid.
9. House Committee on Foreign Affairs, Subcommittee on Asian and Pacific Affairs, *Rural Development in Asia,* April 28, 1967, 90th Cong., 1st sess. (Washington, D.C.), pp. 256–257, 261–262.
10. WHJ memorandum to Eisenhower, June 26, 1954, WHJ Papers, Hoover Library, Stanford University.
11. George C. Herring, *America's Longest War: The United States and Vietnam 1950–1975* (New York: John Wiley & Sons, 1979), pp. 40–42.
12. WHJ memorandum, July 20, 1954, WHJ Papers, Hoover Library, Stanford University.

13. WHJ memorandum, March 1965, WHJ Papers, Hoover Library, Stanford University.
14. WHJ to President Lyndon B. Johnson, March 9, 1965; September 2, 1965; June 2, 1966; WHJ Papers, Hoover Library, Stanford University.
15. WHJ, address at the 1967 Annual Copley Conference, February 23, 1967, Borrego Spring, California, WHJ Private Papers.
16. Ibid.
17. Herring, *America's Longest War,* pp. 172–173.
18. WHJ memorandum to William P. Bundy, October 14, 1967, WHJ Papers, Hoover Library, Stanford University.
19. WHJ, summary of report to President Johnson and Assistant Secretary Bundy, October 16, 1967, WHJ Private Papers.
20. Herring, p. 153.
21. House Foreign Affairs Committee, Subcommittee on Asian and Pacific Affairs, April 11, 1967, p. 249.
22. Herring, pp. 188–189.
23. Ibid., p. 198.
24. WHJ, news briefing at the White House, October 16, 1967, "Weekly Compilation of Presidential Documents."
25. WHJ, "Some Lessons from Vietnam," August 1972, WHJ Papers, Hoover Library, Stanford University.
26. Ibid.
27. Interview with WHJ, May 30, 1987.
28. Anthony Kubek, *The Red China Papers* (New Rochelle: Arlington House, 1975) p. 184.
29. Richard M. Nixon, "Asia After Vietnam," *Foreign Affairs* 46 (October 1967), pp. 111–113.
30. Marvin Kalb and Bernard Kalb, *Kissinger* (Boston: Little, Brown and Company, 1974), pp. 219–220.
31. WHJ to Marx Lewis, February 18, 1969, WHJ Papers, Hoover Library, Stanford University.
32. WHJ to John Chamberlain, February 5, 1969, WHJ Papers, Hoover Library, Stanford University.
33. WHJ to Elmer Anderson, February 10, 1969, WHJ Papers, Hoover Library, Stanford University.
34. Kubek, p. 201.
35. WHJ, remarks before American Bar Association, July 19, 1971, London, WHJ Papers, Hoover Library, Stanford University.
36. Nixon, *RN: The Memoirs of Richard Nixon,* pp. 551–552.
37. Kissinger, *White House Years* (Boston: Little, Brown and Company, 1979) pp. 763–764.
38. Theodore H. White, *The Making of the President 1972* (New York: Atheneum, 1973), p. 59.

39. Kubek, p. 202.

40. *China Report,* vol. 3, no. 2 (April 1971), p. 2.

41. Bachrack, pp. 269–272.

42. *Washington Star,* August 3, 1971.

43. Kissinger, p. 776.

44. Chou En-lai, statement, December 8, 1971, WHJ Papers, Hoover Library, Stanford University.

45. Interview with WHJ, September 11, 1987.

46. *Washington Daily News,* February 16, 1972.

47. *New York Times,* February 28, 1972.

48. Kissinger, pp. 1091–1092.

49. Rozek, p. 308.

50. Interview with WHJ, May 30, 1987.

51. Crozier, pp. 384–385.

52. Keiji Furuya, *Chiang Kai-shek: His Life and Times,* trans. Chun-ming Chang (New York: St. John's University Press, 1981), pp. 500–501.

53. WHJ, "Chiang Kai-shek—His Faith and His Work," remarks, October 7, 1986, Taipei, Taiwan, WHJ Private Papers.

54. WHJ, statement, Committee for a Free China, December 16, 1978, Washington, D.C.

55. WHJ, unpublished article for *Washington Post,* December 20, 1978, WHJ Private Papers.

56. Taiwan Relations Act, Public Law 96-8, April 10, 1979, WHJ Private Papers.

57. Rozek, p. 321.

CHAPTER EIGHTEEN

1. *Report,* Judicial Council of the American Medical Association, October 1971, WHJ Private Papers.

2. *Reader's Digest,* February 1976.

3. CR, December 21, 1970, p. 43148.

4. Interview with WHJ, January 12, 1988.

5. WHJ, address to International Christian Fellowship, July 12, 1977, London, WHJ Private Papers.

6. WHJ, remarks at Charles Edison Memorial Youth Fund dinner, November 12, 1975, WHJ Private Papers.

7. WHJ, remarks at the White House, October 9, 1981, WHJ Private Papers.

8. *China Letter,* August 1982, published by the Committee for a Free China, Washington, D.C.

9. Ibid.

10. Ibid.

11. Interview with WHJ, January 12, 1988.
12. Interview with WHJ, May 30, 1987.
13. *Washington Post Magazine,* January 24, 1988, pp. 26–29.
14. Interview with WHJ, May 30, 1987.
15. Ibid.
16. Ibid.
17. Interview with WHJ, April 13, 1988.
18. Interview with WHJ, March 19, 1988.
19. *Washington Post Magazine,* January 24, 1988, p. 26.
20. *Washington Post,* February 6, 1988.
21. Interview with Douglas Head, June 24, 1988, Minneapolis.
22. Interview with WHJ, April 13, 1988.
23. "China in Transition," seminar sponsored by the Ethics and Public Policy Center, May 12, 1989, Washington, D.C.
24. Remarks by WHJ, seminar sponsored by the Fund For American Studies, July 18, 1989, Georgetown University, Washington, D.C.

Bibliography

Archives and Manuscript Collections

Acheson, Dean. Papers. Harry S. Truman Library, Independence, Missouri.

Bohlen, Charles E. Papers. George C. Marshall Research Library, Lexington, Virginia.

Clifford, Clark M. Papers. Harry S. Truman Library, Independence, Missouri.

Dulles, John Foster. Papers. Seeley Mudd Library, Princeton University.

Eisenhower, Dwight David. Papers. Dwight D. Eisenhower Library, Abilene, Kansas.

Former Members of Congress Oral History Project, Library of Congress.

Judd, Miriam. Private Papers. Mitchellville, Maryland.

Judd, Walter H. Papers. Hoover Institution Library, Stanford University.

_____. Papers. Minnesota Historical Society, St. Paul.

_____. Private Papers. Mitchellville, Maryland.

Kennedy, John Fitzgerald. Papers. John Fitzgerald Kennedy Library, Boston.

Marshall, George C. Papers. George C. Marshall Research Library, Lexington, Virginia.

McNaughton, Frank. Papers. Harry S. Truman Library, Independence, Missouri.

BIBLIOGRAPHY

Stilwell, Joseph S. Papers. Hoover Institution Library, Stanford University.
Truman, Harry S. Papers. Harry S. Truman Library, Independence, Missouri.
Vandenberg, Arthur H. Papers. University of Michigan Library, Ann Arbor.

OFFICIAL DOCUMENTS

U.S. Congress

Congressional Record, 1943–1962.

U.S. Congress. House of Representatives

Committee on Foreign Affairs. *Assistance to Greece and Turkey.* Washington, 1947.
Committee on Foreign Affairs. *National and International Movements, Supplement 3, Communism in China.* Washington, 1948.
Committee on Foreign Affairs. *United States Foreign Policy for a Post-War Recovery Program.* Washington, 1948.
Committee on Foreign Affairs, Subcommittee on the Far East and the Pacific [Executive Session]. *Admission of Red China to the United Nations.* Washington, 1956.
Committee on Foreign Affairs, Subcommittee on Asian and Pacific Affairs. *Rural Development in China.* Washington, 1967.
Committee on Foreign Affairs, Subcommittee on Europe. *The Cold War: Origins and Developments.* Washington, 1971.

U.S. Congress. Senate

Committee on Foreign Relations. *Assistance to Greece and Turkey.* Washington, 1947.
Committee on Foreign Relations. *Legislative Origins of the Truman Doctrine.* Washington, 1947.
Committee on Foreign Relations. *U.S. Economic Assistance to European Economic Recovery.* Washington, 1948.
Committee on Foreign Relations. *United States Policy Toward China.* Washington, 1966.

U.S. Department of State

United States Relations With China: With Special Reference to the Period 1944–1949. Washington, 1949.

BOOKS

Allison, Graham. *Essence of Decision: Explaining the Cuban Missile Crisis.* Boston: Little, Brown and Company, 1971.

Ambrose, Stephen E. *Nixon: The Education of a Politician 1913–1962.* New York: Simon & Schuster, 1987.

Bachrack, Stanley D. *The Committee of One Million: "China Lobby" Politics, 1953–1971.* New York: Columbia University Press, 1976.

Berkov, Robert. *Strong Man of China: The Story of Chiang Kai-shek.* Boston: Houghton Mifflin Company, 1938.

Boller, Paul F. *Presidential Campaigns.* New York: Oxford University Press, 1984.

Botjer, George. *A Short History of Nationalist China 1919–1949.* New York: G. P. Putnam's Sons, 1979.

Brinkley, David. *Washington Goes to War.* New York: Alfred A. Knopf, 1988.

Carroll, Holbert N. *The House of Representatives and Foreign Affairs.* Boston: Little, Brown and Company, 1966.

Cary-Elwes, Columba. *China and the Cross.* New York: P.J. Kenedy & Sons, 1957.

Cheng, Nien. *Life and Death in Shanghai.* New York: Grove Press, 1986.

Chennault, Claire. *Way of a Fighter.* New York: G.P. Putnam's Sons, 1949.

Chin, Hsiao-yi, chairman. *Symposium on the History of the Republic of China.* 5 vols. Taipei: China Cultural Service, 1981.

———. *Proceedings of Conference on Dr. Sun Yat-Sen and Modern China.* 4 vols. Taipei: China Cultural Service, 1986.

Clark, Glenn. *Touchdowns for the Lord: The Story of "Dad" A.J. Elliott.* St. Paul: Macalester Park Publishing Co., 1947.

Clubb, O. Edmund. *Twentieth Century China.* New York: Columbia University Press, 1964.

Cohen, Warren I. *Dean Rusk.* Totowa, New Jersey: Cooper Square Publishers, 1980.

Crozier, Brian. *The Man Who Lost China.* New York: Charles Scribner's Sons, 1976.

Dahl, Robert A. *Congress and Foreign Policy.* New York: W.W. Norton & Company, 1950.

Davis, Forrest and Robert A. Hunter. *The Red China Lobby.* New York: Fleet Publishing Corp., 1963.

Devine, Robert A. *Second Chance: The Triumph of Internationalism in America During World War II.* New York: Atheneum, 1967.

Doenecke, Justus D. *Not to the Swift: The Old Isolationists in the Cold War Era.* Lewisburg, Pa.: Bucknell University Press, 1979.

BIBLIOGRAPHY

Donovan, Robert. *Conflict and Crisis: The Presidency of Harry S. Truman, 1945–1948.* New York: W.W. Norton & Company, 1977.

Dulles, Foster Rhea. *American Policy Toward Communist China 1949–1969.* New York: Thomas Y. Crowell Company, 1972.

Eiler, Keith E., ed. *Wedemeyer on War and Peace.* Stanford, California: Hoover Institution Press, 1987.

Eisenhower, Dwight D. *Mandate for Change 1953–1956.* Garden City, N.Y.: Doubleday & Company, 1963.

————. *Waging Peace 1956–1961.* Garden City, N.Y.: Doubleday & Company, 1963.

Fairbank, John King. *Chinabound: A Fifty-Year Memoir.* New York: Harper & Row, 1982.

————. *The Great Chinese Revolution 1800–1985.* New York: Harper & Row, 1986.

Furuya, Keiji. *Chiang Kai-shek: His Life and Times.* Translated by Chunming Chang. New York: St. John's University, 1981.

Gaddis, John Lewis. *Strategies of Containment: A Critical Appraisal of Postwar American National Security Policy.* Oxford: Oxford University Press, 1982.

Garside, B.A. *Within the Four Seas: The Memoirs of B.A. Garside.* New York: Frederic C. Beil, 1985.

Grew, Joseph C. *Ten Years in Japan.* New York: Simon and Schuster, 1944.

Halle, Louis J. *The Cold War as History.* New York: Harper Torchbooks, 1975.

Hartmann, Susan M. *Truman and the 80th Congress.* Columbus, Missouri: University of Missouri Press, 1971.

Herring, George C. *America's Longest War: The United States and Vietnam 1950–1975.* New York: John Wiley & Sons, 1979.

Johnson, Chalmers A. *Peasant Nationalism and Communist Power.* Stanford: Stanford University Press, 1962.

Jones, Joseph M. *The Fifteen Weeks.* New York: The Viking Press, 1955.

Kalb, Marvin and Bernard Kalb. *Kissinger.* Boston: Little, Brown and Company, 1974.

Keeley, Joseph. *The China Lobby Man: The Story of Alfred Kohlberg.* New Rochelle: Arlington House, 1969.

Kennedy, Robert F. *Thirteen Days: A Memoir of the Cuban Missile Crisis.* New York: W.W. Norton & Company, 1969.

Kissinger, Henry. *White House Years.* Boston: Little, Brown and Company, 1979.

Koen, Ross Y. *The China Lobby in American Politics.* New York: Harper & Row, 1974.

Kubek, Anthony. *How the Far East Was Lost.* Chicago: Henry Regnery Company, 1963.

BIBLIOGRAPHY

_____. *The Red China Papers*. New Rochelle: Arlington House, 1975.

Lasky, Victor. *J.F.K.: The Man and the Myth*. New York: The Macmillan Company, 1963.

Li, K.T. *The Experience of Dynamic Economic Growth on Taiwan*. Taipei: Mei Ya Publications, 1976.

MacNair, Harley Farnsworth and Donald F. Lach. *Modern Far Eastern International Relations*. New York: D. Van Nostrand Company, 1955.

Manchester, William. *The Glory and the Dream: A Narrative History of America 1932–1972*. Boston: Little, Brown and Company, 1973.

May, Ernest R. *The Truman Administration and China, 1945–1949*. Philadelphia: J.B. Lippincott Company, 1975.

Millis, Walter, ed. *The Forrestal Diaries*. New York: The Viking Press, 1951.

Morison, Samuel Eliot. *The Oxford History of the American People*. Vol. 3. New York: New American Library, 1972.

Morris, Richard B., ed. *Encyclopedia of American History*. New York: Harper & Row, 1976.

Nathan, James A. and James K. Oliver. *United States Foreign Policy and World Order*. 2nd ed. Boston: Little, Brown and Company, 1981.

Newman, Robert P. *Recognition of Communist China? A Study in Argument*. New York: The Macmillan Company, 1961.

Nixon, Richard. *RN: The Memoirs of Richard Nixon*. New York: Grosset & Dunlap, 1978.

Payne, Robert. *Chiang Kai-shek*. New York: Weyleright and Talley, 1969.

Phillips, Cabell. *The Truman Presidency: The History of a Triumphant Succession*. New York: The Macmillan Company, 1966.

Pogue, Forrest C. *George C. Marshall: Statesman*. New York: Viking, 1987.

Price, Henry Bayard. *The Marshall Plan and Its Meaning*. Ithaca, N.Y.: Cornell University Press, 1955.

Rankin, Karl Lott. *China Assignment*. Seattle: University of Washington Press, 1964.

Rozek, Edward J., ed. *Walter H. Judd: Chronicles of a Statesman*. Denver: Grier & Company, 1980.

Ryskind, Allan H. *Hubert: An Unauthorized Biography of the Vice President*. New Rochelle: Arlington House, 1968.

Safire, William. *Safire's Political Dictionary*. New York: Random House, 1978.

Schaller, Michael. *The U.S. Crusade in China, 1938–1945*. New York: Columbia University Press, 1979.

Sheridan, James. E. *China in Disintegration: The Republican Era in Chinese History, 1912–1949*. New York: The Free Press, 1975.

Steele, Archibald Trojan. *The American People and China*. New York: McGraw Hill Book Company, 1966.

Stuart, John Leighton. *Fifty Years in China*. New York: Random House, 1954.

Truman, Harry S. *Memoirs, Vol. 2, Years of Trial and Hope*. Garden City, N.Y.: Doubleday & Company, 1956.

Tsou, Tang. *America's Failure in China 1941–50*. Chicago: University of Chicago Press, 1963.

Tuchman, Barbara W. *Stilwell and the American Experience in China, 1911–1945*. New York: The Macmillan Company, 1970.

Tucker, Nancy Bernkopf. *Patterns in the Dust: Chinese-American Relations and the Recognition Controversy, 1949–1950*. New York: Columbia University Press, 1983.

Utley, Freda. *The China Story*. Chicago: Henry Regnery Company, 1951.

Vandenberg, Arthur, Jr., ed. *The Private Papers of Senator Vandenberg*. Boston: Houghton Mifflin Company, 1952.

Wedemeyer, Albert C. *Wedemeyer Reports!* New York: Henry Holt & Company, 1958.

Welch, Robert. *The Politician*. Privately printed by Robert Welch, Belmont, Massachusetts, 1963.

White, F. Clifton with William J. Gill. *Suite 3505: The Story of the Draft Goldwater Movement*. New Rochelle: Arlington House, 1967.

White, Theodore H. *The Making of the President 1960*. New York: Atheneum Publishers, 1961.

————. *The Making of the President 1972*. New York: Atheneum Publishers, 1973.

White, Theodore H. and Annalee Jacoby. *Thunder Out of China*. New York: William Sloane Associates, 1946.

ARTICLES

Baldwin, David A. "Congressional Initiatives in Foreign Policy." *Journal of Politics* 28 (1966), pp. 754–73.

Bax, Frans R. "The Legislative-Executive Relationship in Foreign Policy." *Orbis* 20 (1977), p. 881–904.

Bennet, Douglas, Jr. "Congress in Foreign Policy: Who Needs It?" *Foreign Affairs* 57 (1978), pp. 40–50.

Bernstein, Barton J. "American Foreign Policy and the Cold War." In *Politics and Policies of the Truman Administration*, edited by Barton J. Bernstein. Chicago: Quadrangle Books, 1970.

Bullit, William C. "A Report to the American People on China." *Life*, October 13, 1947, pp. 152–54.

Cohn, Victor. "The Congressman's Scars of Courage." *Coronet*, July 1960, pp. 31–34.

Dulles, John Foster. "A Policy of Boldness." *Life*, May 19, 1952, pp. 146–60.

Green, David. "The Cold War Comes to Latin America." In *Politics and Policies of the Truman Administration*, edited by Barton J. Bernstein. Chicago: Quadrangle Books, 1970.

Herter, Christian A. "Relation of the House of Representatives to the Making and Implementation of Treaties." *Proceedings of the American Society of International Law* 45 (1951), pp. 55–60.

Hitchens, Harold L. "Influences on the Congressional Decision to Pass the Marshall Plan." *Western Political Quarterly* 21 (1968), pp. 51–68.

Humphrey, Hubert H. "The Senate in Foreign Policy." *Foreign Affairs* 37 (1959), pp. 525–36.

Javits, Jacob. "The Congressional Presence in Foreign Relations." *Foreign Affairs* 48 (1970), pp. 221–34.

Kennan, George F. ("X"). "The Sources of Soviet Conduct." *Foreign Affairs* 25 (July 1947), pp. 566–69, 571–82.

Koledziej, Edward A. "Congress and Foreign Policy: Through the Looking Glass." *Virginia Quarterly Review* 43 (1966), pp. 12–27.

Mallalieu, W.C. "The Origin of the Marshall Plan: A Study in Policy Formation and National Leadership." *Political Science Quarterly* (December 1958), pp. 481–504.

Manley, John F. "The Rise of Congress in Foreign Policy Making." *Annals of the American Academy of Political and Social Science* 397 (1971), pp. 60–70.

Nixon, Richard M. "Asia After Vietnam." *Foreign Affairs* 46 (October 1967), pp. 111–125.

Perlmutter, Oscar William. "Acheson Vs. Congress." *Review of Politics* 22 (1960), pp. 5–44.

Quade, Quentin L. "The Truman Administration and the Separation of Powers: The Case of the Marshall Plan." *Review of Politics* 26 (1965), pp. 58–77.

Schlesinger, Arthur M., Jr. "Congress and the Making of American Foreign Policy." *Foreign Affairs* 51 (1972), pp. 78–113.

_____. "Origins of the Cold War." *Foreign Affairs* 45 (October 1967), pp. 22–52.

Index

A

Acheson, Dean, 132, 170–171
  China White Paper, 162–163,
    165–168
"Agrarian reformers," 105
Aid Refugee Chinese Intellectuals
  (ARCI), Judd as chairman
  of, 189
Alsop, Joseph, 106
American China Policy
  Association, 206
American Committee for Non-
  Participation in Japanese
  Aggression, 68–69
American Emergency Committee
  for Tibetan Refugees, 212
Andersen, Governor Elmer, 263
ARCI. See Aid Refugee Chinese
  Intellectuals
Atkinson, Brooks, 103
Austin, Warren A., 138

B

Bageant, Dorothy, 232
Ball, Senator Joseph H., 88, 240
Barber, Benjamin Russell, 42–43

Barber, Miriam. See Judd,
  Miriam
Bay of Pigs, 242–243
Bender, Congressman George H.,
  on Truman Doctrine, 133
Bentley, Alvin, 220
Bliss, Dr. Edward (missionary in
  China), 27–28, 32–33
Buckley, Edgar T., 106
Burton, Senator Harold H., 88
Byrd, Senator Harry, on Truman
  Doctrine, 133
Byrnes, Secretary of State James
  F., 108

C

Carter, President Jimmy,
  administration on China,
  308–309
Castro, Fidel, 242
Chamberlain, John, Judd's letter
  to, 298
Chambers, Whittaker, 158–160
Chiang Kai-shek, 23–41, 46, 52–
  53, 71, 102–104, 106
  death of, 306–307
  and General Stilwell, 98–101

Chiang Kai-shek (*continued*)
Judd's tribute to, 34–35
and post-war China, 109–114
and President Roosevelt, 94–
95
resignation as President of
Republic of China, 166–167
and Sian incident, 52–54
China,
American views on, 91–97,
129–30
Chiang Kai-shek, 23–41, 46,
52–53, 71, 94
"China Lobby," 204–215
formation of the People's
Republic of China, 167
immigrants to U.S. from, 92–
93
Judd reflections on, 33–35
Judd's missionary trip to, 20,
26–40, 48–64
Mao Tse-tung, 36, 50, 109–
111
post-war struggle for power,
109–130
Sian incident, 52–54
Sun Yat-sen regime, 21–23
China Emergency Committee,
206
"China Lobby," 204–215
*The China Lobby in American
Politics* (Koen), 204–205
China White Paper (Acheson),
162–163, 165–168
Chinese Exclusion Act, 91–94
Chou En-lai, 53
Chu Teh, 36
Clarke, Miriam Loretta (Barber),
43
Clubb, O. Edmund, 53–54

Cofer, Timothy, 319
Cold War, 131–155
Committee of One Million, 205–
209, 211–215
dissolved, 303
Committee to Defend America by
Aiding Anti-Communist
China, 206
Communists, Chinese, 35–36,
50–52
Congregational hospital in China,
48–64
Cowley, Malcolm, 85
Crozier, Brian, 104
Cuba. See Bay of Pigs
Cuban missile crisis, 275–276
Currie, Laughlin, 96
Czechoslovakia, seizure by Soviet
Union, 150

D

Dad Elliot, see Elliot, Arthur J.
(Dad)
Davies, John Paton, 102
de Jaegher, Reverend Raymond
J., 105
De Rochefort, Nicholas, 206–
207
Dewey, Thomas E., 107–108,
141
Douglas, Lewis, 144
Dulles, John Foster, 159, 219,
221
death of, 235

E

Eaton, Chairman Charles, 137
Economic Cooperation Act of
1948. See Marshall Plan

Education, of Judd, 13–16
Eisenhower, Dwight D., 169–170
  administration early years,
    219–220
  administration views toward
    Communist China, 210–212
  campaign of 1952, 185–203
  foreign policy, 222–224
  on Judd's defeat, 279
Ellender, Senator Allen, on
  Truman Doctrine, 133
Elliot, Arthur J. (Dad),
  9–10
Emmerson, John, 103

F

Fairbank, John K., 21, 46
  The Great Chinese Revolution,
    95
Fenchow, Judd in, 48–63
Foreign Assistance Act of 1948,
  152
Former Members of Congress,
  311–312
Forrestal, James (Secretary of
  Defense), 118
Fraser, Donald M., 264–265,
  268–272
  defeat of Judd, 278
Frawley, Patrick J., Jr., 284–285
Fulbright, J. William, 91

G

Gauss, Clarence, 95, 98, 102
Gibbon, Edward, The History of
  the Decline and Fall of the
  Roman Empire, 320
Gibert, Joseph, 82

Judd's opponent for congress
  (Farmer-Laborite party), 82
Gorbachev, Mikhail, visit to
  United States, 316–317
The Great Chinese Revolution
  (Fairbank), 95
Greenslit family, 3, 4
Greenslit, Marcia Maria Fuller, 4
Greenslit, Mary Elizabeth. See
  Judd, Mary Elizabeth

H

Hall, Douglas, 128
Halleck, Charlie, 145, 265
Harriman, Averell,
  ambassadorship to Soviet
    Union, 134
  on Judd's election defeat, 279
  on Marshall Plan, 144
Hatch, Senator Carl A., 88, 143
Hays, Brooks, 90, 311
Head, Douglas, campaign
  manager for Judd, 274–275,
  278
Hendrey, Martha Ann, 2
Henry, James, 4
Herter, Christian, 90
  on Foreign Assistance Act of
    1948, 152
Hill, Senator Lister, 88
Hiss, Alger, 158–159
History of the Decline and Fall of
  the Roman Empire, The
  (Gibbon), 320
House Committee on Foreign
  Affairs, Judd on, 136–143
Howard, Roy, 72, 72–73
Hull, Cordell, 73, 96, 98
Humphrey, Hubert H., 83

Hurley, General Patrick, 99, 102, 112

I

Immigrants, Chinese, 92–93
Immigration Act of 1924, 92, 226
India, Miriam Barber in, 44

J

Japan,
  Judd on national character of, 86
  Manchuria seizure, 40
  U.S. policy in, 70–74
  war against China, 52–63, 71–72
  and war with China, 59–64
JCRR. See Joint Commission on Rural Reconstruction in China
Jenkins, Congressman Thomas A., on Truman Doctrine, 135
Jensen, Congressman Ben, on Truman Doctrine, 133
Johnson, Dr. Youbert, 74
Johnson, Lyndon B.,
  administration of, 291–293
Joint Commission on Rural Reconstruction in China (JCRR), 154
Jones, Joseph, 131
Judd, (Deacon) Thomas, 2
Judd, Elizabeth, 2
Judd, Horace Hunter, 1–3, 6–7
  death of, 135–136
  marriage to Mary Greenslit, 5

Judd, Mary Elizabeth (Greenslit), 2, 4
Judd, Miriam (Barber), 18, 322
  in China, 48–64
  personal biography, 42–47
Judd, Phineas, 2
Judd, Russell, death of, 7
Judd, Walter,
  and 1960 election campaign, 245–262
  on Alger Hiss, 158–159
  ancestors of, 1–12
  and Chiang Kai-shek, 34–35
  in China as missionary, 20–41, 48–64
  and Chinese Language School of the University of Nanking, 24
  on civil rights, 226–227, 272
  and Cold War, 236–238
  and Congregational hospital in China, 48–64
  defeat of Oscar Youngdahl in primary, 75–83
  early education of, 8–11
  election defeat of 1962, 263–281
  Europe trip in Sept. 1947, 142–143
  Europe trip in Sept. 1951, 185–186
  on House Committee on Foreign Affairs, 136–143
  and Judicial Council of the American Medical Association, 310
  on Marshall Plan, 152–154
  and Mayo Clinic, 45–47
  and Miriam Barber, 42–47
  as missionary to China, 19–41

nomination to Fifth
Congressional District, 80–
84
personal life, 216–219
Republican National
Convention keynote speech,
247–250
retirement from Congress,
310–324
and University of Nebraska,
10–14
and University of Nebraska
Medical College, 14–16
on Vietnam, 289–296
Warsaw trip, 143
Judd, Warren, 2–3

K

Keating, Senator Kenneth, 275
Kelly, Congresswoman Edna,
233
Kennedy, John F.,
on Communist China, 206,
213
inaugural address, 259
presidential campaign of 1960,
246
Vietnam policy, 290–295
Khrushchev, Nikita, 241–242
Killen, Marcella F., 184
Kissinger, Henry, 297, 303
Kiwanis Clubs, 66–68
Koen, Ross Y., *The China Lobby
in American Politics*, 204–
205
Kohlberg, Alfred, founder of
American China Policy
Association, 206
Koo, Kim, 179
Kuomintang (KMT), 21–41

Kuomintang (KMT)., See also
Nationalist Party of China

L

Lattimore, Owen, 96
Lewis, John Fulton, 285
Liebman, Marvin, 207–208
Lippman, Walter, 140
Lodge, Henry Cabot, 186–187,
243–244
nomination for vice president,
256–257
Lodge, John Davis, 145
Long March, 50
Lu Hsin Ming, 38
Ludden, Raymond P., 105

M

MacArthur, General Douglas,
fired by President Truman,
190
views on China, 178–179
McCarran-Walter Act of 1952,
226
McCarthy, Joseph, 190–192
and "China Lobby," 205
"McCarthyism," 192
McCormack, Congressman John,
on Truman Doctrine, 135
McKee, Frederick C., chairman
of Committee to Defend
America by Aiding Anti-
Communist China, 206
Mansfield, Congressman Mike,
136
Mao Tse-tung, 36, 50, 109–111
formation of People's Republic
of China, 167
Marcantonio, Vito, 137

Marshall, George, 98–99, 113–
119, 132, 144
on Marshall Plan, 148–149
Marshall Plan, 140–144
congressional hearings on,
147–155
Martin, Joe, 196
Marx, Karl, 35–36
Matthews, George, Judd's DFL
opponent, 257
May Fourth Movement, 22
Mayo Clinic (Rochester,
Minnesota), 44–47
Mikoyan, Anastas (Soviet Foreign
Minister), 236
Minneapolis, Judd in, 75–84
Missionary, Judd in China as,
19–41, 48–64
Morrison, Samuel Eliot, on China
and Japan, 70
Mundt, Karl, trip to Europe with
Judd, 143
Mutual Defense Assistance Act,
House debate on, 164, 176

N

National Defense Educational
Act of 1958, 240
Nationalist Party of China, 21–
41, 120
see also Kuomintang (KMT)
NATO (North Atlantic Treaty
Organization), 170
creation of, 164–165
Nazi Germany, 73
Nixon, Richard M.,
on Communist China, 214
election of 1960, 254–257
trip to China, 300–301, 304
Nomura, Kichisaburo, 73

Norris, Senator George, 6
North Atlantic Treaty
Organization. See NATO
Nygaard, Harlan, campaigns for
Judd, 79–80

O

"On the Erosion of America's
Will to Win," Judd speech,
235
One World (Willkie), 92

P

Pepper, Senator Claude, on
Truman Doctrine, 133
Point IV program, 174
Presidential campaign of 1960,
246–262
Price, Harry B., 68
Pudeator, Mistress Ann,
3–4

R

Rankin, Congressman John, on
Truman Doctrine, 133
"Rape of China, The," published
in New York World
Telegram, 72–73
Rayburn, Sam, 90
Reagan, President Ronald, 314–
316
Red Star Over China (Snow),
53
Republican Convention of 1952,
194–196
Republican Convention of 1964,
282–284

Rich, Congressman Robert F., on
  Truman Doctrine, 133
Rising City, Nebraska,
  1–2
Robbie, Joseph, 231–232
Robertson, Walter, in Eisenhower
  administration, 202–203
Roosevelt, Franklin D., 87–88,
  94–95, 107–108
  on Japan, 70–72
  meets with Chiang Kai-shek,
  95–96
Ryan, Thomas P., Judd's
  opponent for Congress, 82

S

Schwarz, Dr. Fred, 271
  *You Can Trust the
  Communists (To Be
  Communists)*, 270
Schwellenbach, Senator Lewis B.,
  on Far East, 70
Scott, Congressman Hugh, 153
Service, John Stewart, 103,
  168
Seymour, Gideon, 80
Shafer, Congressman Paul, on
  Truman Doctrine, 133
Shanghai Times, 30
Shidehara, Baron Kijuro, 39–40
Shipstead, Senator Henrik, 122
Sian incident, 52–54
Sino-Japanese War, 52–63, 71–
  72
Smedley, Agnes, 103
Smith, Congressman Lawrence
  H., on Truman Doctrine,
  133
Smith, Senator Alexander, 186
Snow, Edgar, 103

Red Star Over China, 53
Soviet Union, seizure of
  Czechoslovakia, 150
Special Projects Fund (SPUR),
  238
SPUR, see Special Projects
  Fund
Stassen, Harold, 122, 156, 187
  in the Eisenhower
  administration, 202
Stilwell, General Joseph, anti-
  Chiang sentiments, 97–102
Stimson, Henry L., 68
Strong, Anna Louise, 103
Strong, Reverend William E., 30
Student Volunteer Movement for
  Foreign Missions, 16, 42
Sun Yat-sen, 21–23

T

Taft, Senator Robert A., 128
Taft-Hartley Act, 127
Thomas, Lowell, and American
  Emergency Committee for
  Tibetan Refugees, 212
Thompson, Anders, 231
Thunder Out of China (White),
  54, 140
Thye, Senator Edward, 240
Truman Doctrine, 132–135, 155
Truman, Harry S., 88–89
  administration of, 144
  General MacArthur firing, 190
Tuchman, Barbara, 101

U

U.S.S.R. See Soviet Union
U-2 ("spy plane"), 241–242

United States government,
  on admitting Communist
    China to United Nations,
    210
  recognition of Peking, 205

V

Vandenberg, Senator Arthur,
    134, 145
  on Marshall Plan, 141
Vietnam, 289–296
Vincent, John Carter, 96, 104
Voice of America, 139
Vorys, Congressman John, on the
    Foreign Assistance Act of
    1948, 152

W

Wallace, Henry, 96–97
Wallace Report, 97
Wedemeyer, Albert C., 105, 114,
    118–119
  on China, 162

White, F. Clifton, 282
White, Theodore H., 103
  Thunder Out of China, 54,
    140
Willkie, Wendell, *One World*,
    92
Wright, Congressman Jim, on
    Judd's election defeat, 279

X

"X-ray" exposure, of Judd, 11–
    12, 125

Y

Yalta agreement, 108, 112
Yen, Jimmy, 154
*You Can Trust the Communists
    (To Be Communists)*
    (Schwarz), 270
Youngdahl, Oscar, defeated by
    Judd in primary, 75–82
Yuan Shih-kai, 21